The
Shopping Mall
High School

The
SHOPPING MALL
HIGH SCHOOL

Winners and Losers in
the Educational Marketplace

Arthur G. Powell, Eleanor Farrar,
and David K. Cohen

The Second Report from A Study of High Schools,
Co-sponsored by the National Association of Secondary
School Principals and the Commission on Educational Issues
of the National Association of Independent Schools

HOUGHTON MIFFLIN COMPANY
Boston

For information about permission to reproduce selections from
this book, write to Permissions, Houghton Mifflin Company,
2 Park Street, Boston, Massachusetts 02108.

Library of Congress Cataloging in Publication Data

Powell, Arthur G., date
The shopping mall high school.

"The second report from A Study of High Schools,
co-sponsored by the National Association of Secondary
School Principals and the Commission on Educational
Issues of the National Association of Independent
Schools.''
Bibliography: p.
Includes index.
1. High school—United States—Curricula.
2. Student activities—United States.   3. Personnel
service in secondary education—United States.
4. Individualized instruction.   I. Farrar, Eleanor
II. Cohen, David K., date.   III. National
Association of Secondary School Principals (U.S.).
IV. National Association of Independent Schools.
Commission on Educational Issues.   V. Title.
LB1628.5.P68   1985   373.73   85–7664
ISBN 0-395-37904-0
ISBN 0-395-42638-3 (pbk.)

Printed in the United States of America

MP 15 14 13 12 11

For our children:
Ben, Allie, and Julia
Jeff
Lisa and Sarah

Contents

Introduction

"IT'S A BIG JOB to make up a curriculum that everybody can do." That was how one student explained why her high school contained hundreds of courses and dozens of programs. Her words caught the essence of a widespread American belief that nearly everybody should attend high school, nearly everybody should graduate from high school, and nearly everybody should find the experience constructive. We cannot emphasize too strongly the nobility of these three commitments or how seriously high schools take them.

Nor can we overstate the size of the "big job." To attempt to entice and graduate the entire adolescent population, and ensure that most are somehow the better for it, is a monumental and exhausting task. This book is about how some high schools approach that task. Its central theme is that they proceed by making numerous and different accommodations with students to achieve the result everyone desires. High schools offer accommodations to maximize holding power, graduation percentages, and customer satisfaction.

The accommodations are many because the students vary enormously. Outside observers often categorize this variation by commitment (the alienated, the passive, the motivated); by family background (blue-collar, affluent preppy, poor); or by ability (the gifted, the handicapped, the average). From inside schools, however, group labels often pale before the realities of individual differences that exist within categories. Up close everyone is significantly different from everyone else. Teenagers in this respect are more like adults than like young children. They have lived long enough, grown enough, and learned enough to express actively the distinct personalities they will possess the rest of their lives. Even more than young children they have minds, feelings, and wills of their own. Virtually no other social institution has the task of serving such matured diversity at the same time and in the same place. "The whole society is there," one teacher noted with a mixture of exhaustion and satisfaction. "We've [even] got those retarded kids. We've got kids with multiple sclerosis. We've got kids who can't hear."

Student inclusiveness is the reality most high schools must cope with: the students are *different,* and they are *there.* At the level of institutional policy, schools accommodate to this situation by providing something for everybody. They have expanded almost limitlessly the variety of experiences considered educationally valid. High school catalogs often resemble an amalgam of elementary education, university instruction, technical education, and adult education, plus the offerings of mental health and social service agencies.

The word "curriculum" does not do justice to this astonishing variety; there are really several curricula operating simultaneously. Four deserve close attention. The "horizontal" curriculum, which refers to differences in actual subjects, only scratches the surface of what is available. Subjects with the same title are offered at various levels or degrees of difficulty in a "vertical" curriculum. An "extracurriculum" of sports and other nonacademic or avocational activities is regarded by schoolpeople and students as anything but extra; it is an integral part of the educational program, an often indispensable way to attach students to something that makes them feel successful. And through a "services" curriculum, schools address emotional or social problems deemed educationally valid in themselves or essential prerequisites for other kinds of educational involvement. "There is something here for everyone," students and teachers often say. If they object to variety, the objection is usually that there is not enough of it.

A second crucial accommodation to inclusiveness is to place the burden for choosing among these opportunities squarely on students and their families. Schools assume responsibility for providing opportunities, but most often they place the responsibility for choice and the responsibility for involvement on the students. The opportunities are there, schoolpeople say, but only if you take them. Students commonly claim, "It's all up to you in this school. If you want to learn, this is one of the best places around."

This restricted notion of schools' responsibility — they will press themselves to offer great variety but will not press students to choose wisely or engage deeply — is a deliberate approach to accommodating diversity so that students will stay on, graduate, and be happy. In educational and moral matters, high schools are remarkably wary of telling students what to do. The more student diversity a school contains and the more curricular variety it develops, the less able it is to forge any workable consensus about what educational experiences are of most worth or what kind of mastery is possible or appropriate for all. It is easier to delegate those decisions to students and families. The problem of consensus is not simply that students and families have different ideas about what knowledge is of most worth. It is also that among schoolpeople themselves there is no consensus about these matters. A varied curriculum carries as an inevitable by-product a varied faculty.

Thus these accommodations produce a neutral environment where a do-your-own-thing attitude prevails. High schools take few stands on what is educationally or morally important. Yet one thing they cannot be neutral about is diversity itself. Pluralism is celebrated as a supreme institutional virtue, and tolerating diversity is the moral glue that holds schools together. But tolerance further precludes schools' celebrating more focused notions of education or of character. "Community" has come to mean differences peacefully coexisting rather than people working together toward some serious end.

Such accommodations make many high schools resemble shopping malls. Both types of institution are profoundly consumer-oriented. Both try to hold customers by offering something for everyone. Individual stores or departments, and salespeople or teachers, try their best to attract customers by advertisements of various sorts, yet in the end the customer has the final word. These ideas are developed in Chapter 1.

These institutional policies do not stop at the classroom door. Similar accommodations are available *inside* classrooms. Many opportunities for variety and choice exist there, too. Catalog descriptions are profoundly misleading in their implication that consensus prevails about what a particular subject is and how it will be dealt with once the door is closed. Inside classrooms, teachers and students must come to terms with each other about the extent to which the subjects they mutually confront will be taken seriously or just endured. A multitude of understandings or bargains, sometimes quite subtle, are possible to accommodate the range of preferences of both students and teachers.

We call these different possible arrangements "treaties." Not always explicit or fully conscious agreements, they are at least tacitly made or, if already extant, accepted. Some students and teachers wish to engage a subject to learn and to teach; others wish to avoid subjects as much as possible without the appearance of irresponsibility. Most work out a modus operandi somewhere in between. The different treaties reveal that taking or teaching a course does not by itself imply any commonly-agreed-upon commitments or responsibilities. Often the only common understanding is that passing, and hence graduation, is contingent on orderly attendance rather than on mastery of anything. The need to hold students for graduation and make them feel happy has the effect of disconnecting mastery from the school's expectations. Learning is not discounted or unvalued, but it is profoundly voluntary. The range of classroom treaties and the different reasons why teachers and students enter into them are discussed in Chapter 2.

These accommodations to diversity are generally accepted by the community. Most students and teachers are satisfied with the education available from their own high schools. People can work as much or as little as they wish. Students who do little work can still pass in return for orderly attendance; students and families who want more engagement and push for it can usually get it. The shopping mall high school responds to various kinds of external push by providing specialty shops characterized by greater focus and élan. Some of the most prominent are the top-track or accelerated enclaves, usually frequented by the children of more educated, ambitious, and affluent parents, and the programs in special education or vocational/technical education funded and sometimes man- dated by legislation supported by articulate pressure groups. Teenag- ers designated by some group as special tend to receive special attention. We develop the idea of specialty shops in Chapter 3.

Those who are average or unspecial are usually left alone. They use high schools as they choose, without pressure from either the school or a clear external lobby. Complaints are few. "Why should we?" they say. "We just want to get out." The voices of concern are most often those of educated and ambitious parents whose chil- dren are — at least in school — average. The variety in the shopping mall high school does not displease these parents, but the voluntary nature of commitment does. They oppose notions of individualiza- tion in which adults leave students alone rather than know and guide them. The neutral stance that allows schools to accommodate the preferences of a varied constituency of both students and teachers places too much of a burden on their teenagers to be already self- directed, already proficient in decision-making. They prefer high schools more willing to take educational stands in accordance with their own beliefs, more willing to exert comprehensive institutional pressure on behalf of learning and character, more willing to give personal attention to every student. Instead of a do-your-own-thing atmosphere, even if everything is there for the doing, they want an atmosphere that actively pushes their children to seize educa- tional opportunity. They want a specialty shop of their own.

Sometimes that wish leads to withdrawal from the shopping mall high school, a costly decision available only to a minority. The vast majority who remain are families with neither the resources nor the interest to contemplate such a step. Since they rarely com- plain, little pressure is exerted on the schools to confront their children, who themselves rarely complain, are rarely troublesome, and just pass quietly through. Unspecial students are discussed in Chapter 4.

In a universal public service where those who push for more can usually get it and those who will settle for less can pass through without penalty, incentives for fundamental change are minimal. There is no shortage of innovation in high schools, but it tends to be of a particular sort. It usually aims at further accommodations — at making an inclusive and diverse student population comfortable, willing to stay, and willing to behave. Innovation is rarely directed at challenging existing preferences in favor of making learning itself and learning for everyone the highest institutional priority. The latter kind of innovation upsets the delicate balance of accommodations that make learning and mastery just one among many consumer choices. Reformers who emphasize "quality," and who mean by it higher expectations for all, will be tolerated only to the point where they can find a willing audience; beyond that point they will be resisted. The idea that serious mastery is possible and necessary for most Americans is simply not widely shared. Why this is so — why so many bargains inside schools promote mediocrity and why efforts to change them are so difficult — is examined in Chapter 5. A concluding section considers some implications for educational reform.

It is a truism that high schools are simultaneously very different and very much alike. One effect of our emphasis on themes that cut across schools is that important differences among schools tend to recede into the background. Had we organized our material according to case studies of individual schools, these differences would have been at the forefront and the themes themselves muted. Metaphors like the shopping mall inevitably downplay certain realities of local contexts — realities of social class, race, and community history. We believe that the metaphors illuminate crucial commonalities too often glossed over, but we forewarn readers that they account for only part of high school reality. Not every school, for example, could say that everything was offered, or that everyone was there. Schools with fewer human and financial resources, or less student diversity, were less like shopping malls than others. Similarly, classroom bargains varied widely. Some schools offered special options such as Advanced Placement courses rarely or not at all. Others offered such courses but with startling differences in academic demand. We happened to encounter a few private high schools with practices that were in sharp contrast to those of shopping mall high schools, but not all private schools were that way. Had we focused on small rural schools or on highly specialized urban schools, we doubtless would have discovered further variations.

There is, therefore, much more to American high schools than we have presented and more variety than we have captured. This book is not a census or a sample survey. Rather than a description of "the" American high school we propose a *way of looking* at high schools, and especially at the particular high school closest to the heart of each reader. To what extent does that school resemble a shopping mall in terms of variety, choice, and neutrality? What classroom treaties are tolerated? Who are the special and the unspecial students, and how does the school deal with the differences? Who are the winners and losers (for a school is rarely either effective or ineffective for everyone enrolled)? Is the result acceptable? Desirable?

The argument of *The Shopping Mall High School* was developed jointly by the authors during three years spent visiting fifteen schools and analyzing field notes made on interviews and classroom observations. Arthur G. Powell wrote Chapters 1, 2, and 4, along with the Introduction and Conclusion. Eleanor Farrar wrote Chapter 3, and David K. Cohen wrote Chapter 5. An account of our procedures for data collection and analysis appears at the end. Our numerous debts are described in the Acknowledgments.

This book is the second to emerge from a five-year inquiry into secondary education called A Study of High Schools. Theodore R. Sizer chaired the Study and wrote the first volume, *Horace's Compromise: The Dilemma of the American High School.* Robert L. Hampel's *The Last Little Citadel: American High Schools Since 1940* is the third and concluding volume. The five of us worked closely in concert, even as our separate books reflect somewhat different interests.

1

The Shopping Mall High School

IF AMERICANS WANT to understand their high schools at work, they should imagine them as shopping malls. Secondary education is another consumption experience in an abundant society. Shopping malls attract a broad range of customers with different tastes and purposes. Some shop at Sears, others at Woolworth's or Bloomingdale's. In high schools a broad range of students also shop. They too can select from an astonishing variety of products and services conveniently assembled in one place with ample parking. Furthermore, in malls and schools many different kinds of transactions are possible. Both institutions bring hopeful purveyors and potential purchasers together. The former hope to maximize sales but can take nothing for granted. Shoppers have wide discretion not only about what to buy but also about whether to buy.

Some shoppers know just what they want and efficiently make their purchases. Others come simply to browse. Still others do neither; they just hang out. The mall and the school are places to meet friends, pass the time, get out of the rain, or watch the promenade. Shopping malls or their high school equivalents can be entertaining places to onlookers with no intention of buying anything. Yet not everyone goes to the mall. Unenticed by its shops or its scene, some pass the time elsewhere.

Many contemporary high schools even look like shopping malls. Blessed by a favorable climate, one is a complex of attached single-story buildings whose classrooms open to the outdoors rather than to locker-lined corridors. Between periods students go outside to find their next destination, entering and leaving classrooms as if they were adjacent stores. Another school appears massive and mysterious from the outside, but its architecture looks inward: everything radiates from a lively covered promenade. This mall, in a less forgiving climate, is appropriately enclosed.[1]

It is not surprising, then, that teachers often regard themselves as salespeople. Their business is to attract customers and persuade them to buy. Marketing skills are important; teachers become educational pitchmen. Recognizing that necessity, one teacher lamented, "It would be nice to believe we had a culture that so endorsed the products we have to sell that we don't have to do that." But lacking cultural endorsement, many strive to "build up a constituency" of buyers. They recruit through the reputations they establish and speak of how teaching is "perceived as an art of capturing audiences and entertaining them." Sometimes marketing is directly encouraged by the school, as in the case of one that gives an entire day to a series of faculty commercials for what they hope to teach the forthcoming year. The supply of particular subjects flows directly from student demand. An angry math teacher remembered the elimination of a carefully planned program in technical mathematics for vocational students simply because not enough signed up for it. It is easy to see who really makes decisions about what schools teach: "The kids do."

Not only do teachers compete with one another for the business of students, they also are acutely aware of external competition. Students who always browse but never buy and students who avoid the mall whenever possible are a lost market. A common complaint is that high schools have lost some of their competitive edge for students' time and attention. "School has ceased to be the focus of their lives," teachers often say of students. They have other things to do. Part-time employment, in particular, enables students to work in malls and purchase the goods sold there. Scheduling afternoon classes is often difficult. "A lot of our kids," an administrator explained, "really have no reason to work other than that they just want a car, or they want something special." They insist on attending school only half a day. "They look at you and demand that you approve their half-day schedule." Such students often regard high school, not paid employment, as their real part-time job. "When I have nights off, I study," said one boy who worked twenty hours a week.

Shopkeepers in malls try to coax voluntary attendance through collective efforts that combine convenience and entertainment. Despite competition among themselves, their common goal is to attract people to the mall. Celebrity appearances, live concerts, and food service are only a few of their common strategies. A passive browser may one day become a willing buyer, but no one can even browse if he or she is not drawn to the mall in the first place. So, too, the shopping mall high school is committed to luring and holding the largest possible crowd. Today's casual browser is tomorrow's educational consumer. Compulsory attendance laws, which generally reach only to age sixteen and can be easily subverted through chronic or selective absenteeism, do not guarantee a captive, much less an attentive, audience. Like shopping malls, high schools of necessity offer more than a collection of stores.

One girl gratefully contrasted her school with a local parochial school where "there's nothing to do . . . except go to classes all day long." Browsers like her are drawn to school for social reasons. "I like to come to school because my friends are here," another admitted, "but otherwise than that I don't have any reason." Since "everyone else is in school . . . there's no one to be with" if you stay away. Because their peers are present, teenagers sometimes view high school as "one big party" or a "fun place" where "there is not always reading and writing." Alienated from the educational offerings of his institution, a boy nonetheless emphasized that "school is where it's at. When you put a lot of people in one place, something's bound to happen every day. Right? You can count on having a joint." An exasperated counselor agreed there were "kids who come only to play in our sandbox. They bring a bucket and a shovel and play hour after hour and do nothing. They skip class, . . . go to the bathroom, and stay there."

But complaints about the "big babysitting service" provided by high schools are infrequent. Most educators are resigned to a long-term marketing strategy that helps explain the sandbox approach. School professionals grudgingly tolerate such uses of high schools for the same reasons that mall shopkeepers spend money on live entertainment: no good purpose is served if potential customers stay away. "The kid who just stays in school for seat time," one principal said, "will eventually convert it to learning time; so . . . our philosophy here is to first get students to come . . . Ultimately, what we hope is that while they're in school some of the things that the school has to offer will begin to interest them and involve them, so that they will not only be in school for seat time but will be really learning."

Most educators are proud of the mall-like features of high schools. "The nice thing about [our] school," a teacher explained, "is that students can do their own thing. They can be involved in music, fine arts, athletics, sitting out on the south lawn — and nobody puts them down for it." Here three crucial institutional features are nicely summarized. Schools offer a wide *variety* of consumer opportunities, from curricular opportunities like fine arts to extra-curricular opportunities like sports and noncurricular opportunities like hanging out. Schools place *choice* clearly in the hands of the consumer. Students can do their own thing. In general, the customer is always right. Finally, the institution is largely *neutral* about the choices students make. Adults are unlikely to put them down for their decisions.

But why are these features "really something that helps this school be what it is"? Why is the mall a triumph? Part of the answer, the teacher said, was that the features helped "overcome a lot of the problems that high schools today are going through." The mall is a solution, but what were the problems? The teacher concluded that "there are all different kinds of kids" in the school. Everything follows from that. Variety of opportunities, choice among them, and neutrality about choices are all accommodations made by the school to an inclusive and diversified student body. They are inti-mately related adaptations, successful ones in the teacher's judg-ment, essential ones in any case. A deeper look at these central features is necessary for understanding the logic of the shopping mall high school and for judging its results.

Variety

Sixty-five pages of one high school's typeset and bound catalog were needed just for a brief description of each of 400 credit courses.

With its formal design and total length of nearly one hundred pages, the catalog resembled those of large colleges. Another school catalog looked like a newspaper advertising supplement. Thirty-six sides of 11 × 17 newsprint were required to explain 480 courses and other educational services. The snappy layout and newsprint format were aimed at grabbing the attention of readers who might have other things on their minds. Copies blanketed all corners of the school at course selection time.

Few school professionals, students, or parents master these complex listings; many are astonished to learn the particulars that their school provides. But most are convinced that program variety is one of the best features of high school. "Everything's here," they constantly emphasize — everything that anyone, regardless of destination, would want or need. "There is something for everybody here." Each of their schools "has as much as any school could possibly have." They are convinced that "if you take full advantage of all the opportunities, you can really go far."

They judge the health of a consumption-oriented educational enterprise in the same way they judge the health of a consumption economy: by the sheer variety of goods and services available for purchase. And their favorable conclusion is not a wild exaggeration. Few realms of legitimate human activity lack some formal representation in high schools. No school contains quite the same variety as others; there are variations based on taste, resources, and location. Malls are not identical. But the wish to maximize variety is clear. One counselor thought his school was fast approaching its outer limits. "We have magnet programs, vocational programs, career centers, independent learning centers. We even have a program so far opposite of what the regular program is, . . . designed for a student who can't stand a comprehensive school. He can go at his own pace, wherever he wants to study, in the car, at the beach — he can get a diploma that way."

The official, adult-provided program of shopping mall high schools contains four elements. The most familiar is the *horizontal curriculum,* which consists of the various subjects taught for credit. Courses within the horizontal curriculum readily communicate variety because they have sharply different titles: Beginning French, Tall Flags, Advanced Placement Chemistry, Apartment and Income Properties Management, Calligraphy. But some courses with virtually identical titles are offered at various levels of difficulty. These form a crucial but often less visible *vertical curriculum*. A third element embraces clubs, activities, and sports, which together form the *extracurriculum*. Not considered part of the school's main business, the extracurriculum is nevertheless usually viewed as educationally indispensable by teachers and students alike. Finally, the different kinds of psychological and social services offered by schools make up a distinct *services curriculum*. Sometimes these services are regarded as educational ends in themselves, sometimes as means to other educational ends. Whatever their justification, they extend variety in a fourth important way.[2]

The Horizontal Curriculum

The sheer scope of the horizontal curriculum is one of the genuine wonders of educational history, a triumph of production skills, marketing techniques, and consumption values no less dramatic than the abundance of product lines available in shopping malls. A math course in one high school, for example, covered topics beyond the range of the most difficult version of Advanced Placement calculus. The latter is usually regarded as the equivalent of an introductory calculus course in any of the country's most demanding colleges. The same school offered sign language as one of seven foreign languages, with enrollment restricted to students who could hear. Deaf students had a curriculum of their own, including a course called How to Make Friends and Influence People. But hearing students were not psychologically shortchanged; they could take a counseling course that provided, in addition to theory, practical experience in counseling itself.

The bilingual effort of another school included full-scale curricula in mathematics, science, history, and language arts, each given in Spanish, French, Greek, Chinese, and Portuguese. Students not only could find courses that addressed Decision Making or their "values, aspirations, and life goals"; they could find them taught in Portuguese. The shopping mall high school does not value a limited product line. Consider in particular what two equally committed but very different teachers, Mrs. Jefferson and Dr. McBride, offered for sale, and why.

Only eight of her fifteen students were present at Monday morning's Child and Family class, Mrs. Jefferson explained, because on Mondays "they're tired, whatever." The opening topic was the only child. How, Mrs. Jefferson began, should the only child be disciplined? One boy — half the students were male — volunteered that because only children could be easily spoiled, careful and firm discipline was essential. Mrs. Jefferson jumped in to emphasize that the goal of discipline was to teach. When a child was old enough to reason, the best discipline was to reason things out. Hitting the child, she stressed, was wholly inappropriate. Punishment was sometimes necessary, but never abuse.

What teachers were best for different kinds of youngsters? Robert was called on to speak, and when he proved reluctant Mrs. Jefferson posed a leading question to help him begin: "Why might it be important that a child with a single-parent family have male teachers in elementary school?" Robert answered that he saw no reason why male teachers were so important. Mrs. Jefferson explained that single parents tended to be female, so perhaps a good male role model might be important for a young boy.

But Robert persisted. Being a good teacher was more important, and more unusual, than being male, he argued. Mrs. Jefferson concurred but reiterated that male role models were very important for some children. A girl suddenly interjected that women teachers suffer more stress than men. Laughing nervously, Mrs. Jefferson asked whether she showed stress. Yes, the student replied, she thought so; but then again, maybe not. Mrs. Jefferson said in summary that single parents can often be wonderful parents.

The final topic was handicapped children. What could schools do for children afflicted with Down's syndrome or other forms of retardation? After a few seconds of silence, she answered that schools needed special equipment and specially trained teachers. This prompted a student to comment that we all live in a bad society anyway; Mrs. Jefferson replied that it is certainly a mobile and a rootless one. Another student called out that communism explained why American society is bad. "Well, perhaps we ought to look at this," said Mrs. Jefferson as the bell rang.

Despite eighteen years in the same job at the same school, Mrs. Jefferson stressed afterward, her morale remained high. She performed a crucial educational mission because her students were the kind who had children early: "Some of them will be parents before they leave high school and they have very little idea of how to raise children." She was most concerned about the high rate of child abuse among young parents. Above all else she tried to get home "that it really takes maturity to be a good parent."

Given the parental neglect and poverty that afflicted most of her students, which she knew of in compassionate detail, the message of maturity was neither trite nor easy to convey. She liked to sit next to one boy, she said, because "he likes to be touched, or he'll touch me if he gets upset about things." He was one of ten or eleven children, his mother was unmarried, and he had severe emotional problems. "Some days things are so bad with him you just have to leave him alone. He came in on the first day saying that he was interested in the study of child abuse . . . You can just cry buckets over some of these kids if you want to." He was a bright boy who had had a very difficult life.

Robert had transferred to the school in midsemester with all failing grades. "He wants to do well, he tries to do his work. He's a very likable chap." One afternoon he asked her for aspirin, and she told him to go to the nurse. Although she knew he wouldn't get aspirin there either, at least he could lie down and rest for a while. Mrs. Jefferson was proud that "they feel they can come in for help." Another boy who left class that day to see the nurse had just moved to town and lived with his father. A week after school opened he came in tears to see Mrs. Jefferson. His father was an alcoholic, sometimes violent, and the boy was afraid. She gave him a hotline number he could use day or night in emergencies. "He is a very nice young man. It's very hard for him to cope with his life."

These variously troubled students could "get anything they need here." The available services, she thought, represented high school at its best. Deaf students, for example, were in her classes rather than being kept away from hearing students, "and they do very good work." There were also work programs for those "who need the training of having to fill out applications, talking to people, applying for a job, and how to do their income tax — all of these types of things." She interrupted herself to admit how "very positive" she sounded about the school. "I think school is a wonderful place for them to be."

Mrs. Jefferson felt very positive about her own performance as well. The absence of discipline problems in the Child and Family class, she said, was typical of all her classes. And despite the Monday slippage, she admitted no serious attendance problem. Students came to her classes regularly, visited her outside class, and came back to visit after they had left school. Sometimes, as in the case of a returning boy who wore a pair of trousers he had learned to make in her tailoring course, the evidence of success was direct. She attributed her effectiveness in part to hard work: she had amassed more than one hundred credits above the master's degree and often devoted weekends to school affairs. But she also believed that her success came directly from her personal concern for each child and the fact that she taught "something they really can relate to."

She had no illusions that her success was more than partial. Many students would simply not talk in class, despite sympathy and leading questions. Others couldn't read or write well, and there was nothing she could do about that. "By the time they are juniors and seniors and can't spell or read well, it's hard to plan for them." Furthermore, the brighter students "get bored at the pace we have to go for the slower ones." But on balance Mrs. Jefferson could say, "At the end of the day I feel good about what I am doing and I love it."

When she thought about educational reform, she focused on the fact that Child and Family was only an elective. "We let students go through high school and never take any course in the family." She believed that "food, parenting, and life skills might be more helpful than some of the requirements that they have to take." She quickly added, "Now I'm all for English and math and natural science, but some of these other skills might really be more useful to them . . . With all these babies, they need to learn." Time, she believed, was on her side. She was confident that families and children would be high on the national agenda within five years and that her course would be a graduation requirement for everyone. Even without a requirement, the size of her department had tripled in three years.

About the same number of teenagers attended Dr. McBride's

Advanced Physics class as were present in Child and Family, but no one was absent for the day. The small numbers were caused by gradual attrition over the year. Only the fittest survived to remain. Kara, who was one of them, admitted she often became "pretty lost" and routinely spent ninety minutes or more each night on physics homework. Once you understood the concept, Kara emphasized, it was easy to do the problems. But the understanding part took time and consequently had to be done at home. Her classmate Eric, she said with mild envy, could grasp things much more quickly. Eric agreed that he gave the course only thirty to forty-five minutes a night, always while listening to the radio.

Dr. McBride did not share Kara's modest estimate of her ability. He thought it understandable that she struggled a bit in Advanced Physics, since she had not taken the first-year course that normally was a prerequisite. Her self-perception was based on the fact that in this course she was not at or near the top of the class. But she spoke English as a second language, maintained an A average in other courses, and had been accepted through early decision at MIT. While Kara anxiously awaited word on admission to her first-choice school, Eric could be more relaxed. He had already gained early acceptance to Yale, his first-choice college.

For most of the class Dr. McBride stood in front of the blackboard, facing students seated in conventional rows. The first business was scheduling a test designed primarily to prepare for the Advanced Placement examination now only two months away. "It should be rather bloody," Dr. McBride began, but there's "really nothing like a real situation to get your attention." He had no intention of wasting precious class time on the test, however, and scheduled it for one of the deliberately unscheduled periods built into the school's weekly program. Students with a previous commitment for that period could take the test some other day.

Although Dr. McBride briefly lectured on a mathematical point, he spent the bulk of class time pressing students to ask questions about what they did not understand about simple harmonic motion. His style was to answer questions by asking other questions. When Kara asked about a homework problem she had been unable to solve, McBride asked how far she had gotten and what she had been able to do. He prodded for a reasonable next step, and when

17

she could not think of one, he asked other students to contribute suggestions. Several were made, and McBride offered additional strategic hints without telling the answer. He pointed out, for example, that what students were studying that week in mathematics — he knew that most were enrolled in the same Advanced Placement calculus course — was directly applicable to the physics problem that stumped Kara: "One of the nice parts of this course . . . is that it dovetails with what you're doing in math." He asked Kara to continue to work out loud on the problem. She proceeded uncertainly, then made a mistake, and again he asked other students to pitch in and move things along. He always answered her questions with a question. Kara: "What tells you that's the simple harmonic term?" McBride: "What form is it in?" Kara, after a long pause: "Oh!"

But even then McBride didn't abandon her question. He explained, now to the entire class, an entirely different method of solving the same problem, which employed ideas they had studied earlier in the year. All this was a prelude to a homework problem for that night: "The way they ask you to do it in the text is one of the difficult ways to do a simple problem." Eventually he would show them a clever alternative attack, "but neat ways aren't so good unless you've suffered a bit." Near the end of the period Kara said she didn't like her answer to another problem because, while correct, it seemed "kind of intuitive." McBride almost pounced. "Why do you think that way? This is physics, not math. Intuition is fine."

Kara and Eric liked the class because they imagined it operated the way serious college courses did, a belief doubtless strengthened by their knowledge that Dr. McBride had taught the same course for years in a serious college. They liked the fact that McBride was really tough, wouldn't put up with anything from anybody, and loved sarcasm. He "puts the burden on you to bring the questions to him," Eric remarked. "He expects everyone to know the stuff cold — or to have a question. If he asks for questions and no one has any, he gets angry because he expects everyone to have questions."

His expectation that students be actively involved in material even when they were lost was initially intimidating. But if they played by his rules, the class became surprisingly relaxed. McBride was completely unconcerned, for example, if academically committed students wandered in late from time to time. Nor did he collect, much less correct, homework. Students with questions could raise them in class, and he would discern the quality of their understanding by the quality of their questions. "I cannot pour anything into their heads," he said. He was a teacher, but learning was their job.

McBride's own sense of his classroom objectives and style closely matched the perceptions of Eric and Kara. Physics, he believed, was one of the hardest subjects in high school because mastery required learning a new language. Student opinions were not germane. "They are the uninitiated, and I am there to initiate them, so the style is an old-fashioned style of me at the front board." The hardest thing about teaching was getting students to ask questions about what they did not know. He recalled "long, embarrassing classes where I've simply refused to say a thing until they ask a question." Sometimes he had to wait thirty minutes for something to happen. Able and competitive students did not want to be wrong or to appear confused in front of him or their peers. "Asking questions is really what it is all about; getting the answers is really fairly easy."

Mrs. Jefferson knew intimate details of her students' lives outside school and found her mission in the connection between their daily struggles and what she taught. In contrast, Dr. McBride went out of his way to emphasize that he had no interest in their personal lives at all: "I'm not a counselor." His job was only to teach physics; "it's disastrous to be really friendly with a student," he claimed. To his sixty-five students — down from ninety at the beginning of the year — McBride was sure he gave what they wanted. It was what he wanted, too. Compared with teaching at the college where he had spent his early career, in public high school McBride could work at a faster pace and to a higher level. Students were more interested in the subject — he had no premeds to worry about — and there were fewer of them. He could do what he wanted. For every student who avoided his classes at all costs, there were others who would if necessary bend the system to gain admission.

Jefferson and McBride are committed teachers, respected by the students they deal with, but they are worlds apart in what their high school work is about. They represent the polarities of the horizontal curriculum. In her celebration of "life skills," Mrs. Jefferson is heir to a long American tradition of the practical utility of secondary education, not just to the business of life but to the business of survival in life. She would not be embarrassed to have high school goals include learning the value of taking a bath prior to a job interview. She knows this information is not self-evident. Just as important, she feels comfortable and confident conveying it. There are important things her students simply have to know.

But whenever a student's classroom comment strayed from an expected fact, she became flustered. Mrs. Jefferson ignored Robert's provocative challenge to the male teacher hypothesis, reacted defensively to the interesting comment about female stress, and did not seem upset that the bell rang before she could respond to the crack about communism. Her behavior suggested that she considers students' ideas to be distractions rather than welcome signs of life. They got in the way of communicating the knowledge about parenting that, if firmly implanted, could ameliorate some of life's miseries. These ideas also put her in an uncomfortable no-man's-land, where the life skill at issue is not fact-possession but thinking itself. Faced with faint signals of students' use of their minds, she disregarded them. Responding to the questioning of Robert and the others would have required abandoning for a moment *her* conception of life skills in favor of another. Thinking was not a course goal, nor questioning a method.

On the other end of the horizontal curriculum, Kara and Eric had no immediate need for what Mrs. Jefferson taught. They did not live, like Robert and his classmates, in poor, broken homes. They had no plans for early parenthood, lived comfortably in intact families, and learned from parents all four of whom had professional jobs. The students in the two classes were worlds apart in background and ambition, yet the horizontal curriculum gladly embraced both worlds and many others as well. For Kara and Eric, Advanced Physics was all business; there was nothing esoteric about it. It was at least as close to their lives — "something they really can relate to" — as Child and Family was to Robert's; even closer, if class attendance and time spent outside class on a course are indices of perceived relevance. For a girl who regarded MIT as a second-choice college, the course provided an extra edge. But its uses went beyond the politics of college admission. Kara wanted to be a pediatrician, Eric a scientist. Advanced Physics was clearly vocational preparation for both.

Kara and Eric were aware and grateful that their shopping mall high school offered not merely college-level instruction (all Advanced Placement courses by definition are supposed to be "college" courses); it offered college instruction at a level no less sophisticated than basic physics at the *best* American colleges. The school's commitment to doing this expressed, to Dr. McBride, the American high school at its best, just as its commitment to handling the needs of the afflicted expressed the school's excellence to Mrs. Jefferson. Each teacher was making a practical appeal to a different audience: one offered help in handling the logistics of daily living, the other invited students to join the educational and vocational fast track. The crucial difference was that McBride's approach, perhaps even more than his content, encouraged another "life skill": students' capacity to think for themselves, to feel comfortable with solving problems on their own. This approach differentiated the classes, in the long run, more decisively than the more obvious differences in what their subjects contained. By attempting to meet student and teacher needs, the horizontal curriculum in this instance widened the already wide gap between the Roberts and the Karas.

The Vertical Curriculum

Shopping malls sell not only different products — color televisions and blue jeans, for instance — but also different kinds of TV sets and jeans, with different features and price tags. There is almost as much variety within product categories as there are products. Malls themselves differ from each other not by product categories alone but by the styles and prices of what is sold. There are "upscale" malls for more affluent tastes. In a similar way, high school goods with apparently generic labels — introductory algebra, American history, junior English — are available in different versions within the same school. Each version has distinct features designed to appeal to a particular set of consumer tastes, formed by previous education, ability, motivation, family background, peer pressure, and the blandishments of the purveyors. There are upscale high schools, too.

Not all courses are available in different versions, but most of those that generate large enrollments and require some cognitive dexterity are offered in a vertical curriculum complementing the horizontal. This greatly enhances variety. The vertical curriculum is usually described by "levels"; the word "track" is not fashionable in the 1980s. The names and numbers of levels within a subject vary according to local traditions. Some schools speak of honors, college-preparatory, general, and basic levels. Others use words such as accelerated and regular, and still others employ a letter designation or Arabic or Roman numerals.

Whatever system of product labeling is used, the main purpose is to disclose in advance to prospective consumers the degree of difficulty in courses with similar titles. This is a more subtle undertaking than differentiating between kinds of products — between, say, Child and Family and Advanced Physics — and catalogs therefore often expend considerable effort in making the differences clear. At times the advertising campaign is remarkably candid. Students in one school were told they should elect one level of sophomore English if they were "willing and able to read two or three books a term and to write about experience or books once a week." Another level was appropriate "if you read and write only when you have to," while a third made sense for those who had trouble with reading and writing. At this level, "most of the reading and writing assignments can be completed during class time."

An important function of such candor is to minimize consumer complaints by clarifying in advance the expectations and responsibilities. When courses at various levels have the same name, the descriptions make clear that what is offered and what is expected vary enormously from one course to another. In general, the vertical curriculum is not an instrument to achieve similar ends by different means. Levels usually embody different notions of proficiency and of what a subject is, rather than the notion of different roads to a common destination. One level of junior English often resembles another no more than Child and Family resembles Advanced Physics.[3]

Variety within the vertical curriculum is further enhanced because even courses at the same level are frequently taught by different teachers with considerable freedom to shape their classes as they choose. Students everywhere understand that the experience of a course depends as much (if not more) on who the teacher is as it does on the catalog description. Consumerism allows students in some schools to select teachers as well as courses. Even at the Advanced Placement level, where a common national examination supposedly enforces a common standard, students and their parents understand that dramatic differences exist among teachers and therefore among courses.

In an AP science course, for example, students knew that two teachers brought contrasting philosophies and personalities to the same subject. One version emphasized theory and was designed for prospective scientists; the instructor, like Dr. McBride, was brusque and sarcastic. The other version was more relaxed, proceeded at a slower pace, and had a more hands-on approach and a more nurturing instructor; it was not designed for the budding scientist despite its AP status. Each teacher had defenders and detractors. But in the opinion of students and parents, variety should properly extend this far. "You can't blame them for looking," one satisfied parent commented on the consumerism of his children. An experienced administrator remarked, "There's more feeling now that I don't need to have *you* as a teacher. I can get somebody else."

Junior English as a label masks an extraordinary range of intentions, materials, and methods. Consider three classes; all met the junior English graduation requirement. Applied Communication met the junior English requirement in one school at the level of least difficulty. The class gathered in an attractive theater where attendance ranged from thirty to forty on any given day. Mr. Lynch stood on stage, lecturing and asking questions about comic books as a literary form. Armed with a theatrical flair and considerable knowledge of the history of comics, he held the attention of most students throughout the period.

He began by reviewing the link between comics and the broader themes of the course. "Remember, the function of this is to see how the plot relates to literature. Does anyone know what 'plot' is?" After several seconds of silence, he continued, "A plot is the action of a story — the action that takes place. That's very important." He described two other literary concepts that could be found in comics: "character — people in it" and "setting — time and place, when it takes place and where it takes place." Gradually he increased the complexity of his talk. He reviewed the "three purposes of comics," emphasizing in particular that comics reflected the times in which they were written.

Midway through the period Mr. Lynch changed his approach. He projected on a screen the earliest depictions of Superman. "Superman is one of the most important characters . . . I'd like you to remember Siegel and Shuster." When he asked about Superman's abilities, there was far more response than before. "Faster than a speeding bullet," one student called out. Another asked, "Do we still have to take notes?" "No," Mr. Lynch replied, "this is for your own education . . . This is going to take me about fifteen minutes. Just sit back and enjoy."

The class became pure entertainment. As various Superman strips were projected, Lynch spoke the dialogue with dramatic skill, altering voices according to character. From time to time students shouted out their reactions: "Check out his hair already!" When a response took the form of a question — "Are these the same people writing the comics?" — he swiftly followed it up: "No, let's take some time to talk about this." To reinforce his point, he told the story of how Siegel and Shuster gave up their rights to Superman for one hundred dollars.

Two days later Batman and Robin were the subjects of his scrutiny. Again Mr. Lynch made interesting historical asides about the characters — for instance, he mentioned the controversy over whether their relationship was homosexual — and connected these facts to the idea of plot. Batman could not carry a gun because he could not be placed in a position to kill off central characters, like Joker. Villains needed to live to continue the story line. In this class Mr. Lynch also announced the main writing project for the term. Each student (or pair: two could work together) would create an eight-page comic book. Two pages had to be ads; one had to contain letters to the editor. They would be given seven full classroom periods to execute the project, and he emphasized their obligation to use this time well. "You need to take responsibility," he said. Writing the comic strip was really like writing a short story.

Mr. Lynch knew that the goods available in his class were a far cry from what most people, including himself, imagined junior English to be. Variety in the vertical curriculum allowed for a primary focus on entertainment. Because the content was something that students might relate to, he hoped they would attend, be orderly, and perhaps learn something about plot, character, and setting. Everybody knew the course was a dumping ground for the unproficient and uncommitted. He expected few to buy, and only hoped enough would remain to browse. There were no illusions about product quality in Applied Communication.

Contrast that course with a middle-level or "regular" version of junior English. Unlike Applied Communication, this class was designed as college preparation, and most of the students planned to attend four-year colleges. Mrs. Austin greeted the seventeen students with jokes and puns as they trooped boisterously into her room. She promptly announced that there were two activities on the day's agenda. They would read favorite passages from *The Catcher in the Rye* to each other — selecting the passages had been the homework assignment — and they would play a quiz game.

After everyone's book had been opened to the correct place, a girl read haltingly for a minute. "What does he mean by that last couple of lines?" the teacher probed at the end. The student countered, "Can't I tell you why I like it?" "Oh yes," Mrs. Austin said, "tell us why you like the last part." "The reason is because he finally admits that he likes everybody." "That's right. Who else has a favorite passage?" No one volunteered, so Mrs. Austin read for four minutes in a style nicely expressive of Holden Caulfield's adolescent sarcasm. Everyone listened with evident amusement and many laughed from time to time.

Mrs. Austin liked her own passage because it was humorous and reminded her of contrived, silly movies. The best part was "where he's talking about the lady that cries in the movie but won't take her son to the bathroom. What kind of thing do you think he's trying to get at in real life?" After a long silence she continued,

25

"Psychiatrists are saying now — I've heard it someplace — that people who spend an inordinate amount of time watching soap operas, for example, and living the lives of characters, are often themselves not very humane to other people. They lead a false kind of life, so they can't really feel sympathetic or empathetic with real people. There might be a grain of truth in that, who knows?" Then she asked for more volunteers.

None of the three other students who read aloud remembered to tell why he or she liked the passage chosen, and none was asked to do so. At the beginning of each reading, everyone's visual attention was fixed on the speaker, but during the readings attention noticeably waned. One student surreptitiously opened a package of Fritos and munched away; another nonchalantly combed her hair. Some stared out of the window and a few initiated whispered conversations. Basic order was never lost, though. There were no reprimands or calls for silence. Mrs. Austin later said that she hadn't had a discipline problem in years.

Then the quiz game began. The class split into two teams, with the boys at one side of the room and the girls on the other. The point was for the girls to answer written questions posed by the boys, and vice versa. The questions had been prepared ahead of time as part of a homework assignment. A correct answer earned a team one point; talking among team members gave two points to the team's opponents. The game served as a relaxed review for an upcoming test.

Virtually all of the questions called for the recall of minute plot details. What was the name of the elevator operator? What title did Holden hold on the fencing team? What was the name of Holden's mistress? As the game progressed the noise level grew. Team members talked to one another — more points were accumulated this way than through correct answers — and friendly banter shot back and forth. One boy yelled, "I can't remember, but give me a point anyway." Everyone laughed at that, including the teacher. When another boy protested that the girls would win " 'cause these guys never even read the book," everyone laughed again. When a girl paused a moment before answering, a boy called out, "Hey! Come on!" "Shut up, I'm trying," she yelled back. "Now, now," interrupted Mrs. Austin, suddenly the domestic peacemaker, "no fighting until you get married." A roar of knowing laughter rocked the room.

After class she emphasized the importance of choosing books "that I know they're going to like." Extensive experience with the regular level, at which she much preferred to teach, was that "the pie-in-the-sky *Scarlet Letter* and that type of thing" would just not work. She had assigned it anyway because it was a classic and this was a college-prep class. The students didn't like it but at least they were good sports; "I didn't like it either," she said. *Catcher* was far more congenial to both sides. "We get into the fact that even though it was written thirty or forty years ago, that it is still universal, that it has a lot of truths for today's living." That was her goal. "I tell my students that in reading they learn a lot about themselves. And about others. Even though it's fiction."

This class was a more familiar version of junior English. Students read an acknowledged high school classic, were assigned homework, and discussed the book. Unlike the Applied Communication class, where everyone understood that something other than English was being offered, Mrs. Austin's class had an unmistakable product. But the goods were bogus. Illusions abounded in this middle-level college-prep course. Mrs. Austin did not push her students or herself. She settled for poor reading or no reading; no examination of why passages were chosen; brief answers to trivial questions; and an environment nearly as relaxed and entertaining as that of the other class. Yet she clearly "covered" reputable material. The class was about junior English without taking it seriously. Here was another kind of product available and consumed in the shopping mall high school.

Contrast that product with another level of junior English. Ms. Fish sat in a circle with twenty-one advanced students. The work under scrutiny was Ibsen's play *A Doll's House*, and, as in the other class, students had generated a list of questions. Ms. Fish had duplicated the questions and handed out copies. Her plan was to break the class into small groups to consider some of the questions, and later reconvene to make summary reports. But protests ensued. "We want to hear *everyone's* reaction," one student said. A unanimous student vote confirmed this preference and the lesson plan was discarded.

The first question was whether it was fair to force particular values, such as religious ones, on a child too young to know whether he or she in fact preferred them. Immediately the discussion became animated; six students volunteered responses from personal experience within five minutes. Suddenly Ms. Fish cut the discussion off, skipped over several questions, and finally settled on one farther down. Was it right for Nora to have left her family? After class she explained that her intention at this point in the period was to move the discussion into the play rather than staying with personal experiences. The students were charming talkers, and the danger of neglecting the play was always present.

"No," replied a girl whom Ms. Fish called on, "it was another childish thing to do." From this point on, student comments, which had previously been directed to Ms. Fish, were directed mainly to each other. They began to argue about a highly charged issue: under what circumstances can a parent responsibly abandon a family in order to grow into a more independent person? Some vehemently disagreed with the first speaker. In the family, Nora "never had a chance to be independent." Her withdrawal was not selfish; she merely realized her inadequacies and was attempting to deal with them. Besides, another pointed out, she rarely saw her children even when she was in the family. Such thinking, the first girl rejoined, smacked of the "me-first" mentality of today's generation. Nora was saying that her needs were greater than the responsibilities she had accumulated. "It's childish to say that she's not an ideal mother so let's scrap the whole relationship."

Ms. Fish participated in the debate in two ways. She tried to ensure that a maximum number of students spoke: "Give John a chance and then Blair, who has been extraordinarily patient." And she intervened when necessary, as she later put it, "to get them into the experience of the play and away from intellectualizing." Intellectualizing, like talking only about personal experiences, was a way to evade the play. She explained that there were students who liked to talk but would only talk about the play as a disembodied historical artifact; they would mention, for example, that it had shocked its own generation. When one boy spoke this way, Ms. Fish pressed for a personal reaction to the play itself. "What do *you* think of this? Do you think Nora ought to have left the family?"

"It's heavy." "But what do you personally think?" "She had to leave. Torvald wouldn't have changed. She couldn't have changed had she stayed there." Ms. Fish confronted the initial speaker the same way. "What if she can't change? . . . I'm trying to get you to answer a question you don't want to answer." The girl replied, "I don't disagree with her leaving. I just disagree with her doing it that way." At the end of the hour, a boy said, "Torvald has treated her as something to have around the house — a garnishment." Cheers and laughter followed. "A vocabulary word!" someone shouted in delight.

Afterward Ms. Fish said she was relieved at the openness with which a tough issue had been discussed. She planned to assign Alice Walker's *Meridian* next. This book, about a black woman growing up in the South, was filled with complex racial and sexual issues. Now she thought the students had sufficient sensitivity to begin the task.

The product Ms. Fish offered was more than coverage. By ceaseless questioning, she attempted to engage students in the material. She wouldn't let them alone. Her class was more exhausting than relaxing. Variety within the vertical curriculum thus takes many forms. Students, teachers, and materials can differ profoundly in their conception of junior English. What linked these otherwise different classes was the consumerism they embodied. Each teacher was intent on — and successful at — satisfying the demands of very different consumer tastes. They were all proud of their popularity and pleased by a system that allowed them to teach in a manner that was as comfortable to them as it was congenial to their students.

The Extracurriculum

No high school phrase is more misleading than "extracurricular activities." There is nothing extra about the extracurriculum, whether schools are rich or poor, public or private, large or small. Most teachers and students regard the extracurriculum as constructively educational. It supplements the rest of the curriculum and lures many students and teachers even when academic credit is not given. It is as integral to high schools as food service and celebrity appearances are integral to shopping malls.

Sports are the most visible part of the extracurriculum. Whatever external uses they may have in stimulating community support or providing public entertainment, their internal educational function is widely acknowledged. Curiously, they have supplied the most powerful pedagogical metaphor in recent educational discussion — "coaching" — to reformers with intellectual rather than athletic objectives. And they are defended on educational grounds that extol their usefulness in vocational preparation and in teaching cooperation and personal self-esteem.

One boy assumed as a matter of course that high school should provide vocational education in sports as well as in other fields. "My athletics have really suffered," he lamented, although he found nothing wrong with his school's academic program. There were "a lot of things that I haven't learned that these coaches should have taught me." They "haven't really prepared me for college ball." His sympathetic coaches agreed that the school had not invested sufficiently in equipment, facilities, and qualified instructors. The education of many youngsters had therefore been shortchanged. They thought the problem was not that sports were unimportant in their school, but rather that they were viewed less as a route to college scholarships or eventual jobs and more as a route to developing self-esteem. Achieving the latter goal required little more than the fielding of teams.

The extracurriculum, whether it is sports or some other activity, usually gets better reviews. Andy, for example, freely admitted he was overextended in extracurricular activities. "Really, I'm amazed I make it. But that's one of the reasons I enjoy school that much, because I have something to come to other than the note-taking. Like I say, it's a whole learning experience if you can use that to your advantage."

As a student council member, a position that carried course credit, Andy could try to implement some of his ideas. The council's theme for the year was "Dare!" To Andy this meant "daring for people to attend sports events, and to just become involved." He didn't want teenagers to be able to say at the end of high school, "Hey, the school didn't do anything for me. It just made me sit in the classroom and take notes." He wanted instead "to make school a place where you're not restricted to book-learning, but life-learning."

He would only be satisfied when more students came to high school with the attitude that "you're going to experience so many things that you're going to come out ahead either way it goes, even if you don't take classes or something you need for college." They had to understand that education was more than academics.

Besides the Dare program Andy spent time on a council effort to prepare eighth-graders for entry into high school, founded a youth and government club, and gave presentations to student groups on topics ranging from birth control to values clarification. He did gymnastics, cross-country, and track, and he numbered Advanced Dance and Public Speaking among his favorite courses. He knew his way around the extracurriculum sufficiently well to know that for him, as a black, gaining access to traditionally white enclaves like the student newspaper was too complicated to be worth the trouble. He was proud that various teachers had told him he had a serious future in politics.

Andy's savvy in using the extracurriculum did not carry over to the horizontal or vertical curricula. He regarded these as peripheral to his high school education. Although he fully expected to go on to college, he was taking introductory algebra as a senior. If he failed the course, he reasoned, he would simply repeat it in college. He had had an unpleasant conflict with his junior English teacher and claimed that he had been prevented from taking biology until the end of high school because years earlier the school had misread his reading scores. To no avail he had attempted to take an advanced-level course. This astute young man, who had used one part of the school to his constructive advantage, was at sea in negotiating access to the academic curriculum: "Me on my own, I can't do it." His energies remained in the extracurriculum, where he felt in charge.

Brad also loved high school. "I think I look forward more to school than anything else. It puts order in my life, which I need." High school was his world, and increasingly he found that the best part was the extracurriculum. As a freshman he had dreamed of becoming a veterinarian, but quickly learned that neither math nor chemistry was his strong suit. What he was good at was politics and public speaking. "I just love to speak in front of people," he said excitedly. "It gets me all pumped up inside. It's a great feeling."

Admittedly behind in several academic subjects, he had made deliberate decisions about where to allocate his considerable energy. Student council was his biggest arena; he had ambitions for a major elective office the next year. "The purpose of the student council is to teach you how to be a leader." He was also active in school plays, and a member of the soccer team. He saw all these things in part as vocational education: "I am looking for a career in political science or politics. I'm not going to look in math." But he saw in them a liberal education as well: "I have to be a human being, and I have to be a compassionate human being. If I spend all my time wrapped up in books, maybe I won't take time enough for what goes on around our world. That's what I'm starting to learn from [high school]. That's what I really truly appreciate." Like Andy, Brad appreciated his school's willingness to give him room to find his way. "Of course," he admitted, high school "can't accommodate everybody. It can't look after everybody in the way they want to be looked after." But his school came pretty close to saying "if you want to do this, we are here. We'll back you up." Brad believed "people have chances here."

High schools are proud of their Andys and Brads, solid citizens despite their distance from the academic curriculum. They are institutional success stories. The goods they have purchased are decency and direction, and for the schools that is more than enough. Schools often permit such youngsters to gain substantial graduation credit for their various activities. Student council, the newspaper, the yearbook, the magazine, the debate club, are all usually credit offerings. One school allows students to take up to 36 percent of their credits during grades ten through twelve in Marching and Concert Band. Several others *require* students participating in these activities to take connected courses for credit.

But the penetration of the extracurriculum into the credit curriculum sometimes meets the preferences of those who, unlike Brad and Andy, simply want the easiest path to graduation. One such student, Beth, reduced the number of truly extracurricular activities she engaged in and incorporated them when possible into her regular credit program. By the time she was a senior, her main after-school activity was "to go home and be bored. Because there's nothing to do here and it's more comfortable to sit around at home or talk on the phone." Brad believed that high school gave students chances; Beth wanted only the chance to graduate, and was sure the school would accommodate her wish.

The Services Curriculum

Shopping malls increasingly offer services for sale in addition to tangible products. A walk-in medical clinic, for example, may rent space next to a shoe store. Sometimes the proximity of functions seems surprising and incongruous; but after all, the mall is where the people are. In high school, traditional educational products are similarly offered side by side with an expanding range of social and psychological services. Although it is perhaps the least known, the services curriculum is the fastest-growing component of educational variety in the shopping mall high school. Its specialized sectors and departments rival in complexity those of any other curriculum.

Some services directly address social or psychological problems — grief, child abuse, hunger, alienation. Schools sometimes provide daycare for the children of students. One school has a program to rehabilitate teenage prostitutes, while another has considered creating one to serve the growing number of unmarried teenage fathers who choose to adopt their children when mothers have abandoned them. The possible programs are limited only by the possible problems, for each problem conveys a need for a program.

Other services are for students with "special needs": the handicaps and disabilities recognized by federal and state laws. Only those who are immediately affected care about the particulars of the programs with names like Identifiable Perceptual Communicative Disorders, Significantly Identifiable Emotional Behavioral Disorders, Severely Limited Intellectual Capacity, and Mentally Retarded Significantly Handicapped. What is distinctive about these services is that their existence and nature is mandated by law; eligible students are entitled to them. But the procedures and often the funding come mainly from outside the school districts.

Still other services are directly remedial: tutorials, laboratories, centers, and resource rooms for students in academic trouble. In one school alone, deficiencies in English could be remedied entirely outside the special-needs offerings, in a Prep Seminar, a course called

33

English Maintenance and Improvement, an English Laboratory, and a program called Individualized Reading Instruction. Although the school's test scores ranked high in its district, the principal estimated that 25 percent of the students were enrolled in at least one special-education or remedial program.

These services add to the variety of school programs in part because credit is often given for using them. Even services that might at first seem more appropriate to a clinic than to a school are not only offered in school but offered for credit. Thus a Divorce Resource Group was a course as well as a service, as was an Adolescent Parenting Program designed "for teenage parents and teenagers who are pregnant whether or not they intend to keep their babies." The curriculum included preparing unwed mothers for modern childbirth — "stretching, breathing, relaxing, and various moving techniques." But even when credit is not given, services add to variety because participation in them is how many students and adult professionals spend considerable school time.

Consider the activities of Ms. Devlin, a school social worker. A counselor's referral led to a meeting of a boy who had physically assaulted his mother, the distraught mother, and Ms. Devlin. At the session the social worker provided on-the-spot counseling, a review of responsibilities and penalties under the law, and some practical suggestions on how to avoid further incidents. The next day the boy came to see Ms. Devlin, claiming that the source of the problem was his mother's inability to accept his homosexuality. When eventually confronted with this diagnosis in another conference, the mother admitted that it was true. At Ms. Devlin's suggestion, parent and child agreed to seek outside counseling; she referred them to a local mental health agency. Ms. Devlin was sure the problem would soon be solved. Problems like this arose every day.

In a school that took pride in its reputation for academic excellence, Ms. Devlin's careful records revealed she had seen 17 percent of the student body so far that academic year. Forty-nine students were seen because of poor attendance, 75 for behavior problems, 69 for educational deficiencies, and 55 because of family difficulties. Referrals came from teachers, administrators, counselors, parents, special-education personnel, the school nurse, other social workers, outside social and legal agencies, and the students themselves. Her files indicated that 118 of them had received individual counseling or therapy, 12 group counseling, 74 family counseling, 130 consultation and collaboration with in-school personnel, 87 consultation and collaboration with outside agencies, and 27 referrals to outside agencies.

"I work with students who have problems," she said, "and they're supposed to be school-related problems . . . Whatever interferes with their schoolwork or their school adjustment is something that I take on." Ms. Devlin was also the school's liaison to the local mental health clinic, the juvenile court and criminal justice system, the social agencies, and the health agencies. She coordinated the team conferences for special-education students that were mandated by federal law, and when time permitted she engaged in counseling sessions with parents, students, and sometimes teachers. The biggest recent change in her job was caused by the new services for handicapped children. "By law I'm now required to do so much work with special-ed kids that I don't have time to do the other kind of counseling."

Over the years Ms. Devlin's job had changed in other ways. She recalled that teenage runaways had been a major problem at the end of the sixties but had substantially declined recently. Although the issue of teenage pregnancy had not gone away, it had been recast. Only a few years back, she would refer a pregnant girl to an out-of-school program where she could continue her education until the baby was born. Now there was no demand for such a program because "there really isn't any stigma attached to being pregnant anymore." The girls stayed in school until their babies were born. But since more teenagers were keeping babies instead of putting them up for adoption, new services were needed to allow them to continue their schooling as young mothers.

Social services are by no means the exclusive territory of school-based social workers. A remarkable variety of adults define their own professional identity through servicing social needs. Guidance counselors are usually the most numerous and influential. A typical day for one guidance counselor included meeting with a learning-disabled student who wanted to talk about the inherited disease that had already killed a sister; with a senior about college admissions; with a student leader who was attempting to explain the vandalism caused by other student leaders while on a school trip; with the therapist of a student suffering from anorexia nervosa; and with a student accused of cheating.

School nurses describe their work in far broader terms than providing first aid and doing physical examinations. One regarded physical exams as primarily an instructional rather than a medical task. "It's a powerful teaching tool," she said. "I really take advantage of that opportunity. I don't just zip through the exam . . . I encourage questions, and even if they don't ask questions, then I ask them questions. Everybody has feelings about their body, but most people are so out of tune with their body that they just treat it as an instrument, something that gets you where you need to go."

This nurse's principal stressed that "the kids who come to her don't always have medical problems so much as emotional problems." And her monthly reports confirmed that "counseling" was the reason most often given for student visits. In one month she saw 34 students because of illness, gave first aid to 105, and provided counseling to 152. The bulk of her counseling had to do with health-related issues, especially venereal disease, pregnancy, birth control, and other aspects of sexuality. She was especially pleased by the increasing number of boys who made appointments to talk. But counseling was by no means confined to physical health, narrowly viewed. No problem loomed larger in her mind than severe adolescent depression, which she feared was growing to almost epidemic proportions.

The most striking feature of the nurse's perception of her role was its assured association with the total educational mission of high school. She regarded herself not as mere support staff for the teachers, but as an instructor/counselor in her own right. What she did was at least as important as what teachers did. She claimed to know one third of the student body well and sustained that relationship by active sponsorship of various student clubs.

Other adults traditionally on the periphery of high school life have the same attitude. They too regard themselves as teachers, often with a clearer sense of purpose than those who teach history or math. The security director for one high school deliberately named his office the Department of Safety Service to make clear that he was providing far more than security. "Here," he said with satisfaction, "we are more counselors than we are police officers." He insisted that each of his security guards develop a specialty that went beyond his or her primary responsibility: lifesaving, locksmith skills, rape prevention, bilingual skills, and parking ticket management. Furthermore, he wanted the guards to associate themselves with at least one activity that was educationally central. He himself worked with handicapped youth.

The logic of extending social services is virtually airtight in the shopping mall high school. After all, said one director of health services, a student "can't learn if he has a toothache. He can't learn if he's cold because he doesn't have adequate clothing. He can't learn if he has an overwhelming fear. We try to do what we're able to do to alleviate the effect of these kinds of things." But the director also thought there were reasonable limits. He remembered that the parents of a deaf boy who wanted to play varsity football had argued that the high school was required by law to hire an aide who could sign for him on the field so he would understand the signals. "They wanted this aide not so that he could learn, but so he could play football!" The parents thought that the high school, which had made remarkable provisions to address their son's handicap in regular classes, was as much about football as it was about academics. They wanted whatever they could get for their son, in this case greater variety through a marriage of the extracurriculum and the services curriculum. "Schools are being asked to do more and more all the time, particularly in my department," said the health services director. "We just can't do it." But they would continue to try.

Why are these four aspects of curriculum variety so pervasive, even at a time of declining student enrollments, economic retrenchment, and the beginnings of a national emphasis on basics? Why do schools protest so vehemently the cutbacks forced upon them? For if some of the mini-courses created in the late 1960s were admitted excesses, most cutbacks were viewed inside schools as educational setbacks. When budget reductions forced the elimination of sailing and riflery from one school's extracurriculum, many parents were surprised to learn that those activities had been there in the first place, but some professionals argued that students had been "hurt" by the decision. Counselors who wanted more rather than fewer remedial courses in their services curriculum protested, "We are ignoring the needs of the community."

Schoolpeople, students, and parents like variety in high schools for the same reasons shopkeepers and customers like variety in malls. Variety makes prosperity possible for all. Market research suggests that variety in products and services is necessary to attract potential consumers to the mall, get them to browse, and eventually get them to buy. Potential consumers are different, and if a maximum number of transactions is to be recorded, a variety of tastes and circumstances must be accommodated. If the market is potentially everybody, there must be something for everybody. One science teacher described his school as the kind of place that simultaneously enrolled twelve Mentally Retarded Significantly Handicapped students and five National Merit Scholarship finalists. He even made sure that they were all together for at least one of his classes, when he conducted an experiment high in exciting visual effects. "There is a broad range of kids here," he explained, "but we pride ourselves on being able to deal with each individual kid and to help him move forward in whatever ways are best for that individual." Another characterized his school as a "slice of life." Everyone was there, everyone had to be served, and that moral mandate required enormous curricular variety. A student explained variety by remarking, "It's a big job to make up a curriculum that everybody can do."

Even the most seasoned veterans could not supply precise statistics on the growth of student inclusiveness. One teacher guessed that 20 to 30 percent of the present senior class would have dropped out only two decades before. High school is the one institution in society that not only enrolls the entire population — the lower schools do that — but enrolls people at an age when their diversity is fully apparent. Post-secondary education, despite its mass quality, segregates students into different types of institutions and excludes those at the lower end.

But why should student diversity necessarily require such a varied curriculum in high schools? Why does the idea of meeting individual needs focus so heavily on differences rather than similarities? Why is a need-based curriculum so broad? Part of the answer is that the shopping mall high school cares more about consumption than about what is consumed. Buying something offered for sale is more important than what is bought. The Brads and Andys are valued because they buy something. Whether that something is physics or junior English or sports or music or riflery, schools think it is crucial for teenagers to "plug into something that gives them support." High schools want to provide that something. "Everyone has to feel successful at something," schoolpeople constantly point out. Feeling successful itself seems a valid purchase. That deep conviction alone justifies a varied program because there are so many ways to hope teenagers can feel successful.

Teachers speak less frequently about the resulting variety among themselves. Yet there is no escaping the fact that the variety of customers and products produces a profoundly varied sales force. Disagreements of the most fundamental sort often surface. "There's too much stress on academics and not much time for other things," one teacher complained. "Maybe that was OK when the kids would only live to be forty, but now they're going to live to be seventy or so. Why not let them enjoy this part of their lives? Why push them so hard?" At the same time an equally devoted teacher excoriated a colleague's work: "They have river trips and all that. You can do that, but my concern is, can you read, can you do basic math skills? You know, it's nice to be able to paddle a boat, but can you read?"

Choice

When variety exists in abundance, how choices are made among many possible goods and services becomes a crucial issue. Through expensive advertising, shops attempt to shape choice; but power fundamentally resides in the hands of the consumer. The customer is almost always right. A similar attitude prevails in the shopping mall high school.

Dr. Nelson, an experienced guidance counselor, celebrated his school's "deep, deep commitment and concern that we don't dictate the program to the kid. The kid builds the program around his or her needs." He emphasized that the catalog's clear commitment to honor the individuality of each child was not idle rhetoric. It embodied the democratic ideal at its best. Dr. Nelson was proud that graduation requirements were "very minimal." For the last three years of high school they included three years of English, two of social studies (including American history), one of science, and three (more or less) of physical education. "Everything else depends on the child's needs." With the exception of one English course and two years of physical education, the requirements were only to *take* courses rather than to *pass* them. If students failed them, they could still graduate by accumulating credits in other subjects. Furthermore, the only actual course that everyone had to take was the state-mandated American history.

The school's principal elaborated on why freedom of choice is so important. Adolescence, he suggested, is a time of normal disorganization; it is therefore psychologically counterproductive to impose restrictions on teenagers. "Freedom is a major learning experience . . . We don't believe in restraining kids. We want to give them choices with support, and let them make mistakes." People learn better, he thought, from encountering trouble than they do from smooth sailing. Trouble helps focus attention on problems of morality and justice. It is healthy for teenagers to be exposed to the admittedly unhealthy things that sometimes happen in school, such as vandalism and snowball fights. "The school represents these paradoxes rather than attempts to control them," the principal said. During Dr. Nelson's celebration of freedom he was informed that his son's locker had just been blown up.

The school expressed its beliefs in ways that went beyond diploma requirements. Its open campus allowed students to come and go when they had free periods. Juniors and seniors could spend assigned study halls in a variety of places, including special film showings and lectures. Several excused absences a year permitted engagement in outside political activities. "You're really asked to grow up quickly," a teacher said, "— to make a lot of decisions."

Student choice was central to how teenagers at all levels described the school. One enthusiastic booster enrolled in a vocational specialization said, "You can do whatever you want here . . . You can be a scholar or a total idiot." A friend concurred, emphasizing that "it's all up to you in this school, it's all up to you . . . If you want to learn, this is one of the best places around." A student in the advanced courses agreed: "The education is there for you and it's up to the individual person to go out and get it." If you take the initiative, another said, "it's all at your feet."

When teenagers say "It's here if you want it," they are describing how variety and choice together make the shopping mall high school distinctive. Freedom of choice is a ubiquitous characteristic. The guidance director of a school with flexible diploma requirements said, "The choice of courses is based on the school's graduation requirements and the student's preferences. That's all." Another guidance director commented, "The bottom line is, students can take any courses as long as they've taken the prerequisites. We give them no hassle about it." "You do what you want to here," a student agreed. One catalog assured students of their "right to enroll in any course they feel they need, and for which they are qualified." Elsewhere a parent concluded that "the burden of choice falls on the student," and an administrator confirmed that "the opportunity is here if a student is willing and able to take advantage of it."

These voices regard choice as a distinct virtue. The PTA leadership of one school proudly contrasted its institutional "buffet" with the restrictive "sit-down dinner" of a private school down the road. "Here," they agreed, "you can take any class in the school you want to. There are very few classes you have to be accepted into. There are a couple where you have to qualify, but for the most part, no matter what your IQ is or who you are, you can take that class. You can take as hard or as easy a program as you like."

Substantial choice is possible because graduation requirements are rarely restrictive, because requirements that exist can usually be satisfied in many ways, and because prerequisites (and thus course sequences) are confined to a few subjects. Most four-year high schools require an English course each year, two years of social studies, a year of science, a year of mathematics, and between one and four years of physical education. With the exception of American history and sometimes American government, few specific courses within these departments are mandated.

The range of choices within required areas depends primarily on what is offered in a given year. In one not atypical district,

Advanced Typing could meet the English requirement and Business Arithmetic the math requirement. Possible course sequences are frequently suggested in catalogs, and enrollments are sometimes restricted either because of prerequisites (as in foreign languages and math) or because admission to the honors level is by invitation only. But it is often possible to fail a required course, such as sophomore English, and take junior English the next year. Courses usually tend, as one principal put it, to stand on their own. Rules tell some students what they may not take, but they rarely specify what students *must* take.

In a system where the burden of choice falls mainly on students, the choices students make are shaped by how they, and sometimes their parents and peers, want to use high school. For some uses, little real choice exists. Students intent on vocational preparation in a technical specialization, for example, must meet requirements that often consume half their time for the final two years of high school. Students seeking admission to highly competitive colleges often experience even greater de facto restriction of choice. They "overfulfill" graduation requirements, straining for an impressive transcript that reflects what they think colleges want, more than it does what they themselves want. One able senior decided he had to forgo German in favor of physics because he could not risk college disapproval. "Language requirements are getting stiffened for college, which is why I'm going on in French," another senior reasoned. "That's why I dropped Latin . . . They want a Romantic language." Were it not for college expectations, he would never have taken any foreign language at all.

But the choices of most students are rarely constrained by postsecondary ambitions. Although most regard themselves as college-bound, the entrance requirements of most colleges do not affect significantly what students take in high school. In a school that sent many graduates to local community colleges, one teacher said the dominant student attitude about course choice was, "Things will work out." Why, students would often ask, should they take chemistry when the junior college didn't require it? A dropout could even pass the equivalency exam and enter the community college before his more committed peers had graduated from high school! That, the teacher complained, "cheapens the high school diploma."

The expectations of four-year colleges are not remarkably different. One school told its students that the most selective campus of public higher education in the state required four years of English, two of math, one of a laboratory science, one of American history, and two of a foreign language, plus one additional year of either the language, math, or science. In these courses students had to maintain a B average, with no grade lower than C. The range of the school's horizontal and vertical curricula enabled students to meet these requirements in myriad ways. And since the course grade rather than its level was the crucial college entrance criterion, there was no pressure on students to take more difficult subjects. The tendency was just the reverse. One senior was certain that good aptitude scores would compensate for marginal achievement; inherent smarts could negate laziness. In any event, "there's also a college for everyone," he firmly believed.

Affected only slightly by external demands, most students make their choices for more immediate reasons. Some choose subjects because they like them: "I take every bit of math I can." "I took [Psychology] because I'm seeing a psychiatrist now. I'm having some personal problems, problems with relationships within the family . . . I thought it would be interesting to take the course." "I'm really into music. I want to take music theory and study everything I can about music . . . I don't want to get into a lot of the academic stuff." On ROTC: "It's a new experience . . . It teaches you how to drill. It's fun." On Culinary Arts: "I like to eat." On Foods: "Foods is a good breakfast when I wake up late for school. So I have it the first period I get here."

Students often explain their choices by citing factors unrelated to subject matter. A few enroll in a particular course because it has a special reputation for excellence or uniqueness, but many more enroll in it because it is easy: "A lot of people were there because science was a requirement and they wanted to get through it with as little struggle as possible . . . It was sort of a mockery." One senior said he deliberately took unchallenging courses. "You're going to work your whole life," he explained, so high school should be a place to "enjoy life and have fun." The importance of being with acquaintances in as well as outside class is often mentioned. As one student put it, "I didn't want to leave my friends." The time a course meets can also be crucial, since students who work after school prefer to avoid afternoon classes. In several schools administrators commented that it was very hard to schedule any academic classes after lunch.

Sometimes a student's self-perception dramatically affects choice. "I guess I was scared," explained one girl. "I'm just an average student so I just took average courses." That kind of arrangement seemed the natural order of things. A boy said, "I didn't think I was too smart so I went into [Individualized] English." Sometimes friendships and self-perception work together; students often stick with those they regard as their own kind. Finally, some students don't know why they choose as they do. "I have no idea," one said; another, "I don't remember why I took it." A few cannot remember the courses they are enrolled in or whether, in fact, the courses have names at all.

Some teachers conclude that choice, for many students, is based on profound ignorance. Many of one teacher's sophomores and juniors did not know the difference between regular and accelerated courses, or the meaning of a grade point average: "They didn't know that their academic records were kept, they didn't know what a transcript was." Another pointed out, "Although we have the fabulous course catalog sitting around in the building, my experience has been that the kids don't in fact use it very well. They get overwhelmed by the size of it. And so most of their selections come about by talking with other kids." Many students agree. Although some say they keep their own counsel, most rely heavily on the advice of friends, siblings, and parents. Comrades who had passed through school immediately before them were precious sources of inside information on course demands and teacher personalities.

The involvement of parents in choice varies more sharply. Students whose parents lack a high school or post-secondary education often report that their parents don't know what courses they are taking, don't know the names of their counselors, and rarely come to school for any reason. "The parents from this area never went to school themselves for the most part," one teacher said. "If they didn't graduate from third grade, they have no way of knowing what kids should be doing in high school. They don't know what to expect, what to demand." The involvement of parents who care and are somewhat knowledgeable mirrors their general relationship with their children. Some students said they talked about school choices with parents because they talked about everything with them. Some said they talked to parents because they regarded parents as experts. Others had little choice in the matter. "My folks are grade-point oriented. They made me do it," explained one student about why he was enrolled in advanced classes when he preferred the regular level. "They kind of talk to me about it and show me why I'm wrong . . . They were probably right. I would have gotten lazy and bored."

Many parents play a far more aggressive role in course selection than mere counseling of their children. Where necessary, they will intervene to press for courses or levels they prefer. If you wanted a particular course, one boy said, "you get your mother to call up the school and bitch." Pushy parents are a formidable interest group. Variety and choice work to their advantage because they understand what they want. "The parents from the South Side," a teacher explained, "know just exactly what their kids ought to be doing and what they can expect from their kids . . . They're the ones who push their kids to succeed. Lots of times the others just don't know how."

Indeed, many committed parents only push outside school. Only there are they aware of the consequences of various choices. "Anything I can stick him into, I got him into," one mother said of her son's many activities. Why? " 'Cause when he goes to bed at night his tongue is hanging out. He's so tired he doesn't have time to get involved with anything else. He's got no time for trouble." Despite such commitment, this mother failed to oversee his classroom life; there "he just goofs off." Her confidence in pushiness stopped at the schoolhouse door. One teacher believed that in these circumstances, "we need to make [students] aware of their options rather than increase the number of programs. These kids need [to know] more about what's going on."

But how do they find out? How do schools, as distinct from peers or parents, attempt to engage students with the immense variety before them? How do they educate students about making wise choices? Shopping malls, besides running newspaper ads, maintain directories and sometimes even information booths. What do schools have besides catalogs?

The most important resource they have is guidance counselors.

Advising students is usually regarded as a specialized professional function of counselors. When advising has been described as a legitimate *teacher* responsibility, it has always been within the confines of new, experimental, and controversial programs. One school organized a "teacher advisement program" where classes were set aside to discuss course options, how to read transcripts, how to compute grade point averages, and other practical concerns. Another school experimented with similar classes in which participating teachers received an extra stipend and students received academic credit; each had to be persuaded to join up. Counselors usually believe that teachers are inadequate to the advising task, since they lack training in counseling and knowledge about the full variety of opportunities within schools. Counselors carry the brunt of advising and they prefer things that way.

George, a college-bound senior, said he was lucky to get the counselor he did. His sister had had a good experience years before with a counselor, and his mother naturally requested that George be assigned the same person. But the help that George actually received was of a very minimal sort. He never discussed with the counselor what he wanted to take or why, only whether his choices met diploma requirements and whether they could be conveniently scheduled. George said of his counselor, "If there was something there that showed you weren't going to have enough credits to graduate, then he might stop you. Otherwise, he'll simply sign off on it."

Even though George had many personal problems — he mentioned smashing up a car, seeing an outside therapist, and taking psychology to learn more about himself — it had not occurred to him to raise these issues with the counselor. Nor had the counselor raised them. Counselors, George believed, "don't point you in the direction. They let you go in the direction that you want to go in yourself. They say, 'Your counselors are there *if* you need help.' But I don't agree with that. They should be there for you whether you need help or not."

George thought that counselors were "there" only for students with very serious emotional or behavior problems or for those who were failing — then they would intervene. They would take no initiative for someone like himself. "When I get to college," he resolved, "I'm going to use my counselors a lot more than I did here." He understood that he had not taken the initiative. "I guess that they didn't work for me was partially my fault. I didn't go to them."

Derek, a Vietnamese immigrant, listened quietly to George's account and agreed with him on the reactive function of counselors in most situations: "No one will ever come to you to help you. If you want an answer for something, you have to go and look for the answer." Unlike George, who blamed his own passivity, Derek claimed he had sought help but had been ignored. He knew something about auto mechanics, and the counselor assumed that he should enter that field, "but I want to do something better, but I don't know what." Furthermore, his English was poor and isolated him from people and information. He had asked his counselor if he could be paired with a student proficient in English to practice with, "almost like an exchange student." The counselor said he would think about it, but nothing ever happened. George commented that Derek's counselor wanted to get him out of his office and off his back.

Plainly, Derek's worries were larger than just when he would get to practice his English. He felt lonely and shy, his mother was dead, and his father "left school at about fifth grade, and he doesn't know how important it is." He needed a counselor more than George did: he wanted "somebody giving you a small hint from behind or telling you once in awhile to go along," but instead he had "nobody, nobody." Sometimes, he said, "I even punish myself if I doesn't do what I should. Like I make myself run. I have to just keep running and get my body very tired. Then anything that's upsetting me is gone because I just don't have the energy. But it won't work anymore, because I'm just tired."

Then the boys talked with each other about the common elements in their different situations. They agreed that whenever they consulted any of the adults supposed to help them — counselors, nurses, social workers — the adult's assumption was that something must be *very* wrong. All they wanted was to talk to a caring adult, but the price of a conversation was that they would be considered a problem case. "It just scared me," Derek said. "She asked me so many questions it just made me scared. I don't ever want to go back there again." Not only did they always have to take the initiative to approach the counselors. When they did, the counselors imagined their job as only providing crisis care.

These perceptions are widely shared. The advising received by most students is dominated by the logistics of scheduling and meeting graduation requirements. "It's like you don't even know your counselor," one teenager complained. "You see him at the beginning of the year and that's it. You might as well not be here as far as he's concerned." "You'll see a counselor once," another reported. " 'You doing okay?' And I'll say 'Okay,' and that's that. You won't see the counselor for the rest of the year." In one school a student said that instead of saying, "You should take X or Y," the counselors would say, "What do you want to take?" When one bright college-bound senior in another school was asked why he wasn't taking any math he replied, "Hardly anyone takes it. It isn't stressed." What did he mean by stressed? "The guidance counselors wouldn't ask you, 'Why aren't you taking math?' " A girl regarded her counselor as a kind of traffic cop who told when to go and when to stop, which roads were open and which were blocked: "If I had a problem he'd be the last one I would go to." The reason was, "He doesn't know me. He wouldn't be able to help."

In the shopping mall high school, where variety and choice abound, advising is itself one more consumer good available for purchase or rejection. A parent who admired the variety and choice also concluded that "the reach is from the student to the school and not the other way . . . The arrows don't go both ways." Opportunity was there "if the student is willing and able to take advantage of it." An administrator agreed it was squarely up to parents "to become educated on how to use the resources within a school by taking the initiative themselves in contacting some of the people here."

Many students and families prefer this arrangement. One girl said she realized that her counselor would do nothing unless she took the initiative. And so she made appointment after appointment, asked many questions, and wound up receiving considerable useful advice. If people were not willing to do what she had done, she thought, they had no legitimate complaint. "You have to ask for help, they don't put it out in front of you," another defender of the system admitted. But "if you care enough about getting ahead in life, if you want it, you've got to take it and you've got to find out about it." Certain students, as one parent put it, already "know where they're going and how they are going to go about it . . . They don't require a lot of in-depth counseling."

Counselors agree that, in general, the reach is from the student to the school rather than the reverse. The fact that the burden of choice falls mainly on the student is perceived by them as inevitable and often desirable. Why? First of all, their loads alone render any other system unthinkable. At one school the student-to-counselor ratio was 420:1; at another, 320:1. A school with a 200:1 ratio boasted that it approached the national ideal. The objective of one counseling department was to see each student once a year. These conferences, a counselor estimated, "typically took about ten minutes." She explained, "I don't have time to look over each person to see what their selections are . . . We advise them but we cannot see what they have taken." (In some schools parents do not even have to sign final course selection sheets, and the rule that a teacher should sign off is not enforced.) If sheer numbers is one problem, counselors complain with equal vehemence about the paperwork loaded upon them. One estimated that fully 75 percent of her time was spent keeping records, and others pointed to the significant scheduling and monitoring activities required by special-needs legislation.

But their complaint is not that these burdens keep them from helping students to choose wisely. Rather, it is that they are prevented from giving real assistance to students with pronounced emotional and social problems. Counselors' professional identity rests in clinical psychology. Instead of wanting to mediate how students use a choice-based curriculum, they aim at distinctly psychological or therapeutic objectives such as "developing the whole child" and ensuring that students make a "good adjustment" to school. Guidance adds variety to the school's services curriculum more than it manages consumer choice.

The more sophisticated the guidance department, the greater the pride it takes in its successful extrication from traditional tasks such as scheduling, disciplining, college-admissions counseling, and routine advising. These "distorted the whole counseling relation-

49

ship." They verge on being menial tasks. Psychological ideals, to such departments, are not means but valid ends in themselves. If psychological development is a legitimate end for secondary education, then counselors are as important teachers as the teachers themselves. A common student complaint is that counselors have all the time in the world for people with problems. The squeaky wheels get all the grease.

Changing social forces only accelerate the movement of the counselors along their preferred path. A decade earlier, one guidance director recalled, "there would be less time spent with drug abuse . . . less time spent on counseling and talking about divorce, broken families, and that kind of thing. Probably there would actually be more time spent on dealing with educational concerns and post–high school concerns." In those days there were "fewer acts of violence, and those that occurred were not as intense." In his tranquil and outwardly stable community he estimated that 35 to 40 percent of the students came from broken families.

Psychological attitudes help explain not only why attention to routine advising gets short shrift, but also why too much intrusion into the student choice process is actually thought undesirable. The therapeutic mentality is, first of all, nondirective. One counselor described how he presented his work to students: "You say, 'Look, the service is here if you need it and when you want it.' You have to accept how they feel. And so, fine. Sometimes they're on the street for two months; then they'll come back . . . I don't give a lot of advice . . . I try to respect how they feel and see how they are." A colleague agreed that "informality" was the philosophy of the counseling staff. "It's more of a walk-in place, a 'feel-comfortable' atmosphere. We try to instill a feeling of friendship, good rapport, comfort." Such attitudes were hardly compatible with heavy-handed advice or intentional prying. "The guidance counselors don't want to be the heavies," one teacher said sympathetically. "It's easier for them to get along with the kids if they let them take the courses that they want." Pushing them gets in the way of establishing good rapport.

The psychological mentality also emphasizes the connection between freedom and the development of responsibility. Learning to "take responsibility" is often regarded as being just as worthy an educational objective as learning algebra. Often teachers join counselors in embracing this view; educational justifications for choice are by no means confined to counselors alone. As one teacher rather starkly put it, "You either give kids responsibility and the consequences that go with it, and then they sense power and act responsibly, or you keep the power yourself as adults. Then they don't have any genuine responsibility." "Giving responsibility" meant to her giving freedom to make wise or unwise choices. "Acting responsibly" meant making wise choices. The second could not be learned without the first. Leaving choice to the student was therefore conscious pedagogy.

There were risks, to be sure. A student pointed out that one could choose to be an idiot. And adults could perhaps be overenthusiastic in defending school environments where genuine rather than artificial choices were present. One principal, for example, was not embarrassed to admit that his school had a "major problem with drugs." What others saw as simply a problem, he saw as an educational opportunity: "That's the way we want it . . . If you didn't have these problems, you'd try to create them." The risks inherent in providing genuine choices were worth taking. Too many students, a teacher agreed, deliberately avoided responsibility. That was the real educational dilemma. "They don't want to be pushed out of the role of student. They don't want extra responsibilities." They would say or imply, "What are you being paid for? You're getting paid to run the school, so you run it."

"I'm not saying this is a therapeutic institution," a sympathetic colleague began, but went on to conclude that high school needed to focus more on "developing a sense of responsibility toward your education." Adolescents had been "schooled to be passive for most of their lives, and have no idea how to think for themselves, or how to engage themselves in any sort of procedure to find out their strengths and weaknesses." Too often they simply wanted to be told what to do. A good high school had to resist that temptation; it had to make choices of all sorts unavoidable. Besides, others pointed out, adolescents would be given substantial freedom soon enough in college. "Should it happen at high school?" asked one teacher, who then answered his own question: "Or should it wait until they get into college when there's even more possibility for abuse?"

One other psychological justification for student choice is that an individual knows his or her own needs better than anyone else knows them. Several principals were frightened by what they perceived as a mood of growing educational regimentation in the country. The easy public answer to high school ills, they feared, was more academic requirements. One principal was certain that outside pressure to increase diploma requirements would diminish quality. Students who "needed" particular courses chose them on their own even if those courses were not required for graduation. His school did not mandate English every year, he explained, but virtually everyone in the top half of the class took it — those were the students who needed it. If a fourth year of English was imposed, enormous pressure would fall on those who had failed it before. Such students would have to take two years of English simultaneously, which in turn would make a nightmare of scheduling the classes of students enrolled in vocational programs. The result, the principal said, would surely be that students who needed time to pursue vocational/technical specializations would be discouraged; they might even drop out. Another principal made the same point: "The average kid who graduates takes seventy to eighty percent of what you would expect them to take. Eighty-five percent of the kids are now taking math, but there's no math requirement." Students knew their own needs without adults telling them.

One boy complained that students in his school weren't allowed to make their own choices: "These teachers want me to learn this and learn that, but it isn't particularly relevant to what I want to do." He bitterly objected to "requiring people to take something they didn't want and need" and used therapeutic language to make his point. "I mean, that's a turn-off anyway psychologically. You won't do it as good as something you want to do." This, too, is a common argument for choice: students won't learn anything unless they *want* to. That point is often connected to the idea that students are the best judge of what they would enjoy and therefore be successful at. One dissident teacher criticized counselors who tell incoming students that they can get into most four-year colleges without taking any foreign languages. The "counselors want kids to succeed, and they're afraid they might fail if some courses challenge too much." Choice is seen as a way for students to avoid failure. The prevailing school attitude was, in this teacher's opinion, that "a child can get it if he wants to." It was all there for the taking, but the push to take had to come from the student or his family.

Locating decision-making outside the school — in the hands of students and their parents — is thus another practical accommodation to student diversity. The shopping mall high school provides variety, something for everybody, does not force anybody to choose; it pushes nobody beyond his or her preferences. Those who want to buy can do so. Those who are not sure can browse or bide their time, and still pass through.

Neutrality

Wide curricular variety and unfettered student choice allow the shopping mall high school to accommodate the consumption needs of a diverse population. The institution itself takes few clear stands on whether some products or services are better than others. Each shopkeeper has a legitimate place in the mall; the customer's preferences usually go unchallenged. The school is, for the most part, neutral.

This was inevitable, according to one administrator, because the school had to satisfy many conflicting values held by the customers. Coping with these differences was one of his most taxing duties. His school's catalog communicated the issue with honesty and delicacy. "Several sets of values" — not just one — "emerge from the interaction between school and community," the catalog said. One set was held by those "seriously committed to the values of education." Another was held by those "anxious to work within a more traditional structure than now exists." Yet another belonged to a group "not yet certain of its commitment," which functioned best "outside the regular system of classes and courses and schedules." Other values were held by groups "ranging from the committed to the disenchanted."

In one kind of family, the administrator explained, parents would strongly support disciplinary action taken by the school against a child. In another, the same offense would produce the complaint that a big stink was being made about nothing. The school could rarely take a stand on anything because "we are so fragmented."

He wished that the important people in his community could sit down together and agree on values such as honesty and mutual respect. Even such a modest attempt at "togetherness" would help the school enormously.

Cheating on examinations was, in his opinion, "very bad." But what was worse was the disagreement over whether or not a problem existed. Some students felt that a stigma was attached to cheating, but others plainly did not. The media seemed to teach that no one was honest, no one could be trusted, and everyone cheated if they could. The law seemed to teach that students had many rights, no matter what they did, and few responsibilities. It was often too much trouble and too great an expense to suspend or expel the unruly. Churches and temples had, even in his lifetime, exerted moral influence on kids, but no longer did. Parents did not know what they believed, and they modeled for their children no matrix of a life that fit together. Nobody played the position of "moral quarterback." The prevalent belief, thought a colleague of the administrator, was, "Since life has no meaning, what the hell, why not, anything goes."

Variety and choice in the school permitted students to adjust easily to educational neutrality. They had additional ways to adjust to moral neutrality. Sometimes the unwritten code "No matter what happens, you don't rat" prevailed. Teenagers in the school had an endless tolerance for broken drinking fountains, unusable bathrooms, litter; these were expected parts of high school, things taken for granted. Often students saw problems as unconnected to issues of moral conduct. Some, for example, blamed theft from lockers on the naïveté of students who kept in them things worth stealing.

In another school, a student council faced with intolerable littering also avoided moralizing. When one member suggested punishment — eliminating "open campus" for a week — the others thought this would violate a psychological ideal they held as deeply as some of the staff professionals did. Punishment would be wrong because "we will be telling them that we don't trust them." When someone else suggested that students, including themselves, should simply pick up the litter, the objection was, "I don't mind picking up my own trash, but I'm not going to go around and pick up everybody else's." Besides, someone said, "I don't want to police my friends."

Such value disagreements were resolved by practical approaches that ignored the root of the problem. The school should purchase more wastebaskets, or (employing the psychology of behavior modification) should award points to the class that picked up the most trash, or should appeal to students' sense of school pride.

It is not simply the diversity of students that causes value fragmentation within schools: faculties embody many of the same value differences. Against the lament that school and society had no moral quarterback came the principal's proud claim that in his school "orderliness is a low priority for us." He was "sorry to say that we've participated in a diminution of tolerance for disorder." Since there was no sense of unity in society, there was no reason and no way to promote a sense of unity in school. Not all teachers, for example, want to throw out the most unruly students. One teacher told with horror the story of a boy who commuted daily from jail to school because the judge determined that he had a right to an education. The boy drank in school, extorted money from other students, and cut classes — and nothing could be done. The teacher's conclusion, however, was not that the boy should have been removed, but that the school had failed the boy by not motivating him to attend regularly. "If we could have kept him in class, it would have been different."

In most schools the most diplomatic adult position on troubling moral questions is a tolerant neutrality. A school nurse with first-hand experience in the dilemmas of teenage pregnancy believed that her role was only to present information to students and "not interfere with their lives." When a boy wore a T-shirt that said, "Sex Is Mind Over Matter. If She Doesn't Mind, It Doesn't Matter," his enraged father confiscated it. The boy got it back by arguing that he had bought it with money he had earned in an after-school job. Then the father of the boy's girlfriend objected, and successfully demanded that the shirt never be worn when he visited her house. With such outside hassles, the boy was pleased to report that he could wear the shirt to school whenever he wished. No staff member ever registered an objection. A tolerant neutrality again prevailed.

Even when teachers agree that a particular offense is morally appalling, they are often at odds about what should be done. Several discussed together the proper response to athletes who had painted obscenities on a rival high school. "It's clear to me," one said, "that we really haven't taught them about decent behavior." "We? Or their parents?" rejoined a colleague. "Our job is not to teach morality." A third advanced a different position: "We get them too late to do anything." In another school teachers regarded vandalism of student lockers as inevitable, given the large number of uncommitted and unsuccessful students present. Instead of addressing the problem as a moral one, they sought pragmatic, managerial solutions such as additional faculty hall patrols. One teacher even attributed the problem to the quality of the equipment: "The lockers are so badly made."

Value differences among the adults who work in schools are most pronounced in the explicitly educational realm. A veteran who had built an empire out of ancient history admitted that his subject was exotic and hardly essential to secondary education. The only check against building empires through the sheer force of personality and accumulated reputation was to forge a consensus that "there is a solid core of knowledge preferable for young Americans to know in the social studies." But he was certain that no such consensus, much less the will to force it on students, was likely in his district. One of his administrators thought the faculty would even resist the idea of recommended but wholly voluntary course sequences. "Quite a lot of them have their own turf to protect, their own personal axe to grind, and they resist change."

Indeed, independence — rather than moral or educational cohesiveness — is a central part of the high school teacher's identity. "Teachers," one said with great satisfaction, "have a remarkable amount of independence and autonomy. Teachers have to be completely, extremely, bizarre, far-out, at one end of the spectrum or the other, before anyone interferes." Threats to that independence, even when presented in the name of educational progress, are resisted, perhaps because autonomy is one of the few traditionally "professional" attributes currently possessed by the high school teaching profession. "If the principal were to send out an edict that no late papers were to be accepted," one department chair pointed out, "that would cause a lot of trouble."

Principals rarely think of issuing such edicts. Shopping mall high schools instead promote autonomy — and hence isolation — by leaving their faculties alone. Faculty meetings are uncommon, and are considered useless because there is nothing that faculty members are expected to do together. Departmental meetings, when held, rarely deal with educational substance; the topic is more likely to be teaching schedules or materials allocation. Department heads rarely know one another. And inside departments it is "every man for himself." A Mrs. Jefferson rarely gets the formal opportunity to propose, perhaps in front of a Dr. McBride, that Child and Family become a graduation requirement. Schools have many ways to avoid the many educational disagreements they contain.

In hiring teachers no attempt is made to achieve a consensus of values. The very notion that particular values — as distinct from academic and technical skills — can or should be a legitimate criterion for educational service is alien to the shopping mall high school. It smacks of bygone days when communities had the effrontery and the power to expect moral as well as professional credentials. Once a diverse faculty is in place, neutrality becomes highly functional. Too much is at stake to think of forcing stands or highlighting differences. It is hard enough, after all, to deal with differences among the students.

The one theme that schools can rally around is *tolerating* differences. This is what they are least neutral about. The administrator who longed for a moral quarterback admitted that fragmentation had been accompanied not only by problems but also by increased tolerance by teenagers of differences of all kinds. This was a real gain. Indeed, the only objective officially listed by the school which bore on moral character was the intention that students become "more understanding of the problems of others, and more appreciative of the strengths of others." The "others" included those of different race, religion, cultural background, economic status, talent, sex, and mental or physical capacities.

Because "the whole society is there," emphasizing tolerance is a practical necessity as well as an educational opportunity. In school after school, all members of the community spoke with pride and feeling about the growth of tolerance. Sometimes the dominant images were of including students with physical and mental handicaps, and often of mainstreaming them in regular classes. Under mainstreaming many people felt that the "social gains" for the more fortunate almost approached the educational gains of the handicapped. But discussions of tolerance most frequently concerned racial harmony. Several schools had recently undergone traumas of actual or potential racial discord and had expended considerable emotional and financial resources on that issue. For many teachers the struggle had been the high point of their careers. They were proud of the results: "Here . . . we give kids a really beautiful social education. No one can beat us at that." When racial or ethnic slurs occurred within classrooms, teachers virtually never ignored them. They pounced on them as educational opportunities.[4]

Although it took "a conscious effort to play music that both groups can dance to," overt racial tension had largely vanished. All of the schools were regarded as safe and orderly places, despite the concern in some for litter and vandalism. But tolerance rarely meant closeness. Racially isolated sections had largely disappeared from lunchrooms, but segregated tables were still preferred. And although students spoke about relaxed relations in the halls and on some sports teams, they admitted that integration was rare within the formal curriculum.

In a curiously American, wholly noble, and completely exhausting way, the tolerance of diversity has become the basis for community within high schools. It is not easy to build community on the basis of differences rather than similarities; it goes against the expected grain. It is the burden, the challenge, and to some extent the triumph of the shopping mall high school. But the schools settle for the absence of conflict as the definition of community. Community means an attitude of "Live and let live" more than of people working together. It is another kind of neutrality.

Shopping mall high schools are especially neutral about performance expectations for students. Mrs. Jefferson, for example, would not demand minimum mastery of Child and Family as a condition for passing the course: "I feel it's very unfair if a child comes and really puts forth an effort and is doing his very best and is there every day trying, and yet you defeat him with an F." Failure and defeat were inextricably linked. Despite her genuine commitment to the value of what she taught, the psychological ideal of feeling successful took precedence in her class over learning a crucial life skill. "I am going to do what I can to enhance his self-image and to make him think that the world is good." (Perhaps she was remembering the student who was sure it was not.) "I'm not going to give him F's just because he's not capable of doing what the average student in the room is doing."

Her feelings were shared by most teachers regardless of subject, level, or geographical region. In the shopping mall high school, failure comes from not attending or not behaving. Performance is remarkably irrelevant. Poor performance in fact is sometimes accompanied by acceptable and even honors grades. A teacher of advanced math thought the only way to fail was "not come . . . The kids really have to fail themselves." Those who could not handle the work were simply put in a lower level. Once there, they were graded "almost solely on attitude. If a student comes and has tried his hardest, he will get a B." Dr. McBride said it took far more work for his advanced students to fail than to pass. They had to try to fail, "do it actively." He considered C a "pejorative" mark in the high-level classes, and would give everyone who did decent work an A or a B. Both were officially regarded as honors grades. Another physics teacher explained, "I'm an easy grader. It's hard to get kids into physics in the first place, and I don't want to destroy their GPAs, so I think that a youngster in that class should have no trouble getting a B." High grades were part of his advertising campaign to lure customers. A social studies teacher said that "a kid who's given his best shot" could never do worse than a C, although students who never showed up could fail. After all, agreed a Spanish teacher, "you have to look at kids now from all angles. You can't just look at their performance in Spanish." A girl in her Advanced Placement class was "really not very good at all" in the language. "But she tries very, very hard, and she always attends, and it makes you feel very sorry for her. So she'll get a B or a B minus."

Well aware that passing her course was a diploma requirement, an American history teacher reasoned that "you can't penalize the kids just because we don't have a place to put them." She coped by careful test design. Even though she usually included a little essay question, she made sure "that the kids can pass just by answering the objective portion — pass with a C usually." She did this because many of her students could not write a paragraph. For similar reasons she excluded questions requiring critical thinking in her regular (that is, college-preparatory) classes: "Two thirds of your kids are not able to do that work." Instead, she used questions that "depend primarily on recognition and recall." When asked how her students would ever learn critical thinking, she answered confidently, "The average student never learns it." Bright students learned it intuitively. Others learned it at home. She was "not sure the schools provide it" to anybody.

Students know they will pass in return for orderly attendance because teachers tell them so. There are no covert arrangements here. One group recalled how their history teacher had said the first day of class, "You give me thirty-five minutes [per day in class] and show me you're working and you'll pass the course." Another group remembered that the first words spoken by their eminent English teacher were, "You can just sit there and you'll pass with a D minus." They explained matter-of-factly that "she focuses just on the few who care . . . She doesn't care about the other kids in the class." This seemed to make perfect sense to the students. "I get a lot out of it if I'm prepared," one concluded.

Of course not all teachers accommodate student diversity in this way. "I tell them point-blankly," one dissenter reported, " 'You will pass my final in order to pass my course.' I think I'm one of the few who does it." She thought their reaction confirmed the rarity of her action. "You would think I told them to rape their mother at high noon in the town square." Such behavior seemed rigid and insensitive to many colleagues as well. An administrator explained that "teachers today are more humanistic in their approach with kids . . . A lot of them don't have an ironclad set of standards on achievement. It used to be that if you got sixty percent on a test you were all right, but if you got fifty-nine you were finished." But now they realized that "more and more kids have personal problems, more and more kids have twenty things to deal with as well as school, and they'll take that into account."

Even when students volunteer neither order nor attendance, schools go to enormous lengths to make passing possible. "Most teachers give them a way out," one confided, "or else the system gives them a way out . . . They can go to summer school, they can make up their work, they can take a correspondence course. Miraculously they pass and weasel out." Teachers often don't enforce policies that make failure automatic after a certain number of absences. "I talk to the kid. I tell him, 'If you find the course so distasteful, drop it and take something else.' " At least one school offered a Pass/No Credit course where failure was theoretically impossible.

The shopping mall high school is thus profoundly neutral about mastery. No one opposes it, but few require or expect it. Of course many schools mandate a minimum competency test of some sort as a graduation hurdle. But these test basic skills that have traditionally been the purview of elementary education, are usually first made available to students near the beginning of their high school careers, and are rarely connected to the regular curriculum. Further, there are ways to adjust the competency tests so that everyone may pass. One special-needs teacher pointed out that if a student could not pass the reading test, she could decide what would be appropriate competency for that student: "If I said this student will spell 'cat' by June, and he did, then that student will pass his competency." The regular competency examination was somewhere "between a fifth- and a seventh-grade level. The general public isn't aware of that, and so they assume they're doing twelfth-grade work, and they're not."

Separating passing from even minimal notions of mastery has the effect of making the high school diploma little more than an emblem of good behavior. Despite considerable criticism of this situation by reformers outside the schools and by some professionals in the schools, most schoolpeople do not regard it as scandalous at all. They do not regard the high school experience as exclusively about mastery of the formal curriculum. The centrality of variety, choice, and neutrality in the mall is not seen by insiders as a cop-out, a conspiracy to expect the least. They regard these features, instead, as enabling high schools to meet as many adolescent needs as possible.

Perhaps the need that best explains the commitment to passing is the need to avoid failure. "Failure" in this sense is rarely defined diagnostically, that is, as evidence of some important deficiency whose remediation is at the heart of educational purpose. Failing is never seen in such positive terms. "I believe," one teacher said passionately, "if a kid has done all he can and you fail him, I think you've done him an injustice. He'll feel like he's a nobody. So if he tries, he'll pass my class. A lot of people say kids need to know there are failures in lifetimes, but they're not going to have to spend their lifetime going to school."

Failure is anathema because success — *feeling* success — is so deeply cherished as both a goal and a means to other goals. Many teachers seem preoccupied by the psychological costs of failure and the therapeutic benefits of success. That was what one teacher was talking about when she said, "If you don't get it done, you don't fail. You don't get credit, but you don't experience failure." "The most important thing to me is to make them feel they are human beings, that they are worthwhile," another teacher emphasized. Still another's primary goals were to "build confidence, to build trust . . . I try to affirm them as people." A math teacher prescribed "a daily dose of self-respect." And a social studies teacher explained why he didn't stress thinking skills: "I just encourage them to make the most of their ability to have pride in themselves." In all these instances, the need for students to feel success is disconnected from the idea of students mastering something taught. A wide gap separates the two notions. "Let's face it," a teacher said by way of partial explanation. "A kid could get through their life without having my course." Many teachers believe more in the value of self-esteem than in the value of what they teach. Mastery and success are like ships that pass in the night.

Therapeutic ideology is not the only reason why passing is mainly contingent on orderly attendance, but it is the most noble one. Some teachers also believe, for example, that attendance is more important than course content because it is a marketable skill. Students need to learn "to be on time at their job." Furthermore, these arrangements make life easier for teachers. The bargain is, after all, an attractive one for everyone. Alternatives might cause unwanted conflict. And teachers do not have to work as hard or be as competent if students can do well without learning much.

For teenagers to feel success, pass, and graduate, they must attend. Even in schools where truancy is not a significant dilemma, expensive computers and sophisticated monitoring systems keep track of where everyone is — sometimes before computers are seriously deployed for instructional purposes. "Holding" teenagers is a preoccupation. "They don't want to let anyone leave," a teacher remarked. "They want to bend over backwards to keep them."

The importance of holding students is most deeply felt where transiency is high and family income low. One thoughtful principal contrasted the safety and security of his building to "the street" where "gangs, organizations, prostitution, pimping, drug sales, housebreaking, and robbery" were routine occurrences. Families were simply "no longer there." His primary objective was for adolescents to "survive" better at the end of high school than at the beginning. Mastery in courses was a "secondary goal." After all, as one of his teachers put it, "if they come to class all the time, they must be learning something." Learning was never absent from this principal's mind. But it was a hope, not an expectation and certainly not a demand. High school in his community was a place of last resort, a haven in a heartless world.

Far away another principal agreed: "We're trying to keep kids inside who weren't all that turned on by being in school, so we come up with more programs." Only fifteen years earlier, he recalled, things were different. Then kids were belligerent and challenged authority. Getting rid of some was a survival tactic. Now "the war is over." Order prevailed, for at least a while. He said the current idea was to keep students in school, with the diploma within easy reach, because everyone understood that there was no better place for them to be. High school had become, as the century progressed, not a special place for those who cared about learning and the opportunities that it opened, but the *only* place for teenagers. "The thing I resent most," he complained, "is that society is saying it's our job." Parents would throw up their hands and say, "I can't do anything with the kid. It's your job. Don't call us. Don't bother us."

It was true, he admitted, that in a time of declining enrollments more students meant more dollars for his school. There was "pressure on teachers to maintain their numbers." A cynical colleague concluded, "They aren't trying to keep kids in school because it's good for them. They're trying to keep the kids in school because it keeps their enrollments up. If they don't have enough kids in those seats, it means they lose jobs." But such cynicism disguises the basic reality that the schools that do *not* face loss of population have the same commitment to holding teenagers as the schools that do.

If schools are now judged by their holding power, any attendance problem suggests institutional failure. "It's interesting how it works against you," the principal reflected. "You take a marginal student and do everything you can to encourage him to stay in school and don't drop out of school. 'We'll build you a program, we'll hand-pick your teachers.' So he reluctantly comes on board. And then he's showing up over here as an absenteeism, increasing your percentage of your absentee kids . . . The more you work trying to keep that marginal kid in, the more statistics can make you look somewhat embarrassed." For the marginal student, he speculated, "you could have taken a different tack and say, 'We agree with you.' " You don't have to come. But that approach ran counter to the prevailing wisdom. Suspending students for truancy, the school's attendance officer pointed out, was downright illogical. It would only bring about what the school was trying to avoid. "If you knew you only had to cut a few classes to be thrown out, and you didn't want to be there anyway, that would be the way to do it . . . The kids don't have to go if they don't want to, and there's no way for the school to enforce their attendance. Yet the school clearly feels they ought to be present."5

That is the puzzling dilemma. School and community alike assume that all teenagers should be in high school. High school attendance and graduation are nearly a social entitlement. They are things people take for granted. Perhaps the most valued product offered by high school, the diploma itself, is purchasable for the least effort. "We're successful," one teacher explained, "in that most of them stay in school. They get some minimum degree of skill development. They get a high school diploma. They seem generally happy. They have a lot of freedom moving around the building." These do not seem ambitious indices of success. Another teacher put the matter bluntly. "The problem is, we're trying to retain kids . . . We don't know what to do with these kids . . . Our society doesn't know what to do. The operant goal is to get people to graduate, and they can graduate if they are barely literate."

The neutrality criticized by this teacher captures the successes and problems of the shopping mall high school. In this consumer-oriented institution, students and teachers alike say with considerable truth that everything is there, everybody is there, and there is something for everyone. But it is there only if you want it and will go get it. You can get as much or as little as you choose. If you choose to buy little, the problem is yours, not the mall's. The mall is neutral about the kinds of purchases you make and about how informed a consumer you are. The mall wants your regular presence and your good behavior, and for that alone it will sell you a diploma. From one point of view it is a very good buy. Students, parents, and teachers seem generally satisfied with the deal.

These arrangements, after all, reflect two fundamental realities. First, Americans want high school to be genuinely accessible to virtually everyone, and on a basis such that everyone who wants to can complete it. Second, Americans have profoundly different notions of what a proper high school education should be. There is no consensus at all, no moral equivalent of the early grades' "three Rs." In these circumstances the shopping mall is more than an apt metaphor; it provides high schools with a workable model. In their imitation of the shopping mall, high schools accommodate these two realities with a minimum of friction. But to what extent is this successful accommodation also an abdication of responsibility toward those students and families, who, for whatever reasons, do not make the wise choice that distinguishes between accommodating students and educating them?

2

Treaties

SHOPPERS, SELLERS, AND PRODUCTS interact in various ways as transactions inside stores are conducted. Browsers may scan the merchandise from a wary distance, or they may come close enough to salespeople to provoke the familiar exchange: "May I help you?" "No thanks, I'm just looking." Sometimes they seek and receive considerable advice: "That blouse is just a perfect color on you but it's a bit wide across the shoulders; let me get you the size eight." Sometimes customers know exactly what they want without any help at all. The seller needs only to ring up the sale; no pitch is necessary. Shoppers may patronize favorite sellers or shops, return goods that prove unsatisfactory, dominate the attention of salespeople for long periods of time, or simply walk out. Stores themselves offer a variety of deals: there are discounts, clearances, warranties, alternate methods of payment. Although the mall is not like a Middle East bazaar or local yard sale, where everything is negotiable, it still provides room for everyone to maneuver even at the point of sale.

Inside the classrooms of the shopping mall high school, even greater room exists for the protagonists to maneuver. Any of an enormous number of different transactions is possible. Many kinds of deals can be struck. Variety, choice, and neutrality are institutional features whose effects do not stop at the classroom door.

When classroom doors close, teachers and students are left alone with each other and with the subject that has brought them together. For the better part of an hour, usually five days a week for nearly ten months, teachers, students, and subjects are in the same small space involved in what is supposed to be a joint learning endeavor. They are the classroom's eternal triangle of forces.

The purposes participants bring to class vary astonishingly. Variety in the formal curriculum is very substantial to begin with; but that variety is increased enormously by another, more subtle kind of variety: the range of intentions students and teachers bring to their courses. Although the catalog directory of "stores" in the shopping mall high school is extensive, the directory vastly understates the actual variety of transactions available at the point of classroom sale.

What students and teachers mean by "taking" and "teaching" courses is determined not by subjects or levels alone, but also by the intentions of the participants. Some want to learn or teach. Others want to get through courses with as little effort as possible. Still others are wholly uncommitted. Consumer resistance can be strong even in courses teenagers choose to take. An unusually candid student finally asked his teacher, "Why do we do this all day? You come in trying to teach us. We come in trying not to learn. We bang heads every day. Why don't we all go to McDonald's and forget it?"

The important point is that banging heads every day is the exception rather than the rule. Conflict is rarely the way classroom participants come to terms with one another. Most classes are relaxed and orderly, despite the presence of so many diverse individual intentions. Agreement is far more common than antagonism. Sometimes agreement dominates antagonism because the interests of all parties are similar to begin with. Sometimes it is because, when interests sharply diverge but power is perceived to be equal, peaceful coexistence seems preferable to outright conflict. Sometimes one or another party to an agreement has little choice in the matter: the agreement is really an imposed diktat. To remedy the mix of intentions and preferences they often contain, classes do not have to repair to the neutral turf of McDonald's. Teachers and students have more subtle ways of accommodating either differences or similarities: they arrange deals or treaties that promote mutual goals or that keep the peace.

Some treaties are formal, explicit, and public; they approximate signed agreements. For example, some teachers make crystal clear on the first day what the deal will be. "My advice to them," recalled a social studies teacher, "is, don't get into the class if you don't want to work. It's going to be a rough and rugged class . . . If you don't want to work, find some other class. Take ceramics, PE, team sports." Like many teachers, she preferred wide student course choice because it gave her greater leverage to set the terms on which her elective course would proceed. If they didn't want to play by her rules, they didn't have to take the course. They could negotiate some other treaty elsewhere. Teachers sometimes offer a passing grade in return for the student's "just sitting there." In one class, the fact that passing was contingent only on orderly attendance was publicly stated. Even when the terms are not quite as explicit, students actively try to find out what the deal is and participate as much as possible in the negotiation. Andy, the boy who had extensively used the extracurriculum, pointed out that at the beginning of each term "you found out what teachers were all about. You found out how far you can go." For him a treaty was not always a dictated settlement. Students were represented around the bargaining table and their voices were often heard. Bargaining could be genuinely collective.

But most classroom treaties lack this formal and public character. They are abided by rather than talked about. They are *tacit* arrangements made to accommodate different preferences in a manner satisfactory to all, but they are no less powerful because they are less explicit. Often the signatories are only vaguely aware of the bargain that has been struck. Consider, for example, Mr. Baxter's individualized remedial English class. Each of his twenty-four juniors and seniors was asked to complete eight purple-dittoed worksheets at the student's own pace. The assignment concerned the difference between sentences and fragments — between, for example, "The beavers build dams" and "Their homes at the edge of the bank." When students completed the task they received more worksheets, though some who finished near the end of the period simply walked out.

The work proceeded in a relaxed manner. Students talked easily with one another, passed around almonds and candies, and heard through the walls the distant crooning of Bing Crosby. Mr. Baxter moved around the room, peering over people's shoulders and answering questions whenever they were asked. An aide told students how many absences and tardies they had. Neither teacher nor aide asked students anything. With the exception of two sentences of instruction spoken at the beginning, no comments were ever addressed to the group as a whole. The only evidence of dissatisfaction came when one boy muttered under his breath that the exercise seemed designed for sixth-graders. (The first sheet was entirely about beavers; another was about a little princess who could not cry.) But otherwise a sense of contentment prevailed; there was no need for discipline. At one point a boy walked into the room and talked with a friend for several minutes before leaving. Throughout the period another boy sat quietly listening to a Sony Walkman. With his earphones on and his eyes happily fixed on the wall, he didn't say anything and didn't work on any of the sheets. Neither Mr. Baxter, the aide, nor the other students took any notice.

The class provides an example of one way in which purposes converge. Few students evinced much interest in the importance of complete sentences. Most did not finish the sheets they were given. Their questions were infrequent. One student literally tuned out. Mr. Baxter's interest paralleled their own — he did not press them individually or as a group, did not reward correct or prompt work, ignored interruptions and distractions, and looked at once exhausted and bored. If learning basic English skills was the professed purpose of the class, the behavior of the participants suggested that their real purpose was to get through it. Everyone had made a tacit but well-observed treaty to achieve that end. If the students behaved themselves, the teacher would not push. A student explained that "at this school it's your choice. It's like they can't really force you to do anything, because if they force you you're not going to do it anyway." An administrator noted that Baxter's "worksheet routine" was standard procedure in many other classes. The motives behind the treaty were clear: "Because if you look at kids and say, 'They are out to get me,' and if I keep them busy, if I pass them a worksheet every five minutes, . . . then you have very busy, very quiet kids." The administrator concluded in frustration that "interpretation, analysis, inference, main ideas, are really not part of our educational curriculum." Avoiding those things was the essence of the treaty that students and teacher had willingly, if tacitly, agreed upon.

The practical benefit of tolerating Walkmen was vividly apparent in a science class where the silence of a Walkman in use contrasted favorably with the loud racket emanating from a student's old-fashioned portable radio. A principal in another school succinctly justified this kind of tolerance. The point of the treaty was to "let sleeping dogs lie." A boy serving several days of in-school suspension was delighted that no one objected if he brought in his favorite tapes and played them "real low." "If you can get away with it, then get away with it," he said.

Other students explained in the same way what Walkman tolerance in their school symbolized. One said, "If you want to learn here you can learn good. But if you don't want to, no one will push you." And another: "Not too many people are willing to push it onto you. If you want it desperately, you can go get it. But if you don't, . . . if you want to walk around, flop around — forget it. If you don't want an education, they ain't going to give it to you." Another: "[The teacher] doesn't make you do anything. If you want to get involved, it's up to you. If you want to be interested, that's your choice." The heart of this tacit classroom treaty was, Live and let live.

Avoidance and Engagement

The ultimate stakes in classroom treaties are engagement in learning or avoidance of learning. That is what formal and tacit bargains are all about. How seriously do students and teachers approach the joint endeavor of confronting the subject that brings them together? How much do they really care? How much energy are they willing to expend? Walkman tolerance is an extreme and unsubtle example of a tacit treaty to avoid almost entirely both the subject and the human participants. But classroom bargains in most cases combine simultaneous impulses to avoid and engage. The preferences of students and teachers are often mixed and changeable.

Miss Horton, for example, had taught English for nineteen years. She had amassed 90 credits above her master's, read books as her principal avocation, planned carefully, and knew a surprising number of her 125 students. She prided herself on her clear expectations, her devotion to "time on task," and a no-nonsense approach: "I think I'm considered very old-fashioned that way." A student agreed that "we did what she asked. When we went to other classes we often played around, but we all knew that when it was time to go to English class . . . we'd have to get down to work."

One day the task for her sixteen college-preparatory seniors was to discuss Bacon's essay "Of Love." Miss Horton began by asking, "What were some of the main ideas of the essay?" and then immediately continued by saying that she had extracted some herself and wanted to make sure the class had them. As she read aloud, the seniors wrote down her words verbatim. She read slowly, often repeating a phrase to make sure no one missed her exact language. "One. Drama on the stage often depicts love in both comedy and tragedy. Two. But love in real life creates many problems. Three. Great men do not allow themselves to succumb to the mad degree of love" — and so on through eight points. "Wait, wait" and "Say it again!" cried the students, frantically scribbling. Occasionally "I agree" or "Naw" punctuated her cadences. Everyone was riveted to the task at hand. When it ended there was no discussion; instead, Miss Horton showed a film on Victorian England because it happened to be in the building that day. The students were asked to remember it in anticipation of their study of Dickens later in the term.

Afterward Miss Horton explained that although students had been given class time to read the Bacon essay, some had trouble understanding it and some hadn't read it at all. She decided help was in order. "Later at test time," she pointed out, "I might very well ask them what the major themes of that essay are . . . Everyone is held responsible for the major ideas in that particular essay because we have discussed it." The discussion she referred to was her eight-point lecture. As for the essay itself, "If they want to read it, they can, but that isn't necessary."

Miss Horton was not wholly avoiding Bacon, and her students were not wholly unengaged. The class had to know, and know precisely, an outline of his ideas. No one could deny that this task involved a kind of academic work. But the task also avoided having students think about Bacon. The only use made of Bacon's — or Miss Horton's — ideas was to write them down. But no one complained; Miss Horton never had discipline problems. One of the students, Peter, confirmed afterward that the class was typical of the course and showed an approach he especially liked. It was task-oriented, "to get us ready for a test." Peter understood that goal and accepted his responsibilities for achieving it. Bound for a four-year college, he said "about all I'm going to do" for homework in all his subjects was a total of an hour a night. He ignored English homework entirely, since Miss Horton went over in class everything that was necessary to pass.

Peter and Miss Horton had similar attitudes about engagement and observed a tacit treaty to get along together. Taking or teaching a course meant presenting and remembering facts, nothing more. Everything was predictable; there were no surprises. Peter thought the course was "fun." Miss Horton said that she wanted all her classes to be of the regular college-prep type Peter attended, instead of the more advanced sort. The latter, she explained, required "more work" on her part. Students there could "do everything faster, so I have to do more reading, more paperwork, more preparation." They would actually complain if she was "disorganized or unprepared." Peter's class, in contrast, "wouldn't complain." So she didn't "have to work as hard or do as many assignments. It's easy." Neither of them wanted to work very hard and neither did, but they did not want to admit that they were avoiding work. Their treaty nicely allowed both preferences to coexist.

Peter did not find the same treaty available in all his classes. When he described Mrs. Zukowski's regular Constitutional Law course, he mentioned arrangements that pressed more vigorously toward engagement with the subject. Peter did not list Mrs. Zukowski among his favorite teachers; her class was merely "all right" as distinct from fun. In sharp contrast to Miss Horton's English, Peter felt uncomfortable in Law because he didn't know what he was supposed to know. He found the reading difficult and couldn't get a "handle" on what his response to it was expected to be. Although he avoided homework elsewhere, he did it for Mrs. Zukowski. She was not like teachers who "let you just sit in their room and go to sleep. If you don't do your work, you get embarrassed." Peter could not say why he had signed up for the course, but he was willing this once to play by different rules.

Mrs. Zukowski was very clear about what the rules were. She was the teacher who told everyone the first day how rough and rugged things would be, and that students should leave if they did not want to work. A lawyer before she became a teacher, Mrs. Zukowski used law school classes as her pedagogical model. The main content of the course was twenty watershed cases decided by the Supreme Court. Knowing these cases was sufficient justification for the course, she believed; they contained decisions that shaped students' lives. But she had other educational objectives as well: "They have to learn how to take extensive and precise notes. They have to learn to handle themselves in a dialogue with a professor. They have to learn to handle themselves with the other people in the class. They have to learn to defend ideas, and they have to learn to attack ideas. They must learn to present their arguments in a coherent fashion . . . and analyze a given piece of written material." Learning to do such things meant they were learning to think.

At the beginning of the course she demonstrated how to brief a case, but by the third week groups of students briefed the rest of the class. "They'll have to present those briefs orally and standing . . . They won't have a chance to scrooch down in their seat . . . They really master each case." They had to be prepared to make the best argument for any of the positions in the case, and to make their own argument. She would deliberately challenge their positions. Early in the year they backed off quickly and agreed with her. But when they retreated, "I usually zoom right down the aisle and jump on them." No wonder Peter was confused. The contrast with Miss Horton, with less than ten minutes between classes to adjust, was overwhelming.

Zukowski cared about engaging students with the material. What she hated most was failing to reach them: "I really don't like to have a student sit out there and indicate to me that this is boring. I'm prepared to try and persuade any kid that there is no boring subject matter. There are a lot of boring teachers and boring presentations of subject matter. But I consider it a personal affront and it hurts my pride and my feelings if one of my students isn't affected by my enthusiasm and excitement about learning." If she detected avoidance, "I go after him! I'll go back and be near him, sit on his desk, call on him. It's my job to get him involved!"

She had various strategies besides personal enthusiasm to keep them awake and alert. The most important one was the requirement that they help teach each other. From time to time she also collected their notebooks. "I'll take those notebooks home in big boxes and we correct and grade every one of them. I correct the spelling, I add comments to it, and I grade them." The payoff for a good notebook was that students could use them during the final exam. She went after students outside school, too. When she and her husband attended the theater, they frequently purchased extra tickets and took students along. "The time and the commitment and the enthusiasm — the caring — that you put into it pays off for so many of them. That's what makes it worth doing."

The treaty Mrs. Zukowski announced the first day extended beyond caring. She was sure that "if you maintain any kind of standards at all, they very quickly learn that they have to perform." High expectations formed the centerpiece of her treaty. She hoped that Peter would abide by it and therefore learn. At this early stage, he neither liked nor disliked the course. Puzzled by the absence of right answers to memorize, frustrated that this one course took almost all the homework time he was willing to give the school, Peter's engagement was reluctant and tentative. No one knew how things would turn out. But at least he was willing for a time to observe grudgingly the conditions of her treaty, even as he observed enthusiastically the very different conditions of Miss Horton's.

The classes of Mr. Baxter, Miss Horton, and Mrs. Zukowski represent different treaties, different points on a continuum of avoidance and engagement. Other classes exhibit similar variety and have other treaties with different goals. Both Ms. Fish's English class on *A Doll's House* and Dr. McBride's advanced physics class embody treaties among virtually all participants to engage the subject at an intense level. When Ms. Fish's students saw the isolating danger of small group discussions, they resisted. When she perceived student remarks as avoiding the play in favor of personal experiences or irrelevant intellectualizing, she resisted. Dr. McBride was able to assume sufficient engagement to be casual about collecting home-work and disciplining latecomers. The tacit agreement that physics was important did not make the course easier but, in spite of McBride's Socratic pressure, made it surprisingly relaxed. If Peter was willing to abide by his responsibilities in Zukowski's class, Eric and Kara were anxious to do what was necessary in McBride's.

Faced with unskilled and often alienated youngsters, Mr. Lynch in his discussion of comic books tried to steer a different course. By making Applied Communication undemanding, entertaining, and different from traditional English, he hoped to secure some modest engagement with serious issues of plot, character, and set-ting. The line between cynical avoidance and desperate pedagogy is often thin, as when comic strips are heavily relied upon to carry the burden of junior English. But Mr. Lynch was by no means abdicating all responsibility as he struggled to draft a treaty accepta-ble to all parties.

In her class on *The Catcher in the Rye* Mrs. Austin made it clear that the treaty that was offered substituted relaxation for en-gagement. When she asked a student what Salinger had intended in a passage read aloud, the student objected that the assignment had only been to tell why she liked the passage; Mrs. Austin immedi-ately backed off and did not ask another probing question the entire period. During the quiz game the quality of the questions was never at issue. Since they dealt only with details rather than with plot or meaning, the answers were always brief and always right or wrong. The questions did not lend themselves to discussion or de-bate, and there was none.

Mrs. Austin emphasized her desire to work in an enjoyable, trou-ble-free environment and was proud that neither she nor the school was afflicted with many disruptive students: "We have an attitude here that works. Students have learned to be respectful." Part of the reason for the school's and her own success, she said, was that people had learned to leave each other alone. There was no "authori-tarian" atmosphere: "We don't have big brother looking over your shoulder all the time." Not only were teachers free from administra-tive pressures, but "students don't have pressures from teachers." Everybody gained from that treaty, she believed. "It works out just fine."

She maintained a relaxed atmosphere in her classes by deliberately choosing to teach only regular or average — but still college-preparatory — youngsters. They were "very accepting of what I give them" compared with the "uppity" kids who often took advanced classes. The latter had a "certain amount of arrogance" that spelled trouble and pressure. Often parents were at the root of the pressure: "A lot of time you have students who are under a great deal of pressure from home." That was a problem, because parents would push her as well as them.

The students she preferred to teach were less demanding; they "appreciate what they get." What they appreciated was what she wanted to provide. She contended, for example, that experienced teachers did not need to plan much in advance. "I usually prepare in my head what I'm going to do each day as I drive along" during the commute to school, she said. Further, if students didn't come to class, "we don't hassle them. At least I don't. I don't think anyone else here does." Mrs. Austin was not alone in the bargain she had made. "I think I get along fairly well with most of the kids," admitted a Spanish teacher, "but to be perfectly truthful I think I get along because I don't put a lot of pressure on them." A treaty that resisted engagement while not wholly avoiding the subject was a useful way to get along.

The obligations and responsibilities of the parties to classroom treaties are not often spelled out with the directness of Mrs. Zukowski or the candor of Mrs. Austin. Further, classroom treaties are usually not offered or accepted as single, comprehensive pacts. Instead, different items are negotiated in different ways with different results. Even within the same classroom, some accommodations may emphasize engagement with learning while others promote avoidance. The differences depend on the particular point being negotiated. Three crucial items with which teachers and students must come to terms are time, relationships, and intensity. How much does coursework interrupt the busy lives of teenagers? How do people get along with each other inside classes? How high do courses aim and how much do participants care?

Time

Time is precious to most teenagers, who often seem as fully scheduled as adults: drill team on Monday evening, volleyball practice

Tuesday, a Wednesday choral rehearsal followed by piano lessons. Some even keep appointment books. Large numbers have jobs on weekdays after school. In several schools, paid employment was "damn near universal," as one teacher described it. "The kid who doesn't work is the exception. The hours they work are incredible. It's not at all unusual for a kid to be working over twenty hours a week, and there are kids who are doing forty." With so many opportunities competing for their attention, it is no wonder that many students — and their teachers, whose time is precious for similar reasons — regard school as just another part-time job.

One basic item for negotiation is therefore class attendance. Since chronically truant students rarely pass, there is little for them to bargain about. But selective cutting, or "ditching," of classes is a more complicated matter. Many students freely admit to this practice and think there is nothing wrong with it. "You'll see someone in the hall and they say, 'I'm not in today,'" one student said. One girl would attend or ditch her art class, according to her mood. Some days she felt ready for art, "but there are other days when I don't want to do anything at all. Those are the days I just don't go." She never ditched enough, however, to make failure a realistic possibility.

Teachers approach selective ditching in a variety of ways. A physics teacher announced at the beginning of term that unexcused absences had to be made up either by attending another physics class or by doing an assignment in addition to the regular one. Stiff rules on ditching guaranteed the presence of the serious students he wanted. His policy was in part a recruiting gambit. Besides, since knowledge in his subject was cumulative, missed classes would put students at a disadvantage and place extra work on him to help them catch up. With a load of 120 students and thirty classes per week, this teacher would not assume that extra burden.

A colleague took a very different attitude. When students attended his industrial arts class, he would say to himself, "Well, I'm glad you're here, so let's work as best we can." He couldn't force them to come and didn't want to try. Attendance was their problem, not his. Their absence did not hurt the class, and since the course content was not cumulative, they could understand what was going on whenever they showed up. Moreover, he sympathized with their frequent absences: "A lot of these students are practically supporting themselves . . . I know that a lot of them live in situations that are absolutely deplorable . . . I'm not going to harass a student who's having heavy problems at home if they don't come to school." With such inconsistent practices inside the same school, cutting was far more negotiable than chronic truancy.

The most important way a course affects the time of students who attend is its demands on them outside class. Since few schools have clear policies on homework, policies are established by class participants. At times there is no issue. Many technical courses where hands-on work with equipment is the central task have no homework at all; the time expected of students is the number of hours the course meets. But in most academic courses, time spent out of class is fully as significant as time spent in class. It is when teenagers can practice what is introduced in class or study what will be discussed in class. Class time is only the tip of the learning iceberg.

"Even if I understand the concept we learned in class," said one student, "it takes me a few problems to understand and get used to using it." A boy explained, "If you just saw him do it in the class, you can say that you understand every step that he's doing, but then when you have it on a test you don't have the practice of actually doing it yourself. It's like driving a car. It's different between knowing how to do it in your head and actually knowing how to do it." To such students homework is not a ritualistic adjunct to classwork but the course's center of gravity. Many spend between thirty minutes and an hour per night on each major course. A total weeknight commitment of at least three hours is not unusual.

But others took the opposite view, that school had absolutely no claim on their time once the last bell had rung. "When I'm out of school I'm done with school . . . If I did get it at home, I wouldn't do it," one student said. The majority expressed reluctance but took no hard-and-fast stand. "I don't want to [do homework] because there are so many other things to do, like track, or maybe working."

The physics teacher who demanded attendance demanded homework as well. Others in his position, such as Dr. McBride, were sufficiently confident of the operative treaty that they didn't bother to correct or collect it — it would be done, they assumed, because students knew they needed to do it. Doing homework, as one said, was "their part of the deal." But most teachers struck a different bargain. They spoke of the need to be realistic. One said that his students always passed in what he assigned because "I pay attention to how much they'll be willing to do." He thought teachers who had trouble with homework were those with unrealistic expectations. A biology teacher who had learned the same lesson said he gave homework only two nights a week because "if all of their teachers gave them homework every night, there would be no way they could get around to it." Some learned that it was senseless to assign any because no more than half would ever do it.

Flexibility was extremely important, teachers claimed. "When I came here," a history teacher recalled, "I learned from the kids that they don't get homework on the weekend . . . When it came right down to what they could do, I'd have to get where they are. I'd have to be more flexible. They are capable of more, but the more I ask, the greater [the] number of students who won't do it. My goal is to run a classroom where learning takes place, without losing students. One problem of pressing the kids is that then you'd start to lose some. I also think you could anticipate some behavior problems . . . I have hardly any now." He negotiated successfully to keep students from tuning out or acting out.

The same reasoning was offered by a Spanish teacher who admitted that it would be good for his students if he assigned more homework. "Then why don't I? Because there are enough of the kids who will tell me to go to hell if I try to get too strict with them, so I take the easier way out." He wasn't really afraid of them and didn't undervalue homework. But the reality was that he had to bargain in order to achieve a lesser but still worthy goal. "I'm trying to make it so the kids will come to class, not be afraid to enter the class, and know that I'll be accepting if they did not do some of their work. At least they come." Getting them there in exchange for not working them was the best deal he could make.

Shifting positions somewhat, he said that he thought the whole homework issue was irrelevant, since "if the kids don't want to work, they're not going to work. They turn it off." His wouldn't work because they were "tough kids, you know . . . they come

79

from broken homes." His sympathy began to emerge. The treaty was not only realistic, it was humane. "Sometimes they come to school and they've just watched their father beat up on their mother, and we expect them to sit there and be perfect, docile little kids. And it's not going to work out that way." It was absurd, he concluded, to think that a crackdown in the name of standards and homework would have any positive effect at all.

The more teachers perceived students' home life to be difficult, the more they believed that homework was unrealistic. A math teacher pointed out that parents couldn't help, even if they were at home, because they didn't know any math. "The big problem for these kids is getting to the school in the morning, bringing their books, and being polite. Adding required homework would be too much, and the students simply wouldn't do it regardless of whether I flunked them." You had to "teach them where they are." Some teachers used exactly the reverse argument to justify not assigning homework: the parents would help too much, to the point that teachers could not know if students' written work was really theirs.

Teachers who abandon or relax homework demands usually understand that the function of homework cannot wholly be abandoned if courses are to have any integrity at all. They accommodate this belief — and student preferences as well — by relocating homework to the classroom. Class time is used for activities that would otherwise be done out of class. The time demand of a course on students is halved and, usually, the time demand on teachers as well. Remedial classes like Mr. Baxter's often assume that students will do nothing outside class. Their worksheet approach often reminds observers less of school than of groups of students doing homework together in libraries or around dining room tables. School takes on, along with so much else, the function of homework. Whatever the intention, the usual effect is less work for everyone and the belief that at least something has been accomplished.

"I like this," said one English teacher of a new policy that required college-preparatory juniors to read four novels a year in class. Students were given class time to read *The Scarlet Letter, The Red Badge of Courage, Huckleberry Finn,* and *The Great Gatsby* because many would not read the books if they were assigned as homework.

Parents had complained that such homework was excessive. Pressure from them might even bring the teaching of the books to a halt. "I like this," the teacher continued, "because I can see that they've read the books. We can discuss them. We give them a week to read the book in the class and I'll give them a paper to do and they will have read it."

A colleague admitted he had first thought the new policy ridiculous, "but now I realize that if you want them to read, especially the longer assignments, you have to do it in class. And even then some won't do it. I would like to have said it was class time wasted, but if they enjoy it, they'll keep reading." The treaty was "maddening" but worth arranging. Teachers had to be practical. "If you can't get them to read at home, you do the next best thing. It has to be done. It's like the football coach who likes to score on every play. If you can't do that, do the next best thing. That's what we do . . . I'm trying to be optimistic and say we're building up their expectations in school." Homework done in class is like sales promotion — it gets students to buy into the assignment so they may actually consider doing some of it at home.

Uncommitted students prefer using class time for homework not only because it eliminates out-of-school obligations but also because it eliminates classroom obligations. "I don't like sitting in class without doing homework," one boy remarked. "It's boring just sleeping." Classes where students read or wrote or did problems on their own were also classes where further negotiations were possible. Students were sometimes permitted to move around, talk to friends quietly about other matters, and, especially toward the end of the period, avoid the assignment entirely. More committed students usually dislike the practice, not because they love to work but because they find classrooms uncongenial places to study — they prefer more private places where they can think, take breaks, listen to the radio, or call friends on the phone if they have questions.

The most striking effect of these homework treaties is that they widen rather than close the existing gaps in student proficiency. Those with the fewest skills and commitment get the least work. More homework is assigned to students in higher-level classes, and more of it is expected to be done outside class. Two sophomores explained how it worked: "When a student has a higher average than others, the teacher she would probably expect more. Like if a person was getting a D, she probably would not expect them to do her homework." "And the person who's getting an A, she would probably expect them to turn in every assignment and her homework. If you're getting A or B in class, she expects more out of you."

Teachers often saw more clearly than others that treaties which acknowledged avoidance also promoted it. The dilemma was painful, and most felt impotent to do much more than accommodate. One poignantly spoke of how she had learned disengagement as a form of self-protection. "I've had to force myself to disengage. Not get involved when they don't do their homework, for example. Not get involved when they flunk all their tests. Not get involved when they do nothing." She just talked with them occasionally. "Like why aren't you doing your homework? But not be the driving force because they're not going to do it unless they want to do it. And you're not going to be able to force them. That's what I had to realize. Although I take responsibility, I can't take too much responsibility. I can't constantly blame myself for what they don't do." The treaty she had made was as much with herself as with her students.

The time that teachers control most is class time itself. "Time on task" is a popular catch phrase for the idea that classes should start at the bell, end at the bell, and focus throughout on the business of learning. One of the classic bargains for avoiding the subject of a course is to delay beginning a lesson and to hasten its end. The most enthusiastic moments of many classes occur at the start, when a teacher may reveal the latest exploits of his mischievous dog or the students may insist on recapitulating the previous evening's basketball game. And a palpable sense of relief is often felt when classes end early not because a lesson has come to some conclusion but because everyone wants to drop the material. "I'll tell you what I'm gonna do," one teacher announced to his delighted audience with seven minutes to go. "Nothin'. I'll give you the couple of minutes." The gift was welcomed by both sides.

Not all delay is intended to avoid learning. The organization of school days into periods separated by five- or seven-minute intervals places enormous pressure on students and teachers to make rapid physical and mental adjustments. Mr. Glynn was an unusually gifted English teacher who understood that some transition or warm-up time was not only civilized but could promote engagement. He always began his class with a recording of an operatic aria, and he asked students to ponder a variety of quotes he wrote on the board. ("Without the fireside, there is no human advancement.") Sometimes the students were asked to choose a quotation they liked and talk about why. At other times Mr. Glynn explained why one or another moved him.

None of these activities had a direct connection with most lessons. They were designed to create a mood, cast a spell, sharpen the distinction between the world of Glynn's class and the outside world that students had come from and would return to. Whatever images of humanity barraged his students from the mass media, Glynn wanted them to begin English every day with the idea "that man can also be sublime." Brad, that prominent user of the extracurriculum, had been "immune" to opera at the beginning, but now thought the opening routine was "neat." Everyone in the class appreciated the fact that Glynn was sharing something special with them.

There is another kind of delay that is not evidence of a treaty to avoid learning — a delay imposed from outside. Interruptions routinely come from the public address system, from students coming and going with messages and passes, and from unscheduled surprises such as "visual screening time" for all class members or a visit from counselors to discuss course options for the next year. Teachers complained about these interruptions but saw them as inevitable. One was completely unfazed when two students suddenly barged into her class to hawk the latest student newspaper. They stopped her cold in the middle of reading a Spenser sonnet. Two minutes elapsed while the money was being collected. The treaty she quickly negotiated with the students was that she would end class early so the paper could be read, and in return, students would not read it when her lesson resumed. That, she said later, was the way things were done. In a different school, a teacher's response to the same interruption was to apologize to the intruders for not having correct change to pay for her newspaper.

The most pervasive way in which class time is used for delay is digression. Students and teachers covet it because of its ambiguity.

Digressions often do not delay brazenly, and thus they create the illusion that teaching and learning are proceeding when the reverse is true. Halfway through one period, for example, a history teacher asked his students to close their books, take out a sheet of paper, and write on it the numbers 1 through 20. "Ooh, you didn't tell us," students groaned, expecting a spot quiz, but were quickly reassured that the teacher was only giving an assignment for extra credit. For the next fifteen minutes he laboriously dictated an assignment that could have been duplicated and passed out in seconds. The students wrote down various historical names — Milton Berle, Gorgeous George, Roy Rogers — in order to interview parents or grandparents on who they were. Not surprisingly, students had difficulty spelling names they had never heard before. Making sure everyone had them right prolonged the project still further. When the task was finished, some time still remained; at that point the teacher simply stopped and gave students the rest of the period to do as they pleased. Digression can also be employed at the end of an assignment, as when a class spent twenty minutes tabulating the results of an opinion questionnaire that had been filled out as homework.

The most subtle form of digression is when a class veers off the subject just enough to sabotage it without avoiding it entirely. Ms. Fish was always poised to thwart such attempts, but many other classes welcomed them. An advanced-level Asian Studies class polled its members on their attitudes toward death and funerals, in order to illuminate the contrast between Western attitudes and the various religions of the East. No digression was permitted in tabulating the results — the teacher had done that himself the night before — but the lively and attentive discussion never went beyond the students' opinions; and it never touched the East at all. When the teacher reported that most kids wanted to be buried in the mountains and that he too wanted his ashes scattered there, someone said it was probably illegal. When he reported that most students believed that the soul existed separate from the body, he commented, "Where it goes is up for grabs." Someone yelled that souls usually go on United Airlines. There was loud laughter when someone else suggested that only Christian souls went to heaven. The teacher mentioned a scientific study purporting to prove that souls existed because dead people were slightly lighter in weight than when they were alive. An animated discussion on the existence of souls was summarized by the teacher: "Who knows?" The lesson had clearly digressed from the comparative question but had held everyone's attention. "The temptation," another teacher explained, "is that sometimes someone brings up something that everyone's interested in. The temptation is to go with that . . . At least they are talking."

Digressions like this are usually explained as necessary to stimulate interest and are often planned in advance. A student thoughtfully alerted a visitor before the start of an honors literature class: "You are in luck. You are about to hear about [the teacher's] post-pubescent love life. We just finished with JoAnne and are about to go on to Jane." And indeed the teacher did begin with Jane and with how "my sole desire was to get rid of her." The kids yelled out that he was repeating himself from the day before. "I know. Don't you know in a two-part story they always review a little?" Amidst the laughter he went on, "Anyway I was down at [the] Club." The kids interrupted: "Oh yeah, this was the girl who was in the car with you." "No," he corrected them, "this was a different girl. We were dancing slow to Johnny Mathis, real close. She squeezes my hand. I was in heaven." No one's attention wandered.

He explained later that lecturing on his teenage love life was a way to introduce honors students to a unit on love in literature. His previous units on love had "always bombed." Though he doubted that this approach was "pedagogically sound," it certainly was worth a try. At least one student felt he had succeeded, but not quite at what he intended. The only flaw, the student believed, was mentioning the unit on literature — that "broke the drama of the story."

Relationships

Even when time demands are minimal, teenagers and an adult are together in the same room for several hours a week. Arranging that time so that it is tolerable to all — relaxed rather than tense, friendly rather than uncomfortable — is of high priority to everyone.

Students and teachers are exquisitely sensitive to how relationships among them contribute to a relaxed and tolerable atmosphere. What those relationships are, and especially how they affect engagement or avoidance with the subject of the classes, are crucial items for negotiation. Many different treaties are in force.

Behind all the treaties lies a deeply felt preference by most students and most teachers for relations they usually call open, friendly, and caring. No student definition of a good teacher was more common than someone who could "relate" to them. "When you have a relationship with someone it is much easier to come to school," one student said. In a different school a particular teacher seemed "the best, not an asshole like every other teacher," because "he knows you. He cares about you." But another teacher, who admittedly knew her subject extremely well, was considered "a drip, a wet blanket" because she was "so introverted — she only gives a certain amount to the class." Students would have liked her better "if you knew something about her." Relating well requires self-revelation as well as friendliness. Teachers like her had "a steel wall around them. They know that the kids can't relate to them, but they don't care, and they don't try to relate to the kids."

Teachers tended to agree. One said, "You've got to be personal, you've got to be friendly. It helps the kids get interested. You can't be nasty. 'Sit down. Shut up. Do the work.' " Another summed up the general mood. "Kids want to be dealt with openly, and they want people to be straight with them. I find that dealing with things directly, getting angry, taking the kids seriously, giving and taking and being vulnerable, is what a teacher needs in order to be able to get along with kids in school today . . . The kids want to know they're cared for."

Differences in age and authority are downplayed in favor of informality. One student latecomer explained aloud that his tardiness was caused by "some problems . . . girl problems." "That's okay," the teacher reassured him, and began the class by recounting a recent professional meeting. "There was good food, a bar. We had a good time." A student interrupted: "I hope you didn't drink?" "Well," replied the teacher, "I must admit that I did partake." "How much did you drink?" "Well, I have a low threshold. I don't have to drink too much before I feel real good." With complete seriousness the student remarked, "I don't drink, but I know where you're coming from."

Another teacher observed that few things had changed as significantly in high school as relationships. In the past students "never had the nerve to do or say things in school that the students of today do not hesitate to do or say." Just as students preferred closer and more informal relations with teachers, so, too, had teachers themselves become "much more approachable." Sometimes they had little choice, the teacher said. She remembered her roommate in the hospital maternity ward after each had just given birth: the roommate was the sixteen-year-old wife of one of her English students. Professional distance was no longer possible when even the birthing experience was shared. Teachers often find the informal relations a welcome change. One veteran admitted, "I enjoy dealing with kids now more than I did" near the beginning of his career. Even though it was harder to get them to do homework, they were "easier to talk to."

What is at stake in most classroom negotiations about relationships is thus not informality itself; with few exceptions, teachers and students prefer relaxed, friendly, and caring relations. Different kinds of treaties are worked out, instead, about how relaxed relations among people affect their relations with the subject of the class — that is, with learning itself. Friendly and relaxed relations can be employed to engage or to avoid learning. "Having good relationships is essential to a good class," a teacher argued, "or they just turn you off." But the critical issue is what a "good class" is expected to be.

Mr. Glynn was one teacher whose conception of informal relationships went beyond a relaxed classroom atmosphere to embrace learning. He saw informality not as a pleasant end in itself, but as a necessary trigger for engagement. Nowadays "you've got to be very vulnerable to be an effective teacher." Students had to know their teacher "as a person and like what they say or perhaps commiserate with some of the things they say. Then, if they like something that turns them on, hey, maybe there's something about Shakespeare or Keats or whoever because I like this teacher and the teacher likes it." His point was, "They have to get turned on to him before they get turned on to the subject matter." Getting students turned on to him took more than friendliness, so he brought all his personal experience into the classroom: "I tell them about my life, my loves." He needed openness to sustain his own energy as much as the students needed it to sustain their commitment.

The problem was that he could communicate something about himself to his students in a group setting, but could not learn enough about *them*. The organization of high school made it almost impossible for teachers to know very many students as individuals. Friendly relations guaranteed little knowledge beyond surface geniality. There was simply not enough time. "If we could just take five minutes a day and spend it with just one student, and do it every day, we could help some of them open up." But if Glynn did that with each of his 125 students, the effort would consume more than ten hours a day.

One of his colleagues left classroom teaching for school psychology precisely because he didn't feel he could know his students well enough to teach them effectively. The average load of 125–130 made it impossible. Furthermore, "you look at thirty kids in the classroom . . . the five bright ones in the front row who are paying attention, fifteen others who are half asleep, and ten more who are really snoring. You're not teaching a class then, you're teaching five kids. The rest of the kids are nowhere. That's ridiculous!" His only answer had been to change jobs.

In the absence of structural change that Mr. Glynn could not imagine, a class taught by another English teacher, Mr. Rodriguez, made the kind of treaty about relationships that Glynn had in mind. Mr. Rodriguez began the term by announcing that the treaty he hoped to enforce had less to do with homework or attendance than with "codes of conduct" centering on mutual responsibilities. "I have important things to share with you and you have important things that you want to share with me. The only way we can do that is to have a forum. That means when I speak, you quietly listen whether you agree or not, and vice versa." By a forum for sharing Rodriguez meant joint *obligations* to the business of the course. "If students don't listen," he said, "I'll stop teaching. I'll make an example of the rudeness." All he was doing, he confided outside class, was using "pop psychology as a control factor, using politeness, manners, and social interaction as a base. I never raise my voice."

Mr. Rodriguez once asked for their reaction to his willingness to reveal feelings. He had told them, for example, "I've had a bad weekend. I've got a hangover. I just broke up with my girlfriend and I feel miserable." One savvy student answered that such talk was all right because he didn't do it every day. He didn't excuse himself that often. "There are teachers who have that syndrome every day," the student said. Rodriguez pressed on to make his point. "I'm a human being and you have to know that and that I go out and that I don't feel well sometimes, and at other times I stay home late and I'm well prepared." He wanted reciprocity but often didn't get it. "I do all my homework and I prepare all my lectures and . . . I don't feel that you're prepared to take in all that I've done. And I want you to know it." He told them he had become increasingly forthright with students. "I present myself as a human being." In so doing he tried to persuade them to agree to his treaty.

Rodriguez's preoccupation with feelings carried over to the ways he tried to engage students with materials like *The Odyssey*. His basic strategy was to make the book accessible by emphasizing its psychological aspects. The class considered, for example, why Telemachus left to search for his father. "And yet," Rodriguez began, "he's told continually that he's not his father, he's not as strong as his father . . . He is a puny soul who'll never measure up." Then he made a psychological jump. "And what happens when children are told these kinds of things?" One student called out, "They get depressed"; another, "They get insecure. They fail. They can't live up to their parents' expectations." One retorted, "Athena helps against that," and Rodriguez — instead of asking, "How?" — shot back, "What could Athena be? What's Athena in your lives, our lives?"

The class continued in the same vein. "What is Telemachus doing? He is going out to prove that he's a man. He's looking for his father, but really what is he doing? He's looking for whom?" The students replied, "Himself." "Let's be amateur psychologists now," Rodriguez went on. "How do you, as young people growing up now, relate to what Telemachus is doing? Did you see this as a quest for identity before we discussed it today?" One replied, "Yes. He's getting out from under the shadow of Mom." "Is it hard?" "Yes, you're leaving what's known." "What do you need to do it? Do all people go out eventually?" "Yes, unless they're wimps." "Some people take a long time to do it." "You need purpose. Telemachus used the excuse of looking for his father to give him a reason to leave."

At times Mr. Rodriguez stopped the discussion to summarize where they were, and perhaps to reassure them that they were somewhere. "Telemachus has two forces. Internal conflict, the fact that it's time for him to grow, and an external conflict, the need to look for his father. You all have internal and external conflicts . . . You're being torn in adolescence and you don't know what to do." But, he continued, Telemachus searches in a positive way. "What does Homer portray that makes us know that Telemachus has what it takes?" More discussion followed about the complexities of love between parents and children.

As the class neared its end Rodriguez asked for some of Telemachus's weaknesses. "He didn't tell his mother he was leaving," one student said. Rodriguez: "But he told her to go to her room. How many of you could do that? Also, he cries in an inappropriate situation. If you remember from *The Iliad,* Greek men can cry but they have to do it appropriately." A student interrupted: "He told people to leave, he asserted himself." Rodriguez: "Yes, he asserted himself. Then, when people didn't leave, he started to cry. It's kind of like birth. It doesn't just happen. Whether it's the birth of a baby or the birth of a self, it takes energy and pain and relaxation and tension, and what happened to Telemachus was, after he asserted himself, when things didn't go right, he started to cry." He told them they should write an essay the next day on the discussion just concluded, since he would be absent. They all yelled that they wanted to continue the discussion instead, but he jovially insisted that they couldn't have a discussion without him. "Go to your room," they scolded affectionately when the bell sounded. As they trooped out, one said aloud, "This is a good class."

Mr. Rodriguez's substantial reputation, a colleague suggested, rested on his capacity to marry charisma with intelligence: "He turns the kids on. The kids idolize him. He's one of them, and yet he's their idol, however he manages that." At the same time, "he teaches them to think. He's the only one that I can think of in the English department who does." Both Rodriguez and Glynn understood the danger of overemphasizing feelings, intimacy, close personal relationships. Those could become ends in themselves, ways to avoid engagement in the subject, unless teachers also had mastery of their fields and commitment to use relationships to help students understand subjects. Rodriguez considered himself "a real purist, a real classicist." Glynn insisted, "You have to be able to draw the line. You have to be able to shut it off. When you want to get serious, they have to get serious . . . Some teachers just can't do this."

Many cannot or will not; informal and friendly relations for them stand alone as the heart of classroom accommodations. After all, there are no codicils requiring that these relations be in the service of engagement with subjects. The logic of avoidance through relating was nicely put by one student's explanation of his teacher's behavior: "If he gave homework every night, put a lot of pressure on the kids, they would naturally hate him. So he keeps things under control by being more personal with the kids, being more natural." This kind of treaty is far more common than those negotiated by Rodriguez and Glynn. The English teacher who discoursed on the intimacies of his post-pubescent love life is one example. "He's fun," one student concluded. "You can bring donuts to class and chocolate-covered pretzels and all that sort of good stuff. We eat a lot in most of my classes." Mrs. Austin, too, loved openness, friendliness, and informality above all else. Relaxation was not a means to an end; it was the only end. "It feels kind of good," she said, "to walk down the hall and be able to say hello to people and know who they really are; they're not just faces." And in truth she knew who was going out with whom, and had no more reserve about referring to these social relations in class than her students did.

In many schools the use of relationships to avoid engagement in learning almost approaches institutional policy. One teacher remarked that "every class is supposed to be an I–Thou encounter." This led to a high energy level but also to "big BS sessions." Students quickly learned to be good at that, but "they're not as good at disciplined attention to anything." At another school a teacher complained that "the official first priority of the district . . . is human relations . . . There's no emphasis on academics." Students who described their school as "relaxed" often simply meant that "everybody knows everybody else . . . We don't stress academics too much." If the place had a motto they thought it might be "Enjoy yourself."

Getting along by relating is the path to many relaxed classrooms but not to all of them. Some teachers and students bargained to get along by ignoring each other's personal lives and feelings altogether. Dr. McBride did this in physics but still maintained a relaxed class. Students like Kara and Eric not only tolerated his arrangement, they preferred it. They spoke disparagingly of another teacher's excessive warmth and sympathetic caring toward students. She was accepting of everything, nurtured too much, didn't know how to shut people off when they were wasting class time, wasn't tough enough. Fully committed to the subject, Kara and Eric required only relationships focused upon intellectual understanding. McBride was not mean-spirited; he simply didn't want or need to intrude feelings into the class the way Rodriguez and Glynn did.

There is a difference, however, between being merely uninterested in students' personal lives, as McBride was, and being personally insensitive. One insensitive teacher often lashed out bitterly at students for being rude, asking poor questions, not paying attention. His aggressive style of insulting them when he felt they deserved it produced, as a colleague delicately put it, "great personality conflicts." The colleague thought that variety in student-teacher relationships was inevitable and good. "Everybody," he pointed out, "isn't going to be always going around patting you on the back. Some of them are going to use, not a negativistic approach, but they're going to be a little bit rough at times." The teacher in question was appreciated by some for the demanding and successful Advanced Placement preparation he provided, but loathed by others, who moved heaven and earth to avoid his classes. Few teachers of this sort are successful with students who do not bring substantial commitment and competence to a subject to begin with.

There is another way to minimize classroom relationships that is too often welcomed by all parties: human contact can be eliminated entirely. Isolation — anonymity — is sometimes a more acceptable treaty than content-laden badgering or even content-free bantering. Mr. Baxter's beaver-worksheet class was relaxed because relationships were deliberately avoided. Each student worked alone at his or her own pace and was even allowed to do nothing at all, as long as basic order prevailed.

"Every week we go through the same sequence," another teacher pointed out. "On Monday students read and take notes in class . . . On Tuesday they do worksheets from their notebooks on the chapter. On Wednesday we discuss the chapter, on Thursday we have a film on the chapter, and on Friday there's a test." For 80 percent of the course, therefore, no spoken relations between students and teacher, or among students, occurred at all. The teacher never even initiated a discussion of the lively *Sixty Minutes* segments that were shown during the Thursday movie hour, because she was "reluctant to express my views on what the film has to say . . . I don't think it's good for me to impose my values on the class." The treaty of silence in her course and Mr. Baxter's was one more way for everyone to get through the day.

These various accommodations all concern relationships between students and teachers. But, Mr. Glynn stressed, it is among students that relationship treaties promoting engagement with learning are especially difficult to arrange. There is no absence of student relationships in class. Socializing with friends is a major use many students make of school. Since most school time is class time, they naturally try to use it for friendly chat. Mr. Baxter's class embodied one kind of bargain. There, a student not in the class could just walk in, carry on a conversation, and leave without anyone taking notice. Another arrangement tolerated quiet social conversations among small groups as long as they did not disrupt the class as a whole. Those who wished to tune out could do so. Still another arrangement was simply to tolerate interesting but irrelevant talk. One boy said he liked going to English a lot because "it's comedy. Seriously, it's comedy." It was comedy not because the course was about comedy, but because "the kids make you laugh in there. It's funny because you know these two guys who come. They're both funny."

Thus the issue Mr. Glynn was raising is not whether students relate to one another in class, but rather whether they are willing to relate to one another around the subject under scrutiny. Hard though it is for teachers to show openness and vulnerability, it is even harder for students. "They are so afraid of being exposed to their classmates that they just won't take a chance," Glynn said. "They like [vulnerability] in teachers, but they won't get there themselves." Peer pressure was the great inhibitor. "They're more afraid of their peers than anything else. It's the biggest thing in their lives . . . They think more highly of them than they do of their teachers or their parents."

Students across all levels are frequently reluctant to speak out or to listen to one another. Two identified as potential dropouts resented a teacher's inclusion of class participation in the grading process. "Some people just naturally get into what is going on but I just like to sit back," one said. The other thought class discussion was pointless. If teachers wanted to know what she knew, they could simply give her a test. A middle-level student commented that "everybody is afraid to answer" because "your friends will think you are a dipshit if you screw up." Top-track students worried, one reported, " 'What if it's wrong?' They don't want to take the chance that people will think that they're stupid." Teachers agreed with Glynn. "That's so critical, that peer group. It's more important than Saint Peter."

The most convenient teacher accommodation is simple acquiescence. One teacher explained, "I provide them with ways to save face if they screw up. I don't back them against the wall in front of their friends." Because so many of his regular (but still college-prep) students "won't get up and talk," another teacher eliminated all oral individual presentations and kept discussions to a controlled minimum: "When you have discussions, you don't want to really pose any threats." You also had to be very careful about correcting anyone; if you did, "that's the end of the discussion." Teachers like Mrs. Austin obtained active participation from all at the price of serious engagement from anyone. Students talked often to one another, but their serious exchanges were usually social.

Pedagogies officially designed to maximize student interaction — such as breaking the class into small groups — are used by some teachers, but often a group is allowed to avoid its official task. The task of small groups in one advanced English class was to update in their own language a Tennyson poem. For an entire week students worked in groups of three or four, with the teacher watching the proceedings from a distance. One group took the task seriously and worked closely together. In another group one student did all the talking. In a third, a boy stared straight ahead in silence for the entire period, another perused the school newspaper, and two others competed with each other to create the most absurd rhymes possible without transgressing local obscenity standards. At the end each small group had a product, but the objective of maximizing participation had been forgotten.

But some teachers, hoping to forge different treaties, begin with ground rules about courtesy and cooperation, just as others have ground rules about homework or attendance. "There are no put-downs of any sort" is the one big rule for an English teacher. She tried to emphasize that talking was an act of trust; if someone talked, everyone else had to listen. "The more I can get kids talking, the better the class, because they get each other going." A colleague was "very explicit about the need to talk to each other, to listen to each other with respect." She was pleased that overt put-downs were infrequent, but discouraged that "at the most they will talk to me. *At most.* And they won't listen. I mean *no one* will listen . . . There is no communication. It's incredible." "Students don't see that they have any responsibility for the class as a whole," another teacher said, echoing the complaint of many. "Their responsibility is to do their work, be quiet, and cooperate. That's it. They have no responsibility for other students. I ask them, 'If so-and-so isn't doing well, what's your responsibility?' And they say, 'None.' "

Mutual responsibility is often best cultivated when working together is indispensable to success. Curiously, the importance of teamwork is more apparent in the extracurriculum than in regular classes. A coordinator of a media program, whose products were visible for the whole school to see, felt fortunate that students counted on each other to come through: "If the kids don't act responsibly, they're letting a whole team down." The same attitude prevails in sports, drama, and music. In classroom learning, however, valued and visible group products are so rare that individual isolation and competitiveness seem almost intended.

A few teachers attempted to make interaction and even confrontation among students a central instructional goal. Some rearranged seats so students would look at one another. In a biology class

95

teams of students were required to research a topic and teach it, without notes, to classmates. Teams were evaluated on the quality of presentations, the quality of test questions prepared on the units, and the quality of notes taken on the presentations of other groups. Mrs. Zukowski also employed peer teaching to good effect in Constitutional Law. Yet in none of these cases were students judged on how well their classmates understood what they had taught them. There were limits to the responsibilities that students were expected to take, even when arranged by the most creative teachers.

One team of veterans from the alternative-school movement of the late sixties defined "attitude change" as the goal of an experimental class. They regarded social studies in part as learning to confront each other's differences — deliberately vast, in terms of race and class. "We worked very hard . . . on getting kids to respect one another's ideas, to talk to each other, and to give each other a chance." At first there had been tremendous hostility. "We have had some very hot discussions in here that have ended . . . with kids in tears, and kids walking out." The teachers were proud to report that a girl had written recently that they "had finally gotten to know each other well enough so that we could have a good fight." The beginnings of trust were evident: two previously warring girls had been found in the bathroom together illegally smoking cigarettes. Student engagement with each other, these teachers believed, was at the heart of educational purpose. But this was one of the hardest treaties to conclude. Especially when serious differences of class and race existed, students preferred to avoid each other. Relationships among them tended to evaporate when they were employed to promote learning rather than just sociability.

Intensity

No classroom treaties are more important than those that reflect how much the participants believe their time together really matters. How much do they care about learning and how much do they put out to secure it? To what extent will they settle for going through the motions? In the extracurriculum and especially in sports, coaches and players commonly describe energy, drive, and commitment as intensity. Intensity is the difference between the capacity to perform

96

and the will to perform, between a passive and an active attitude. It signifies desire, sweat, and hard work exerted toward well-understood personal or group objectives. Those who lack it may make the team but often sit on the bench. In classrooms, this quality is more elusive than on the playing fields and less talked about. Nobody gets benched, much less cut, for lacking classroom intensity.

The classroom equivalent of athletic intensity is how seriously students and teachers approach their subject, whatever it may be, as a means for developing, practicing, and demonstrating the capacity to think. One teacher emphasized, "You have to set expectations for individuals that are just a little too high for them to meet comfortably, but not so high that they become discouraged." Setting high standards was hard, but harder still was holding onto them. "It's easy to let them slip, to let things get in the way, and to have the standards stay down. But it's essential that you keep them up, both for your own sake and for the kids'. You have to continue to resist taking the easiest course."

Mr. Snyder was one teacher who understood that mutual intensity was the most crucial part of any classroom treaty. At the beginning of his course he explained not only to students but also to their parents that literature was "basically an excuse for conversation, for thinking, and for writing." He told them that the faculty's goal — not just his own — was to "hold kids to a standard of excellence, no fooling around . . . We'll do what needs to be done to help you, but we expect you to really try hard to accomplish these goals and learn these skills."

Students understood this proffered treaty very well. Although it was unusually demanding, it was worthwhile. "He digs at you until you finally come out with it," one student said. "He doesn't shove it down your throat, but he won't let you go without knowing it. He just makes you understand. He tests you and makes it come out of yourself. He doesn't care as much about grades as he does about learning." But in other classes, a comrade pointed out, "you just talk about the facts. You don't worry about the idea so much." They knew that Snyder modeled for them an attitude toward learning that he expected they would reciprocate.

Like many teachers who strive for intensive classrooms focused on thinking, Mr. Snyder had a teaching style that involved posing significant questions and clarifying the responses. He made class participation by all more likely by arranging chairs in a square so that students faced one another. One day his sophomores encountered an Emerson poem called "Give All for Love." "How many people do you know, and perhaps you want to think of yourself first," Snyder asked, "who are likely to follow Emerson's injunction to give all for love, to give up everything to follow your heart?" Some replied that many did; others answered that many said they should but never really did. Laughing, Snyder retorted, "If they have the inclination to, but really don't, why do you think that is so?" "Because it's irrational." Laughing again, Snyder asked, "Is there something wrong with being irrational?" "Yes! It messes you up," one student answered. Another added, "All throughout school and everything you're taught how to use your mind in a logical way . . . So to follow your heart is to go against everything you've learned all along."

Snyder: "He seems to be stressing something that is rather foreign to our backgrounds. Is that it?" Student: "Yes . . . it's more like what you might act if you followed human nature, if you haven't been educated." Student: "You can make a lot of mistakes if you follow your heart. It can hurt you." Gently, Mr. Snyder moved the discussion to taking gambles and risks, and to how many risks this group was willing to take. Not many, it turned out, and he said, "But if you are not taking risks, how are you living?" "In a steel safe," admitted a boy, alluding to something the group had studied the year before. "Your mind is a steel file. To open the steel file and to go out is to open your heart, and follow your heart instead of just living in a closed world."

Snyder moved back in to ask how the discussion fit in with the other Emerson pieces they had been reading. "It seems to me," one began, "that his analogy of be thyself — " "You mean 'injunction,'" Snyder cut in, and then the student went on to point out that you must please yourself and not go along with the crowd. "If that's the case," Snyder pressed, "how does a person ever love someone else?" The student said he didn't know: "If you do that, then there is no room to love anyone else." Snyder pushed further: "How do you put those two together?" After confused discussion, he intervened again: "Maybe what we have to do is to ask what it means to love another person. Then . . . we'll have some idea of what he is talking about." He asked what audience Emerson was addressing. "People who are educated," one replied. "But educated for what?" Continuing in this manner, the discussion moved toward the conclusion that giving all to love meant loving someone who dared to be true to himself and his own ideas.

A student called out that it was more than that. You shouldn't love someone just for being himself or herself; love meant bringing out individuality in the loved one, helping that person become himself. Snyder beamed. "In a way, you've gotten right into describing a true relationship. You're respecting who that person is, the uniqueness and the individuality of that person, and not trying to impose your feelings or ideas of what he should be on that other person." "Right," said the student, "it's an unconditional love for their individuality." Snyder replied, "Indeed, and isn't that what makes it possible? Look back to the text," and off they went reading aloud from Emerson.

The most striking part of the class was not that these fifteen-year-olds exhibited any special insight or brilliance, but that virtually everything they and Snyder did confirmed that the task they were mutually engaged in mattered. Despite the relaxed atmosphere, the class took its responsibilities very seriously. Not everyone participated, but most did, and all were attentive. Snyder talked less than several students, but his words were always crucial. He responded to every comment in a way that moved a potentially aimless conversation in an orderly progression. The discussion had direction, moving ever closer to an understanding of one side of Emerson's thought. The students listened. They seemed to respect one another's comments as much as Snyder respected theirs. The responses were serious, if sometimes puzzled, and were directed at the issue under examination rather than away from it. Students spoke mainly in complete, sometimes imperfect, sentences. By referring back to material learned as freshmen and also to other works of Emerson, read earlier in the course, students conveyed the sense that the class was not an isolated moment in their lives. The class had a collective memory from which it drew. All of these qualities are evidence of shared intensity. Snyder was exhausted at the end, as most good teachers are after a serious discussion that stays on track.

The students were exhausted, too. Emerson is often "a little boring" to sophomores, and these were no exception. But the pace and expectations of the discussion kept them involved.

Living by the terms of this kind of treaty is not easy. It requires hard work by everyone, even when undertaken in friendly surroundings. It also entails large risks. Teachers must be knowledgeable enough and quick enough to bring off-track comments back into the mainstream of serious discussion, yet they must also be able to admit they sometimes do not know the answers to unexpected but germane questions. Students must be equally willing to make mistakes in front of both peers and their teacher without fear of humiliation. The product of such serious effort on both sides is often exhaustion.

It is wrong to associate intensity too closely with any particular teaching technique, even though Mr. Snyder was most comfortable with the discussion approach. There are many different ways in which classes can develop, practice, and demonstrate the capacity to think. Even a lecture can electrify, can stimulate interest where none existed before. Nevertheless, teachers who take seriously the goal of thinking rarely allow students to be passive for long. They press for activity — in particular, activity that emphasizes speaking and writing. Mr. Snyder not only expected students to speak in sentences, but corrected one student in midsentence on his use of the word "analogy." Dr. McBride stressed oral discussion of physics problems that students could not understand. Mrs. Zukowski paid attention both to the notebooks her Constitutional Law students compiled and to their oral briefings of cases to each other.

But treaties for mutual intensity are the exception rather than the rule. Teachers and students tend to bargain for less taxing obligations. The absence of intensity is most obvious when teachers and students behave as if nothing they are doing really matters. The throwaway line "Who knows?" — as employed, for example, by Mrs. Austin or by the Asian Studies teacher in the discussion of the soul's existence — has also the clear implication "Who cares?"

In an American history class the teacher's discussion of a filmstrip on political campaign posters was based entirely on questions and answers contained in a guide that accompanied the film. Her main goal was to get through the list by the end of the period. A typical question was, "From this poster, can you decide what the Democratic Party's attitude toward big business was?" "Pro business" was the right answer. When it was given, the teacher repeated it with the accompanying reinforcement, "Very good, class," and moved quickly to the next question. The pressure to get through was overwhelming. When wrong answers were given, the teacher would say, "Yes, that's right," and then rephrase the answer so that it was correct. Faced with the question, "What were the economic conditions of most Americans between 1877 and 1920?" one student called out, "Mixed up." This answer, perhaps brilliantly appropriate and in any case an invitation to follow up, was greeted with the stern admonition, "Will you kindly listen to the question? I said economic conditions." The answer she accepted was, "Pretty good." This kind of mechanical discussion and student acceptance of it suggested that American history in this class was nothing more than a burden for everyone to endure as painlessly and briefly as possible.

The sense of a mutual and onerous burden was caught in another painful history exchange in a different classroom. The teacher tried to start a discussion on whether American industry was sufficiently prepared for World War II. "Once the war starts, what effect does that have on the average Joe?" asked the teacher. Silence. "Okay. Wait. Let me ask you this. What did most people feel about Vietnam? Was it a popular war? The overall feeling in America about Vietnam was what?" Silence. "Tell me. Talk to me. What about World War I? What happened in World War II that made it different?" Finally a student said, "We got riled up." The teacher was happy to settle for that level of response. "Once we were attacked," he agreed, "it's payback time." The class slouched on to something else.

More specific accommodations to avoid thinking involve mutual expectations about how students speak and write. Consider classroom oral discourse. Silence is the most extreme treaty to avoid talking, but not the most common. A more frequent arrangement is for teachers to permit or encourage students to express themselves orally in single words or short phrases rather than in complete sentences. These responses rarely lend themselves to further discussion. They are self-contained, and that is what is intended — on the part of both teacher and students. The teacher in one class, for example, was preoccupied with the correct identification of such terms as rugged individualism, stock market speculation, and the Federal Farm Board. When she asked what the Depression was, hands shot up and students called out, "Hard times," "Problems that blacks had," "No money," "Loss of jobs," and so on. But all their answers were pronounced wrong. The teacher announced that the correct one, which students had to know for test purposes, was "Economic collapse." She was willing — even determined — to settle for particular one- or two-word memorized answers. Knowledge was self-contained in bits and pieces.

As this class progressed, it exposed a second way in which thinking can be avoided by what kind of discourse is tolerated. Remarkably brief attention was given to a remarkably broad range of topics. Extended attention to any one of them was avoided like the plague. The very notion of a conversation was absent. Sometimes one phrase was enough to justify moving on to the next topic. Coverage was everything. This one class period "covered" the Good Neighbor policy, the Thirteenth Amendment, the Emancipation Proclamation, treatment of returning World War I veterans, Vietnam veterans, the Triple Entente, the Falkland Islands war, American armaments, socialists, communists, and Huey Long.

The teacher complained that the quality of her students had declined over the years — they now lacked analytical skills. They were able to handle the material in one textbook, where a typical study question would be "Name the three presidents of this period," but they could not manage another text, where the question would be "What factors might have influenced a particular event and which ones were most important?" The latter question called for an answer not provided explicitly in the book. Yet she saw no connection between students' lack of analytical skill and her own classroom practice. By emphasizing what she thought they could already do (remember disconnected facts), she was helping to perpetuate what they could not do (carry on a conversation about the meaning of facts). She proudly insisted, however, that standards had not been compromised. It was very hard to get an A. The lesson began exactly when the bell sounded. There was no fooling around. Homework was assigned, collected, and graded. She helped convince the students and herself that these requirements and high standards were synonymous. She would have been delighted to hear one student's description of her. "Nobody's made an A in many of her classes this year. You have to do the tests, daily work, and the exams and you have to get a perfect score." Another student said the main things taught were "attendance, conduct conducive to learning, like when she asks us a question, how much answer we give her back." When asked what else the teacher wanted, she replied, "Well, I'm not sure."

No one said she was a favorite teacher, but all agreed she was among the school's most demanding faculty. They had all settled for an ersatz intensity. Where speaking in class does not require complete sentences, and where the words that students speak are not grounded in a longer conversation permitting follow-up, the uses of speaking to develop, practice, or exhibit thinking are compromised.

The wholesale absence of intensity about thinking is especially noticeable when there is no relation at all between one classroom comment and the comments that follow it. Mr. Snyder used each student answer to formulate his next question. His questions were not random; they represented split-second judgments about how to move a discussion forward in a constructive way. But in many classes there is near total randomness in what is said. The mood is one of desperate chaos. Anything goes. Nothing matters, except keeping things going until the end.

A class about the de Maupassant short story "The Mask" lurched into chaos from the outset. To get at the theme of older people trying to stay youthful the teacher opened with the question "How do people try to stay young today?" The class contributed remarks like "They dress young," "You dye your hair," "Worrying a lot turns your hair gray." The teacher wrote all these on the board, adding to them face lifts and cosmetic surgery. Students then began to discuss the pros and cons of face lifts. The teacher contributed that "Gerald Ford's wife had her face lifted," that the back of the hand shows age, and that he himself had "age spots." This kind of talk, with the short story wholly ignored, continued throughout the hour.

Getting students to write is even more problematic than getting them to talk in complete sentences around topics that might be followed up. When students write they produce concrete products that must be read and assessed. One superb but exhausted teacher — for her the notion of "burnout" meant she was just plain tired — admitted that "papers haunt me." She spent every weekend correcting them, getting up at 4 A.M. on both Saturday and Sunday to begin the task. If she went away for the weekend, she took the papers with her. She once stayed up all night correcting them so she could have one weekend day free. But she couldn't imagine teaching English without having students write and she couldn't imagine being responsible without reading them herself. She felt she had compromised enough by requiring only one paper a week from her less skilled students, as opposed to the two assigned to her higher-level classes. Exhausted but unwilling to compromise further, her thoughts turned to leaving teaching.

A more common treaty is not to assign writing, on the grounds that students cannot write. "I can't bear to read the papers," one teacher admitted. "When I have to stop to teach grammar . . . I gave up instead of flipping my lid." Not only are papers eliminated, but in-class written work is dominated by the same penchant for one-word answers that characterizes spoken discourse. Worksheets and exams are often of the multiple choice or fill-in-the-blank kind. Even when a quiz emphasized factual recall ("Who was George?"), a student asked, "Do we have to write in complete sentences?"

Further, writing is usually regarded as the exclusive responsibility of the English department. A history teacher said he told his class that "if they want guidance in the writing of their papers they should go down the hall to the other department who are the experts . . . 'cause if you gave me an eighth-grade comma quiz I'd probably miss fifty percent." Writing was for experts. Often teachers invoked the importance of specialization not to promote quality but to disguise ignorance. One principal thought, in addition, that parents might complain of unfairness if a history teacher used spelling as a criterion in grading history papers, but would not object if English teachers did it.

Visual media often replace both speaking and writing. A surprising fraction of classroom time is spent watching films, filmstrips, and videotapes. Many of these materials have been competently produced, and students often prefer them to live teachers. "I'd rather watch them than listen to him," one admitted. "He gets off the subject. He talks about things from the news . . . He's not an exciting speaker." Teachers who want some brief respite from the labor of teaching, as well as teachers who wish to avoid those labors entirely, find the visual media a godsend.

One teacher explained that he liked to use film because it exploited a skill teenagers already had rather than ones they didn't have. Students were "visually literate," he argued. They were "very good at watching films, because they are trained." Another pointed out that his middle-level college-prep students would "view *The Scarlet Letter* . . . but they won't read it." They might read it if they could read it in class, but even that didn't work well. "TV works better than spending one month in class getting them to read it carefully."

The classroom uses made of visual media after the viewing are often the most avoidance-prone aspects of the process; the materials themselves are the lesser part of the problem. Sometimes there is no discussion or follow-up at all. And sometimes discussions mirror depressingly the discussions held about things students have read. A thoughtful filmstrip on China, "Different Roads to Socialism," was followed by a discussion that did not mention China at all. The teacher emphasized instead the superiority of America to Russia and Czechoslovakia. The latter was included because the teacher had recently visited it and could talk confidently of his impressions of the country, as distinct from China, which apparently he knew little about. The class avoided the film just as completely as the class on "The Mask" avoided de Maupassant.

Even in schools where the concept of demand is more vigorously academic, thoughtful schoolpeople sometimes distinguish between an academic intensity that measures success by external test scores and an intellectual intensity that measures success by the extent to which a subject is viewed as a means to promote thinking or understand human experience. Academic intensity in this sense is not uncommon in some top-track classes; indeed, it is pursued almost desperately by a minority of ambitious students and parents. But intellectual intensity, as defined by a Snyder or a Zukowski, is admitted almost everywhere to be "very rare."

Intensity is thus expressed in various ways. Treaties are often arranged that regard subjects not as vehicles for the development of thinking but as materials to be endured with as little passion and commitment as possible. The object is to do just enough to get by, or to do what is necessary to acquire the grade or score. Many teachers deceive their students — often unwittingly, and hence themselves as well — into believing that merely requiring work from students without giving attention to the character of the work is a serious form of educational engagement.

The Stakes of Negotiation

Classroom treaties are understandings about the degree to which subjects will be avoided or engaged. A course may require more time or less time. Personal relationships may be employed to relate to the subject or to ignore it. A teaching method may approach the subject intensively or passively. Participation in class carries no general expectations for either students or teachers. Why not? Why the multiplicity of treaties surrounding time, relationships, and intensity? Why is so much open to private negotiation, and why are so many tacit or explicit deals in fact struck?

For students the reasons are not complicated. There are different treaties inside classrooms for the same reason that there is great curricular variety in the catalog: different students have different commitments to classroom learning. One student explained that "you have the kids who try to excel. And then there's the others who are here. They have their own thing. They just want to graduate and get out and do whatever they're going to do." Students assume that both kinds will be in high school and must be taken care of. They regard high school attendance as the natural consequence of being a teenager. Rather than a privilege, even a modest one, it seems a right — a rite of passage. Rather than a stage of learning, it is a stage on which the drama of adolescence is performed. Admission, continuation, and graduation do not depend on commitment or performance: they depend mainly on age. "The point," one said, "is that the teacher's there to babysit. You're on your own. If you get it, fine. If not, that's okay too." Some want to learn, some don't, some don't know what they want. Internal classroom life, in addition to the curriculum itself, has to be arranged to accommodate each preference. Each, in students' opinion, is okay.

Most students believe that the availability of very different classroom bargains is a fair and realistic policy. If they choose not to work hard and bargain instead for avoidance, they contend, it is their problem because it is their life. Besides, they are convinced schools can't force them to work. "Teachers can try to force you, but it doesn't work. It's up to the students," said one student. Nor could schools force students to learn. "Kids don't learn nothing if they're not interested in the class," said another. They think students will work as much or as little as necessary to meet their personal objectives. "Most students take upon themselves to learn what they have to. They do enough to get by."

Some choose to do a lot. But most candidly express uninterest in schoolwork and a preference for avoidance over engagement. They have no reasons to act differently — "we just want to get out." Sometimes they even see an incentive for doing poorly. In a school that urges students with grades better than C to take more demanding courses, students concluded, "If you want to avoid moving up then you have to keep your work at the C level." Asked about student interests, one boy replied that "the majority of students are interested in putting chrome wheels on their cars. If you're asking what's popular, cars are very popular." In another school the main student issue was the inconvenience of speed bumps in the parking lot. Elsewhere a teacher locked up the soft drinks stored in her class overnight but not the minimum competency tests. A colleague explained that she thought students might "steal the sodas and not the tests, and she's probably right." A senior there who had suffered from "senioritis since eighth grade" figured school was "no big deal . . . I let it slide."

Neither high school nor the outside society provides a carrot or a stick to challenge classroom passivity. High school is no big deal. The impact of what used to be called "higher" education on student incentives has diminished, in part because post-secondary education has become nearly as much an entitlement — that is, an expectation conferred by virtue of age and good behavior — as high school itself. "As long as we have students here who know that they will get into junior college, even if they don't have good grades in high school, there won't be pressure on them in high school," a teacher commented. "Lifelong learning" is a growth industry with an ironic stake in high school failure. The more high schools fail to educate, the more remedial opportunities — and hence adult employment — have to be provided outside the schools. High schools in the same way ironically profit from the failures of the lower schools, since many high school jobs would be unnecessary if students entered with grade-level skills.

In a buyer's market, students interested in four-year colleges also understand that the pressure is off. Only a tiny number of colleges have admissions requirements that force students to work hard. One student admitted with disarming candor, "I put forth an average amount of effort, but I will never kill myself unless it's something I enjoy doing. I might be in the mood for calculus and do a whole set, but it's not because I'm a diligent student. It's because there's nothing else to do and I feel like doing it."

But why do *teachers* not press for more? Why do they so frequently settle for treaties that emphasize avoidance? Why, as Mrs. Zukowski put it, do they allow students so often to "take a whole period and just sit around and rap and rest and play"? One common reply is that teachers are powerless to do anything else. As one teacher put it, students have gotten "the word that they can do anything that they want, that the system will still be around to take care of them." "The kids are willing to do less, and the adults are just adjusting to that," another teacher said. So, in a reversal of roles, "we've had to respond more to them than the other way around." Teachers say they have to put up with "almost any kind of behavior that can occur. Even on a day when a kid comes into class and you can tell at a glance that he isn't going to be able to get along with you, you have to let him [stay] there."

Thus a major teacher incentive in negotiating treaties is preventing conflict. Although people exaggerate the discipline problem in most schools, the potential for active resistance and debilitating classroom battles is never far from teachers' minds. Everyone remembers the isolated horror story more than the normal routine. "There's a kid who took a science teacher and bashed his head against one of these walls," a teacher recounted. "The kid was back in three days, threatening to get the teacher again. A judge won't keep them out for more than three days." Most negotiations about class-room treaties have some connection with conflict prevention.

One teacher, for example, reported that she acquiesced to a "cook-book" approach to math rather than one that emphasized "the whys of it" because she feared students would become "rebellious" if she stressed the latter. A remedial teacher settled for silence rather than discussions that might cause "confrontation" because "as soon as they feel threatened, they lash out." Not assigning homework was justified on the grounds of avoiding "behavioral problems," and not disturbing students who were under the influence of alcohol was tolerated as long as they did not "get obstreperous." Going along with kids avoided problems and hassles.

Conflict prevention is occasionally an incentive for engagement. Students often work harder for a teacher whose power they fear. And parents sometimes force teachers to work harder than they want to. In several schools administrators admitted that pressure from pushy parents was their main lever to maintain faculty quality control. Inept teachers could be shaped up by parental badgering, or transferred out of the school, even when the system itself provided no serious deselection procedure.

Teachers also negotiate avoidance treaties for a less defensive reason: they feel a genuine sympathy with adolescents encountering problems and pressures. They are often as child-centered in their values as they are subject-centered, and accept to a surprising extent the therapeutic goals of counselors. The administrator who longed for a moral quarterback to curb value fragmentation also believed that psychology was as powerful an educational force as pluralism: "Our society is so aware of psychology that it really isn't capable of punishing people. We always find reasons for not doing that, and that's the kind of thing you find in a classroom today." Years ago, he believed, teachers were tough, but today they were "aware of so many other variables in a youngster's life besides a French lesson." He was conflicted himself about the proper attitude to take. He disagreed with students who claimed they could learn only from teachers to whom they could "relate," but also believed that the most important quality of good teachers was their ability to relate to students.

As an example he pointed to an English class that mainly enrolled alienated youngsters. "There's an element of great anger in these kids. The expectations of the society work against them. They see what these expectations are, and how far away from them they are." They needed a teacher who was clearly perceived by them as a "whole person," always respectful and caring. The teacher of the class, who fully met that criterion, believed that "most kids will forgive you a multitude of sins if they perceive you as a person." Caring inevitably meant spending far more class time on their lives and behavior than on nouns and verbs. Therapeutic ideals came first. "In their gut, these students think they're losers." The formation of "self-respect" had to precede academic engagement. This was no easy task, because the source of the problem was at home, beyond significant reach. About one third of the parents, he judged, were supportive of his strenuous efforts; "another third can't help themselves, let alone their kids." The last third, he said, decided that "there's nothing more that they can do, they have done everything they can."

A history teacher of these students felt the same sympathy. They had been losers in school for so long that they had given up. More than history they needed "some sense of accomplishment." The extraordinary variety of the school's offerings was not enough to meet their needs. He refused to reinforce further their sense of failure by overemphasizing academic learning. The absence of homework in his course was more than defensive conflict prevention; it expressed sympathy, and bewilderment about what more could be done. The psychological ideals he had incorporated prevented him from writing off uncommitted students but offered little, beyond intensive caring, as a practical approach. "School isn't for everybody," the teacher concluded with more than a little bitterness. "In reality it's still for smart kids."

Conflict prevention and sympathy are very different incentives for teachers to emphasize avoidance rather than engagement. But behind both motives is the common idea that student diversity is the root cause of varied classroom treaties. Teachers say that some students will work hard, some will do something, and some won't do much of anything. Yet they are all in school. Some students can't be expected to engage with schoolwork. They suffer from poverty or neglect. They have more compelling things on their minds than school. Or they can't be expected to engage because they lack sufficient scholastic ability. Yet they, too, are all in school. Most teachers reason that accommodations inside classes must be made for those who *won't* or *can't* learn. If everyone is in school, at least the pain that many experience there can be minimized.

Teachers differ immensely, too, in what they *wish* to negotiate. Some want treaties for engagement, know how to achieve them, and will not settle for less. Some have the commitment but not the capacity to teach. Some lack commitment entirely; they want to avoid the process of learning just as much as their students. One principal believed that an informal but crucial process of matching teacher and student incentives took place. It was "kind of a natural selection." The prevalence of agreement rather than conflict — of treaties rather than wars — was in part the result of like finding like. People who preferred similar classroom arrangements regarding time, relationships, and intensity often found each other.

Teachers who press for engagement tend to be enthusiastic and knowledgeable about their subjects, teenagers, and teaching. They were usually successful students in school, were educated broadly rather than as narrow specialists in college, and are passionately devoted to their work. Teaching seems more a calling than a profession. Work taken on outside school, whether paid or unpaid, is typically an extension of their work in school. If a teacher has two jobs, he or she still leads one life. They write novels or papers, play an instrument, do scientific or computer consulting, practice their trade, teach in local colleges.

The teacher haunted by correcting the weekly papers assigned to less-skilled students, for example, still vividly remembers the pleasure felt in high school when she first discovered "the life of the mind." An all-A student, she went on to a demanding college where "I thought I'd died and went to heaven." It was heaven because she spent three hours outside class preparing for every class meeting. "I went to class, rushed home, studied from one P.M. to one A.M., and loved it. It was an addiction. I couldn't stop." She remembered the styles of good teachers there, not just in English but in physics, biology, and history, and thought of those styles even now as she prepared for her classes. Mr. Snyder, the teacher of Emerson, majored in philosophy because he would read all the English books anyway for fun. An addiction to the life of the mind does not guarantee excellent academic teaching, but it usually is a necessary condition.

Teachers with this background and addiction are a tiny minority, no more numerous than teachers who admit to having been trouble-makers or academic failures as high school students. "I was just like these kids," said one teacher in explaining why he preferred to teach below-average youngsters. Another characterized himself as a former "derelict" and poor student. He enjoyed teaching students who reminded him of himself as a boy. "We're a good family unit. They use me as a backboard about their fears, their problems." He knew a "lot of very intimate things" about his students, such as how much they drank on weekends, and was proud of his friendly relations with them. They were as screwed up now as he once had been. That affinity helped him "relate" to them. They could see "I'm not a perfect human being, sitting at a desk, who knows everything I'm supposed to be doing." They knew a lot of intimate things about him, too.

His goals for them and for his own teaching were products of his life experience just as much as those of the teacher addicted to the life of the mind were of hers. Within the vocational specialty he taught, he had no interest in teaching students to think, and only passing interest in the content of the specialization. He empha-sized instead the practicalities of getting and holding a job. Employ-ers, he told his students, wanted employees who could perform under minimal supervision, were prompt and cooperative, had good personal hygiene, and knew how to take orders. The written home-work he gave once every two weeks stressed such things as how to fill out a job application. He wanted above all to keep his students out of trouble, and was pleased that students sympathetic to these goals were available for him to teach.

Sometimes teachers, unlike this one, prefer classroom treaties that welcome avoidance because they are as alienated from their work as their students are passive about it. A math teacher liked his job only because "I wanted to do something easy, something where I wouldn't have to work too hard," and arranged classroom demands on himself and his students accordingly. Often low morale is an excuse for not working hard. One teacher reacted to low status and staff reductions by refusing "to give of myself . . . I'm not extending myself any more."

Another teacher, Mr. Cleveland, was unusually candid about his resentment against colleagues, students, and the community. Whatever academic reputation his school might have, he contended, was certainly not due to the teachers; many of them even believed they were as bright as the admittedly bright students they were teaching. But they were only isolated "castles" with no capacity to work together. Department meetings were held "as seldom as possible" and it was "inconceivable" that one teacher would talk to another about a better way to teach something.

His students were "lazy" and he "despised" the community. Parents angered him because they sometimes challenged his interpretations; he would then have to go to the library to "check it out." More important, the community simply did not value its teachers. "When a bus driver or a plumber is making more money than I am, I'm going to be bitter about it . . . My world basically is not giving me anything in return . . . I don't get the inner self-satisfaction." He wanted to be regarded as a professional — "I'm not a priest or a social worker." But as long as society refused to do that, "I'm not going to do any more than I have to."

All his incentives were to avoid work. He admitted to no interest in promoting the faculty colleagueship whose absence he deplored. If the principal ever asked him to become the chairperson of his department, he would immediately decline the offer. And when he spoke of his teaching he admitted that advanced students should be required to write more, but "I don't have the time I'm gonna spend on it." He probably should be spending more time with the regular students also, but that would "increase the amount of work that I would personally have to do . . . that frankly on my salary I wouldn't be willing to do." He spent no time preparing for classes and refused to accept anything longer than five pages for the single research paper he assigned.

In spite of his alienation and shattered morale, Mr. Cleveland had no thoughts of leaving teaching. "At this point, I've got too much into it. And I've got businesses on the side. They are producing income." Besides, he pointed out sarcastically, his behavior was accepted and even expected by his students. Bright kids with pushy parents would learn what they needed without him. The others were satisfied with what they got. He allowed them to read in class three out of every ten periods, and showed films as often as possible. Treaties for mediocrity were welcomed by both sides.

Withering and articulate in his denunciations, Mr. Cleveland was by no means poorly educated or ignorant of his field. Teachers with less education but more commitment often settle unwillingly for avoidance treaties not because of cynicism but because they cannot do any better. Sometimes they are aware of the problem but are trapped by personal limitations beyond their control. One teacher who took on Advanced Placement American history when another teacher retired admitted that he couldn't "really do justice" to the course, but there was no one else to teach it. "I don't have a major in history. I have social studies." He tried hard but was exhausted. "I had never read the book before, so I have to spend so much time reading." He neglected his family.

He tried to rescue the situation by avoiding the subject. Personal relationships became very important. He was unusually caring and ran a relaxed classroom. He compromised on intensity as well. Classes increasingly emphasized facts and rote knowledge. An up-coming test would be "kind of picky," he told the students, because it would deal with such things as which was the last state to ratify the Constitution. "So you should know the material cold . . . How many people participated in the Constitutional Convention? Fifty-five!" He thought things would get better later in the year, when he would compromise on time. By then he could arrange for guest speakers to come in and discuss their jobs in fields like law, engineering, and fashion. Although this wasn't quite American history, it would allow him to "mellow out a little bit." Students understood that he didn't know his subject but liked him anyway.

At least he knew he was unprepared and tried to cope. But many teachers whose classrooms reveal even more profound avoidance believe they are doing good work. Mr. Hicks also had little training in history — his major had been public speaking. He organized his college-preparatory class by a predictable daily routine. Students spent Monday in the library writing. Tuesday and Wednesday were lecture days. Thursday was given over to "enrichment," when things close to student interests — "emotional things, like gory details of assassinations" — were covered. Part of Friday's class was a test, the other part a film.

Although lectures dominated three fifths of the course and student discussion was virtually nonexistent, Mr. Hicks nevertheless asserted, "I don't think lectures have a place in high school." He used them, he said, only as "reinforcement" of the text, and he meant that in the most literal sense. On one lecture day Mr. Hicks was relaxed and friendly, and his students absolutely quiet. As he talked on, with the textbook open before him, some students began to gaze around. Others read quietly. Everyone was orderly. No one seemed restless. No one took notes. It was easy to tune out. Instead of providing background information, the lecture seemed only to provide background noise. On he went.

"Grant established the first Civil Service Commission. Grant was honest, but his appointees and his advisers were unscrupulous. Scandal followed. Garfield ran on a reform platform. After Arthur took over, he also pressed for reform, though no one thought he would. The Pendleton Civil Service Act was passed and still holds. It leads to really good jobs that are secure with good pay. Okay. That's it for civil service reform. Does everybody get it? Now let's talk about currency. It's complicated, and I don't really understand it, but let's go. There's hard money and soft currency. Is everyone following me? Am I losing anyone? I think I'm losing myself."

At this point four students were sound asleep. Mr. Hicks did not seem to notice, but if he did he took no notice. "The Grange. It's not a labor union, it's like a first association. In a way it's like a labor union. It's on the left-hand side of page 309." He moved on to child labor and early social reform. Two students asked questions but he did not respond. He just pushed on. "The U.S. didn't become socialistic or communistic, as in Europe, because though factory conditions were bad, they weren't that bad." Noticing some mild restlessness, he paused to reassure them: "Hang on, we're almost finished." Then he suddenly switched gears to an animated and detailed account of the pain and suffering experienced by President Garfield as he lay dying. Now everyone snapped to attention; the sleepers were wide awake. Even an interruption by a girl who wandered in and asked permission to talk with a friend (she received it) did not break the spell. The class ended with a flourish when

Mr. Hicks announced that Garfield had finally died from infection.

Mr. Hicks's proud explanations of his techniques capture many of the motives that drive teachers toward treaties that avoid learning. He thought it essential to understand that none of the students wanted to be in the room because of the course: "The majority are here because their friends are." Given the absence of student interest, preventing conflict was a first duty. "When you work in a setting like this, you have to be careful." Since "having good relationships is essential to a good class," he used humor a lot and made sure not to "back them against the wall in front of their friends." Although most were bound for post-secondary education, he eliminated essay questions on tests because they couldn't write, and eliminated an "analytical approach" in favor of "knowledge" because they couldn't think. Whenever they were restless, he knew how to entertain them. They all got along well together.

But his strategies were more than responses to their preferences. They were ways to accommodate his own ignorance. Mr. Hicks knew little about American history. His lectures "reinforced" the text simply by repeating many of its words verbatim. He could jovially admit he was "losing himself" without admitting incompetence; nothing on currency would be tested and few students were listening to the lecture. He avoided discussions and thus interaction entirely, and ignored the only questions asked during his talk. Nothing about the subject mattered to him at all. To him, the sleeping students exemplified their own lack of interest more than they confirmed his incompetence. Although he talked sympathetically about how school was a safe haven for troubled and neglected teenagers, it was he who was safe from any scrutiny.

Mr. Hicks preferred to teach average students who accepted without question the terms of classroom life he offered them. His principal, whose metaphor of "natural selection" had called attention to how like could find like, elaborated on what he had meant. "There are teachers who can't teach bright kids. They kind of drop out. They don't tell you they don't want to do it, but what they do is to take the easier, less preparation, more kids with lower abilities . . . They can't keep up with the kids." Another administrator was less circumspect. "There are quite a few of the walking dead here. The administration knows, but can't do much." Hicks was one of the walking dead. He was not an able cynic who shamelessly confessed laziness, like Mr. Cleveland, or a teacher who was frustrated by but aware of his limitations; he firmly believed he was a good teacher of college-bound adolescents. Uncommitted to his subject and keenly aware of the need to be sympathetic and to prevent conflict, he had overwhelming incentives to settle for mediocrity.

The most notable feature of classroom treaties is that they expand immeasurably the already immense variety offered by the shopping mall high school, and do so in a quasi-secretive manner. High schools are proud and unapologetic about the variety expressed in their horizontal, vertical, extra-, and services curricula. They have no trouble justifying the existence of Child and Family and Advanced Physics under the same roof. Virtually everything officially offered, they know, has the potential to engage students seriously in learning. Virtually everything offered has the potential to engage the minds of students and help them develop to their limits the capacity to think.

Treaties are about the extent to which classroom participants want to realize that potential. Many do, but most do not. High schools accommodate diverse student purposes not only by offering a broad choice-based curriculum, but also by offering different levels of *commitment* to that curriculum. Their ultimate accommodation is to allow students and teachers to avoid or engage in learning. These often-subtle understandings about time, relationships, and intensity are less talked about. They are not part of official variety at all, for this kind of variety cannot be easily celebrated as an educational benefit. Despite curricular variety and choice, many students have no incentives to learn what is offered but wish to graduate nevertheless. And many teachers with little commitment or skill wish to retain their jobs. They use student passivity as an excuse to cover up their own passivity. It is one kind of problem to strive for institutional esprit when students and teachers are equally committed to engaging with many different subjects. It is quite another to forge a community of learners when the issue at stake is whether learning itself is valued. When even that is subject to many different negotiations, coherent institutional purpose becomes blurred almost beyond recognition.

3

Specialty Shops

STORES INSIDE SHOPPING MALLS differ from one another in several important respects. Some sell a wide range of products and are large enough to be comprehensive department stores. In others only a particular line of items, such as designer sportswear or kitchen equipment, is sold. Some stores, even if they are multipurpose, pride themselves on offering extensive customer service, while others deal with customers only at the cash register. Stores with a particular product line or with unusual attention to customers are specialty shops: they are special in what they sell, how they sell it, or both. The existence of these specialty shops is for some shoppers — even though they spend time buying or browsing elsewhere — the central lure of the mall.

Specialty shops are very conscious of their preferred customers. The "regulars" receive announcements of sales before the public advertisement. They are invited to take out special credit cards or to attend special events. Sometimes customers become special because the shops seek them out through market research or targeted advertising; sometimes they become special because they insist on special treatment. Whatever the reason, some customers come to occupy a more privileged position than others. They demand, need, or are given extra resources and services.

High schools similarly offer specialty shops: the students who

118

shop in them are regarded by the school as special, as preferred customers. A disproportionate fraction of adult time, energy, and resources is lavished on them. The character of their school experience tends to differ from that of students who make fewer demands or have neither the abilities nor the disabilities to make them stand out. As one teacher remarked, "If you have to say where the resources or energies are concentrated, I'd say the resources are concentrated on the high track and the low track."

In this chapter we take a closer look at the major specialty shops and the services they provide. Why do certain individuals become special, and how is that specialness related to the treaties or accommodations made between them and their teachers?

The Shops

The Top-Track Shop

Most high schools have at least one program that caters to the school's brightest or most ambitious students, the top-track shop, where the subject matter is demanding and the teachers are willing to work hard for their students. The students in the top-track programs have to be committed to the academic purposes of high school; in return they are recognized by being given a variety of services, resources, and privileges not available to others. Top-track students are a special group, and many teachers believe that it is this group that is best served by the school. One history teacher confided, "You know, it's the top kids that get the gravy!"

Top-track programs have developed because preparation for college is no longer a truly distinctive high school purpose; being college preparatory is no longer sufficient to make someone special. So much has the expectation of college attendance become the norm that many school districts have set their graduation requirements to meet the entrance requirements of the state college system. One administrator recalled that in his district this practice began in the late 1960s, "when the minority kids felt that they were being tracked according to grade scores. They were having opportunities closed to them, so it was decided that all students would be prepared as if for college." Even in a district where the requirements for leaving high school were not the same as those for entering college, a principal remarked, "If there's a youngster who wants to go to college in this state, there's a college for him." To be college-bound and special today, students have to reach beyond the ordinary college-prep program.

Top-track programs vary from school to school in the ways they are organized, the number of courses they offer, and the intellectual and time commitments they require. Some programs are self-contained to provide interdisciplinary study with a few teachers for several hours daily, but most offer a collection of honors and Advanced Placement courses taught by different teachers. The Delta Program was an example of the first. It served only the most elite students in a suburban high school where almost one quarter of the students had been identified through testing programs as gifted — that is, with IQs of over 136. The program's fifty-three sophomores, juniors, and seniors were taught by two teachers — the class size was thus about ten students fewer than the school's average — who used an interdisciplinary approach to teach English, history, art history, and French in a largely ungraded setting. The Delta Program had a long waiting list for admission, even though the school offered six other programs for the gifted as well as honors-level courses for each grade in each of the major subject areas.

Academic work in the Delta Program was grueling for both students and teachers. Most of it was highly individualized. Students studied and wrote about authors or historical events that interested them, and teachers discussed ongoing work with them, reading drafts and finding secondary sources to refer them to. As sophomores, students worked as a group on assigned novels, such as Melville's *Billy Budd.* The final papers, on analytic themes like symbolism or character development, were distributed to classmates for written comments, which were then discussed in detail by the group. Participation in these lengthy assignments was a condition of continued membership, and few failed to meet it. "In a six-week period, we work with about eight books, three three-page papers, a fifteen-page paper, and a history exam," reported Mr. Burns, one of the teachers. "And we do that with three different classes!" The workload was heavy, but the time students spent on it seemed to pay off. Of all twenty sophomores who took the National Merit Scholarship qualifying examination, nine were eventually chosen as semifinalists and the other eleven were commended. The six seniors who had graduated from the program the previous June were all admitted to very selective colleges.

The teachers, too, invested unusual amounts of time — about ten hours a day plus a weekend day, in Burns's estimate: "It's too much and not enough." Those hours were spent working with students and grading papers. The teachers also met twice a year with each student's parents, interviewed prospective candidates (with their parents) who had been sent over from the junior high, and managed the Delta Program's separate budget.

It was generally agreed that students who gained admission to the program were given a great deal in return for their commitment. But there were some skeptics: one of the school's regular teachers, for instance, commented that the Delta Program students received too much "handholding and caretaking" and studied so much that they didn't participate in extracurriculars and were "not very well rounded." She thought they'd be better off in honors classes. A teacher in the program insisted, however, that these students needed and deserved the school's extraordinary investment in their education: "These kids are just as different from average kids as is the kid who is retarded."

The ungraded and individualized organization of the Delta Program is unusual among top-track specialty shops, but the classroom treaties that these students and teachers abide by are found in many of the more conventional top-track programs. These treaties are characterized by an eagerness to teach and learn for understanding rather than for simple recall and by close working relationships built on a common understanding that achievement and competency are the main objectives. Randy, a student in another school, liked to wander in after school to chat with Mr. Rodriguez, a teacher in the top track, about literature that was not read in class. "It's not that I don't feel I can talk to him about his life," Randy said, referring to the more usual topic of after-school conversation between students and staff. "It's that I'd rather talk about *Crime and Punishment.*" He expressed a view of school that is not uncommon among top-track students when he said, "The teacher and the subject matter are the most important. School is to learn. I take the hardest classes offered, just short of killing myself . . . to milk the most I can from these years."

Randy liked the intellectual give-and-take, the learning process itself, but to some students "milking the most" means grade-grubbing, and mastery is sought chiefly for tests and college boards. "If you want to do well, then school has to become your first obsession," one girl insisted. "Grades are your label." Admission to selective colleges is the incentive that drives many top-track students; one group admitted that whenever they thought about getting involved in sports or school activities, they considered first how it would look on their college applications. Whatever their motivation, most top-track students are determined to make school a successful academic performance and are quick to uphold their end of the classroom treaties. "I have a responsibility to myself to learn the material," one boy asserted. "I mean preparedness. This class is a commitment and I'm going to push myself doing that."

Coming to class prepared is one expression of commitment; so is sharing ideas with classmates — many top-track students expect their teachers to make that possible. They use classroom relationships to promote learning. "It's counterproductive to learn sitting in rows listening to somebody and looking at the blackboard," one boy explained in talking about how the Delta Program differed from others in the school. "Delta has an atmosphere where learning is not just something that is told to you, or you get in a book, but is something where you sort of absorb in an interaction with other people of your own mental caliber." Another student contrasted her top-track English course with other, "restricted" classes. There, "people have to raise their hands. It's cut and dry. In honors we do Chaucer interpretations, we can talk out. In the regular classes, the teacher lectures and people fall asleep." Students raised their hands in the regular classes because the teacher could not assume that everyone was prepared and would participate, and each question there had a "right" answer, a short one. Chaucer interpretations were not "cut and dry" because people shared ideas that took the discussion in many different directions.

Top-track students set treaty terms they expect the teachers to uphold as well. Teachers like Dr. McBride and Ms. Fish do indeed accommodate these students and press the treaty terms even harder. But teachers quickly admit that their own commitments to the top track are exhausting, even though they get considerable satisfaction from teaching these students. Sixty-four-year-old Mr. Burns, who had been teaching exclusively in the Delta Program for fifteen years, said that the work didn't get any easier. He left the program three times for a year's sabbatical because the work was "so terribly taxing." Yet he came back because working with these students was so rewarding and because he couldn't find other teachers who were willing to stay for more than a year. Teachers like Mr. Burns do the work and often do it well, even if they are ambivalent, balancing what they get from students against the toll it takes. What they get is students' commitment. "That's the joy of AP," one teacher said. "It's that they want to be here. There's little I have to do to motivate them because they're self-motivated, and it's been a pure joy this year teaching them."

But students appreciate their top-track teachers only if the teachers meet the expected standard of performance. Trying isn't enough; teachers have to be able to deliver. This adds to the performance pressures that many of them experience. A history teacher newly assigned to teach the AP history class told of "getting through the regular classes pretty doggone good, but the advanced classes — I can't even measure the hours of preparation." He had to prepare lecture notes, write questions to guide class discussion, and turn to reference books to research issues. This, combined with reading and grading essays, left him with little free time and no social life: "My children are suffering; I'm pooped all the time." One of his students complained, "I really hate it when I ask the teacher a question and he doesn't know the answer, particularly when it's about basic stuff . . . He's not knowledgeable enough for the AP classes." One student who felt it was her duty "to tell the teacher if I think what he's doing stinks" complained to a physics teacher who had introduced historical and biographical material into the top-track physics course. The teacher said he wanted the material "to bring the subject to life for them as it does for my regular college-prep students," but then "toned things down after [the students'] half-year evaluation. They wanted systematic homework assignments. And they don't like the artsy-craftsy stuff." One administrator even arranged the master schedule so that every one of his top-track seniors could take honors English with a particular tough, eccentric teacher whom the students respected. "The kids here are under academic pressure to have a course that is *really* a course. They kind of attack and become very aggressive when things aren't right." These students want teachers to challenge them as well as to prepare them for college entrance examinations.

This frequent insistence on rigorous academic treaties in the top-track enclave sets these students apart from others in the high school. "We're in a little world of our own," one girl said of her honors group. Another observed, "On Monday, certain cliques come in and talk about the parties they attended on the weekend, while others come in and talk about their English essay." "We get what we want," another student asserted. "It's kind of compromising. A lot of the kids who are not in [the honors program] don't get what they want."

The top-track enclave provides a place where special students can get what they want from the school while avoiding what they don't want or won't tolerate. Like some of the shoppers in the mall, top-track students occasionally shop in the other stores, but they spend most of their time in the specialty shop. Moreover, the terms and conditions of the shop's treaties form the basis of their commitment to the school. The existence of top-track courses as a prerequisite even for attending the school was expressed forcefully by one parent who was concerned about discussions in the district to eliminate advanced classes: "Any trend that would say that with integration we've got to get rid of these advanced classes . . . If that happened, I think the system would collapse, at least with parents like us. I think we would say, 'We can't do that. Hey, no way!' " For these students and their parents, the specialty shop *is* high school. They browse in the mall and partake of some of its side shows, but their main event is in the enclave where the workload is "entirely different." The high school had much to offer her daughter, one parent said, "assuming that she's on the fast track." Many people, then, consider the top-track enclave not only a special place that delivers a special product to its customers but the essential feature of the shopping mall high school, the reason they are there.

124

The Special-Needs Shop

A special-needs teacher, Mr. Weiss, received a telephone call early one morning from a student's mother; she was worried because her son Chris would not get out of bed to go to school or to his job placement. He had skipped school the day before, too, and the teacher had known where to find him. But again Chris was reluctant to leave the house. After his mother talked with the teacher for a minute or two, Chris himself got on the line with Mr. Weiss. "Hi, Chrissy-guy! This is Ralph. What's the matter?" said Weiss. After several minutes of probing, Weiss realized that Chris was afraid to go to school because he hadn't gone to work, and he hadn't gone to work because he hadn't received his paycheck on Friday as the rest of the employees had. In the past Chris had lost his paycheck to bamboozling co-workers and had gone home empty-handed. Mr. Weiss had worked out a system whereby Chris was paid earlier in the week. But Chris didn't understand that; he thought he ought to get his check early in the week and on Friday too.

Mr. Weiss suggested that Chris come over to the school for a talk. After lunch they would together go to the employer's: "You and I and Linda [the employer] can have a talk." That wasn't satisfactory to Chris; he wanted to wait until Monday. "Monday's too far away," said Weiss. Again Chris refused. "Come on, Chris, we've got to get you back to work. You need the money." There was a pause in the conversation. "You don't want to work any more?" asked Mr. Weiss. "Oh, come on. I tell you what. You just stay on home this morning and I'll come on over after lunch and we'll have a talk about it. I want you to do good, Chris. So does your mom." Another pause in the conversation. "No," said Mr. Weiss, "we're not going to suspend you. We're just trying to put a little pressure on you so you'll do a good job for us. Come on, you're one of our best guys out there." Chris was not comforted, but he continued to hold on to the telephone connection. They talked about why Chris didn't want to work, why he didn't want to do that kind of work, why he was upset about not getting paid. Weiss remained concerned and gentle but pushed more and more firmly for a face-to-face conversation. The upshot was that Mr. Weiss visited Chris at noon.

The telephone conversation took fifteen minutes. The visit to Chris's home and the trip with Chris to the employer's office took another three hours. According to Weiss, Chris has intellectual handicaps and a lot of emotional problems. "He's a real mess. That means we have to stay real buddy-buddy with him. We have to provide a lot of extra support for him if he's going to be able to make it out in the world." The number of hours Mr. Weiss spent that day on Chris, persuading, explaining, and reassuring, was remarkable but not unusual. Special-needs staff often make extraordinary efforts to help individual students resolve their problems or confusions, trying to build self-esteem at every turn. Services of this sort, combined with personal warmth, caring, and loyalty among members, are the distinctive features that make the special-needs enclave stand out in the shopping mall high school.

The problem of students like Chris was highlighted as a special challenge for Americans more than a decade ago. With the passage of Public Law 94-142 in 1975, the federal government required local schools to identify students whose disabilities prevented their full participation in regular classrooms and develop individualized education programs for them. Schools now provide an extraordinary range of services to students with physical, intellectual, and emotional handicaps, students who would not even have been found in public schools a few years ago.

Many schools provide programs for others who have brought their "special needs" into the schools: pregnancy, lack of familiarity with the English language and American customs, drug and alcohol abuse. Some schools receive state and/or federal funding to support these sometimes extensive programs and services, which include prenatal care coordinated with health agencies, daycare for students' infants, bilingual classes, and individual and group counseling. But even in schools in which these services are available, students classified under PL 94-142 have access to a wider range of programs and resources. They are more comprehensively and consistently served than the others, and thus form a specialty shop.

The most extraordinary of the services for PL 94-142 special-needs students is a mandatory procedure that requires schools to develop an individualized education program for each of them. For each student the school district must convene a team consisting of the special-needs teacher, a counselor, a psychologist or social worker, an administrator, and sometimes health care professionals. With the parents, the team works out an appropriate course of study. This contrasts with standard school procedures, in which programs are put together by students and counselors are rarely involved except to be sure that students have signed up for required courses.

Special-needs teachers are also obliged to talk with classroom teachers about their students. "We spend a heck of a lot of time talking to [classroom teachers] and getting to know them and telling them what our kids can do," a special-needs teacher reported. One of his four special-education colleagues concurred: "[We] spend a lot of time convincing them that they're not going to take on a raving maniac," he said. Person-to-person communication with school staff happens regularly, so the classroom teachers often learn more about their mainstreamed students than about many of the other students they teach.

Mainstreaming, which requires schools to enroll students in regular classes whenever the students can handle the work, sometimes calls for additional special services. In many classrooms a second adult stands at the front of the class, presenting the lesson in sign language for a mainstreamed deaf student. Special needs mandates lower student-teacher ratios, and these small groups of five to ten students may spend most of the day working closely with the same teacher. In addition, parents are regularly informed about how their children are doing. All of these processes and services convey unusual attention to the children who qualify for this enclave. "It's fabulous," said one special-needs teacher. "But all these special services are for a small number of kids."

Special treatment often extends well beyond the requirements of federal or state mandates. Many special-education teachers have an extraordinary sense of caring and compassion for these students. Miss Marks began working with learning-disabled children as a volunteer while she was in college. "I'm an LD kid. I couldn't read as a youngster . . . I didn't have any other way of getting interested in it. I think if you talk to most special-ed people, they have been touched by a handicap someplace in their lives. You find with people teaching special education there is a dedication and almost a — I hate to use the word fanaticism — but almost a missionary zeal that very frankly you don't see a lot of in the teaching profession any longer."

This dedication takes many shapes, but one form is the constant search for the right balances — for work that challenges but does not discourage, for support that is honest but not gratuitous. Finding the balance and holding it is like walking a tightrope in a high wind. When students are mainstreamed, many teachers feel that their work is undone because other teachers don't share their high expectations. To circumvent the mainstreaming requirement, Miss Marks developed a social studies curriculum for special-needs students in grades ten through twelve. "That's something I fought for like a tiger because I found that teachers were giving these youngsters [easy] grades, and learning-disabled kids are too smart. They don't want gifts, and so they have to work hard for their grades. And we make them work hard!" At the same time teachers must bolster students' morale and confidence, which have often been damaged by years of defeats and disappointments. "The failure syndrome is a devastating thing to them. I tell them, 'No, you're not dumb. You have a quirk and we'll work around it.' " One of Miss Marks's colleagues said, "I never, *never* use the word 'wrong' or 'incorrect' for an answer. I emphasize that no answer is completely wrong, especially in English. I try to establish a good atmosphere about making mistakes." Work in the special-needs enclave, perhaps more than anywhere else in the school, requires great faith and firm commitment in the face of what often seems to be small progress.

Although the school regards these students as special, school is still a painful experience for many of them. Brent, a senior, told in slow and measured phrases his story of the grades he had had to repeat as a youngster, epileptic seizures in class (which one teacher treated by putting him in the cloakroom), and disappointments. "I wanted to work with cars [after graduation]. I wanted to be a mechanic, but I think that is out. I wanted to get some experience here in high school, but you have to pass two courses and I didn't pass the tests so I couldn't get into the program." Brent's classmate said, "This [LD] teacher helps me to read." In a mainstream class, she explained, the teacher "says, 'Read so many pages,' but I can't do it. It takes me forever to read one page and all the other people keep on reading and doing the questions and I can't." "Being in the LD unit has helped me out quite a lot," Brent said. "My reading has improved a little — not that much — and my writing has improved a lot. I still write like a third-grader and still reverse letters." Another student commented, "I love it. I wouldn't be where I'm at if it weren't for the LD help that I've gotten. They put everything at my level so I can work at it and do my best." And one of Miss Marks's students who had gone into a vocational program said, "I think I have a positive attitude in life. I've got a trade background behind me now. I'm proud about that, and about myself."

These students know that their teachers and teaching are special, despite the struggle they have with learning, and some are deeply grateful. As one teacher noted, "I had one student write me a note last week, and she said, 'It's so nice to have a teacher who is a good teacher and also a good friend.' And it is that sort of thing that really is rewarding to me." Miss Marks felt so strongly about the rewards of teaching in this enclave that she said, "If they repeal 94-142, I will lie on the Capitol steps and let the Congressmen step over me!"

The Vocational/Technical Specialty Shop

For students who want to develop work-related skills, there is a third special enclave, the vocational/technical program. Most comprehensive high schools offer traditional business and vocational courses of one sort or another, but in recent years many districts have created far more focused efforts, often in magnet programs intended to increase racial integration and often housed in special facilities. Some of the programs now offered are fashion and merchandising, performing arts, science and technology, communications, and agribusiness. In addition, more specialized programs in modern electronics, the aircraft trades, and the hotel-hospitality industry have appeared alongside the familiar vocational education menu. Certain of these newer vocational/technical programs share with other specialty shops a number of characteristics: students who have chosen to be there; teachers who are willing to work individually with students and to coach them; and the special feeling of accomplishment that comes from learning a skill, becoming competent, producing a visible product. Some of the programs have entrance requirements, although these often are less concerned with special abilities than with discipline and attendance records. Nevertheless, one counselor who couldn't place as many students in the voc/tech program as he would have liked grumbled, "The kids they accept are so super that I could send them to Phillips Andover Academy."

Miss McNair runs a communications and media vocational/technical program that draws students from all over a large city district. She and her colleagues work with 214 students in a year-long, half-day course that covers all phases of television production, from operating equipment to writing, directing, and on-screen performing. Their media projects appear as a twice-weekly news show aired on a local cable TV network and a daily news bulletin shown on the school's TV monitors. A tall, striking woman who enunciates her words with traces of professional training, Miss McNair had just returned from a two-year leave of absence spent working as a producer and on-camera reporter for television stations in California and Texas. She looked the part of a charming big-time on-camera personality.

Miss McNair liked this kind of work experience in the program; it put students "out into the real world, where they get to explore a lot of areas and meet a lot of people that kids in general do not have the opportunity of doing." Her program's goals were to "educate, to socialize, to make them literate and give them coping skills — but on a somewhat higher plane." She also taught basic academic skills. "We read a lot; we write a lot, because nothing in TV is ever spoken before it's written; we orally communicate a lot. We just happen to do it through the most popular current media."

A group of reporters who had been out in the field searching for a person they were to interview trooped into the room and told Miss McNair that they couldn't find their subject. After brief explanations she said to them, "Get back in your car. Go find her." It would take two hours to shoot the story after they found her, and forty-five minutes to edit it. They would be working on this project well after school was dismissed because it was scheduled to be aired the next day. There was an understanding — a treaty

— in McNair's shop that no one would leave until the job was finished. "After all, these kids have chosen to come here," Miss McNair said. "Therefore, you can demand more from them, just as you can from gifted kids."

Students in McNair's voc/tech shop took risks: they committed themselves not only to long hours but also to the task of learning enough to conduct intelligent interviews with strangers and to the exposure of themselves and their work to classmates, teachers, and TV watchers in the local community. "It's not like regular classes, because there is no pressure there," McNair believed. "If you fail, you fail . . . but this is the real world, and that's where you learn these kinds of things." In return, the program offered incentives of the sort that students said they missed in other classrooms: a visible product, a public performance, and results that people talked about. Students also got away from classrooms and the unswerving routines of school life. These risks and incentives made McNair's treaties much like those of music directors and football coaches, whose work yields public rather than private performances.

Despite the program's deliberate effort to appeal to students, Miss McNair had difficulty recruiting. The problem, she believed, was that many students didn't like leaving their "home" schools for even a few hours a day. One of Miss McNair's students explained that he disliked the bus ride and leaving his friends; he liked the program better than other classes, though, because "you're on your own. Your head is not always in a book. It seems kind of natural." One of Miss McNair's colleagues attributed recruitment difficulties to parents' reluctance to abandon college hopes for their children. Persistent strivings for higher education and concerns about the second-class status of vocational education and its long-term worth keep some students from becoming involved in programs like McNair's. Although these programs offer many unusual and attractive features, many students don't want to be special in this way.

Even in the most selective programs, many voc/tech students are different from top-track students in one important respect: for them, school has not been a winning experience. They are students who haven't really learned to cope. As a result, "social skills" or "survival skills" have to be emphasized — the rules of work and community life that top-track students already know and largely respect. A twenty-five-year veteran of the auto mechanics shop had each potential student and his parents sign a contract, his formal treaty, acknowledging the program's rules: students were required to maintain a C average in both academic and voc/tech courses, wear safety glasses and work clothes, maintain the work area, and avoid illegal drugs. The contract also outlined the school's attendance policy, which he said caused many students to lose interest; ten absences could mean expulsion from the program (but not from the school). By sticking to this rule he had few problems with student absences.

These standards for entry to a special program and the possibility of forced exit if performance is not up to snuff — a possibility that does not exist in the school's regular programs — combine to create a sense of specialness in these vocational/technical programs, and an incentive to do well. But the existence of treaties that are more demanding than the usual accommodations doesn't help to minimize the skepticism frequently expressed about voc/tech programs. They may teach useful vocational skills, but the content of voc/tech academic courses is often watered down by work-related material. The courses are designed for students who don't like academic work, and so the content is changed to emphasize job or career information and to include activities such as filling out job application forms. Still, voc/tech teachers resent the suggestion that what they teach is easier and feel it prevents them from attracting even better students and raising standards and status even higher. "It irritates me that this [program] isn't on a par with [honors] courses," one vocational teacher said. "That keeps some kids out." He also felt that defining the program as "regular" unfairly downplayed the academic quality of the course. "I go through trigonometrics and circuitry. It should be [honors]." A boy enrolled in another voc/tech program complained, "Our vocational math is harder than academic math. We have different formulas, harder formulas, like the rates of speed of feed . . . Our electronic math is harder, too."

But despite criticisms that voc/tech training is a poor substitute for academics and research that says that vocational education doesn't deliver on its promises for better jobs and employment, students believe that they are learning usable skills. They see clear connections between what they are learning and work they want to do. "When you're doing something in the shop, it's not like somebody told you something you might forget," one aspiring carpenter said. "If you're cutting a piece of stock and you break your cut, then you've got to figure out why. You know, you've done it once. But if someone tells you that in a classroom, you might not catch on." "Some of my friends, they wish they were in the carpentry class," his friend observed. "They get sick and tired of just sitting in the other parts of the building and not doing anything." The third member of this group said, "In a classroom you write papers that eventually get thrown away or burned. But if you're making something, like a carpenter makes a house, he can see it twenty years later and tell his kids that he made that house."

These students receive unusual services in the shopping mall high school because there are a number of people, and their Congressional representatives, who believe that work-related training *is* somehow superior to bookwork, that books and papers don't stand up like houses. And many students feel good about skills training and think they learn best that way. Others disagree. This educational debate has been running ever since federal vocational legislation was passed in 1917 and is not likely to be settled soon. Particularly in the current climate, where many people want education to be more practical, more immediately useful, the public resources that ensure the existence of this special enclave are likely to keep flowing. The mall will continue to offer special status to some students who are not interested in academic work.

Extracurricular Specialty Shops: Band and Football

Pete, Matt, and Eileen were doing well academically and were also heavily involved in school activities. Pete, the senior of the group, was president of the student council. In addition he was active with the debating team, varsity soccer, baseball, and the national honor society. Matt, a sophomore, participated in debating and a political discussion group, played on the soccer and tennis teams, and served on the student council. Eileen, a junior, seemed the busiest of the three. She was involved in debating and the political discussion group, played on the tennis and track teams, edited the

133

sports section of the yearbook, and occasionally wrote for the school newspaper. None worked after school and all planned to go to college.

When the trio described their school and its students, Pete said, "It's hard. We're certainly a sports-minded school. We have seventeen varsity sports and just about everyone here is involved. But there's drama, too — we do six or seven plays a year. There are a lot of very involved students. People aren't here just to go to school; they're here to do other things." Matt chimed in: "When Pete and Eileen and me did the debate team and won, it was a real sense of satisfaction. I get a lot of satisfaction out of planning an activity and seeing it come off. I don't know what motivates me, though." Pete added, "It's hard to say why one person does it. A lot of people don't like the school." Eileen agreed. "I would hate school if I weren't involved. It would drive me crazy."

High schools offer an array of clubs, teams, and performing groups to students like Pete, Matt, and Eileen who want something from school besides academics. Students and teachers observe that intense participation in a single activity — sports, newspaper, band, student government — frequently provides students with a source of school satisfaction that they would otherwise lack. In some places, however, extracurricular activities seem to be just as important as the academic program. "When we force kids to choose between an activity like band and an advanced diploma — we shouldn't put kids in that position," one principal asserted. Activities are important because they are thought to foster school spirit, build student "commitment," and "help keep many of them in school," in the principal's words. They also have educational value: sports are said to teach some of life's important lessons, which transfer from the playing fields to other dimensions of school life. "If you have a good extracurricular program, that's great and it will carry over to other areas. We preach to the kids that we're going after the best, and in the long run, we'll come out better for it," said one athletics director. "It doesn't do us a whole lot of good to be ten and zero if we play the Sisters of the Poor all the time." Sports, he believed, could establish a notion of excellence that students could grasp. The performance is concrete, the results unambiguous. "Even as activities detract, they add," one principal said with conviction.

134

Football and music stand out as specialty shops among the large collection of extracurricular activities because they tend to involve the most students and they are the most popular and visible. One young man who participated in neither thought that those who did were special in his school: "It's the sports and performing groups who get the show. It's a national trend." There is a clear link between band and football — each helps to make the other possible, each helps connect youngsters and community to the school — because these are the activities that most people really care about. "There's athletics and then there's football," one principal explained. "Football is almost a way of life" — so much so, in fact, that it is not unusual to see six thousand people attending a football game in this school whose student body is just a fraction of that number.

The football-band combo also expands the possibilities for building customer loyalty when major academic goals and purposes are not widely valued. In this high school, sixty boys are "dressed" for each football game; an additional twenty-five or so play on the junior varsity team. Almost 30 percent of the boys in the school are on a football team, though many of the team members don't actually play. The suiting-up ritual is in itself a curious compromise between real participation and mere spectatorship. Then there are one hundred fifty students in the band, ten cheerleaders, eight in the ROTC color guard that performs at games, and twelve or so others who run concessions or the PA system. In all, 41 percent of the students have some duty at a varsity football game. Most of the other students are in the stands, along with a sizable fraction of the surrounding community. The voters and taxpayers, many of whom have no formal allegiance to the school, are an important school constituency, particularly as enrollments decline and the population gets older. At football games the school makes a public accounting, pays back the community that supports it. Football is local entertainment; it's also a way up and out for some young athletes and musicians. "We can afford [this program] and other schools can't," an athletic director commented. "I feel bad for the kids in city schools who are missing out because programs are being cut. And a lot of those kids lose their chance for scholarships. It's a rotten shame."

Band-football possesses many of the characteristics found in other specialty shops. Participants come to class prepared; they have practiced their instruments or team plays. They keep in shape. One counselor reported that many athletes are among the 50 percent of students who take early-release time: they run and weight-train before practice begins. The serious work under way in this enclave is acknowledged with departmental status and course offerings that carry credit. Distinctions are frequently blurred between this work and academic coursework, complained one guidance counselor, who lamented that in her school, students could "major in music," because the department offered many credit courses and the requirements in other areas were minimal. The importance of music in this community has elevated it to a high-status program that competes with other departments for students, often wins, and has a waiting list.

The teaching arrangements in the band-football enclave are exceptional, too, as students' skills are worked and refined by teachers who care about how each person plays and how well the group plays together. "Coaching" is a term increasingly used to describe good academic teaching; it has long characterized teaching in the sports and music enclaves. Consider a description of coaching in a band class: "The students are participating in warm-up drills with much concentration. The band master is at the podium directing with his baton. He goes through G-flat and C-flat, and grimaces. 'Let's play C-flat in intervals.' He makes them play again until he is satisfied with the sound. He continues — 'C-major' — and the group is very disciplined, following his baton until he signals to stop. There is no random tuning of instruments or rattling of sheet music during this period. The band master raises the baton and says, 'Just air.' They respond by blowing air without the instruments. 'Now, that's not together. Can't you hear it? It's not together.' He makes them do it until they get it right, then, 'Now, with your instruments.' The band plays. 'Good job. Nice control. You're going to be great tonight!' "

In the music specialty shop, students are coached not only to play better but also to recognize a top performance and not settle for less. "Part of my job," one music teacher said, "is making them want to move toward excellence. We see things through our own experience, and if we've never experienced excellence, there's no way that we can determine it. I have to help them know what excellence really is." Teachers in these classes have an advantage other teachers lack: the public accountability of an on-stage performance. It provides students and staff with a powerful incentive to do well. The symmetry between what these enclaves do and what society cares about gives an unusual degree of intensity to the work that goes on in this specialty shop.

Mr. Appleby, the band teacher in another school, enumerated a few modest needs: music paper, decent band uniforms, more than just basic instruments, and some money to fix them when they broke. For twenty-five years Mr. Appleby had developed a different musical repertoire for each of the band's ten performances during the football season. He couldn't buy expensive sheet music, so he wrote the music from Top 40 hits heard on the radio, devising the parts for each instrument in the 130-student band. He had even written out each of the parts by hand until the band booster club gave him a photocopying machine. But Mr. Appleby had what he needed most: motivated players. "When they come they are motivated. When they're in junior high, they see the marching band perform and they can't wait to get to high school to be a part of it." He thought it was easier to get students to work hard for the band than for English classes: "For example, when he goes to English class, no one really sees what he or she is really doing except the English teacher. But when he performs, he is performing for the public. Public sentiment plays a big part." The visibility of the product and of the performer motivated the students; it also provided the drive for Mr. Appleby, who was rewarded by having a band that was known citywide year after year.

Football and music have become high school specialty shops for reasons that parallel why the top track became special: people care enough about these things to want schools to invest in successful programs. Just how much they care can often be measured by how much space the shop gets, both in the physical plant of the school and in the formal curriculum. In one school the ubiquitous display case in the central hall contained over three hundred trophies, forty plaques, and various other testaments to the school's musical accomplishments, including a regular spot in the parade of a major bowl game. The music complex at the far end of the campus provided storage lockers for every student and several special practice rooms. The main rehearsal studio was wired with top-of-the-line recording equipment and sound systems of various sorts. Music in this school was a serious extracurricular pastime and an expensive business.

Music was also a substantial part of the school's formal curriculum. The school supported a marching band, an orchestra, a percussion group, a chamber ensemble, and several ad hoc jazz and rock groups. Students could select from thirteen music courses that carried credit. But the school's course catalog warned that of the 165 course credits that students had to accumulate in high school to graduate, not more than 60 could be earned in band and orchestra. According to the principal, who was quietly trying to upgrade the quality of the school's top-track academic program, some students participated in music courses for three or four hours daily; they had to take at least two music courses if they were in the band. "The performing groups are in conflict with academic excellence," he concluded, but because of music's popularity he proceeded cautiously in de-emphasizing it. One of the things he was planning to upgrade was a public-speaking program. By modeling it after sports and music, with public competitions, he hoped to generate the same kind of community enthusiasm and support for the program as the sports-music performances received. Here, as in many other communities, academics did not fare well when measured against the visible specialty shops.

Troublemakers and Chronic Truants

Many students are troubled, depressed, even self-destructive, school-people say, but that in itself is not a qualification for special treatment. The troubled students who receive attention are the school's serious troublemakers and chronic truants — those who cannot or will not agree to even the most undemanding of the high school's treaties. When these students act out, the school must respond, as one vice principal illustrated when she confessed to knowing only the names of the school's stars and its troublemakers. The troublemakers must be attended to, if only for the school's own self-defense. The school's way of dealing with these students suggests that they, too, form a special enclave.

The fact that students must create a problem for someone else in order to qualify for unusual services is illustrated by two examples drawn from the same high school. David was a junior regarded by his school as a potential dropout. Fashionably dressed in black, from his hat and shades to the soles of his hightop sneakers, he was unsmiling, tough, and commanding. David's records indicated that he was very bright but had discipline problems and a poor academic record in junior high school. In high school things improved: his grades went up and he was on the honor roll, he stayed out of trouble, and the vice principal called him a "guy with real leadership potential." The principal appointed him to a district-wide advisory team on race relations. Then, in his junior year, things soured. His grades plummeted and his record turned to D's and F's. He started to skip school, but not excessively so. David's explanation for this turn of events was math. He wanted to attend college and major in computer science, but Algebra II was doing him in. He hadn't asked the teacher for extra help. His guidance counselor had not requested to see him.

According to an administrator who knew David and cared about his future, his problem was drugs. Sometimes he came to school stoned, but most of his drug use occurred out of school. She knew it was drugs; she knew the signs. Yes, she talked to David, but no, they didn't talk about drugs. "There's no point in trying to give him a lot of help if he doesn't want it," she said. "If he comes forward and asks for it, there are things we can do for him. Until then, we'd be wasting our time." David's problem was his own, not someone else's. He used drugs out of school, attended with tolerable regularity, and was not a discipline problem. David received no special attention. Since he was not a serious troublemaker, he was not in a specialty shop.

By contrast, Bill had been a problem in the school since he arrived three years earlier. He had an "incident" record that went back to elementary school: fights in the schoolyard and halls, disruptive behavior in classes. One of the high school's vice principals knew him well and came to know his parents as the result of several meetings. The vice principal tried to keep the lid on, talked to Bill informally, sought him out in the courtyard at lunchtime. He thought they were friends. One day he heard a commotion outside his office and found Bill engaged in a serious fight, sitting on his adversary's back and smashing the boy's head against the pavement. He pulled Bill off and an ambulance was called. He spent the rest of that day and part of the next on Bill, driving him home, explaining the seriousness of the incident to him and his parents, and initiating the paperwork for an expulsion hearing that would subsequently consume many more hours of his time. This incident was the last straw; the vice principal was clearly depressed and disappointed. He had tried hard but had not succeeded.

David and Bill were both troubled, but the one who made his problem the school's problem received more attention. As a teacher observed, "It's the ones who don't care, the ones who get in trouble, who get the attention." High schools contain more Davids than Bills; in fact, most schools are generally peaceful. Nevertheless, every school contains some students whose behavior is threatening and disruptive, students who fight, are openly rebellious, disturb classes and corridors, and otherwise aggressively break the rules. Unlike students in other special enclaves, these do not have advocates who approve of their behavior, although some schoolpeople take pleasure in working with them and they have powerful allies such as the courts, civil rights organizations, and community members who sometimes actively lobby to keep these students in school. As a result, expulsion is uncommon.

Schools tend to deal with their troublemakers through an elaborate set of administrative procedures that move them from one status to another, gradually distancing them from the rest of the school. First come in-house suspensions, then a special self-contained in-school program. Sometimes the final step is a separate no-frills continuation school, and sometimes the reverse movement back into the school is made if a student is showing signs of improvement. But the behavior of unruly students rarely gets better. Schools know who they are and learn to monitor and massage the very small but stable corps of troublemakers, more to protect the shopping mall high school from them than to protect them from the mall's allures.

One school runs a half-day, self-contained program for its troublemakers — "students [who] can't walk a hundred yards without getting sidetracked into some kind of trouble," as one of the teachers put it. Four teachers cover all the academic subjects, follow up on truancies, and provide counseling services to forty-five students. The program was started for youngsters who seemed to need more structure and attention; the idea was to make it harder for them to cut classes or cause a stir and vanish into the great anonymous mass in the school. "By putting them together in this program, you at least know where they are," said one of the teachers. He thought that teaching English was the easiest part of his job, that more energy went into confronting students and teaching them to look at the consequences of their actions. Still, his daily diet of fist fights and shouting matches was not without its rewards. "It makes you feel overwhelmed," he said, "but out of the conflict comes a bond. Affection comes out of the confrontation if you do it consistently and if you show the kid that this is the way it is." He thought students hated the struggles, "hate it when you're on their back all the time, and at first they feel picked on," but then they were appreciative when he supported them in conflicts with other teachers.

This unremitting attention helped some astonished students take home B's for the first time; however, this teacher worried about the undesirable group norms that developed in the program despite its success. Behavior dropped to the lowest common denominator, and the intensive attention only made it harder for them to function in the mainstream school in the afternoon. He also worried about his own fatigue and stress and their effect on his family. The program takes a "tremendous toll on the people who work with these kids," but it also "takes tremendous pressure off the rest of the school because there are forty-five kids in it that [administrators] know are being taken care of for half the day." The program provides protection for the school and the troublemakers, but the high concentration of school resources — the ratio of one teacher to 11.5 students — is remarkable, matched only by ratios in the special-needs program.

The larger and perhaps more exasperating group of troublemakers consists of the chronic truants who drop in and out of school according to whim or the weather, or, more maddening still, attend school but drop in and out of classes. "Good morning, John," one teacher remarked during roll call, "it must not be a good beach day." These reluctant students also consume school resources — truancy staff, phone calls, expensive computer installations, special programs, city street sweeps — even though many administrators believe that by high school the prognosis for chronic truants is grim. One reason for these remarkable investments is state funding practices based on average daily attendance, which create a strong incentive to keep attendance up, particularly as overall enrollments are declining. Another reason is the tight link between attendance and academic performance, which in turn is associated with school retention. Schools pursue truants to prevent dropouts.

The roll call is one line of attack aimed at "class-ditchers" whose occasional disregard of classes is thought to sometimes augur more serious day-long truancy. Most schools take class rolls partly to identify these casual ditchers and their more determined colleagues and partly as a deterrent. In one school the roll is delivered to the main office at the start of each period, where the attendance clerk records the information by computer. With 120 teachers and five class periods a day, a full-time attendance clerk processes 600 roll reports each day, or, at thirty students per class, 18,000 names — a remarkable indication of the school's determination to address the attendance issue. The attendance clerk demonstrated the magnitude of the class-ditching problem here by picking a day at random from her records. Nearly one quarter of the student body had been absent from class for one or more periods that day, yet the official average daily attendance rate for the school was 93 percent. What did they do when they weren't in class? "A lot of them are around here but not going to classes," the counselor reported. "They like coming to school and meeting their friends, but don't like the regimented routine of classes and assignments. For the most part, the kids come to school and hang around, or at least drop into the school during the day when they are truant." One vice principal and a counselor worked nearly full-time in following up on the most flagrant cases.

A second strategy for dealing with self-designated part-time students includes counseling sessions and telephone calls to their homes, day or night. This may be followed reluctantly and inconsistently by legal action against the parents of youngsters still under the official school-leaving age. But schools much prefer to try alternative programs — work experience or programs individually tailored to accommodate a student's tolerance for school. "You're attempting to work out some program for them, some kind of alternative program whether it is in-school or out-of-school," one counselor explained. "You don't just say, 'Since you're not coming, leave!' No, you don't do that. You have to respect where they are in their own life."

Schools go to great lengths to accommodate chronic truants and troublemakers because they fear the community, the courts, and the effect of declining enrollments. But their response is not entirely self-interested; they also believe that being enrolled in high school is better for teenagers than most any non-school alternative, and the alternative represents the institution's failure. Shopping mall high schools are committed to finding something legitimate for everyone and, just as with top-track or special-needs students, will try to provide whatever is needed to keep troublemakers there. The prescription in this instance isn't clear, and many schoolpeople feel that what they do is insufficient. Still, the programs, services, and personnel devoted to holding and perhaps reforming these students are considerably beyond what is available to the mall's regular customers.

Specialness

Specialty shops usually serve very different student constituencies; nevertheless, they share several important characteristics. Membership is often highly visible; participation usually conveys a certain luster or distinction — though of very different kinds. Beyond this there are a number of threads running through the specialty shops, threads that help explain how specialness itself is conferred and how the high school experience is shaped as a result.

One of these threads is advocacy. Most of the groups are special because of pressure from somewhere, both inside and outside the school, to make them so. Lobbies or supporters lurk in the background for all of the specialty shops.

A second thread is that all specialty shops have an admissions process of some sort. Not everyone qualifies. In a mass institution where everyone is welcome, this sets them apart.

A third thread reflects what the specialty shops do *not* offer. The range of choices within them tends to be restricted. Top-track students choose from a fairly small number of courses that prepare for academically demanding colleges. Focused curricula also exist for both special-needs and vocational/technical students. A complex web of arrangements is used to handle troublemakers. Students who want to excel in an extracurricular activity such as music feel pressure to take many music courses, which limits other choices.

Fourth, adults — both parents and teachers — provide more attention for specialty-shop students than other students receive. Adults oversee their course choices and provide more guidance. They know the specialty-shop clients more intimately, often because they spend more time with them and share more deeply their interests and situations.

Fifth, the specialty shops permit participating teachers to become more special themselves. These teachers may acquire a certain mystique because the students they work with have it or because the teachers have special training, public visibility, or more desirable work arrangements. Sometimes they work actively to develop a certain style or reputation to draw students, since their jobs literally depend on the continued existence of the shop. Sometimes, and of equal importance, their morale depends on it.

These five components of specialness characterize all the high school specialty shops, with obvious variations in degree and style from shop to shop and from school to school. These variations should not be underestimated. Top-track enclaves are not equally rigorous in all high schools. Football and band are not all-consuming passions in all communities. Voc/tech programs are more or less selective from place to place; some high schools do not have them at all. Still, these components help explain the special cachet that surrounds the shops and make it easier to understand why people in the rest of the mall are often ambivalent about the shops and their participants. As a public institution, the high school aims to make its services available to all and has multiplied its offerings in an effort to provide equal or equivalent services to its full range of customers. But not all clients are equally committed or able to take advantage of the school's willingness to provide. Under circumstances of unequal will or ability, the specialty shops are the natural outgrowth of the desire of some customers (or their representatives) to obtain what they want.

Advocacy

Each specialty shop has potent advocates working to ensure that the shop provides top services to its constituency and obtains the resources needed to do it. A guidance counselor in a school to which many top-track students had been redistricted spoke about the role their parents played in getting what they wanted for their children: "Our library had to be the worst library in the system before integration. When the white parents came over and looked around, they said with incredulity, 'This is your library? Why, separate really isn't equal after all, is it?' Very shortly afterwards, we were able to add a lot to our media center and our library. They also said, 'Where are your labs? Where are your microscopes? Look at those charts on the walls. We used those charts when we were in school twenty years ago!' If their children had to come here, they were going to make sure that they received a quality education. They looked around, and when they saw that, things got done."

Parents are usually the most powerful advocates at work on the shops' behalf, but teachers and administrators, the local community, and various special-interest groups that operate at the federal and state level also ensure unusual treatment for some groups. In some schools, the very existence of a shop may depend on the efforts of its lobbyists; in others, the shop's standards are raised or maintained by vigilant watchdogs both inside and outside school. The pressures that these supporters bring to bear on schools are not always adversarial; to win what they want, they seldom have to overpower a resistant district. More often they succeed because they have brought their concerns to the district's attention, raised them on its agenda. The parents whose top-track children were moved to the new district got what they wanted not by forcing the school to implement improvements it had previously sought to avoid, but by working closely with administrators for changes that no one had ever pushed for before. In the same school the voc/tech parent lobby followed with a similarly successful ploy. A voc/tech teacher said proudly of his assertive parents, "They're the ones who will say, 'What do you mean we don't have a computer? Everybody else has a computer . . . We want one too.' And then they push for it." Pushing counts when the enclave's advocates do it.

Sometimes supporters bring about improvements that affect the entire school. In one case, parents raised money for a new auditorium and gave the school computers. These parents would have done even more, school staff said, but the district would not approve it because its other high schools could not be equally endowed. But most schools face a different problem: parents who want services or resources that benefit a small number of students. Administrators in another district had decided to eliminate advanced math and science courses from individual high schools and offer them only at the magnet science and technology program some miles away. Teachers balked, but it was the organization of angry parents that made a difference. Quietly, the school continued to offer the advanced curriculum under other course names and numbers. "In some circumstances, we're encouraged to be deviant and to not go by the book," an administrator explained. People suspected that the district office knew but looked the other way to avoid confrontation with influential parents. In another school a teacher recalled that a similar proposal to eliminate the advanced track "produced an outcry from the parents that was real loud indeed. The X track is with us. We have to learn how to deal with it, do better with the kids and the situation. We just can't do away with the X track. People threatened to remove their kids from the school, and it was just a very unpopular notion."

Parent-advocates sometimes work in groups, but more often they work individually to get what they want for their children. School guidance staff say that much of their contact with parents revolves around schedule changes because parents or students don't like assigned classes or teachers. "If the parents come pounding at the door, then they make sure that those kids get the best program. And if the parent won't be pounding at the door, they get what's left." Schools try to avoid these changes because of the resulting paperwork and unbalanced classes, but as one student observed, "You get your mother to call up the school and bitch. Your parents carry so much clout."

Parents like these can use influence to good advantage because they're very well informed about the school. They and their children know who the good teachers are; they talk about it to friends, their children and children's friends, and teachers. "We have a better science department," one parent said knowingly as she compared two close-by schools, "and I understand from talking to parents and teachers that we have a better math department — I don't know about that — and that we have a better history department except for one person. Our English department is better. Also, I've heard arguments back and forth. Have you heard them?"

Such parents want their children to make high grades, and some of them will push the school for that, too. One top-track teacher revealed, "You always have to be very careful of the grades because of the political situation, meaning the parents. You have to be careful that there aren't too many low grades. They must have them — that is, the grades. They must have them." He added that when a teacher gives low grades, the principal "comes around very gently and he'll let you know how your grades are comparing with somebody else's on the computer. The message is, if your grades are out of line, then you must be out of line." The pressure from parents for high grades was "extraordinarily strong" and a "constant tension" that teachers and administrators had to deal with. He told of one case in which the principal stood by him because the principal agreed that the parent was wrong. "But she put a lot of pressure on him. The personalized stationery, the phone calls, the threats. And the pressure came to me directly from the mother. She called me up and I told her where I stood. She said, 'Okay, this is where you stand, this is where I stand. I'm not going to let this matter rest.' " A lot of teachers avoid this "by making sure that the grades are high enough to begin with."

Parental pressure is also keenly felt within the special-needs enclave, where the federal requirement that parents must be included in developing students' individualized learning plans has created many well-informed and active lobbyists for their children's interests. One counselor mentioned a deaf college-bound student for whom the school had hired a sign interpreter to accompany him to all classes. The counselor explained that the student's parents were also deaf, were very assertive about their rights, and had gone directly to the school board to press for what they felt was legitimate for their son. The district paid for this expensive special service but would not have hired anyone if the parents had not pushed.

Since most parents do not push, it is easier for schools to respond to the specific and well-focused interests of parents who do. "The only thing they can't do is get rid of teachers," one teacher observed with a mixture of admiration and regret, "and they ought to be able to do that." Schools accommodate these parents to maintain harmony and peaceful relationships, but they're ambivalent. They sometimes welcome such direct evidence of parental commitment and sometimes resent its intrusiveness. Regardless of how they feel about it, however, they realize that such pushing is atypical. It helps create and maintain a special status for some of the students in the shopping mall high school.

Teachers and administrators can also be powerful advocates for specialty shops. These are usually the teachers who work in them or counselors and administrators who feel an affinity for what a shop teaches or the kind of student it serves. Such administrative support can affect the teaching assignments of more able teachers, the number of courses a shop can offer, or prime-time course schedules and student assignments. Administrators' and teachers' preferences for some shops over others influence how the school's resources are deployed, and these decisions can influence which groups are more special.

Teachers, of course, have strong incentives for lobbying on behalf of the enclaves they are mainly associated with. Survival is one reason, particularly in shops that are not mandated by law, but many also strive for high standards or interesting, exciting courses that will provide a richer educational experience than what is generally available in the school's regular programs. One top-track teacher lobbied to maintain the academic integrity of her program, which had been called exclusionary because few minority students were enrolled. The district wanted to move the program downtown to a magnet school, but she successfully resisted by arguing that her students wouldn't go because "they'd have to spend an hour and a half daily in transportation" and that was "very dear time to them." She didn't want to lose her job, but she also didn't want her students to have to enroll in the less demanding alternatives that would remain in the high school. Mixtures of self-interest and a belief in the importance of the enclave's special services create strong and active teacher lobbies.

The question of standards prompted the special-needs teacher mentioned earlier to develop the social studies curriculum for her students because she felt that teachers in the mainstream classes gave them "gifts," graded too easily. In another school an English teacher complained that most of his colleagues had "abysmally low standards for the kids, and the kids who have any curiosity or enthusiasm to learn don't have much chance." He developed a new film and literature course for them to take the following year: "I have a class of sophomores who are good, and I want to keep them together." He was willing to spend time designing the course and running it through various channels for approval in order to provide better service to his top-track students. Another English teacher in the school provided, beyond his regular load, an independent study in American history to top-track students who were unhappy with the quality of the advanced course that was available.

Many teachers who work in the specialty shops, whether with honors students or troublemakers or those headed for vocational/ technical careers, demonstrate an unusual commitment to their shops and students through efforts of this sort. The schools offer many other examples: a teacher negotiating for hours to repair a troublemaker's latest stew, a vocational/technical teacher giving students "real experience" by inviting them to join him on his weekend jobs. Some of this arises from the high school's enormous adaptability, from the like-finds-like phenomenon that the mall's freedom of choice encourages for everyone. Smart top-track teachers are drawn to the ambitious and inquisitive students they themselves once were. Voc/tech teachers talk about their own troubled history with academic courses and are often as deeply committed to helping their students learn trades as the former special-needs youngster, now a teacher, is to helping her students rise above their disabilities.

At an administrative level, such commitment can be controversial, viewed as favoritism to some students and a net loss to students in other programs. As one guidance counselor remarked about the principal's move to add honors and Advanced Placement courses in a school where only one tenth of the graduates go on to four-year colleges, "I don't think this is an appropriate priority for this community. We need more entry-level courses in shop and business." The superintendent concurred: "It's a little overstated, when you consider the number of students who go on to work." Still, staff who believe in a specialty shop and will work to advance it help ensure its privileged status.

In many cases it is the community at large that acts as an advocate. "We're very fortunate to have a community that is interested in its young people," one superintendent said. "They support our school very well. We are really fortunate in these economic times to have the community support nineteen varsity programs. That's a lot! That's not to say that we're sports-minded, but we are. It plays an important part in town. It's big; it really is." Every school is surrounded by a large and potentially useful lobby, people who may or may not have children enrolled but who pay taxes and vote bond issues. The school can often cultivate the support of the community through its major extracurricular specialty shops, sports and music. By developing successful bands and teams and inviting the community to join with them at public performances, schools make a claim for the allegiance of the local population; schools become visible and real to people who might otherwise ignore them.

"In this town," the superintendent continued, "there's a pecking order, and you see it . . . at the football games." Choice seats in the stadium are a prestige item, and "people even will their seats to other family members." There is not only considerable community enthusiasm for sports here, but also a generous gate: football games regularly draw five thousand people and receipts of $61,000 a season, and basketball brings in another $37,000. Together they support the entire annual cost of the athletic programs in the district's three junior highs and the high school.

Athletics also help schools develop community support for essential but less popular school services. When this district's citizens balked at a bond issue to replace funds lost by state cuts in education spending, administrators responded with a threat to cut eleven coaches. When the bond issue subsequently passed, all eleven coaches were retained and four new ones were hired. Most of the money was spent on staff salaries and underfunded academic programs, but local people didn't notice. Administrators had used the community's favorite specialty shop in the interest of educational needs community members cared less about. The district has also successfully cultivated the town's major industry, which underwrote the costs of the new football stadium and provided an endowed fund for its annual $60,000 upkeep. The company's managers "are always reminding people that they don't want any second-class equipment or cut-rate products going into the stadium," the principal commented. Local businesses also provide many non-sports-related things for the school, such as discounted computer time and heavily subsidized data analysis and accounting services.

This school has been unusually successful with community constituents, perhaps because it is in a one-high-school town that is miles away from the nearest college and professional teams. But, although loyal, the community focuses its interest chiefly on the specialty shop it cares about; the community does not happily support a bond issue to benefit other shops, much less the mall in general. Local citizens are not very interested in nonathletic school affairs, according to local journalists. "If the newspaper can write about schools or something else," one administrator lamented, "they write about something else." This community's loyalty to its schools finds expression primarily through supporting its sports-music specialty shop.

Lobbies of one kind or another thus help to ensure the preferential treatment specialty shop members receive. Some lobbies are individuals. Some are local groups that convene on an ad hoc basis when the shop is threatened or needs something; some are more formal groups, like the band boosters in one community, who help to raise money or speak on behalf of the school's music program at school board budget hearings. "It depends on the issue," a principal observed. "If the board is contemplating changes in the honors program or academic requirements, the intellectuals and parents from the university turn out in strength. If it has to do with sports and extracurricular things, the PTA and social parents show up."

In addition to this local lobbying, state and national special-interest organizations have invested considerable money and professional talent to persuade the legislative branches of government to appropriate funds to benefit particular groups of students. Those who advocate on behalf of children with handicaps or special needs are perhaps the most effective, but other lobbyists are effective, too. Advocates for gifted students, for example, have seen to it that federal and state funds are earmarked for developing and supporting programs for the gifted and talented. Some states now require districts to operate such programs, sometimes with specially credentialed teachers.

Truants and troublemakers, in contrast, lack advocates who approve of their behavior, but there are people who lobby for their retention in school, some school professionals believe. These advocates operate from a mixed set of motives and beliefs about why schools should be at pains to retain their problem students. Some worry about street crime; there is little doubt that teenagers figure prominently in these statistics. A teacher told of one student who had stolen a car but was released by the police, only to be caught stealing a purse at school two days later. "Why should she worry about me catching her stealing a pocketbook?" the teacher said despairingly. He thought there was no place for students like that except in school; teenagers in school can commit crimes only in school, which at least contains it.

Others want troublemakers in school for more charitable reasons: it protects them from the temptations of the street and may save them from a criminal life. At the very least, school serves as a safe, caring environment in which, with luck, they will grow wiser and more sensible and which they will eventually leave with a diploma. Still others, particularly members of labor organizations, worry about out-of-school youngsters flooding the job market and displacing older workers. Lobbying on behalf of schooling for students who don't behave as if they want it has been a particularly effective labor union strategy. Labor deserves much credit for the current minimum school-leaving age of sixteen, which has also had the happy consequence of keeping younger teens out of the full-time labor market. More recently, the courts and various civil rights organizations have joined the chorus of advocates for troublemakers, arguing and hearing cases and admitting *amicus curiae* briefs on the arbitrary and often discriminatory actions of schools in excluding problem students who too often are from minority groups. Together, these strange bedfellows have quite effectively kept truants and troublemakers in school, or at least made them harder to get rid of, even when their behavior suggests they would rather be anywhere else.

Each of the high school specialty shops has such advocates, and the schools respond. "The key to it is interest," one parent said about advocacy. "There are people who can make decisions and have an influence on decisions. They want something done, and they get it done. That's the reality we all must accept."

Admission

The specialty shops cannot serve everyone; to be in a special program, a student has to be admitted. How do the admissions processes work? Who gets in?

Some students are admitted as a result of testing or other diagnostic activities. Based on objective data alone, or on some combination of data and the opinions of staff or other experts, they are found to have the special characteristics required for membership. Other students simply choose to join. But that decision always has to be accompanied by a willingness to agree to the terms of the classroom treaties in that specialty shop; students must play by the rules.

Relatively clear-cut performance or ability criteria govern access to the top-track programs in some schools. One school that offered a very limited honors program claimed to admit students according to how well they did on the district's achievement test. Teacher or counselor judgment was not a consideration, nor could students push their way into the program. Access to the top track at such schools is supposed to be as strictly controlled from outside the school as admission to special-needs programs is, which is almost always based on test results established by states and districts.

But access to the top track is most often determined by a more complicated set of factors. One school, blessed with an abundance of bright and ambitious students, limited access to its most exclusive academic track to students whose test scores placed them in the category of "gifted." Objective data determined eligibility, but decisions about who among the eligible were admitted rested with the teachers. "It is completely subjective in the end," a program teacher admitted. "We're trying to build a family unit and will take the kids who fit into it." At another school, the chairperson of the English department explained that assignments to the sophomore honors program were based on the recommendation of the ninth-grade teachers, with whom she and a colleague met each spring. "We honor those recommendations. If a parent comes in and says, 'I want my youngster in honors,' even though the junior high doesn't recommend it, I've gotten away with saying no. I don't have any legal right to say that, but I've gotten away with it because I then say, 'But as soon as he performs for us at what we consider to be an honors level, we'll move him into honors.' And so far I have gotten away with that." Yet she admitted that very few students were moved up — maybe five a year; the placement process worked well. The school followed the same policy in mathematics. If a parent pressured, the rule could be waived, a math teacher said — but he had never seen it happen in his twenty-six years of teaching there.

Why do some students and parents go along with those decisions when others do not and insist on admission to honors classes? Teachers accuse schools of obfuscating the issue of ability levels to avoid any appearance of tracking and thus of not providing students with enough information to make informed choices. They think that many students don't know what doors will open or close when they apply to colleges, don't know that more selective schools and even some programs in state universities will be closed to them if they have not taken honors courses. One teacher pondered whether students know that classes are arranged by ability level, that honors courses cover different material, and that participating in those courses may mean different future choices: "I'd say yes and no. We thought we were being indicted for tracking, so we tried to do away with it. But in effect we're still tracking." The school maintained tracks, each assigned a different name or number, but it carefully avoided discussing the differences between levels to avoid questions about who gets assigned where and why. It's up to students to figure out the distinctions between levels. "The kids at the top know," she commented. "They know the teachers they want and the courses. The high kids know every single track and what's available. I think the low kids tend to know but don't talk about it." A teacher in another school believed that because no one officially talked about different levels, some students didn't pay attention to them. But the smart kids did: "The smart ones become aware by the time they are juniors with whom they should take honors English or honors literature, and they make sure they get the classes they want. But most kids are not aware of the differences."

Some teachers think that schools avoid pointing out the differences between course levels because more students would try to enroll in honors courses. The honors-level faculty in several schools did feel that too many unqualified students were enrolled in their courses and that they should be more selective. The less able ones couldn't keep up, they said, and when more than a handful were enrolled, the bright students suffered. One teacher said that he tried to counsel students out of his honors English class when a review of their records suggested that they'd have to struggle. Another said that heterogeneous honors classes were hard to teach, and he had to spend too much time after class with students who wanted to do the work but couldn't without extra help. A school psychologist working in a high school where there were many ambitious students — and parents — commented: "I've seen so many kids who are of just average ability but who are in the accelerated classes. They're nice, solid kids from nice families, and they do credibly in school. But they may be in three or even four accelerated classes. They shouldn't be there. They're just not that bright." Many were succeeding, but the cost seemed too great; they would be better off and happier in less demanding classes, he thought.

But many teachers feel that schools should try harder to accommodate the less special in the honors enclave. In their opinion, students who want to work hard should have access to classes with better students, like tennis players who try to improve their game by seeking out better players. An English teacher said that in her honors class she had "several kids who are very marginal for honors," but they were a welcome addition because they were willing to work hard: "Ability is not the best criterion for tracking; commitment is."

Why do parents want their children to be in the top track? For one thing, they think the instruction is better there. Second, they hope that the top-track program will reinforce their children's commitment to working, interest in studying, and aspirations for competitive colleges. Another important reason is that in some schools grades are weighted (that is, extra points are assigned to honors classes), which means that the top-track students have higher grade point averages and higher places in the class ranking. In fact, one principal thought that many students took honors classes entirely for the accompanying weighted grades and class ranks.

It is probable, too, that many parents look on the top-track enclave as a place where the racial and class lines within the school can be maintained. One teacher in a top-track class speculated, "It almost seems at times that the honors classes are a thing to bypass integration." Parents didn't mind having their child attend an integrated school "as long as he is in the honors class."

There is disagreement about why most of the top-track programs are predominantly white. Do minorities who could do the work choose to stay away? Do the counselors who make the selection discriminate against blacks? One teacher said she had had many minority students in her regular classes who could have been in honors sections; they were invited into the top track but chose not to go. She agreed with their decision. The regular classes helped develop "good self-esteem," she said. But one black student in the school had tried and failed to get his counselor to enroll him in honors classes; he thought the system was unfair: "The counselors discriminate against a student whom they don't think can handle it. Making that judgment before they even know for sure . . . I would love to have the chance to be in an honors-track class." If his mother had come in and "pulled strings, they would do something. But me on my own, I can't do it." Since pushy parents often can and do overturn the counselor's admissions decisions, why didn't this student's mother push? A black teacher in the school thought the explanation was that poor families tended not to value education; that, she said, was why there were so few minority students in the honors classes. But a white social studies teacher disagreed. He thought that most black families trusted the schools to do what was best for their children, and that the few who tried to push were quickly intimidated. Successful pushing, he thought, required confidence.

Admission to other specialty shops is less often the result of student or parent push and more often because students have special abilities, disabilities, or behavior problems that meet the program's selection requirements. The characteristics these shops look for are often identified through formal testing programs or other performance measures. Special-needs programs are required to base admissions on the results of several objective tests, and vocational/technical programs rest their decisions on some combination of applicants' grades, attendance records, and teachers' "behavior ratings." Commenting on the admissions process in his voc/tech program, a vocational counselor observed, "Intensity is essential to build skills, and intelligence is needed for this program. It's not for slow students. That's why it's so important that we screen the students carefully and make sure that they are not misplaced." Admission to the troublemakers' specialty shop is the consequence of undesirable behavior: excessive truancy or disciplinary incidents. It is the absence of the positive or even of the merely ordinary that puts students in this special enclave.

Admission to the sports and music specialty shops parallels admission to the troublemakers' enclave, except that the movement is in the opposite direction: troublemakers have to get worse to get in, athletes and musicians have to get better. One coach said that he tried not to cut students from teams — if one hundred showed up for the tryouts, then one hundred would make the team. There were exceptions, of course, but the school's goal was to have as many students as possible on each team. Yet not all these members played; only those who were both exceptionally able and committed saw action as varsity players. As an athlete, one is only a special participant when admitted to varsity status, just as the college-bound are only special as members of the top-track enclave.

A good illustration of admissions based on program selectivity is the special-needs specialty shop, where the admissions process is virtually the same from school to school: a student is referred for an initial screening which may be followed by the administration of a complete battery of tests with cutoff points that determine admission. When one teacher began teaching fourteen years before, "special education was just a dumping ground for any kid who didn't fit." Admissions, then, were based mainly on a single test score, or a teacher's opinion. Now students were thoroughly tested, and "if a student can perform at a certain level, then we know he belongs in one or another program."

The constraint on admission is perhaps the most troublesome issue surrounding the special-needs enclave. Schools contain many students whose learning problems make them plausible candidates for special-needs programs, yet they do not meet the admissions criteria. According to one counselor, federal cuts in Title I supplementary reading and math programs were disastrous for these marginal candidates: "We were forced to place them in regular English classes, where we knew in advance they were going to fail." But these students could not be admitted to special-education programs, she said, because the admissions requirements were so "severe" that most simply would not be eligible. In another school, a counselor reported that the special-needs classes filled so quickly that eligible students were placed wherever space was available, although failure and discouragement for most in these placements were practically guaranteed. There was often great frustration that the law (and limited resources) prevented some from gaining admission who would profit immensely by being defined as special in this way. If only, many special-needs teachers have said, the same procedures available to those who qualify could be applied to those who barely do not — and even to larger numbers who clearly do not. A teacher who asserted that "low ability has the money" thought that an informal pattern of his school was to send the bottom of the regular students to the special-needs classes if they needed the extra attention. In such cases the immense federal and state investment might bring larger and more visible returns for these marginal students. Several schools reported that they used to place marginal students in special-needs classes, but that recent cuts in federal funding for special education, combined with increasingly stringent eligibility requirements, had virtually eliminated this option. Even students who met the special-needs admissions criteria that had existed three or four years before were now enrolled in regular classes.

All admissions procedures generate discontent. Some students don't like the constraints imposed by the troublemakers' enclave and try to avoid membership, sometimes by dropping out of school. There are students (and their parents) who don't understand why they didn't make the orchestra or the varsity team; they try hard, practice faithfully, and feel they perform as well as those selected. Some vocational/technical program candidates are disappointed by decisions that they feel have closed certain careers to them, while some students and their parents won't accept disappointment and push for admission to the top-track enclave. Admission to the specialty shops is controversial precisely because advantages accompany membership: special treatment, a better education, higher status, more recognition. The existence of admissions processes makes evident that the specialty shops and the services provided in them are not accessible to everyone. More broadly, it indicates that students are not equal and that schools recognize and respond to student differences in ways that modify the egalitarian ideal of high school.

Constraints on Choice

Most students in the mall can take virtually any course at their grade level that interests them, but the specialty shop customers have less choice. Students there cannot browse, cannot pick and choose randomly among the wares that appeal to them; they cannot follow impulse. They are more likely to take a prescribed or expected program of courses that has some internal logic to it, that is structured to build skills and knowledge toward some objective. A vice principal reported, "We find that the accelerated kids or the ones in the AP track do follow a sequence of learning. However, the other kids do not." A math teacher in the top track said, "Kids have to have Algebra I in the eighth grade, geometry in the ninth grade, algebra and trig in the tenth, and advanced math in the eleventh. And for a kid to take algebra as an eighth-grader, he has to have an OK from the seventh-grade teacher."

Vocational/technical programs have similarly specified curricula. Courses on television equipment operation and repair precede courses on program production and film editing, which precede courses on script writing and on-camera roles; students in the media magnet program must take the entire sequence. In the extracurricular specialty shops as well, sports practice and music rehearsals that begin during the last periods of the school day also limit participants' choices.

The wish to be part of a specialty shop often keeps students from trying as many different courses or teachers or activities as others do. And if a student wants to participate in two shops simultaneously — the honors program and sports, or voc/tech and music — choice is not merely restricted, it virtually disappears. These students — the "lock-ins," as one vice principal calls those whose programs won't or can't vary much — shape the design of the master schedule that other students' programs must fit into. The mall's broad variety is not suitable for the specialty shop students, so high schools must pay close attention to the narrow range of offerings that are designed for them alone.

In some shops the constraint on choice is a by-product of mandated processes that effectively leave the decisions to adults, as with special-needs students. For other students, course possibilities are fewer because they hope for jobs or colleges for which there are well-understood, if not prescribed, programs. Positioning oneself as a serious candidate for admission to a selective college, for example, requires preparation beyond the school's graduation requirements. These are too "lenient," said one top-track junior; she and her classmates "overfill" the requirements because they don't "demand enough." The limits on the top-track students' choices are de facto and self-imposed, bound by what is available in the tough academic curriculum and what they know the selective colleges want. The physics teacher Dr. McBride said that in his school, "there are a number of students who are résumé-builders, who take this course and then leave [it] at the end of the first term. These students are very competitive about getting into college, and they want to be sure they have the right courses on their transcripts." These students' choices are limited by the number of "right" courses on their transcript. They don't take others even though they would like to. One would "love to take auto repair" but took creative writing instead. She said it was her own choice; she was in a very academic college-prep program that she loved.

A mother with two children in the top track admitted that they felt a certain "drudgery" in the accelerated program. They wished for more freedom, more flexibility in the courses available to them and in the work they had to do. Both would have preferred to take some classes for fun, but didn't because they felt "so programmed into the college preparatory classes." One of them wished she "could have tried the other courses, but once you drop out of the accelerated courses, you can't get back in." In her senior year, with college applications in, the burden was lifted. "Now I'm taking the things I'm interested in."

Troublemakers find their choices restricted in ways that are meant to keep them out of trouble and to move them toward graduation. High schools do not usually mandate programs for their problem students, but as an implicit condition of continued membership in the mall, troublemakers may be persuaded to enter a special program — in some schools their last chance before an alternative or continuation school that is located outside the mall. Students who don't want to leave don't have much choice; courses and teachers are selected for them and offered in half-day, self-contained programs where structure and supervision are tight. A teacher in one such program said its goal was to see that students earned "a core of credits" which most didn't have when they arrived. They had to be in the classroom; they had to do the work. In fact, choice was so constrained in this program that students were eventually asked "more and more to make choices" so that they could better negotiate choice once they returned to regular classes.

One effect of these constraints on choice is that some specialty-shop students are more likely to graduate than if they stayed in regular classes. Restrictions protect them from the temptations of choice and prevent them from leaving the mall empty-handed. Other specialty-shop students profit from restricted choice by becoming accomplished or unusually knowledgeable — in mathematics or auto mechanics or the flute, perhaps. The specialty shops are designed to encourage achievements of this sort, but though they produce many accomplished teenagers, some of the courses students forgo for those achievements — the things they haven't learned — suggest that restricted choice does not always benefit them. Some athletes and musicians, for example, invest so heavily in the sports-music enclave that their academic work leaves them ill-prepared to handle the more difficult work of college. Stories of illiterate college athletes who fail in the classroom appear in the press all too frequently, and colleges admit that remedial tutoring for athletes is virtually expected. De facto restriction on choice in this specialty shop can have disastrous consequences for students who are encouraged by fans and coaches to view academic work as a distraction in their hell-bent quest for the major leagues, for stardom. But constraints on choice in the specialty shops more often produce a happy ending. They provide students with a coherent and useful education, one that leaves them prepared for what follows high school.

Attention

The correlate of less choice for those in specialty shops is that they receive more attention from school staff. Lower student-to-teacher ratios, as in the special-needs, vocational/technical, and troublemakers' enclaves, help make this possible. Teachers work with small groups — from six to perhaps fifteen students — and have the time to teach and coach them individually, the energy to focus on the particular strengths and weaknesses of each. Students in these shops are also likely to spend several periods of the day "block-scheduled" into a sequence of courses with the same teacher, as in elementary school — an arrangement that helps people find a niche and develop close working relationships.

When half-day classes in the troublemakers' enclave are over, students who are now free to wander about the mall receive attention from security guards, counselors, or others assigned to monitor their activities. One "student adviser" in a city school patrolled the corridors from before the school day began until well after it ended, watching out for just such students. "I see this role primarily as a way to keep kids out of trouble, not get them out once they've gotten in." Counseling students is a central feature of these jobs. "Here we are more counselors than we are police officers," reported the director of security and safety in another school. He said they tried not to involve the police or the courts but rather tried to deal "in house" with various crises that arose on school grounds. He visited homes because he didn't believe "in dragging parents to school"; he looked around for teenagers after school and pulled them into his car for "little talks"; he also spent considerable time "hanging around in pinball arcades with students and just shooting the breeze."

The senior member of an English department thought about the relationship he established with his top-track students, the attention he gave and what he got in return: "I play a role . . . The role is to really care, to be really tough about learning, that no one has been tough enough. I'm saying, 'Hey, I'm different, and you'd best be, too.' They learn that insult is a form of caring. I tell them, 'I want you to be ready, to toughen up, to fight for your ideas, to believe in the idea, to have it have meaning for you.' Their biggest problem is commitment . . . I now list many, many kids who have gotten Ph.D.s in English over the past sixteen years."

His satisfaction came from the success of his performance, on terms that he personally valued — by convincing students to make a Ph.D.-level commitment to their work. The personal investment of specialty shop teachers in their students usually takes the form of some sort of special attention, attention that may help the students to grow in particular ways. A football coach spent time with his athletes out of school, mostly by taking them to various sporting events. He did it, he said, because it was important for youngsters to be exposed to the world beyond their neighborhoods "from which they really don't venture very much." He used the things he valued — sports events — as the medium for paying attention to his students. A history teacher and outdoors enthusiast took his top-track students hiking in the mountains and on rafting trips, trying particularly hard to entice his black and Hispanic students to join because they had never done these things. Each teacher expresses caring and commitment in his or her own way.

Although attention is often given freely, that is not always the case; sometimes it is mandated or required by the program, or is given because students or their parents push for it. "For the advanced kids, I have to be the mother and the father and the teacher," complained a history teacher; he said that his students had been "pampered" and "babied" by teachers more than students in regular classes. They wanted attention and they were used to getting it. One area in which top-track students receive a great deal of attention is counseling: they expect counselors to spend time helping them select and apply to colleges, and to write recommendations. A college and career counselor reported that she couldn't do everything and had "jettisoned" certain responsibilities: "Anything to do with technical schools, junior colleges, or the military. Any information that involves referral to anything [other than] a straight four-year college has to be put aside." Top-track students got her time individually; she met with other students only in groups. In another school an administrator observed that "counseling is structured in the school such that the squeaky wheels, or the very bright kids who are constantly pushing for advice, see the counselors." "Fast-track kids get the best counseling," agreed two graduates of the school, now Harvard freshmen.

Special-needs students, too, "tend to overuse the people that they know," one counselor explained. He and other administrators in his school believed that because of federal requirements they gave more to special-needs students than to average ones, mentioning the example of an autistic boy who got private tutors for English and math and whose mainstream teachers were specially trained to communicate with him. "A small number of special-needs students take a high proportion of our time — sometimes about half," another counselor said. Only 30 to 40 of her students — a small fraction of her total load of 240 — were special-needs. "A dozen kids could consume you. You could spend all your time with these [special-needs] kids." There is some debate over which group, special-needs or top-track, should have more counseling, but there is little doubt that both groups receive extraordinary attention from the school, in the form of the bureaucratic tasks of keeping records and writing recommendations as well as the personal contact maintained through counseling.

Special Teachers

Teachers who work mainly in the specialty shops often feel different and are regarded as being different, just as their students are. Many of them can be distinguished from their colleagues in the same ways as their students differ from others: they are more ambitious or committed, more concerned that the school satisfy their preferences. They are not necessarily better teachers (though many are), but through their personal styles or standards or their ability to work successfully with special students and their parents, they acquire a certain luster, which some are able to use to negotiate privileges or more favorable work conditions. In the shopping mall high school, where the conditions and rewards of work are often standardized in order to minimize distinctions among teachers, those who are able to get more for themselves become special. Privileged teachers are not found exclusively in the specialty shops, but teaching there makes it easier for a teacher to get what he or she cares about.

Mr. Rodriguez candidly admitted, "A lot of people resent me. I'm a spoiled teacher. I do what I want. I come late. I leave early. I get the best courses and the best students." Some teachers become special because, like the students they teach and those students' parents, they insist that the school provide them with certain privileges. They are particularly committed to and successful with special students, and so they believe that the rules that govern other teachers do not apply to them. "This school provides me with the kind of personal freedom I need to be a good teacher," Rodriguez continued. "That's what I value most about it. Because of that, I find very few personal concerns here." Rodriguez is aware that he is unique, knows that high performance in the top-track enclave confers status, and he uses both to get what he wants.

Another teacher felt protected by his association with the top track. He took students on trips despite administrators' disapproval and wrote letters to the local papers condemning the latest district-sponsored reorganization plan. "We're untouchable," he said of himself and a few colleagues. "We may be renegades. And they're afraid of us. But we have a fair amount of power both in the school among our students and in the community." He linked the status and power of this small group to their association with the powerful — top-track students and their influential parents. Top-track students and parents "protect me." They wanted him in the school because he was a good teacher; their values coincided. He observed that other teachers' power may have been linked to funding sources, such as those for special education; their work with distinctive and influential groups conferred power on them as well.

The feeling of empowerment is especially pervasive in a high school containing several advanced and gifted programs and serving the community's most influential families. An administrator concluded, "This school is more autonomous than the other [high schools]. We don't have to do the things that the others do: in fact, we are encouraged to resist going by the book . . . The teachers feel the same way." He attributes these feelings to "snobbishness, or the needs of the kids, which are different from those of other kids in town, depending on who you talk to." There is an attitude of entitlement in the school, a belief that the faculty has the freedom to make its own policy, which may or may not in fact be true. But they act as if it is. They feel special and therefore act as if they are.

Power and privilege are derived from public visibility, from teaching the things that the community considers truly important. In this sense, coaching a team or directing a band makes a teacher special in a community where these activities matter. Recall the principal who spoke of moving cautiously to reduce the amount of attention paid to music in his school. The principal's guarded approach was due partly to the music director's influence in the community, his power to create a local stir because he had a responsive constituency and had used it effectively in the past to protect his interests.

Coaching has clear performance criteria by which its quality can be judged; that makes it easier for coaches to derive not only personal satisfaction from their work but also public acclaim and sometimes job offers. This visibility is not always pleasant; when a football team loses, the coach would certainly prefer more anonymity. Unfavorable visibility is not a problem for regular classroom teachers, many of whom are not visible enough. But those in special enclaves can and do gain public recognition. One English department chairperson said that some of its top-track teachers had been saying for so long that they were the greatest — "like Mohammed Ali" — that people had begun to believe them. He said that parents decided which teachers were outstanding, often on the basis of what teachers said about themselves, and spread the word in their social networks. Another teacher in his school recalled that for his first few years in the program, advanced students treated him "like a substitute. They tore me apart. I was unsure of myself and they went after me, the parents in particular." But he felt this "made me more professional. Even my vocabulary has improved since I've been here. They teased me when I used incorrect English or spelling." Now he no longer wanted to teach the lower tracks: it would be a "downer type of experience to teach the less able."

Some of the shops' faculty are encouraged to feel special by the added years of graduate training required for certification to teach in certain enclaves. The federal special-needs mandate has spawned a new breed of teacher who works as psychologist, diagnostician, and social worker and feels more closely allied with the higher-status health care professions than with classroom teachers. "I don't associate with the English department," said one special-needs English teacher, who works mostly with her special-needs colleagues and their outside consultants. Vocational/technical teachers also are specially credentialed, as are the top-track teachers in some states that require "gifted and talented" credentials to work with the most able students.

Many of the shops' faculty are encouraged to feel special because their work is thought to be more pleasant than that of regular teachers. Most teachers work in self-contained classrooms and have few opportunities to collaborate with others or to deviate from the fifty-minute-period, six-period-day routine. The work is structured, the schedules set. But teachers in the enclaves are often required to break from these routines to work with other teachers, with people in other schools or the district office, or those in public agencies or the local business. They can get out of their classrooms, even out of the school during the day, to recruit students for magnet programs, search for job placements, or monitor students at work. The coordinator of an international business studies program got "tired of staying in the classroom going through the same routine all the time. Now I can get out and mix with people and find it's added a good bit of zest to my work." Much of the appeal of her job was its break from usual teaching patterns. "After sitting in class for ten or eleven years, anything that comes along that at least diversifies the system, regardless of what it leads to, has got to be appealing." Many voc/tech teachers do not feel as locked in to teaching because they spend time outside the classroom and because they have skills that will transfer to industry if they want to move. One staff member of an industrial arts department said that this mobility makes him feel "pretty doggone independent."

In addition to having greater mobility than regular teachers, specialty shop staff have more satisfying work conditions inside their classrooms. Smaller class size and block scheduling make it possible for teachers to get to know their students, both personally and academically. Like student performance criteria, measures of teacher performance are more explicit in the specialty shops: coaches have game scores; top-track teachers have the College Board Achievement or AP test results; voc/tech teachers have finished products. In all these, teachers can see their contributions. Finally, the specialty shops are relatively free of teachers' most difficult problem: resistant, passive, or hostile students. Students who are there usually *want* to be there.

Each of these conditions is hard to find outside the specialty shops. Many regular teachers feel demoralized, manipulated by administrators or students, and unable to do much about it — in short, powerless. Morale problems are not absent from the specialty shops, but there they tend to be associated with low salaries, limited time, or the feeling that too many important corners must be cut in the scramble to cover the material. Yet most teachers thrive on the pressures imposed by the accommodations expected in their enclaves. They are special in the school because the school needs them. One administrator believed that his school's virtual survival depended on these special teachers. "There are some real demoniac parents here. And we have some very, very interesting teachers who are academic, able, and even very traditional. And they're very good at dealing with the parents." In return for their special skills, these teachers received certain privileges from the administration. One administrator confessed that "the better teachers get to teach the better students that they want, and we put our weaker teachers with low ability groups." In another school where the same system was at work, an administrator proposed to break this pattern but knew he was headed for trouble. "Very strong individuals survive here because they can handle the community. But in terms of dealing with those people, changing [their schedules], you have to have somebody who's willing to get in there and arm-wrestle." The top-track teacher Mr. Rodriguez admitted, "I'm being recognized in lots of ways by this administration." Teachers in the specialty shops not only feel special and empowered by their students, then — they also get tangible things from their administrators.

The rewards that go along with teaching in the specialty shops help explain why many of the shops and their teachers are so controversial. Regular teachers sometimes resent the smaller teaching loads in the shops and, in the case of the top-track programs, the special teachers' opportunity to work with the most able students, which in turn means that regular college-prep teachers don't have them in their classes. And even though most regular teachers are grateful that they don't have to work with special-needs students and trouble-makers in their larger classes, the smaller teaching loads there are a source of friction. The ways in which administrators sweeten the pill for some enclave teachers do not go unnoticed. The existence of these resentments toward the specialty shops, the fact that it is mostly these teachers who are referred to as "prima donnas" and gossiped about by other teachers, suggests that the envies students have for each other are shared by their teachers and are often even more deeply etched. Many of the specialty-shop teachers have found a way to make the system work for them — sometimes by design, often by accident — and are as special in the school as their students.

The cumulative impact of all the ways in which specialness is created and maintained is to separate the clients of specialty shops from the rest of the shopping mall high school. The separation is some-times accomplished by setting aside particular building areas or classrooms, but even when there is no spatial separation the sense of tight group identification has the same effect. Many students know high school as members of an isolated enclave; the notion of "comprehensiveness" is a distant abstraction about school as a whole, not a description of how these students usually experience school. "The kids in the accelerated track are together all the time," a teacher observed. "They live together, study together, eat together, and die together." His words suggest a sense of community and even of family.

Membership in an educational community legitimized as such by the school gives those who belong to it a niche that is nearly an end in itself. One counselor believed her school best served the student "who has an interest or a purpose that get him in touch with a segment of the school — whether it's the athletes or the kid who's into music, a kid who skis, or can join a club — some sense of belonging." Two students who derived great satisfaction from membership on the debate team couldn't say what motivated them to engage, aside perhaps from winning. But they asserted they would "hate school" without involvement with a group and the resulting task of "planning an activity and helping it to come off." If you belonged to a specialty shop and had a problem, another student said, you could simply go to other students. "Anybody would help," she emphasized with absolute certainty. School professionals often say that a group is not essential for a student to find some productive attachment, that individuals on their own can make contact with something important. Some individual students certainly do, but for most, group support and camaraderie matter a great deal.

But the stakes of a "sense of belonging" are higher than the prevention of individual loneliness and alienation, even though that is an attractive feature. Belonging to a specialty shop makes educational engagement itself more likely, because students are less on their own to make their own way. They have a host of formidable allies. Some allies are people: parents, teachers, members of advocacy groups, other students. Other allies are procedures: admissions standards, or expectations for students and the adults in school who work with them. All these allies not only reinforce specialness, they reinforce learning whatever the specialty shops teach. They challenge — for students affected by them — the neutrality of the shopping mall high school.

Not everybody belongs. Not everybody has advocates outside or inside school. One administrator was appalled to find a boy with strong test scores enrolled in a slate of low-level courses where he was doing well. He said he wanted to be an engineer, but his counselor had told him he couldn't do the work. The administrator knew from experience that "if the kids come from homes of privilege, then you can expect them to assume some responsibility for these things. But if the kid is from a poor family, the counselor must take him by the hand and help him to secure the best education that he can." And the counselor hadn't. In this case neither parent nor counselor was an advocate; the boy had no educational allies. He was wholly on his own.

Or, rather, he was at the mercy of different forces, the forces of class and race that keep some students away from specialty shops. An athletics director was distressed that vocational students did not go out for football in his sports-conscious school, even though he knew from watching them play ball at lunchtime that many were naturals for the game. He planned to try recruiting but admitted that in his school football happened to be the traditional province of the college-bound. Values keep students both in and out of the shops, and schools seldom push those who are different into them. In leaving choice to students and their families, schools unintentionally perpetuate the distinctions that high school is supposed to eliminate.

4

The Unspecial

THE LOOK of Miss Lowell's office was either lived-in cozy or hopelessly chaotic, depending on one's taste for tidiness. She explained the mess without being asked, as doubtless she had often explained it before to disapproving fellow administrators. One chair served as a student's locker, another as a place to study. Students used the room all the time for all sorts of purposes. It seemed more like a disheveled family room in a large household than an efficient management haven. "I don't mind if kids are here studying while I'm on the phone," Miss Lowell said. "I don't mind if kids are here when I'm not here." The only thing she minded was kids going through her files.

Miss Lowell loved to play "Big Mama" to the several hundred students in her immediate jurisdiction, not only because she was that way but because she thought they needed it. She fully understood the remarkable assets of her shopping mall high school. Variety and choice allowed it to offer strong programs for the handicapped and strong programs for the talented. Size enabled those services to exist, but size, she also knew, could breed an impersonal atmosphere. She tried to prevent that by getting to know her students and building a homey environment inside the mall. Making her office a family room was only one of many ways she did this. At graduation she made sure to kiss every student to whom she handed a diploma. The practice took so long that her students were always scheduled last on the program, so that other families could leave the ceremonies early if they chose.

Despite her impressive caring, Miss Lowell remembered being "blown away" by an event the year before. A girl near the end of her senior year had been caught smoking illegally and was sent to Miss Lowell for discipline. She had been under Miss Lowell's jurisdiction for several years, but she appeared in the office as a total stranger. Miss Lowell had no idea who she was; neither did any of the other building counselors. The lesson was that "kids get lost."

Not all kids, Miss Lowell emphasized, but a certain kind of kid. Not the students on the top nor the ones on the bottom — everyone knew who *they* were. The kind of youngster who could be invisible even to such a sympathetic administrator was "the middle-of-everything kid, the unspecial kind of kid." Parents usually knew what was unique about their children. No child was really unspecial to them. But the unpleasant truth was that school professionals like herself "don't always know." She recognized that "an average kid can go through and make no impression"; some teenagers were simply not "distinctive in any way." The unspecial constituted "that great mass in the middle that education has dropped the ball on for years."

The Unspecial and the Shopping Mall High School

Few characteristics of the shopping mall high school are more significant than the existence of unspecial students in the middle who are ignored and poorly served. Teachers and administrators talk a great deal about the problem. "We do very much for the top, top students and the real problems," one teacher asserted, "but for these average 'nice' kids with low motivation we don't do much of anything." "Honors kids are fine and kids with handicaps are fine, but what are we doing for the average kid?" another said. An administrator made the same point: "We're doing a lot for the accelerated kids, we're doing a lot for the student who needs special help, but this kid in the middle gets the least attention." Another teacher concurred: "If you had to say where the resources or energies are concentrated, I'd say the resources are concentrated on high track and low track and the ones in the middle are lost." A school psychologist believed that "the great reservoir of kids who need help are not the few who appear in dramatic ways. I think it's the quiet group that you never hear about."

Parents, too, are concerned about those in the middle. In one school a parent commented that "we do take care of our superstars and those on the lower end of the spectrum, but there are lots in the middle who get lost." Parents at another school were proud that "top-flight kids" had "every range of thing that they can take . . . and a lot of attention is paid them." The same was true at the other end. "If you need help, there's someone to come and help you with remedial this or that." But "in the middle, you know, you're just — you're there, you're surviving."

The unspecial often remain as collectively invisible as the smoking offender had been to Miss Lowell. One veteran believed her school could take the greatest pride in the fact that it had "found enough ways to support the weak and give freedom to the strong." It was as if her entire awareness of the student population was confined to these two extreme categories of specialness.

Everyone agrees that the unspecial is a sizable group. One counselor first estimated that 70 percent of his school's student body fell into the category, but then added that he did not mean to imply that the school served well only 30 percent of its enrollment. Three quarters of that middle 70 percent at least had an "attachment" to something of a constructive nature; they were not entirely disconnected from school.

In school after school, definitions of the unspecial were vague. Indeed, one important characteristic is the very absence of precision about exactly who they are. They were variously the "invisible people," "the middle class," and "that great gray-mass area, those people who don't belong anywhere, the people who don't fit into any . . . categories." Words like average, middle, normal, and regular were often used to describe quite different kinds of adolescents. Some schoolpeople primarily meant the large number who were enrolled in college-preparatory programs but were not in advanced or honors classes. Although preparing for college, they were no longer special because post-secondary education was a mass expectation: college preparation had become bifurcated into special and unspecial divisions. In this view, the problem of the unspecial was a problem of the college-bound.

Others saw the unspecial as a contemporary version of traditional "general" students whose lives in school were shaped neither by clear college expectations nor by clearly-focused vocational purposes. A parent remembered, "In the high school I went to, . . . I was in the general course. You know, the general course. You're not college and you're not business and nobody had time for us. And they gave us nothing to take away from that high school and into life." For such students high school might be "their last concentrated spot of education" prior to a wholly vocational post-secondary experience or no future education at all. It was the only time for a liberal education in "how our government works, the arts, music, poetry, all those things." She saw no change from her day in how these students were treated.

Still others thought the unspecial were those on the top end of the bottom of the school's spectrum. They weren't handicapped enough, or delinquent enough, to be eligible for the services that conveyed specialness on their more needy peers. Yet "slow learners [who] are not special education material" could often profit immensely from exactly the programs for which they were not eligible. And the programs designed for them were often those most vulnerable to sudden termination of outside funding. Many teachers shared the view of one who said that for every student technically identified as learning-disabled, ten with disabilities were not identified. They were in regular classes, left to fend for themselves. "Isn't it too bad," ruminated an administrator who spent hours each week arranging evaluations and team meetings for the officially handicapped, "that every kid can't have one of these conferences?"

"This is terrible to say," apologized a counselor, but "it's not fair that all the money be put into many youngsters that will never be the doctors and lawyers and the leaders of society." The society's priorities were wrong, although the emotions that set them were understandable. Her "very idealistic" approach would be to deflect

175

some special-education money to average students who might really take off if programs analogous to special-needs were made available to them. But without a severe reduction of student loads, she could not imagine an individual "educational plan" being written for average students. Teachers who saw 125 students a day couldn't remember enough about each one to implement educational plans even if they existed.

Characteristically, the unspecial were usually defined by relation to some other group. Thus regular college-prep students were not accelerated students, either because they did not meet formal eligibility requirements (such as being invited by a teacher to take honors English) or because they chose to remain in regular classes. And students with real but not profound learning problems were not eligible for mandated programs with highly detailed admissions requirements. The unspecial had not been admitted to anything where admissions conferred specialness. The only thing they had been admitted to was high school itself, but this carried no cachet because admission was virtually automatic.

The allotted role of the unspecial often seems to be to call attention to the specialness of others. They made up, for example, an important part of the audience for Friday night football. Spectatorship was their lot, and most played the role happily. Only rarely did students complain that team sports were usually accessible only to talented athletes. One teacher even thought that spectatorship, in the stands and in the classroom, was sound preparation for life. Such students would play roles in life requiring a "passive position." While in school they were "already orienting themselves to the environment in which they're going to be." It was sound pedagogy to know that "they respond better if you don't try to force them to take over."

Another fundamental characteristic of the unspecial is that they have no important allies or advocates. One counselor stressed that top-track students were blessed with a "strong constituency of parents." The handicapped, those with highly focused vocational interests, even the unruly, also had their spokespeople, usually organized lobbies or political groups that generated money or mandates from legislatures and courts. The local community was a formidable advocate for other students, notably talented athletes, who gain recognition in return for providing entertainment and boosting local pride. But average youngsters have none of these advocates. Parents are always a potential lobby, a potential source of advocacy, a potential counterweight to in-school invisibility — but only a handful choose to play that role. Some parents are wholly absent from their children's lives. Even if they are available, "they are too busy trying to survive to try to tell the schools what to do," said one counselor. To schools, these parents are profoundly unspecial themselves; they are as invisible as their children.

Yet most care deeply. A typical mother spoke of the lengths she would go to make her son a good citizen and keep him out of trouble. She drove the somewhat reluctant teenager to a popular youth hangout miles out of town. She took a sleeping bag and pillow with her and slept in the car while the boy danced with his friends. She did this often enough to know all the security policemen around the parking lot, and made sure that her son arrived home safe and sober. But her oversight flagged when it came to schoolwork. She had enough commitment to sleep in the car but was not bothered by the fact that her son received poor grades and ditched classes frequently. He had many friends, liked school, and had a job three and a half hours a day. "Sixteen is such a difficult age," she said, laughing. "He may be a late bloomer like I was." She praised the school for informing her of his many absences. "I really appreciate it. At least I know what he's doing." The boy was very special to his mother, but unspecial when it came to schoolwork. She and other parents like her trusted the experts, not knowing what else to do, and sensed no real urgency in their children's poor grades, cutting of classes, goofing off, and rejection of opportunities to take more demanding classes. Such parents, one counselor knew from experience, were "not the ones with political clout or even particularly good street fighters. They expect the school to do the job."

The educational background of parents strongly influences their capacity to be an informed and effective pressure group for their children. One group of educated parents who knew how to push remembered a "middle kid" with a "lot of potential" who "got into bonehead English when he really didn't belong there." His parents did not "bother to push at the beginning . . . maybe even didn't know how to go about doing that." Their children had a palpable advantage. "That's the kind of thing that nobody in this room would allow to happen to their kid." Without advocates like themselves, they wondered aloud, where would pressure on behalf of average kids ever come from?

Many self-proclaimed ordinary students understand that they lack forceful advocates. A group of them talked of how their parents didn't know what courses they were taking or the names of their counselors. One said defiantly and perhaps defensively, "It's my life. I want to take care of it anyway." But another expressed frustration and called for help: "It seems as if all the kids who were successful and do well at school are the ones who have been successful over the years. They come from good homes. Their parents had a good education and they expected to do the same thing. What I would like is for the school to find a way to reach the students who don't come from this kind of family. Maybe by our age it's too late. Maybe they need to start earlier, but I don't think they are getting a chance." In another school an average student who admitted disliking schoolwork described the same problem. "In order to get a kid really going," he argued, "you have to get after him. They expect the parents to do that, to chase after you, but they have to do it too, because what about the kid who has alcoholic parents, or parents who are never there? He's not going to get anywhere."

Parents with several children of their own in the same school were often most aware of the very different impact the shopping mall high school could have on different individuals. Variety, choice, and neutrality could be constructive and liberating for some of their children, but just the opposite for others. "Everything's here," one mother said succinctly, and "the burden of choice falls on the student." The system worked extremely well for her son. A top-track student, he made wise choices, did well, and posed no problems for anyone. "But then, he's so smart," she said.

Things had not worked out as well for her daughter. A pattern of ditching classes began when her schedule forced her to take driver education, lunch, and study hall consecutively. Somehow driver ed was rescheduled and another study hall assigned in its place. That left a block of "almost two hours of dead time." She began to cut the entire block, but her mother didn't know: "I was naïve enough to think they went to study halls if they took them. Apparently nobody goes — nobody. It's not considered important enough to let you know about, either." Once used to ditching, "she started cutting classes that counted . . . she had been a good student up to then." When the mother finally learned what was happening, she merely told her daughter to talk to the counselor. She assumed there would be intervention by the school, but there was none. The daughter cut more, began to be rebellious at home, and felt discouraged about herself and school.

One problem with the school's reaction, the mother thought, was that counselors were simply too busy to handle minor problems. "If your kid isn't really in *bad* trouble or what someone defines as bad trouble, they may put their name in asking for counseling sessions and they may not get picked up for three, four, or five days. If that's a whole week it can get pretty critical by the end of the week." Beyond that, she disliked the time lag in teachers' getting information about her daughter's behavior to counselors, and the time lag in counselors' informing parents. For example, she didn't learn for a long time that her daughter "cut forty-five study halls . . . that she dropped out of French because she had a fight with her French teacher." Her point was that "the immediacy of follow-up — and some of these kids really need that — is missing."

This parent was careful not to seem too critical. After all, she had taken little initiative herself. And her son hadn't had any problems with schooling. Not everybody needed follow-up. "The student who is motivated," she concluded, "will find what he needs and will do it. The student who is a little bit confused and a little bit unsure of himself, I think the arrow points the other way." Choice had proved most burdensome for the least special of her children, but the school had neither the means nor the inclination to respond.

Another parent admitted that she had not been "very aggressive" in pushing for her youngest son because the older ones had done well on their own. But when he got "lost between the cracks," no one told her or tried to find him. Neither a troublemaker nor a failure, he simply became alienated from schoolwork. "I know teachers are tired, but a call from a teacher or an approach for a conference would be helpful, and I just don't see it happening."

Perhaps it was impossible, since teachers often saw 150 students a day. But she was sure more could be done. Perhaps they could create a buddy system, as in swimming, where teenagers could be paired and taught to reach out to each other: "We want you in class. Where are you? We need you." Perhaps teachers and counselors could reach out to parents beyond the reporting of problems to say, "Your son or daughter wasn't in class. Let's find out why and see what we can do about it."

A third mother was outraged to learn only at the end of the term that her daughter received a D in a course. Institutional practice was to inform families of top-track students at midterm if their grades were D; other families received an early warning signal only if their children were failing. If one cared about D's in that school, it helped to be special. "They assume," she concluded, "that kids are ready for more responsibility than they really are. This is an enormous school, and an enormous set of curriculum choices, but if the kids don't follow through, they drop it." The adults didn't follow through any more than the students did. She valued the school's freedom. The answer was not "leading them by the nose, but you have to guide them, and show them what their options are, and help them to make a choice. Now that's not the same thing as telling them what to do . . . When they're in high school you have to watch over them gently without suffocating them . . . You have to go after them." What she and the other parents wanted for those of their children who in school were average, normal, and unspecial was something between freedom and regimentation. They accepted the basic premise of choice amidst vast variety, but wished for more assertive direction and personal attention from the adults.

For the middle student, a school's neutral stance on pushing students has the effect of making minimum requirements maximum standards. One group of parents of top-track students said the system benefited their own children but "cheated" average students. When this group tried to "tighten it up" by adding a second year of required math, the educators resisted most — they would say, the parents claimed, "No, you'll discourage them. We'll lose too many. They'll drop out. They'll get discouraged. They'll fail." Increasing requirements frightened educators, these parents thought, because they increased the possibility that someone might not be able to meet them. They were not sure whether the "tremendous efforts to keep children in school — and they are really extensive" were due to fears that lost numbers would mean lost teaching jobs, or whether educators genuinely believed that high school was good for everybody. But when their school did respond to demands for "standards" by adding a second year of math, it made sure to allow courses like Consumer Mathematics to satisfy the requirement. By increasing requirements, the school could respond to periodic outside pressures without really increasing demands on middle students.

How do schoolpeople react to requests from students without supportive families for help, or to parents frustrated by the fact that some of their children make far better use of high school than others? Most recognize that the unspecial are the Achilles' heel of the shopping mall high school. Dr. Nelson, the counselor who celebrated variety and freedom as the central components of true individualization, understood that "the individualization breaks down when you get to the middle kid." He knew from experience that "substantial numbers" of "quiet and passive" teenagers simply "pass through." A colleague who praised the school for providing "enormous opportunity" admitted, "Jesus, kids drift . . . For years they drift. Finally . . . they scramble and get their minimum credits and graduate and have done very little." Most seemed happy enough to spend their high school years that way. They had great "tolerance for boredom" while they were there. But at the end, many graduates felt embittered. "You hear . . . , 'Nobody made me work. I was allowed to cut and skip and drift and I didn't turn in my homework and got C's and nobody did anything.' " That happened a lot, he thought, and most frequently with students in the middle.

Average kids, another school's counselor admitted, were the most vulnerable ones. "These are the ones who with the right pushing can take off and fly, but without it, simply fall back and get nothing done." Wise decision-making, another explained, "isn't so much a problem for the kids who are near the top of the class. It's not often that a kid who wants to go to Yale hasn't taken courses. It's more likely to be the one in the middle who wants to be a physical therapist and doesn't realize that they need to take a lot of science." She remembered a girl who wanted to be an accountant but stopped taking math after tenth grade. Nobody pressed her because she had met the minimum graduation requirements.

"There's no one to push them" — that is the widespread belief about schools' reach to the middle student. Parents agree, schoolpeople agree, teenagers agree. One boy remembered that when he failed a course, the school called home to say, "Hey, [he] got an F. Bye. Click." Although he claimed he would not work harder regardless of school policy, he missed at least some attempt on the school's part to push him. Other middle students knew they were supposed to push themselves, but it was hard to do so "when you know you won't get into trouble" if you didn't.

One school's internal survey revealed that middle students' academic programs over the entire high school span were disconnected and nearly random. In contrast with teenagers at the extremes, they were "taking a conglomerate of courses with no sequential learning." The middle student was variously described as "unfocused" in choosing, unable to use school well, and "not sophisticated [enough to] choose the kind of quality that a lot of the kids who know the teachers, and know how they teach, do." Their frequent ignorance of basic knowledge about school organization and career requirements was a major barrier to informed self-direction.

Yet within schools there was no consensus about what to do. Some schoolpeople contended that parents who wanted high schools to push students or reach out more to them did not understand what schools could realistically do and what they could *not* do — they didn't have the resources to reach out to adolescents who were only "marginally" at risk. What schools needed to do more, one counselor said, was to educate parents of these children to "use the resources within a school by taking the initiatives themselves in contacting some of the people here." Ideally, she "would want parents to call and make appointments with teachers and find out what's going on in the classroom, to call and make appointments with counselors, and maybe even make requests for progress reports each week that the student would be responsible for picking up on Friday and bringing home."

She admitted that only a few parents understood that it was legitimate to be this active, and fewer still who would actually initiate an appointment with a teacher. Those who knew how to do this were rarely parents of unspecial children. Her last suggestion was to write down on paper all these options and distribute them to parents. When asked whether counselors and teachers would welcome such a document — some teachers in the school already complained about parents who were *too* pushy — she smiled and said nothing. "The irony," she concluded, "is that we turn to parents for support, but they put it back on the school, saying they need *us* for support. They're not always passing the buck, but have real problems in dealing with their kids and hope that we have more authority to help the kids straighten out than they do." But in the end the reach had to come from parents, she believed, not the school. Parents had only their own children on their minds; the school had hundreds, sometimes thousands, of kids.

But others in schools thought that approach was too simplistic. Some counselors saw their responsibility as being "to make an effort to be sure we see the kids in the middle," even as they admitted they did not succeed. A school psychologist believed there was insufficient reach by teachers toward these students. Teachers never asked, "What's going on?" The average kids weren't "bothersome" enough to be noticed, "yet that's the kind of student that potentially you're in the best position to help." One teacher was more direct: "All kids are not as mature as others when they come in . . . They're lost . . . We lose them. They drift away. This is where we fail . . . We have machinery to find out if a kid is absent but no machinery to find out why or what to do." In her judgment schools could not abdicate responsibility for knowing more about the lives and motives of all students.

Others emphasized academic expectations in addition to personal attention. The ever-louder calls for higher standards usually affected only those at the extremes: more programs for the talented to keep America ahead, more minimal competency tests to minimize the awkward reality of illiterate high school graduates. "At all levels of the scale," one teacher emphasized in contrast, "there should be a demand for excellence."

But a few believed the problem was exaggerated out of proportion. They attributed the "lack of inclination" to deal head-on with the unspecial to a feeling that in the long run things would even out.

Average kids had a "perseverance and steadiness" that would stand them in good stead. The top-track student might have his day in school and perhaps in college, but would often fizzle out under the pressure to achieve. Push was not necessarily positive or important. The average student would eventually run the country. In this view passivity in school is hardly an insuperable barrier to future happiness or success.

Classroom Treaties

Treaties for avoidance rather than engagement dominate classes attended by the unspecial. Little is usually expected of these students, and little is done to change their lot. High school attendance thus perpetuates and confirms unspecialness. Contrast, for example, two senior English classes taught by Mr. Cleveland. During first period he showed his advanced students a thirty-minute film version of *The Red Badge of Courage* and then led a twenty-minute discussion. He repeated the procedure second period with his regular senior English class. Both groups were mainly bound for four-year colleges. Despite surface similarities, the classes seemed worlds apart. They were "really very different," he commented — "wow, really different."

Mr. Cleveland began the advanced discussion with "What symbolism did you find?" and the regular discussion with "What did you like about the film?" In the first class he followed up by asking what the actions of various figures in the story revealed about their characters. Students seemed eager to participate. They spoke in sentences, sometimes in paragraphs. Some students asked questions of their own about such topics as the connection between the film and the Civil War. In the regular class Cleveland had trouble getting a response to his initial question, despite attempts to rephrase it in various ways. Few students wanted to talk. No one spoke in complete sentences. At least one worked on homework, another sat so far in the rear corner that he seemed not a member of the class at all, and many others fidgeted. Midway through the discussion Cleveland abandoned it and conducted a short lecture on weaponry. When he spoke of the Civil War as a transition in arms from rifles to ironclads, attention perked up, though the lecture had nothing to do with the film. With ten minutes left he ended his talk and told them to work at their desks until the bell rang.

Cleveland adjusted classroom procedures in various ways to accommodate the two groups. The regular students received no more than twenty-five minutes a night of homework and the advanced students double that amount, though neither group got homework every day. Many advanced students would submit five-page term papers — the maximum Cleveland allowed — while he would accept from regular students a term paper of eighty words. He felt regular students did not like to talk, so he held discussions to a minimum and required oral presentations only in the advanced class. When discussions did occur in the regular class, they emphasized concrete details rather than analysis. Regular kids, Mr. Cleveland explained, preferred more variation in classroom activities than the advanced class. If he employed two activities during an advanced class (say, a film and discussion), he would often use four in the regular class (film, discussion, lecture, and seatwork).

In his view, regular students also liked the "security" of a predictable routine that varied little each day; they wanted to be told exactly what to do all the time. They would become upset if a writing assignment was given without a specific subject to write about or specific instructions on the number of words expected: "Without that some of them were paralyzed." The advanced group, on the other hand, tolerated or even welcomed unpredictability.

In most classes for the unspecial, not just Mr. Cleveland's, all of the crucial areas of teacher-student negotiations are settled in favor of avoidance. Time demands are held to a minimum. Regular classes have far less homework than advanced classes, even though both groups of students are often bound for post-secondary education. Much more class time is given over to homework. Distractions of every variety are accepted, sometimes encouraged; they serve as additional activities to vary the pace and cope with short attention spans. A friendly and relaxed classroom atmosphere is often ensured by leaving students alone. "They don't want to be put in the position to talk," one teacher said, but "in the honors classes you have people fighting to talk." And regular students are rarely willing to talk with each other about the subject. "They don't want to draw attention to themselves," a teacher explained. The best strategy to get them to talk was to talk about something other than the subject.

Passivity rather than intensity predominates. The lecture method is popular in classes for the unspecial. One teacher said that middle kids were "desirous to have me lead"; they liked to "just sit there and listen and take notes." They also liked to stay with facts and details. "They'll get edgy when you start to get in," said one English teacher who encountered resistance to probing questions. "They say that you're destroying the story." Since they preferred to "stay on the surface," he accommodated by giving classes and tests that dealt with "pretty much fact . . . I want them to tell me that they read the play and they understand what happened." They often preferred "busy-work" such as worksheets because it's "controlled and structured and they can get immediate feedback and build up marks." Their teachers rarely mentioned thinking as a class objective.

Why do teachers settle so readily for these treaties? Why does their classroom practice perpetuate rather than attack passivity? Mr. Cleveland, for example, saw no contradiction in his behavior, only inevitability. How did he explain why his classroom treaties for regular students were so dominated by avoidance?

First of all, he said he was constrained by the reality that these students *would* not do more. They were "unenthusiastic" about learning and "won't get up and talk." Discussions didn't work because "everybody just sits." He couldn't stay with any activity for long because, having been raised on TV, they would tune out at a moment's notice. He couldn't make more demands: "If you try to overwork them, they balk." Teachers with high demands had low enrollments.

Teachers in general often do not push for more because they, like Mr. Cleveland, believe average kids "won't do it." They could almost feel the absence of motivation: ordinary teenagers just didn't have the "drive" of aggressive, special kids. All that interested them was "jobs and sports." Students didn't see how working hard at school was "going to influence either their present or their future lives," one teacher said. "They tend to be satisfied with what they're given," another reported, "and they don't demand as much." Another teacher claimed, "They just don't like to rock the boat. They quickly assess what is expected of them in class and will do exactly that and no more. They're not motivated to try harder, so just getting by is enough." Treaties that accommodate lack of motivation are thus among the easiest to negotiate.

Special students at either end of the school continuum had some "clearly defined purpose." Sometimes the purpose was felt directly by the students; it came from within or from the push of families. Sometimes the purpose was established by outside forces such as legislative mandates. But when no educational purpose at all was in evidence, and the task was to create one for each student, teachers were at a loss. It was hard to find materials, or teaching methods, that would appeal to so many different personalities and life histories.

Mr. Cleveland emphasized the great diversity among students in his regular class. No single quality described the middle student. Several could handle the advanced class but did not want the work or the competition. One "con artist" wanted to transfer to a lower-level bilingual class even though her English was excellent and she probably could handle more advanced work. Alienated from school and frequently absent, she wanted the easiest route to a diploma. Others with very modest skills had been pushed up into his regular class because they had become exhausting disciplinary problems for their remedial teacher. She wanted only to get rid of them.

Another teacher thought that her school could communicate fairly clearly its purposes for students at the extremes, but had no "clear and definite" objective for those in the middle. And one who regarded the latter as the most difficult and challenging group to teach admitted, "We don't have a curriculum for them." Institutional neutrality affects with its fullest force those in the middle. That situation makes the unspecial at once *easier to manage* — a circumstance that Mr. Cleveland well understood — but *harder to teach.* It is easier to settle for classroom avoidance, which unmotivated students prefer, than to stimulate engagement. One teacher explained that worksheets were the perfect pedagogy: the kids liked them and thus were orderly, and worksheets meant less work for her. The middle students' preference for structure and predictability also means less work for teachers. The more the structure — as defined by worksheets, lectures, films on certain days, reading in class — the easier classes are to manage.

The problem goes deeper than motivation; it is not just that average students won't do more. Mr. Cleveland took pains to emphasize that most *couldn't* do more. He didn't use an analytic approach because they couldn't understand it. He didn't assign *The Scarlet Letter* — he showed the TV version instead — because they would need a month of class time to read it. Even if they read it, he couldn't stand the thought of boring discussions that had to be confined to the "busy-work" of plot summaries. "I have taught it, and I've broken it down chapter by chapter using the good old worksheet. 'Why did Hester do X?' 'Why is he named Dimsdale?' 'What happened after Y?' " To avoid this pointless boredom he used the film: "TV works better." It took account of what he believed to be their limited analytic powers.

He was hardly alone in this belief. "By ninth grade, if they haven't picked up academic skills," another teacher remarked, "then forget that. Put them on an assembly line, give them on-the-job training, make them feel that they're accomplishing something, so that when they get out of school they feel that they have a job, that they can go right into society." A teacher concluded simply that "some students can and some can't. In teaching the regular classes last year, it was impossible altogether to have discussions — they have lower ability, lower attention span, and so on." Teachers used words like "smart" and "slow" not to describe differences in upbringing that a just society might correct, but differences in human endowment that were not subject to remediation. There certainly are clear limits to educability. But since the unspecial are such a large and varied population, those limits for particular individuals are wholly unclear. Yet the average student is usually lumped together with others in a great gray mass, and, as an individual, effectively written off.

Like many teachers, Mr. Cleveland understood that "the problem has always been the middle. They get the least money and the least extra services." He readily admitted those students were underserved. Many teachers go beyond Mr. Cleveland's distant sympathy and explain their aims in their classes for the unspecial in deliberate psychological and therapeutic terms. Students in the middle *won't* work, teachers say, because they are unmotivated; hence the importance of psychology as a motivational tool. Students *can't* perform, at least in part, because they lack supportive social or economic environments outside school. Lacking the capacity to attack frontally these environmental barriers — teachers cannot easily remove children from them or intervene directly to change them — they sympathetically fall back on therapeutic ideals as their only tool.

What such sympathy usually means in practice is the wholesale replacement of academic goals by therapeutic ones of self-esteem and feelings of success. One able science teacher, for example, said that her college-prep middle students did not want or expect a "fully high-powered college-prep biology course." So she concentrated instead on topics that "matter to them personally," such as the human body. Sometimes she felt guilty about leaving out topics that she considered central to biology, but when she thought about self-esteem and kids encountering success, "then I stop feeling guilty." An English teacher who tried to "affirm" her average students "as people" would never have used the same words about advanced students. A history teacher justified her extensive use of charades as pedagogy, her elimination of a term paper, and her tortoise-like pace through the text by saying that her course objective was to build self-confidence.

Mr. Cleveland made none of this effort, which often requires herculean labor of a particular sort. Instead, he candidly admitted that he didn't push his regular classes more because he wouldn't push himself more. More demands on the middle student (and they constituted three fourths of his teaching load) would mean more contacts with parents, more preparation for classes, more follow-up afterward. On his salary he simply wouldn't do it. One of the advantages of teaching *The Red Badge of Courage* to undemanding kids, he explained, was, "I don't have to reread that damn thing." Because they didn't push him, he didn't have to push himself. Advanced students, in contrast, might "sharp-shoot you." He remembered one such class that met early in the day. The students were always "ready to go and I wasn't." Their parents also had forced him to be on his toes. He resented this and did his best to avoid a recurrence.

Unspecial students are thus an attractive market to teachers who are unspecial themselves. Miss Horton, Mrs. Austin, and Mr. Cleveland were all remarkably candid about why they preferred average students: such students did not demand much and did not threaten their own passivity. At the same time the most proficient teachers usually prefer to teach the most able students. Mr. Cleveland complained that the prima donnas of his department — those regarded by students and parents as the best teachers — wanted only the advanced classes. One had even said that regular kids were "unimportant." Just as the students were divided into the haves and have-nots, so were the teachers. The attitude of the haves toward their colleagues, Cleveland reported, was, "I have all the advanced classes and you also teach at the school — I think." He resented this reality even while admitting he preferred things that way. The process of "natural selection" — of like finding like — is another powerful incentive for classes that enroll the unspecial to be unspecial.

How do the unspecial themselves respond to these classroom treaties? At one school six seniors and three sophomores talked together about their classes. In an institution with three levels of instruction, all of them had taken their courses in the middle division. They differed from one another in sex, race, ethnicity, and dreams for the future. Six anticipated post-secondary education immediately after graduation, and half of those thought a two-year institution was most likely. Their career interests ranged across elementary school teaching, the military, automotive trades, air traffic control, and commercial diving. But despite the differences in their backgrounds and interests, their views about schoolwork were remarkably convergent.

These were not alienated youth who disliked school or ditched frequently. But they were tolerant of chronic ditchers; they were not like them but had no criticisms: "It's their life." Nor were they like the higher-level kids and did not want to be. One said she had refused an invitation to take more advanced courses "because I'm lazy," and another said she had moved out of such a course in order to "slump off" but still get a B. But they did not criticize peers who chose the higher level. Everyone had made and should be allowed to make his own choices. Their own regular classes, one said to everyone's satisfaction, were for "normal, average, everyday" people. She had been one of these "all my life." Their school, they said with pride, was a "do-your-own-thing school."

These self-proclaimed average students thought that friendly and tolerant relationships were the most important thing about high school. "The school is relaxed," one said, and others chimed in that "the social life is great" and that "Enjoy yourself" best captured the local mood. "Everyone gets along pretty good." One explained, "We're Americans. Why argue? Let's all have fun." They pointed proudly to the abundance of clubs and sports. Yet they also reported that *they* did not participate in these activities, or, rather, they participated only by attending athletic events. Some explained this by the time demands of paid jobs they held, though not all had jobs.

When they discussed the school's educational program, they stressed that what you got out of a do-your-own-thing school was determined by what you put in: "You got to do it yourself." "Nobody's going to push you." "They'll help you if you want help." If you didn't, "they'll leave you alone and let you fail." These students liked things that way. "Kids don't really try that hard." For themselves they chose courses that were easy, met at convenient times, and enrolled their friends. They did homework, as long as it was not too much. (One estimate was a total of two or three hours per week for all courses.) A boy said he deliberately constructed his schedule to avoid homework, so he would have time to "work, play, and be with my friends." They never complained when little was expected of them. "Why should we? We just want to get out." They thought their teachers probably felt the same way. They were as much "goof-offs" as the students, as much anxious for the end of school so they too could begin their second jobs. Avoidance treaties were mutually advantageous — like had found like.

Most of the seniors in the group expressed a tinge of regret and perhaps more than a tinge of anxiety: "I wish I hadn't goofed off." "I could be doing better. I would take harder classes." "I wish I would have taken more college-prep classes." "I wish someone was there to push me. I just kind of slacked off." Yet these ambivalent feelings did not convince them that the school should apply greater push. They opposed cracking down on chronic ditchers. And when asked what needed changing, they mentioned nothing about classroom life. Instead, they said the facilities needed upgrading. The gym was too small. There was no pool. Sports equipment was not of top quality, nor for that matter was the coaching. They disliked seeing late-term pregnant girls walking the halls. The school, they agreed, was too big. But the problem of bigness was not impersonalism; it was a complex time schedule that many found hard to incorporate into their out-of-school activities.

Specialty Shops for the Unspecial

Not all average students are so satisfied. Mike and Rita were juniors with C averages in middle-level courses, and both lived with their parents as the youngest children in large families. Mike's father was a bank executive, Rita's a fireman. Neither mother worked outside the home. Mike had no after-school job but played on his school's football team. He wanted to go to college, but he didn't know what kind of college or what he would study there. He was not achieving at the level his test scores indicated he might; and he was walking, as a teacher put it, a thin line between being a thug and being a student. Rita did not participate in extracurricular activities but worked after school as a supermarket cashier. Her plans were to become either a model or a junior high school teacher. She was sometimes angry at teachers and other students, thought little of herself, and perhaps had experienced some violence at home where her father was a heavy drinker.

They were not at all satisfied with the do-your-own-thing mentality of their high school. Kids like themselves, they stressed, "get lost in the shuffle." They were quick to point out that not everyone got lost. The top-level kids wanted to go to class and knew what they wanted out of life. Good teachers would always "be around for those kinds of kids," Mike said, and were really "rooting" for them. Teachers did more for them because they realized they wanted something from school. That was their incentive to negotiate treaties for engagement. The school's "juvenile delinquents," in their estimation, also got a lot of attention. The school would do anything to keep them from dropping out.

Those priorities were why "everyone else gets lost . . . They're leaving out the regular kids who just go to classes and fall asleep, who aren't getting anything out of it." Sooner or later teachers

192

gave up on those kids — kids like themselves. "They feel nobody wants to learn; they feel students don't care, so why should they?" Rita added that "kids who are just doing their own thing, that at least are trying to participate, aren't getting anything." Unlike Mike, who thought that teachers were accommodating their own behavior to the passivity of their students, Rita believed it was often the other way around. In many classes, the teacher was not giving his best shot, and "that sets the mood for the kids not to care either." But despite their different views about causation, they agreed that "teachers are not pushing middle kids." They felt ignored and wanted different classroom arrangements, but felt powerless on their own to bring them about.

A few teachers in their school started a special program called Beta to address this situation. Beta was nothing more elaborate than a conjoining of two junior-year American history and English classes. The courses met back to back, and the two teachers involved worked closely together inside and outside class. Enrollment was small, and the program took up only a third of the school day. Beta was special because its intended clientele was the unspecial. Average students with low motivation were invited to participate. They were not causing real trouble to the school but were not excited by any of its curricula, either. Many, said one of the teachers, "are kids who have been passed by in their average class of twenty-five to thirty. Teachers would have seen them as nice but quiet, or nice but slow. We wanted to pick this type of student and give them more attention and support." That they had found the "type of student we don't do much for" was perhaps confirmed by the fact that most teachers in the school didn't know that Beta existed.

The teachers had approached Mike and Rita as ideal candidates, and the two agreed to sign up. After nearly a year, they pronounced it "real comfortable" and a sharp contrast to the rest of their school lives. One appeal was a sense that they *belonged* to something. They were not anonymous. Someone considered them important. In her other classes, Rita remarked, "you're just a number, not a person." And Mike, still more sympathetic than she toward teachers, added, "They'd like to care but it's just so bad and there're so many kids. How can they think about kids? . . . You feel you don't belong. In junior high at least you mean something. You're a person." Although their Beta classes were slightly smaller than the regular classes, the feeling of belonging derived mainly from arrangements and attitudes that transcended class size. Rita noted, for example, that students always sat in a circle in her Beta English class and the teacher sat in the circle with them. At first she thought the circle was silly — she felt uncomfortable looking at fellow students — but eventually she came to appreciate the closeness, the conversations about the subject, and the greater courtesy among the students. Mike agreed the circle helped immensely to "bring the kids together, make a group."

A second appeal was their conviction that the Beta teachers really cared about them personally. It was as if attitudes toward them which they saw in teachers compelled complementary attitudes in themselves toward teachers. As Mike put it, "They're putting out for you so you have to put out for them." In other classes they observed that neither students nor teachers really wanted to be there at all. There, all participants had the attitude, "I've just got to drag myself through this class." That was the more common high school treaty.

The Beta teachers emphasized caring as both an end and a means; they were fully committed to therapeutic ideals. One of them characterized progress over the year as "caring about one another, as opposed to September when they would just put one another down." The other agreed, "We're building some trust." Their most fundamental ground rule was to eliminate put-downs and discourtesy. They knew that average students were especially unwilling to talk in class about the subject, so a major objective was to get them to speak out. By emphasizing that "talking is an act of trust," and that students and teachers alike show respect by listening carefully to one another, they hoped to cut through the vulnerability that kept the unspecial silent. The English teacher who cared enough to persuade Mike and Rita to give her subject a chance was the same teacher whom Eric and Kara, Dr. McBride's physics students, had dismissed as inept because she was too soft in an advanced class where they were also her students.

Neither teacher regarded Beta as a panacea. After nearly a year Rita was still frequently turned off and still had a short fuse. Mike was still not achieving according to test-score potential and had not finally decided whether to be a student or a thug. Perhaps Beta "may be tipping the balance" between avoidance of learning and engagement in it, but it was too soon to say. At least they came to class, read real books, wrote a short paper weekly, took vocabulary tests twice a week, and gave a speech to the class once a term. They were still C students but were "getting a good deal and obviously I'm pleased with the way it's going," said one of the teachers.

The most striking thing about Beta is that programs like it are rare in shopping mall high schools. Consumers are offered wide variety but are hardly ever offered this kind of specialty shop. There is not much demand — Beta had to actively recruit. There is also a reluctance to supply; Beta's two teachers were heroic exceptions to standard practice.

But consumerism in education is a deeply ingrained social attitude. Some families who want programs like Beta, or programs more substantial than Beta, exercise the ultimate consumer decision: they look beyond the shopping mall high school for institutional specialty shops that cater without apology to average children. Such parents are often sophisticated consumers within the mall. They look there first for the right kind of specialty shop for a particular child and, if it is available, gain entrance by pushing the child and the school. But if it is not available there, they have no problems taking their educational business elsewhere. Though they profess general loyalty to the ideals of public education, and often send their more special children there, the choice they make for average youngsters — if they have the means and the commitment to consider choosing — is a private school. There they believe such children are less likely to get "lost in the cracks." There they believe, if students are reluctant to push themselves, they will be pushed.

One family's story is typical of many. When a family had moved two years before, the parents naturally sent both sons to the local public high school, whose reputation for excellence, the mother said, was both enviable and well-deserved. One of the boys had previously attended a private school where he had been "the fair-haired boy, the bellwether of the class. There they expected great things of him, and they told him, and they told [us]. They pushed and they squeezed every last ounce out of that kid. And he loved it. He thrived." But after enrollment in the new school, "nobody cared who he was or what he could do." For example, he had always thought of himself as a good basketball player, and he made the team in the new school. But he wound up sitting on the bench, because he wasn't good enough to play regularly. "There was a star system there" — that was how his mother phrased it. "No one down there thought he was too special."

It was that way in classes, too. His former specialness evaporated. "He didn't get much support. It was a very difficult year." So, while maintaining that the school was indeed excellent for many students, she concluded that it didn't suit this particular child. She switched him to a neighboring private school, where, in class and on the court, he became special again.

Like most parents who described this costly decision, this mother resisted generalizations about public and private schools. She knew the common stereotypes were wrong — that public schools were dangerous jungles, and that private schools were filled with students easy to teach. That kind of silly talk missed the entire point, she said. The point was the practical consumer problem of matching a particular child to a particular school. She believed that no school was better in a general sense; indeed, the public school had worked out marvelously for her other son: "There are some kids who need more scope, who need a bigger learning environment, and there are some who absolutely need a small school." Other students "have certain needs that could be met in both public and private schools."

The very idea of a school that is good for everyone seemed flawed to parents whose children are not clones of each other. The son who thrived in the public school "just wanted to be anonymous . . . He didn't want too much personal attention." And he was doing very well. Many kids were like that. "They've had too much of people knowing who they are and what they are about." For them, the shopping mall high school was a welcome refuge.

That private schools often act as specialty shops for students who otherwise might be lost in the crowd is obvious to families who use them, schoolpeople who work in them, and many public school professionals as well. Certainly a few private schools are specialty shops for the already special. They attract the talented and committed, in the way that urban public examination schools do, or the handicapped, the learning-disabled, or the alienated. They are private specialty shops that replicate public specialty shops which, for one reason or another, do not exist in a local public school or seem unsatisfactory to parents.

But most private schools do not cater to such very special populations. Even when a school is not exclusively for the student in the middle, it recognizes him or her as being part of a sizable, distinct, and legitimate constituency. At the school that the unspecial basketball player switched to, for example, the principal asserted, "We do well with the average college-prep child who would be swallowed up in a big school . . . The one who doesn't need us is the bright, well-motivated self-starter who will do well anyway." The admissions director agreed that "the public school can't be beat if the kids are really great, but when they are round about average, we can do a much better job of providing individual instruction." Another administrator confided, "If I had a child who was at the top of his class . . . I'm not sure I would put down the [money] to send him [here]."

What were these schools attempting to do that lured parents who could pay tuition from the shopping mall high school? What did families think they were receiving, and what did they receive, from this substantial consumer investment? And, in light of the existence of Beta, was such a withdrawal inevitable, or was it merely a reflection of the incapacity of the shopping mall high school to perceive and respond to yet another consumer demand? Three themes run through the answers given to such questions. All suggest that the unspecial are often best served by institutional arrangements that contrast sharply with those most prominent in the shopping mall high school.

Instead of a neutrality shaped by conflicting values among school participants, private schools seek agreement about institutional purpose. Ideally families and schools are fused in a single community of values. Instead of accommodating different preferences by offering deep variety and wide choice, the private schools typically restrict variety and choice and substitute for them active adult push. And instead of promoting individualization by the presence of boundless opportunities and the absence of restraints, private schools attempt to promote it by giving intimate personal attention.

Purpose

Two boys who lived in the same town, Glenn and Carlos, were like ships that passed in the night. A self-described "public school kid," Glenn left the local high school after a year to attend a private school. His old school, he explained, "caters to the supersmart but not to persons in the middle like me." Carlos, on the other hand, withdrew from Glenn's private school to attend the same public high school Glenn had abandoned. At both institutions Carlos ranked near the top of his class. He had traded one kind of specialty shop for another. In the public school he now took all accelerated classes, was pleased to find more students like himself in the top-track enclave, and claimed that most of his former private school classmates could not have handled the advanced work on which he thrived. He emphasized that now he played in a school orchestra good enough to go on tour in Europe.

The boys traveled in different circles but had remarkably similar views about the two high schools they each knew first-hand. They agreed that the public high school had no clear purpose. You could do your own thing and nobody minded. For most students, Carlos thought, the closest thing the school had to a purpose was a "big babysitting service." The private school, in contrast, had an absolutely clear mission: learning, and especially the kind of learning that prepared for four-year colleges. A girl who made the same transfer as Glenn agreed that students used the public school for many purposes. It was for some "a playground, a social place. Many people go there to have a good time." The private school was in contrast simply "a school, a place to study and to learn."

The difference in purpose was what drew Glenn to one school and Carlos to the other. Carlos felt constricted, babied, and spoon-fed by endless private school rules and expectations that constrained his freedom. Self-directed and academically talented, he prized the choices that the neutrality of the public high school made possible. The very absence of a single purpose allowed him to make his own way. And he had suffered no apparent ill effects from the move to the public school, since he was part of the top-track specialty shop where peers and teachers were willing and able to work hard and successfully. He was glad to get out of the private school but asserted that students without his drive or ability would be better off there.

Glenn, who was just this kind of student, readily agreed. The private school environment was a "pampered" one, he admitted, but also a "perfect" one for him. At the public school, "to do well you have to work harder to learn." It was easier to learn at the private school because "you don't have as many things to overcome." People like himself — not everyone, not a supersmart boy like Carlos — had a better chance to learn if they attended a school which made unmistakably clear that the purpose of being in school was to learn. The boys agreed that common institutional purpose could be either stifling or the key to growth. It depended on the student. Neither school was right for everyone, so it made little sense to argue in the abstract about which school was better than the other.

Agreement about school purpose is especially important for average students. But many teachers accept as inevitable and desirable the neutrality of the shopping mall high school. It is the price that has to be paid to accommodate the entire spectrum of adolescent values and capacities. One teacher admitted that his school had no clear commitment to learning, only a clear commitment to accommodating student diversity. Although personally committed to academic values — he was a first-rate teacher of top-track students — he thought the "social gains" made by sacrificing an institution-wide commitment to learning outweighed what had been lost. He would never turn the clock back, and expressed pride that his school had "made enormous progress as a community in becoming sensitive to people with disabilities of all sorts." Tolerance itself was the closest thing the school had to a common purpose. For him this was more than enough. Commitment to other purposes was a responsibility for individual students to assume, not the school.

But this was not enough for parents of average students who sought a supportive atmosphere that placed less total responsibility on their children. They wanted an environment that stood for "a common focus in life or a common goal, that is the goal of learning." One admitted that if she had kept her children in the local high school, they would certainly have learned a great deal about social diversity and "street life." But in the end, she said, "what would they have?" They would learn much of that out of school anyway, and she certainly did not object. But she wanted school to be a different place, a special place that did not mirror the real world but stood for something different — for the importance of learning. She felt that the real world of conflicting values and varying adolescent cultures would confuse and even overwhelm the average and impressionable child; that world would perpetuate unspecialness. She regarded too much diversity and neutrality as a threat to her children, even while she admitted that the shopping mall high school was an enormous opportunity for other teenagers. Parents like her wanted a place apart.

That is why such parents usually approve of symbolic expressions of common purpose. Dress codes, which all the private schools maintain to some degree, are one expression of common purpose. They are most often justified as a way to convey the idea that school is a special place with a special function. In this view, schools are different enough in function from the outside world to demand of students a different *look*. Dress codes are a strategy for teaching that membership in school confers particular responsibilities on all students.

Teachers in schools with a common purpose are more likely to see their institutions as countervailing forces to the outside world. One music teacher, for example, regarded his school as engaged in constant battle against mass culture to "develop taste," a battle that he freely admitted was usually lost. He loathed the idea that high school should be "democratic," accommodating endlessly to the preferences students brought with them from the outside. It should stand without apology for different and coherent values. "Anything that the students are exposed to around here," he said without embarrassment, "are things that the faculty have decided are good for them." His fear was not that a common academic purpose was constricting or elitist. Even with a common purpose, students spent most of their time outside school, beyond its influence. "We have them a very small percentage of their musical lives. The rest of it occurs during the hours when they listen to the radio, television, and ride on elevators listening to music." The school could not exclude pop culture from the home, but it could stand unabashedly for an alternative.

If there are limits on how far a common purpose can extend, these schools nevertheless attempt to exact a time commitment from all students that goes far beyond the voluntarism of the shopping mall high school. Many private school students said that school responsibilities consumed most of their waking hours. "Your whole life centers around school," one student said. One private school went so far as to prohibit students from holding after-school jobs unless permission was obtained from the principal. In another, most students used a portion of their earnings to pay school tuition. Even when they worked, they were meeting school obligations.

These schools and the families that use them often strive for a common moral purpose in addition to an educational one. One institution, for example, characterized its situation this way: "This is an age of changing styles of behavior; however, the eternal truths of honesty, kindness, and fair play do not change. We all need to live within the rules of our society and be governed by firm, consistent, fair, and kind discipline. The responsibility rests with both the home and the school. We want our young people to develop into unique individuals, and we consider the formation of character to be the fundamental duty of the home and school alliance."

Such a statement might seem minimalist and secular to schools with a more specific ethical or religious tradition, but it would have delighted the public school administrator who longed for a moral quarterback. Its importance lies less in the specifics of what good character is than in the assumption that character formation is a proper function of high school and that families and schools have mutual obligations to each other. Sufficient agreement prevailed about moral purpose that a few simple rules did the job. Breaking them was not tolerated; it threatened one's membership in the community. One student visitor to such a school was struck by the presence of attractive plants in a common room "without their being pulled apart or thrown around." A school that had little worry about petty vandalism could afford to upgrade its notions of moral conduct to include, for example, concern for teenagers' "meanness" toward one another.

Whether educational or moral, a common purpose makes the institution *itself* an active factor in the educational process rather than merely a neutral physical setting in which education goes on.

Glenn remembered that when he first went to high school, he kept his elementary school friends and emulated them. They settled for just getting by and he went along. He said he was simply "not strong enough" to resist the peer pressure that sometimes led to cutting classes in order to party at someone's empty house. In his middle-level classes he could "do what I wanted" and still pass. The peer group pushed him toward avoidance. But in the private school the peer group changed. There, "rowdy" friends were replaced by those who "all do their work." He didn't have to deal with friends who were "real frustrated, and they don't know what to do, so they take it out on the building and each other." He didn't have to overcome the tug to associate with rowdy but enjoyable peers because they were rarely there. Any high school, he said, had a real advantage if most students were there to learn.

Many unspecial students who switch schools as Glenn did say that the biggest difference is the impact of peer pressure. And many parents say that the most important thing they are purchasing in private school is a supportive peer group. Peer pressure is never absent, it is just different. Left to their own devices, students like Glenn would prefer not to work. One said, "If people around you are not working, are not doing their homework, you feel, 'Why should I?' " But in his private school "I feel you've got to keep up with your peers, since everyone else is working." At one girl's old high school "the competition is to see how little you can do; here it's to see how good you can do." And another student stressed the big difference between school pressure and peer pressure: "When I came here I got involved not because you have to but because that's what everyone else was doing and I did not want to be out in left field."

"The people here are safer," one boy began. "Safer as far as your peace of mind in learning, since you're here to learn. You go to school to learn." Another boy who was listening pressed for clarification. "You got cut down, is that what you're saying?" The reply was, "I got ganged up upon . . . But in this environment you're not exposed to a crowd that's going to be harmful to you . . . There's the same motivation in everybody. Everybody has to work here. Whereas you have to make a decision in the public school. 'Am I going to work or am I going to lay back and be

202

with the crowd, because there are both groups?' Whereas [here] you really don't find both types of people." He did not say he worked because he wanted to learn. He did not say that most people did not work in public school. He said he worked now because he feared rejection by his peers if he didn't.

The point of these accounts is not that positive peer pressure is the exclusive preserve of private school, since it is not. The point is that, for average students, the potential effects of negative peer pressure are minimized by the existence of a common purpose. A common purpose understood by students protects them from their own inclination to avoid rather than engage in learning. The peer culture supports a willingness to work that many students say is more important than the capacity of teachers to motivate them to work. One way that a common purpose is sustained, therefore, is by the students themselves and the families in back of them. Those that value a common purpose of a particular sort seek a school that proclaims that purpose. Like finds like, and diversity of values is minimized at the beginning.

Further, parents of private school students know that they have more inherent power than they would have if their children were in the public high school. Even though their children are often educationally average, the school cannot ignore them. Their children are a crucial constituency because the parents are primarily responsible for the school's solvency. They — not the local community as a whole and the taxpayers of the state and nation — pay most of the bills. They are the true consumers that the school must satisfy.

And since tuition, in general, is the same for all students in a school, all have the same claim on the school's resources. One private school teacher hated the elaborate written reports on all students which he had to prepare several times a year, but he did it — because "that's what the families are paying for." When a group of parents protested what they considered lax discipline, the principal called a special faculty meeting to say that if teachers couldn't enforce the published rules — considered to be a contract between school and family — they should resign. The notion of a "contract" makes the school's relations with families just as central as its relations with teachers.

Students often have similar expectations. A teacher who recently switched from a public to a private school remarked, "Here the students expect competence. They expect you to go beyond the classroom. If they need extra help they expect you to give it. They expect you to be there when you need some assistance. But in a public school system they don't. There, they think it's wonderful if you're competent. They appreciate that and appreciate it when you go beyond." At times student expectations in private schools verge on a sense of *entitlement* to competence, but most teachers do not resent that. It comes with the territory and is not the same thing as selfishness or arrogance. Indeed, student and parent expectations often make teachers feel respected and valued. Parents and students not only help sustain a common purpose, they help sustain an even application of that purpose to all students by all teachers.

But how do schools themselves create and sustain a common purpose rather than a neutral, do-it-yourself environment? One important way is through faculty appointments. It is rare for a public high school principal to regard a "shared view of education" as a significant criterion for teacher employment, but common for a private school principal to do so. Educational and often moral values — such as beliefs about what knowledge, skills, or environments are of most worth, or about the time commitments involved in teaching, or about the importance of the unspecial — are rarely important qualifications for appointment in public high schools. Indeed, in cities of several high schools at a time of declining student enrollment, principals have remarkably little discretion about who their teachers are. Seniority is the main criterion. Any search for purpose in such institutions must occur *after* teaching appointments are made.

In contrast, the private schools replace technical professional credentials — credentials that by definition are intended to be appropriate in any school — with a less formal set of credentials that are specific to a particular school. In this way private schools curiously perpetuate an older public school tradition, associated mainly but not exclusively with smaller towns, which cherishes the values of teachers as much as formal professional credentials. If embittered teachers like Mr. Cleveland justify passivity by arguing that teaching is not sufficiently a profession, many private school principals believe that it is one to too great an extent already. They see in the idea of professionalization an exclusive focus on technical proficiency, which neglects the idea of teaching as a "calling" or "vocation" where values, commitments, and even personality should assume a significant place.

Parents who patronize private schools often speak favorably about the values of teachers — they are "responsible, knowledgeable, and interested in students," and they "respect" students — and also speak about a greater across-the-board consistency in private school faculties. It is not that the private schools have more brilliant teachers, but that extremes in faculty competence are less apparent there and a sense of common purpose more apparent. For parents of average students, no value is more important than the willingness of good teachers to work hard with their children. Mr. Snyder, the teacher of Emerson, was exactly what they wanted. "The most interesting" students for him were always "the ones at the back of the room with their arms crossed and their feet up and saying, 'Teach me, I dare you.' When I see one of those I try not to smile because then I give it all away." These were the "kids who initially don't want to have anything to do with English . . . the middle group who are more prone to frustrations and whatnot." They were very hard to teach — getting even the most proficient students to engage with Emerson was never easy — but Snyder wanted them in his classes: "We can do something with these kids that they wouldn't be able to do on their own, and it's very satisfying."

A widespread belief in private schools is that a sense of community within the faculty is essential to maintaining any common purpose. Although departmental fiefdoms are common there, many teachers spoke of wider academic colleagueship. Departments heads talked more with each other about educational issues, and within departments teachers talked about education as well as about book allocation and schedules. Faculties met together more often, and had considerably more power than public school faculties. Even though private school principals also had more power than their public school counterparts — on teacher appointments, for example — that power did not come at the expense of faculty educational authority. One teacher explained the existence of colleagueship simply by the fact that he respected his colleagues. They shared his educational values and were, in general, people he enjoyed being with.

One school communicated moral values, a principal said, by faculty example. The key was "what we do and how we treat [students] in the school environment" rather than "making speeches" about proper conduct. Teachers and families could agree enough about conduct to enforce, for example, requirements that students themselves work in the lunchroom and help keep the school clean.

A single, well-understood purpose is further sustained by deliberate efforts to strengthen the idea of a community of school and families working together for a common end. The "alliance" between family and school is a fundamental institutional treaty that requires constant effort to maintain. "It's a family-oriented school," one teacher pointed out, "and you get all members of the family together as often as possible." Through potluck suppers and other devices, these schools make the same effort to involve parents which is usually associated only with elementary education. Mr. Snyder made clear that family involvement included classroom learning. "I encourage the parents to read along with the kids so that they can pick up on the discussions in class at home . . . It's a nice thing to [get] into raging arguments in class which go right home to the dinner table and then come back the next day."

Even within private schools the effort to create and sustain a common purpose associated with learning is sometimes resisted and resented. Many recognize the tradeoffs that are made. "The environment we've created here," one student said with deep ambivalence, "is such a bubble. It's such a perfect bubble . . . It's just such a perfect environment sometimes you get really protected and sometimes people don't know how to deal with the things in the outside, the real world." An administrator complained that the common purpose of his school was only "to hold back time, to inoculate these children in some way from having to come to grips with everything the twentieth century means." He wanted more diversity of purpose, more freedom for students to learn by making mistakes, less protection from temptations. He wanted to burst the bubble, and he envied the spirit of the shopping mall high school.

Carlos agreed and switched schools. But no one environment works best for all. For Glenn, a sense of common purpose was constructive. Its existence shaped the terms with which students and teachers came together. It reduced the number of areas open to private negotiation. Some treaties had been arranged outside and prior to classroom life. They were formal rather than tacit, and reduced his freedom to maneuver. That is what he, his parents, and similar teenagers often want — protection from disabling distractions and above all from the fate of neglect. More specifically, they want, beyond a common commitment to learning, a common commitment to push and personalization.

Push

Glenn's private school attempted on a day-to-day basis to achieve its purpose through what he called "the system." The system was different from the informal but effective peer pressure that partially explained his willingness to work. It was the formal set of rules, regulations, and expectations by which the school expected all students to abide. The system was how the school pushed its students. There were clear expectations, for example, about the amount of homework Glenn normally had per night, and even regulations about personal neatness. At the beginning he had been "astonished and outraged" when teachers told him, at age sixteen, to "tie your shoes. Tuck in your shirt."

More palatable were regulations that minimized "disruptions." He appreciated the infrequency of fire drills and the absence of long waits on line for lunch. Eventually he "learned how to play the game" and worked much harder than he had before. His grades, however, were no better, since it was far harder to get an honors grade of B than in his former high school. What he got for his hard work, be believed, were not high grades but "study habits" that he hoped would stand him in good stead later on.

Carlos had loathed the system. He had been required, for example, to hand in all his math homework, which seemed to him ridiculous busy-work because he could learn the material without doing every problem. In the public school he was now free to do it or not. Since it was neither collected nor corrected, he did it only when he needed to practice something difficult. He liked the attitude of top-track teachers who assumed that intelligent students should be able to figure out what they needed to do to learn. In the private school, Carlos said, homework was often assigned, collected, and corrected merely to inculcate good study habits. Glenn had mentioned study habits as a positive educational outcome, but Carlos asserted he knew how to study and had the track record to prove it. Instead of being "spoon-fed," he now had to assume responsibility for his own learning. At the private school, "they tell you all the tests you're supposed to take, what you're supposed to do to get into college, whereas here you're kind of on your own."

The educational push on Carlos was self-imposed rather than mandated by the school. And his assessment of the two schools' different approaches to push was confirmed not only by Glenn, but by others in a position to know. An administrator in Carlos's present school lamented that "we are really ignoring the middle range of kids who are getting C's and who could be getting B's if someone pushed them." He volunteered that those kinds of kids were usually better served in private schools. Two girls in the same top track as Carlos said, "If you try in a public school you can get just as much out of it as you can in a private school. Especially here because . . . it is a very good school. But in a private school they really sit on people and make you work." One of Glenn's teachers, when asked what might happen if a student didn't follow the system, replied, "The shit would hit the fan pretty quickly."

Differing attitudes toward push do not make one school better or worse than another, but raise in many parents' minds the question of which approach best matches the needs of particular children. One such parent had always taken public school for granted, but a change in circumstances made private school a possibility for his daughter. Partly out of curiosity, he had her take the required admissions test and was surprised to learn she did poorly even though she always got A's and B's in her classes. Perplexed, he asked one of her teachers how she could get honors grades but perform ineptly on the test. The teacher explained that her section didn't deal with the materials covered by the test. Only the other section did.

Suddenly the light began to dawn. "So she gets a B or an A but that B or A is relevant to her group," her father said. It had nothing to do with what she really knew or could do. The private school accepted her and, after a year, he was generally pleased. Her grades had plummeted, and she spent vastly more time on

208

homework — three hours a night — than ever before. The father noted that she spent more time on homework than some of the quicker students precisely because she received the same homework as they did. It just took her a bit longer. Indeed, the only students in the school who admitted doing less than the expected two to three hours of homework a night were those near the top of the class.

To her father the lesson was clear. In the new school, "even at the lowest level, you are forced to work." Even at the lowest level, there were standards similar to those for the more proficient. Standards were evenly applied across the board. Yet he didn't want to be misunderstood. "The point I'm making is that it is available in the public schools and you can get it. But having it in this situation here, it is more driven home." He recalled his own experience. "It's just like in the Marines. Yeah, everybody can get in shape, but when you're in the Marines you don't have an option. You get in shape. [Here] they don't give you that out and I guess that's sort of the comparison."

He also understood the costs. It wasn't easy to work harder than ever before and receive non-honors grades as a reward. And working hard in school was not the only important thing in life. "There's a childhood here too," he said almost wistfully. But she was learning more, and no stigma was attached to being an ordinary student. Everyone had taken the admissions exam and had been selected; everyone in that sense was equally special. One student in the school said, "There's nothing wrong about a slow learner. He just needs a little extra time to grasp some information."

The Marine analogy was well understood throughout the school. Images of strictness and regulation peppered students' talk. They often felt "under constant surveillance." Teachers agreed that students were "hand-fed." "When a kid steps out of line here," one said with perhaps excessive satisfaction, "the situation is going to be dealt with." An administrator explained that adult push was what parents wanted. They frequently told him, "I will put my child here because if you leave him in a total free environment, if you don't put the pressure on him, and if you don't constantly ask him questions seeing if he's prepared, he's going to flounder a little bit because I don't think he's self-motivated." A nearby high school was deservedly proud of its high achievers, but at the same school students could graduate "and there is no guarantee that they'll be able to write a coherent paragraph." His school, he asserted in contrast, was "able to make demands and follow through" with all its students. It could assure parents that graduates would have a good foundation in speaking, writing, a foreign language, and mathematics: "It's practically a guarantee." An approving parent, with one boy in the honors track at the nearby high school, sent a second son to the private school after learning he was "floating downstream with the crowd." The main difference between the two institutions was the relentless push exerted by the latter on "each student to perform up to their potential."

How do such schools apply push in a uniform manner? One important part of their "system" is a simpler, leaner curriculum than that of the shopping mall high school. In one private school, for example, everyone took the same four-year English sequence, though an Advanced Placement option was available for seniors. Although several consumer-oriented English electives such as "Psychology in Literature" were offered, these could be taken only in addition to the required sequence rather than in place of it. Three-year required sequences in math and foreign languages were similar to the English sequence in that final-year options recognized differences in ability and interests. In language, for example, one third-year option emphasized conversational skills for those who probably would not go on in the language and wanted only speaking ability. An analogous option in math emphasized computer and statistical skills for those with limited mathematical dexterity. There was also a two-year history sequence and a two-year science requirement. Additional required courses in the arts, religion, and physical education — not all of which were specific course rather than area requirements — meant that 90 percent of the units needed for graduation had to be specific courses or from specific areas. Choice was by no means absent — there were three foreign languages to select from, and work on the newspaper carried course credit — but it was limited. Nor were decisions about the choices that did exist placed wholly in the hands of students. Teacher-advisers "won't wait for you . . . They'll go to you and say, 'What's going on? Why aren't you doing better?' They don't pamper you, but they seek you out," one student said. Push about which courses to take was almost as important as the push inherent in a limited curriculum.

In one sense, schools with a limited curriculum deprive students of the greater variety of educational opportunity available in the shopping mall high school. Talented in science and math, Carlos accurately observed that he could delve more deeply into those fields in the public high school because more advanced courses were offered. But those opportunities are often deceptive for average students. A French teacher in Carlos's school told a visiting private school senior that her Achievement Test scores in French were lower than those of any student taking senior French in the public school. The teacher's intention was to celebrate the academic excellence of those who took advanced French as seniors, a source of considerable departmental pride, but he was also saying that students with the visiting girl's scores simply didn't take senior French in his school. Unless they were especially talented, they dropped out or were counseled out. For her, the opportunity to continue taking a subject that she enjoyed but did not excel in was at the private school. There she was encouraged to go on even though her performance was not distinguished.

The encouragement of continued participation in activities deemed educationally beneficial extends in most private schools to the extracurriculum. It is routine for large numbers of their students to remain at school, engaged in some sort of activity, until late afternoon. Curiously, participation in sports often seems more pervasive and less voluntary than in the shopping mall high school. Students are expected to be participants and performers rather than spectators. Sports and other activities are viewed as training not only in self-esteem but also for a life of participation. The reason that Carlos's private school orchestra did not get invited to Europe, in contrast to his public school orchestra, was that it contained many members who liked to play but were not that good. But they played. Athletic teams were also not just for the talented. The mother of the unspecial basketball player was perfectly willing, as was the boy, to trade benchwarming on a good team for starting on a less skilled squad. He wanted to play, and the private school cared deeply about developing the habit of active participation rather than passive spectatorship. Even the athletically unspecial might have their chance. This too was a form of institutional push.

Beyond the shape of the curriculum, push is promoted by explicit rules governing classroom obligations. The rules are designed to apply to everyone, and guarantee that comparable if not identical expectations are imposed on both the most and the least swift. Neither students nor teachers have much room to negotiate private treaties. One teacher summarized, "There's a constant reinforcement of what's happening." In one school, for example, homework was assigned on a weekly basis. The assignments were passed out — students did not write them down in class — and were also reported to an administrative office at a stipulated time. The homework expectation — a minimum of thirty to forty-five minutes per academic "solid" per night — was a school rule distributed in writing to students and teachers alike. The school further stipulated in writing that "homework assignments should be given over the weekend and should be the equivalent of one night of homework."

Published rules also governed dates for major tests and papers, the purposes of final exams, and grading calculations. Similar rules addressed not only the consequences of student misconduct (one class cut yielded three hours' detention) but faculty responsibilities. The latter covered the amount of time permitted between the submission of written work and its corrected return, and the duty of teachers to be at once well-prepared and well-groomed. Sometimes teachers regarded themselves to be as spoon-fed as the students. They both worked in a "controlled environment." They were pushed too.

Often the most informed descriptions of this aspect of push were given by students who had resisted it and had withdrawn to the shopping mall high school. One who had switched to an accelerated public school track said it was easier there because "teachers don't pressure you to do things like getting your homework in." In her old school, "they track you down . . . but they leave you alone here. It's up to you to get your homework in, or your grade will go down. It's also up to you to learn . . . You can get a good education here, but you can also blow it. At [the private school] they told you you had to do it. All the rules were there for you to follow and you had no choice of classes . . . They told you so

much about what to do that you didn't have to pay attention. If
you didn't get something in, you didn't have to worry because you
knew they'd track you down." Another who had switched emphasized that "nobody really cares" if he worked or not in the public
school, whereas he used to be "pestered" if he was late with anything.
He liked the new arrangement and so did his teachers. It did them
"a favor" because "they have so many students so they have to
leave a lot up to you." Further, it was more like "real life because
you are in charge of yourself. People don't tell you what to do."

Average students like these were also happy that their grades
usually went up when they changed to the shopping mall high
school even though they worked less. And often students who stay
rather than switch schools are ambivalent about this tradeoff.
"Sometimes I would like to change some of the pressure," one
ruminated. If somehow teachers could genuinely motivate everyone
— "get 'em really interested" — then all kids might actually learn
more. But few teachers in private or public schools could do that
by themselves. The reality was that most students preferred to do
other things than schoolwork, even when taught by very skilled
teachers. So "if you remove the pressure, people just don't do as
much. I know I wouldn't. I wouldn't work as hard." In the end
he was glad things remained as they were: he needed to be pushed.

Inside the classrooms of private schools, actual pedagogy tends
to be uncomplicated and no more imaginative than in shopping
mall high schools. One private school teacher noted that her school
was "rather old-fashioned in its approach to education, and that
doesn't bother me very much. There are no gimmicks. The classrooms are straightforward and disciplined. They expect homework
and paying attention in class. The one disadvantage is that it's a
bit of spoon-feeding." Indeed, private school classrooms are notable
for their remarkable resemblance in teaching procedures to public
school classrooms. It is as if "the system" that governs everyone's
behavior when they *enter* the classroom is more important to student
learning than the particular skills a teacher exhibits *during* the
class.

Carlos and Glenn agreed there were significant differences between the private school system and the neutrality of the public
school. But they also agreed that the quality of the teaching was

about the same. And while parents often praised the commitment of private school teachers to average children, they rarely mentioned teaching skill per se as a factor that differentiated the two kinds of institutions. They did not expect individual teachers to motivate children to work as much as they expected the system of push to do it.

Good and less-good teachers can be found in both kinds of schools. If the private schools happily have their Snyders, the public schools happily have their Zukowskis, Fishes, Glynns, and McBrides. The value of a system of push is that it compensates somewhat for inevitable differences in teaching skill. Not every private school student can get a Mr. Snyder for English, or every public school student a Ms. Fish. But the expectations set by formal and informal rules make up for some of these differences in the private schools, while no comparable mechanism reduces the chance of getting an avoidance treaty in the shopping mall high school. This is why students who switched back and forth between private and public schools generally (but not exclusively) reported working harder in the private school, even when their public school experience was in the accelerated track. The differences were usually attributable to the system. "Participation" is paramount in private schools; that is a crucial treaty. "There's no way that you can come to class unprepared, withdrawn, or not paying attention," asserted a private school principal, "without having some notice taken, because you're bound to have to participate." Students who switched one way or the other agreed that in private school they participated more in class discussions, read more, wrote more, and spoke more. The more they were asked to participate, the more intensity a class contained. The frequent difference in classroom expectations for average children — not necessarily a difference in teacher skill — was between "completion of assignments and talking about the story rather than analyzing it"; more specifically, between questions like "Where was the house located?" and "Do a psychological analysis of a character's motivation."

"We want our kids to grow," one teacher said succinctly, "and one of the ways they grow is if you throw tasks at them." Students in the middle grew best, in this view, not by exercising free choice and facing the consequences but rather by making habitual the responsible behavior that was forced upon them. Another teacher believed that rules which seemed oppressive on the surface actually gave teenagers "the freedom and responsibility to be themselves, and to act according to their own dictates. They don't have to feel unprotected. They don't have to feel that the other kids will force them to be wise or smart-alecky." Stiff rules, paradoxically, were designed to liberate.

Virtually nothing about push was directly concerned with making learning pleasurable. The kind of engagement that most private school classes emphasized was academic engagement rather than intellectual engagement. The distinction was important. Students worked to get good grades and scores, to become a "perfect work machine." Good study habits, more than enthusiasm about the content of classes, was what most parents wanted and what most schools sought to provide. Private school teachers complained no less than their public school colleagues that "students today are more passive and unquestioning than they were in the sixties and seventies, and that's both good and bad. They are more productive but also more acquiescent and not probing." They wouldn't experiment or take risks "when they may get a D and that D goes on the transcript." Carlos disliked what he considered a near anti-intellectual attitude in the private school. His was a harsh overgeneralization, but it contained a kernel of truth. It is enough for most private schools to engage the unspecial in learning. Institutional push does not require them to enjoy it.

Personalization

For Glenn and other average students, the sometimes relentless surveillance of adult push was softened by a complementary institutional commitment to providing genuine personal attention to everyone. Personal attention, he thought, explained much of his school's ability to get him to work and learn. Carlos made the same point. Teachers, he recalled, would always "rush to help you" in the private school if you were not doing well — "that was part of their job." Teachers in the public school would help too, of course, but there, you had to reach out to them. Carlos didn't mind that arrangement at all. He noted, for example, that even though his classes were now somewhat larger than they had been in the private school, that fact made little real difference. He asked and answered questions in class just as frequently as before, and arranged outside conferences with his teachers just as easily as before. If he took the initiative, attention would be paid.

Personalization is as important as purpose and push to parents who use private schools. They noticed in these schools, at least for their children, a different kind of teacher-student relationship than they had had before. "They talk to each other, they eat in the same cafeteria. They relate to each other as individuals . . . They deal with each other with respect, which is a very important part of learning respect for one another." Public school teachers often said the same thing. Miss Lowell and several colleagues believed that, for the unspecial, the most significant difference between their school and a private school was that teachers in the latter "are being paid to know your kid." Another teacher said the main difference between his school and a private school was "the quality and quantity of personal attention." And a counselor recalled the unrealistic expectations of a mother whose son had recently transferred from a private school. The boy started cutting classes, and the mother visited his counselor to find out what was going on. But the mother, said the counselor, didn't understand "why I don't know where he is all the time." The problem was, "She doesn't understand the role of the counselor."

All high schools profess full allegiance to the ideal of individualized education; it is a pervasive American commitment. But in the shopping mall high school, individualization is usually defined by providing variety and removing barriers to choice. Individualization means the freedom to do it yourself. Except for students deemed special in one way or another, it is usually an anonymous process. Whether by choices made outside of class or worksheets in class, individualization is carried on without much knowledge of the individual. It is almost the opposite of personalization, which is what many parents and students really want. One student said, "I like a lot of attention. I want someone who's really familiar with my work, familiar with what I'm capable of and my style. I want them to have all the information — so that when they approach me, they can do it in the right manner. When a teacher knows you well, they try and stretch you more."

One private school informed its teachers that parents were often inspired to pay large tuitions by "their confidence in the faculty's

216

specific attention to each child's education." It was insufficient to individualize by giving students freedom. "Back work, failed work, and incomplete work are never entirely the student's responsibility, since this school may at any time be asked for an accounting of the measures it has taken to help that student bring his work up to date. No criticism of an independent school is more frequent than the criticism by parents that they were advised too late in a deteriorating situation and that the school did nothing earlier in the way of remediation." The trick, said the principal, was to persuade teachers to put the well-being of all students above every other concern. "Like a doctor or a psychiatrist, they have to be able to say that the patient — the kid — is the only real issue."

It is hard to be anonymous in a private school. The implementation of personalization depends both on institutional structures and on values. Most private schools are small; a senior class of under one hundred is not uncommon. One virtue of smallness is that the same students can be known to teachers who know one another. Teachers can only share knowledge about particular students with each other if they teach them. This shared knowledge was one of the purposes of the Beta program, but in a large high school such a program turns out to be a scheduling nightmare. The possibility of creating a critical mass of teachers who know one another and the same students is further diminished if student transiency or turnover is high, as it is in many public high schools. When students constantly come and go because of the instability of parental employment, even the most heroic efforts to know them are doomed. Of all the external social forces that subvert the aims of schooling, few are more damaging or beyond the power of day schools to remedy.

Smaller classes can also increase the chances of personal attention, but a far more crucial factor is the total student load of each teacher. Small classes are significant in large part because they shape total student loads that are much smaller in the private schools. If a typical teacher in the public schools has a load of roughly 125, the private school teacher usually teaches between 60 and 80 students. The number of sections taught affects student load as much as class size. Private school teachers usually teach four classes, public school teachers usually five.

A final structural feature that affects personal attention is the number of times a course meets per week. Half of the private school major courses met four times a week; only one of the public schools met on other than a daily basis. Thus a private school teacher often taught sixteen classes per week, while his public school counterpart taught twenty-five. The resulting "free time" was rarely used for preparation, which was assumed to be an out-of-school responsibility, but for individual conferences and tutorials that made one-on-one contact a routine part of school life. The private school teachers typically were "not so overloaded that they can't see [students] during their free periods . . . You can't follow through on thirty kids when that's followed by another thirty and another thirty and another thirty." An underlying assumption was that class meetings were but one part of a course, and that the flexibility gained in having courses meet less as a class outweighed any loss. Another assumption was that classes were not primarily custodial arrangements. If students were not in class, they could productively spend time elsewhere in the building.

When student loads were larger and teachers spent most of their school time teaching classes, personal attention had to be rationed carefully. Not surprisingly, it usually went only to students who, like Carlos, took the initiative to seek it out. When student loads were smaller, a common private school assumption was that personal attention was available *especially* to those who needed extra help. Some private schools needed to be explicit about just how much extra help a teacher could reasonably be expected to provide. One stated in its parents' handbook that, beyond a certain number of individual tutorials, the school would provide (for a supplementary fee) tutors for students doing work below C. Since it did not consider C an inferior grade, it made no institutional effort to secure tutors for those working at or above C level.

The most decisive pedagogical interventions for the unspecial can often be found in this shadowy area of out-of-class extra help by teachers or tutors. It is rarely noticed, since its existence is unusual in most schools and sometimes involves an extra outlay by parents already paying substantial tuitions. But personal attention in the form of direct coaching is often mentioned by average students as the most important reason for improved performance.

Personalization is further implemented by specific procedures that are sometimes dependent on small student loads and sometimes not. It is routine in many private schools, and virtually nonexistent in public schools, for parents to receive written comments (as distinct from letter grades) several times during the school year. Often these are accompanied by a summary written comment from a student's adviser, and often a school will mandate that such comments be made whenever there is a significant change in student performance. Even with small loads, this detailed feedback from school to family is enormously time-consuming. One faculty almost revolted when the free day they traditionally had been given to write the comments was replaced by a day devoted to parent conferences. The assumption was that they would spend their evenings writing the comments in addition to preparing for classes.

Feedback among teachers about each student is nearly as important as feedback to parents. Most of the private schools designate faculty meetings during the year when each student is discussed by the faculty as a whole. "By getting together and comparing notes, we can make suggestions to each other about what to do and how to save that student with what we found that works, and so forth . . . It's not a day when we complain about students. It's a day when we probe and try to see what we can do for the students." One transferee from a large public school saw the difference. In the old school, "anything that I did was perhaps praised by one teacher alone but none of my other teachers knew how I was doing in any of my other classes or how I did on the whole. Whereas here, I think everybody knows." The closest analogies to written comments and group faculty discussions in the shopping mall high school are the educational plans and team conferences mandated by law for special-needs students. One public school attempted to make team conferences available to all, on a voluntary basis, but found that the students most in need were those least interested in taking the initiative to arrange them.

A practice that encourages personal attention without any dependence on small student loads is student advising. Advising in the private schools is regarded as an integral duty of the teaching faculty, rather than a task for specialized counselors. Since virtually all professional staff have some advisees, the ratios are usually less than 10:1 as distinct from the 300:1 student–counselor ratios common in the shopping mall high school. The premise is that the kind of advising students need most is not technical counseling or therapy but the time of "an adult friend who pays particular attention to an individual student." The adviser was "not expected to be a master of counseling techniques or to handle serious, deep-seated problems." Instead, he or she was simply a "ready listener" whose expertise was "common sense delivered in a caring, unthreatening way." Elsewhere, advisers were told to know students by "listening, by keeping in touch with teachers, by going to games and plays, by caring." The adviser's central task was to establish a genuine personal relationship with an advisee, and to take initiative even when no obvious crises were apparent. One school expected advisers to have met the parents of their charges before one month of school was over.

This commitment to personal attention contained little of the therapeutic mentality so common among those who taught the unspecial in the shopping mall high school. The "adult friend" was not expected to become too friendly. Teachers were warned about creating or imposing "emotional dependence." More to the point was a reluctance to admit the emotional lives of students as a fit concern for secondary education. Teachers could be "friendly, sensitive, helpful" at the same time they admitted not liking "to touch the psychological." *Liking* particular adolescents seemed more important than *knowing* about adolescent development. "I think we all hold to the philosophy," one said, "that good hard work is a tonic, it's a medicine when you're feeling down or low and have some other problems, and that business as usual can often be the most supportive way of going about things." A colleague agreed that "mental and emotional states should be dealt with outside of class, not in class." Even this school's part-time psychologist, charged with dealing with serious emotional problems, resisted the notion of a services curriculum. He even opposed sponsoring groups to talk about social issues such as divorce: "It is not the school's job to be putting together groups of kids to talk about home problems." Expanding the institution's purpose, in his view, weakened it.

Personalization, in short, was not to be confused with sympathy for the full range of issues teenagers face in their lives. School had a more specialized and limited focus. It was an ally of the family rather than a substitute for it. "We're not a trendy school," an administrator admitted. "We don't talk continuously about relevance and about making our primary goal the happiness and emotional well-being of students at every turn." In place of a "preoccupation with self, preoccupation with the latest trends about personal well-being," his school valued "pushing students toward goals they might not achieve otherwise." Sympathy toward the problems of the unspecial was not its style. Personal attention was not synonymous with child-centered education. If feeling successful was important, the success that should be felt in schools was not just any success, but academic success.

Thus personal attention, as applied to the unspecial, is to know them but not make excuses for them. Push is the best therapy, and though teachers need to be "sensitive about how much you should push," sensitivity shouldn't become sentimentality. "Relationships can get in the way when you start feeling sorry for someone because you know him well. You may excuse the weaknesses or you don't want to hurt them. In this way you can impede their learning." Push is not antithetical to personalization in the private schools. The two go hand in hand.

But the private schools' unapologetic amateurism in how personal attention is conceived ("common sense"), as distinct from any psychological orientation, makes a surprisingly small impact on classroom practice itself. Despite the commitment to personalization that is at the heart of market appeal, actual classroom pedagogy does not differ from that in shopping mall high schools. Teachers lecture just as often and conduct teacher-dominated discussions just as frequently. Classes, though usually arranged to minimize students' hiding from the teacher and one another, are no more likely to emphasize the students' responsibility for each other's learning. Politeness and individual participation are the most conventional treaties. And despite their concern for knowing individuals, teachers are rarely interested in exploring whether psychology and psychometrics provide any diagnostic tools to reveal differences in learning styles. Generally suspicious of psychology, the private schools rarely imagine that it might be harnessed to their interests. Personalization is at once extensive and confined.

Persistent Unspecialness

Modifications of the shopping mall high school that emphasize purpose, push, and personalization work reasonably well for many average students like Glenn. They respond favorably to environments where it is not all up to them and where education is there regardless of whether they want it. At the same time many very special students like Carlos profit enormously from the shopping mall high school. Both boys are lucky. Both had the opportunity to choose among very different kinds of schools, and both seemed to have chosen sensibly. But the grafts do not always take, the matches do not always succeed.

If Americans are beginning to accept that there is no one best educational system for everyone, they must also accept education's present inability to find a workable school environment for every adolescent. Even when the will and the resources are available to seek the right match, the end result is sometimes failure or ambivalence. This is a sobering lesson that private schools can teach to anyone who believes that the central characteristics of these schools make private schooling a universal cure for educational unspecialness. And since private schools are so much more dependent on consumer satisfaction than public schools, it is also a sobering lesson for themselves. Consider the very different cases of Bruce and Thomas.

Bruce was skilled enough to pass examinations in his private school while also violating fundamental institutional treaties such as completing homework and attending classes. It did not take a therapeutic frame of mind for his teachers to realize how troubled and angry he was. A messy divorce found him living with a stepfather he hated and a family situation from which he desperately wanted to escape. Emotional issues overwhelmed him and neutralized the remarkable personal attention lavished on him by the school (which included professional therapy administered inside and outside the school).

Peer pressure, rules, and nurturance had little effect. Further restrictions on his already limited freedom — such as confining him to the main building during free periods so he would not wander outside and (some feared) take drugs — only exacerbated his ditching and his resentment. The impossible home situation rendered laughable the idea of an intimate family-school alliance; it wasn't even clear in his case who the relevant family was.

When all of its systems had broken down, the school began to ponder whether its own institutional treaties might have to be renegotiated. It did not want to lose Bruce, to fail with him, any more than shopping mall high schools wanted to lose students. One senior teacher close to the case wished she could somehow say to him, "Okay, Bruce, we know that you know the joke. You know what we're up to. We can't pull anything over on you. We'll make a deal with you. We will realize that you know the game we are playing and we'll just ask you to cooperate . . . If you don't want to do your homework, don't do your homework." In return, she would want a commitment from him that at least "I'll go to class and I'll get there when I'm supposed to get there." That would be enough. "He really needs to negotiate. I have to provide a way for him to work this through in which he has some power to negotiate." Perhaps, for him, greater freedom was the only way. "For now he has to try it his way. Let's not get in the way any more than we have to." In a crisis her personal commitment to him conflicted fundamentally with what she called the "enforced pressure" of the school's system. Maybe even students who had chosen the school and been chosen by it, she thought, were different enough from each other to render a uniform system unworkable. Maybe he, and others, needed to be held to different expectations on things like homework. Maybe he should have more, not less, choice. "There may not be enough room," she said, "to fail in the right kind of way."

Here was a boy who was not failing anything, but who ditched some classes and did not complete homework. In many schools he would not have been singled out for such major attention. He would have been a classic example of the unspecial. But in this school he was a problem because he was not performing as well as he could, was obviously unhappy, and violated certain institutional norms that were fundamental to its structure. If the system had been willing to bend enough to accept some ditching *and* no homework, in return for order, passing grades, and reasonable attendance, perhaps Bruce might have been held. If it had allowed more flexibility in curriculum choice — Bruce loved music and would have spent far more time with it had he been permitted — then perhaps he could have been held. But in the end there were limits beyond which the institution would not negotiate, and he dropped out to go on the road with a rock band.

Thomas, in contrast, had dutifully played by all the rules. His presence in the private school, his mother said, was a family decision based on the hope that the push and attention he received would enable him to perform to his limits and improve his self-esteem. And so he struggled year after year to get C's and some D's. Near the end the mother admitted doubts. "When," she cried out in frustration, "do you stop giving him C's and knocking him down? When do you start stroking him a bit to give him the bit of self-confidence that he needs?" She knew he received considerable personal attention, but she saw that building self-esteem involved more than just pushing teenagers toward goals they might otherwise not achieve. She wanted some therapeutic sympathy, too.

Thomas had struggled to make the varsity basketball team, his first love and the activity at which he most excelled. But his grades suffered because of the practices so he finally quit the team. Instead, he gave his all to a major senior paper that his mother claimed would have been a straight-A effort in the regular college-prep track of his local high school. But it received a C. The teacher's final comment on it — it had been very thoroughly read — was, "This paper is written so well that I cried that I can't give it an honors grade."

The grade and comment "took the stuffings out of him," and his mother as well. Why, just this once, couldn't the teacher have eased up? she wondered. "When is somebody going to go up to Thomas and say, 'You did a beautiful job this year' on something?" She complained to the principal, not because she wanted the grade changed — that would do no good — but because she wanted to vent her anger. The result was that the final written comments on Thomas's course performance stressed his improvement. She and he appreciated that.

But she still wondered whether the experience had been worth it. Were extended and informed comments ending with a C really better than briefer comments, no summary comment, and an A?

Perhaps the first was better after all. "I think I have seen him by virtue of the struggle come to terms with himself," she said. Whatever the rigors of high school, college would surely be much easier as a result. It was well known in the school that students admitted to even the most selective colleges (which Thomas would not apply to) worked less hard than in high school. But she still had doubts. Thomas had certainly learned much about his limitations. It was less clear from the "struggle" what he had learned of his strengths.

Bruce's school had clearly failed to engage him in learning. Thomas's school had pushed him to his limits, but in the end the benefits were uncertain. Clearly purpose, push, and personalization are not panaceas. Even though the parents might admit that schooling could not wholly satisfy everyone, the fact was that *they* were not satisfied customers. This is a problem all schools face, public and private alike. It is an especially troubling one for schools whose tuition charges imply a near guarantee that everyone will be successful.

But private schools also face a second problem, one that threatens their ability to retain the very characteristics that make them effective with at least many of the unspecial. Internal and external agreement about purpose is crucial to their functioning, but many show signs of erosion of that agreement. They are by no means immune from the broad tendencies affecting public high schools — diversification in the student body, for example. All of the private schools examined had made within a decade major institutional decisions leading to more inclusive student bodies. All had merged with another institution, and in so doing had abandoned more specialized missions in favor of more comprehensive ones. Where once they were single-sex, or boarding, or military, or unambiguously religious, they were now all coeducational, day, nonmilitary, and quasi-secular. Although each school remained relatively homogeneous economically, student backgrounds had diversified along ethnic, religious, educational, and racial dimensions. One had diversified so much that it could no longer take for granted that graduates would immediately go on to post-secondary education. Their faculties had become more diverse as well.

This pluralism brought with it a diversity of values that most of the schools had not known before. Despite the sense of common purpose they all wished to project, doubts about mission accompanied diversity of constituency. One teacher thought the administrators wanted her school "to look right but they're not even sure what that means. A nineteenth-century finishing school, or intellectual, or an academy with soccer team winners and trophies, or what?" In another school an administrator admitted, "I think we're not sure what we're doing. I think some of us think success is measured by that college placement record. I think some of us think that success is measured by the number of students who return after having graduated and say thank you. I think some of us believe that our success is measured by the percentage of increase we get in our salary." In a third school a senior teacher commented, "It's hard for young people to know what kind of values to hold. I don't know what kind of institutional response to make. Thank God we're not a boarding school. I guess we assume that the parents deal with these issues."

One principal of a secular school longed for "a basis of faith around which we can rally," but schools with religious traditions faced the same problem of finding value consensus "in a completely pluralistic community." Even in a school with religious ties, it was not easy to be charged with responsibility for developing moral character. The job "really drains . . . really burns them out," a departing chaplain explained. Some students, parents, and teachers were wholly indifferent to religion and would eliminate it in a moment if they had the opportunity. Others were caught up in the new religious fervor of some Americans and were champing at the bit for more rather than less "soul stuff."

When one chaplain spoke to students on the scriptural passage "Blessed are the pure in heart," a teacher chastised him for not directly advocating sexual abstinence before marriage. The chaplain felt caught in a no-win situation. He didn't want to offend the devout; they were an important school constituency. But he also "wouldn't touch that with a ten-foot pole in chapel . . . Our culture obviously doesn't support sexual purity and I just think it would be an impossible task to do that." Not only did the culture not support sexual purity, neither did the chaplain. He remembered with embarrassment that a popular female teacher had shown in class slides of a camping trip she had taken with her boyfriend. It was well known that the extensively photographed two-person

226

tent used on the trip had been loaned to the couple by the chaplain. Parents who wanted the school to value abstinence could not even assume that the school's moral leader was on their side.

Problems of values consensus were accompanied by growing problems of educational consensus. Some began to regard the simplicity of the curriculum as excessively narrow. At the beginning of a national revival of interest in academic values, one private school teacher asserted that his school instead needed "more courses for living." Sounding like Mrs. Jefferson, he complained, "We don't offer Health here, no Home Economics, no Shop, no Auto Mechanics . . . Life is simply much too academic." Others valued "hiding places" in the curriculum; they were "places to breathe" away from academics, such as Child Psychology or Contemporary Issues.

The idea of push no longer was universally praised. A teacher complained, "We're piling too much on the kids . . . They don't have any time for social life or for relaxing." "Kids have so many worries and complexities to deal with anyway," said another private school teacher who thought her school assigned too much homework. "Things having to do with adolescence, tension before the dance, 'Oh, I'm sick to my stomach because of the dance,' that kind of thing. We've got to remain sensitive to that." At the same time some also had second thoughts about personalization. "We're always in touch with the kids," Mr. Snyder pointed out, but sometimes "the kids feel that there's too much, that we know too much about them." Many students felt "overobserved." There was "no place to get away, no place to be yourself . . . All the teachers know you." One school seemed "too personal. You can't do anything without everybody finding out about it."

The subtle erosion of institutional agreement also found expression in classroom life. Some teachers believed that the traditional treaty — that students would do what they were told — was increasingly being violated. "We can't expect as much of them. They are less willing to study, and I find that I have to push and motivate them in ways that were just not necessary back in the days when you could just give them an assignment and know that they would do it," said one. In the old days kids reacted to a D by crying. "Now they hate you . . . They put the blame on the teacher." The schools were well aware that the incentives that drove families and students to accept institutional treaties for engagement were fragile. If, for example, a more diversified student body began to attend nonselective colleges in large numbers, their agreement to accept an adult-dominated structure might diminish. Pressure for a more varied, relaxed, and choice-based education might rise.

Private schools, then, face several major problems. First, they do not always succeed with the unspecial. Given that their customers are such self-conscious educational consumers, that is a nontrivial problem. Second, the values of those who attend and work in private schools are increasingly pluralistic, thereby confounding the consensus about purpose, push, and personalization which is their major strategy for educating the unspecial. What, if anything, do they do about these dilemmas? They usually take one of two approaches. One is to soften their traditional characteristics and to become increasingly like shopping mall high schools. The other is to eliminate the problems at the source: to rid themselves of unspecial children as quickly as circumstances permit. They become enclaves only for the already talented and committed.

Recall that Bruce's adviser did not want to rid the school of his kind but rather to renegotiate the treaties that students had to abide by. Indeed, experience with students like Bruce helped provoke in her school a "process of liberalization." The principal, responding to a common perception that kids "have no time to breathe," wanted to reduce the "anxiety and tension about college entrance, or College Board scores, or the like." The school subsequently began to relax requirements, increase choice, and widen variety. "We want the kids to begin to take a stronger role in mapping out things that are interesting to them in designing their own curriculum." The ambition, with students like Bruce and also Thomas in mind, was to find something for every student to do well so that "success is a part of every kid's life." The principal explained that "psychological maturity is what we really ought to be working on."

So the therapeutic mentality is present in private schools, too; shopping mall high schools have no monopoly on it. At least to some extent, classroom participation is as much a voluntary student choice as a clear student responsibility. Persuasion by teachers is therefore necessary. "I try to meet them where they are," one private school teacher explained, "because otherwise I would lose them

. . . The staff must be more aware of motivating students and meeting their needs." At times, private school teachers would also like to act more like counseling psychologists than adult friends, but fear they don't know how. Many private schools are gradually increasing the on-site psychological services available to students.

In the realm of moral conduct, a more tolerant neutrality sometimes competes with focused purpose. Schools spoke increasingly of "clarifying" student values rather than standing for anything — and clarification is a form of neutrality. Disagreements about values were sometimes considered as much an educational asset in the private school as they were in the shopping mall high school. "It is hoped that the tensions can be creative and that all may contribute toward each person's spiritual journey," a school serenely announced. The role of religion in one school, according to a veteran who had known a different day, was "more a matter of keeping it in the forefront of our consciousness . . . than acting on it in a particular way." Chapel services were required less often, and were more "philosophical" than "theological." The most that one chaplain could hope to do was find secular proxies for religion that most constituents could support: caring, courtesy, social responsibility. This was hard enough to accomplish. But if he had his choice he would give up the pretense that the school stood for anything in the moral realm and instead work with the minority who cared about God.

These accommodations make the schools who use them more like shopping mall high schools, but there was another very different direction to take. Few private school tendencies are more ironic than the rise of meritocratic admissions policies. Most of the private schools examined reported significant shifts toward a more academically special student body at the end of the 1970s and, indeed, that process continued apace afterward. Catering to large numbers of unspecial youngsters — in talent or motivation — had previously been a necessary consequence of their applicant pools. When the pools enlarged, the schools had more choice about whom to admit. Given that choice, the schools invariably opted to admit as many already-special students as they could.

A principal explained that "our credibility as a quality academic institution is the primary thing at this period in the school's history, at some cost to some other things." At one school, for example, 30 percent of incoming students in 1975 had IQ scores of below 110, and twelve of those individuals were below 100. By 1981 the fraction of new students with IQs below 110 had fallen to 15 percent. The same meritocratic transition had been experienced by many prestigious colleges during the 1950s and by a tiny number of prestigious private schools during the 1960s.

The process was inexorable because educational prestige and all the financial advantages that accompany it are increasingly built not on what schools do with those who enroll but on where graduates go afterward. Schools by the 1960s were judged more on who their students were than on anything else, and this standard grew exponentially by the late 1970s. If the ethos of many private schools — purpose, push, personalization — was built historically from the responsibility to develop to their fullest whoever could pay the bills, that ethos was actively opposed by significant factions within most private schools by the late 1970s. One articulate college counselor defined the combatants. There was an older faction in his faculty — often childless women — "for whom the school was their family." They actually *preferred* an atmosphere where the academic program was little more than "remediation" for "indifferently gifted children." They were committed to an "ethic of sharing and nurture and help along and nudging, and teachers tutoring day and night and giving you tests over and over." They were the true advocates of the unspecial. But, he thought, their time was past and he for one was delighted. "If we want to send these people now to MIT . . . then we have a different act."

People like this college counselor wanted smarter students and a less nurturing, more high-powered faculty. The values of community which the school had held over the years seemed now anachronistic; they had to give way to competitive and individualistic ones. Traditional pedagogies employed for the less swift — such as going over rewritten papers again and again — seemed no longer proud coaching but unworthy "hand-holding and coddling." One teacher sympathetic toward meritocracy but dubious about its impact on his school said, "If we got all these brilliant kids . . . some of these teachers wouldn't be able to handle it. They'd have to find another job. After all, the brilliant student makes more work."

He meant more intellectual work, not more time expended. Getting rid of unspecial students meant cleaning out the teachers too. If nurturing now meant mere coddling, then the coddlers obviously had to go.

One young teacher observed in his own classes the tension between trying to help everyone and being a referee in a competition to sort out life's winners and losers. Teaching strategies designed to help the unspecial, such as rewrites and retests, were often regarded as unfair by the more proficient students, who saw class less as a chance to learn than as a race to be won. His school had quietly abandoned a curriculum effort to design serious courses for the unspecial (such as a language course that took things at a slower pace and gave a half-year's credit for a year's time) because the changing student body made such attempts no longer necessary.

Other younger teachers welcomed the chance to renegotiate classroom agreements. They regarded the tradition of student "participation" as merely a stultifying euphemism for carrying out an assigned task, like "quietly taking notes . . . and feeding back one week later what they have just learned." One teacher who had no use for old-fashioned notions of nurturance in basic skills and study habits wanted in his classes "argument . . . sparks . . . anger . . . terror . . . sadness, frustration, and energy . . . I tell them, 'What you learn in class isn't the end product of your work, it's the starting point. If you finish at the starting point, you're not succeeding.' "

But he couldn't mandate this kind of intellectual engagement the same way the school could mandate straightforward academic engagement through rules about homework. The intellectual intensity he longed for required a different system. It required *voluntary* participation on the part of the student, and the capacity to excite and motivate on the part of the teacher. If he had his choice this teacher would combine both kinds of pulls on private school traditionalism. He would recruit more talented students with the brains to engage in argument and spark, and he would move in a mall-like direction to offer far greater variety and choice. He saw no real conflict between the two pulls. Both could work together. He wanted a school full of students like Carlos, Kara, and Eric and a faculty full of Dr. McBrides.

These private school tendencies are on the periphery rather than at the center. They are minor rather than dominant themes. Perhaps they are straws in the wind, perhaps not. But both pulls have one thing in common: they make the place of the unspecial just as problematic as it is in the shopping mall high school. If the private schools move too far in either — or both — directions, the educational loss to average youngsters will be immense.

The private schools might choose to exorcise a no longer necessary burden. Ordinariness among students, after all, does not create enviable school reputations. The country prefers clear winners. What could be more reasonable, assuming a choice, than not admitting the unspecial at all? Alternatively, they might move toward all the qualities of the mall and the risk that, as they accommodate a pluralistic society, no institutional press will be applied to prevent the student in the middle from being lost. Already there are a few disquieting signs. One private school teacher admitted, "We're good with the very talented and with the kid in trouble. Some kids in the middle, who are not outstanding in any way, can just get lost. We don't get to know them, and it's difficult for them to find recognition here." It sounded too familiar.

5

Origins

ONE THEME of the preceding chapters is that most youngsters who are old enough to be in high school are there, and another is that they are in class, quietly. Teachers and students come to terms with each other in classrooms, and for the most part they do so decently. Accommodations, not exits or rebellions, are the rule. Another theme is that these accommodations vary remarkably. Some classes stand out because students and teachers work hard together, others are notable for the absence of academic activity, and most spread themselves between these extremes. Still another theme, though, is that high school students and teachers generally settle for mediocrity. Most classwork is modestly demanding of energy, minimally demanding of intellect, and utterly lacking in flair. Yet most students say that they like their classes and their teachers, and nearly all teachers claim to like their students and their classes. What explains this seeming paradox? If so many classes are undemanding and uninspired, why do students and teachers seem so satisfied?

Earlier chapters have answered these queries chiefly by pointing to various features of high schools and the people in them: most students' modest interest in academic work; most teachers' heavy workloads; many teachers' modest competence; and most schools' celebration of tolerance, their virtual neutrality about the quality

233

of academic work. But how did high schools come to be this way? Were most students always uninterested? Were most teachers always overworked and underprepared? Have high schools always encouraged or permitted mediocre work? Have there not been school reforms that solved these problems?

This chapter pursues these five questions. I focus first on the earliest four decades of the twentieth century, for that was when America built its system of mass secondary education. Those were years of furious activity for educators — in forty years public high school enrollments shot up from about half a million students to about six and a half million students, and an entire system had to be built to accommodate them.[1] But those were not years of furious controversy about how to do the job. After early arguments, a remarkably broad consensus was quickly forged about what the purposes of a mass system would be, about how schools should be organized, and about what sorts of work students and teachers should do. In the first half of this chapter, I describe this new system and the consensus that it embodied; that view of the foundations of mass secondary education will provide some answers to the five queries.

But the answers will only be partial, because life has not stood still in high schools since the 1940s. Two noteworthy features of the postwar years have been the almost incessant criticism of secondary education and the succession of movements to reform the schools. If the prewar decades were marked by rather broad agreement about the aims and shape of secondary education, the postwar years have been marked by terrific divisions of opinion: about what was right and wrong with high schools; about what should be fixed, and how; and therefore about what the most important purposes of high school education should be. The second portion of this chapter portrays those shoot-outs and tries to assess the effects of criticism and reform.

School Expansion in the Prewar Years

Where did all the students come from between 1900 and 1940? In a 1911 study of New York City high schools, an observer wrote

234

that he was astonished to find that many students had parents who were "struggling for the bare necessities of life." Perhaps they came to high schools as part of "a grand struggle upward," he speculated. "From boys whose parents are struggling with poverty will come successful merchants, lawyers, doctors, college professors . . . From the girls whose parents are working hard to keep the family fed and clothed will come many successful teachers who will in turn repay all sacrifices with later support."[2] This is a familiar story for Americans, and one that has the ring of authenticity: many students went to high school because more education was believed to be a great advantage in the struggle for social standing and economic advancement.

But when George Counts published one of his classic high school studies a decade later, he offered rather a different answer: "There is practically no place in modern industry for a child under sixteen or seventeen years of age." Like many others of his time, Counts believed that economic changes were pushing thousands of children — who would have gone to work a few decades earlier — into secondary schools. He argued that "since there is so much that needs to be done in preparing these young people for the many and varied . . . activities of life, it seems the better part of wisdom to enrich their lives and equip them . . . through the agency of the secondary school."[3]

Counts's view is also a familiar one, though less in the popular folklore of education than in academic arguments about schools. In this view high school attendance boomed chiefly because the economic alternatives to education had diminished, not because youthful hunger for academic learning had grown. Changes in the structure of industry and in technology during the first half of the twentieth century reduced the unskilled jobs, which adolescents had filled. Economic prosperity and later expansion of the welfare state eased the pressures that once made adolescent labor a near necessity for poor and working-class families, and changes in culture and communications made many jobs for which adolescents would once have scrambled eagerly seem dirty, demeaning, or distasteful. Another reason attendance grew is that society encouraged it: by World War II the laws governing work had effectively closed youth out of the market for jobs in manufacturing and for much other

unskilled and semiskilled work. The laws were in part a humane
effort to protect youngsters from exploitation, but in part a self-
interested effort to protect their elders from cheap competition.
Still another reason is that firms gradually raised the entry-level
educational requirements for jobs. Some of this was merely the
fashion in a society that fancied itself "knowledgeable." Some of
it was due to real increases in the skill requirements of some jobs.
And some of it reflected employers' sense that school completion
was useful indirect evidence of character traits that they preferred
in workers: obedience, stick-to-it-iveness, and the like. Teenagers
went to school, then, because economic change had reduced the
jobs they might get, and social and political changes had reduced
their access to whatever jobs there were.

August Hollingshead, a well-known academic, revisited the question nearly two decades after Counts wrote, at the very end of
the 1930s. He studied high school–age youth in a Midwestern city
— he called it "Elmtown" — and emphasized still another point:
Americans had few agencies that helped adolescents to become
adults. There were no generally accepted rites of passage that helped
older children to prepare for adult responsibilities and formally
inducted them into adult roles. Agencies that did such work existed
in most preliterate societies, but the economic changes on which
modern America was built had swept away even the vestiges of
such rituals. In the world that was left, adults worked, children
attended primary school, and adolescents lived in what Hollingshead
called a "no man's land," in between. Virtually the only formal
agency standing in that ambiguous land was the high school, a
relic of earlier times when a few young people used it to prepare
for the pulpit or other learned careers. Willy-nilly, as the number
of adolescents grew and society's capacity to occupy them with
work shrank, high schools were pressed into a new service. They
became the place, in the no man's land of adolescence, "where
the maturing person works out the . . . tasks of freeing himself
from his family, making heterosexual adjustments, selecting a vocation, gaining an education, and — for a considerable percentage
of young Elmtowners — establishing a home of his own."[4]

Hollingshead's account, although not logically opposed to
Counts's, is in certain respects quite different. It pictures high

236

schools as an agency in which teenagers have improvised solutions to the universal tasks of social development, coping there with the loss of other agencies that were once better suited to the job. But both authors agreed on one crucial point: whatever the reasons most students had for coming to high school, a hunger for academic learning was not high on the list. Most of the students who poured into high schools between 1900 and 1940 went because the other things they might have preferred to do a few decades earlier were unavailable, or were unavailable without a high school diploma, or because high schools had become the place where adolescents could park while working out the social problems of becoming adults.

One implication of this view was that vast economic and social changes pressed secondary schools into service as social centers for otherwise unoccupied adolescents. The schools had become the only game in town — the place where one's friends were likely to be, and thus where social life and entertainment could reliably be found. Whatever high schools might have been or might have wished to become, they were forced to solve the social problems arising from the huge pool of surplus youthful labor and from the lack of other institutions that could help.

How could schools solve such a problem? If most kids did not come to school to learn, could they be expected to learn much in school, or to try hard? Observers who studied high schools during the first half of this century gave a straightforward answer: one could not expect much in the way of academic effort. Robert and Helen Lynd's renowned studies, for instance, reported that Middletown's high school students were little interested in schoolwork in the 1920s and 1930s. The Lynds found that even straight-A students in this small Indiana city didn't work hard at their classes, and they reported that only a few students saw learning as a primary or even secondary aim of school attendance. The Lynds also noted that while most students did very little homework, they got through school quite nicely — even in the top academic courses. And the Lynds recorded a common lament: "More than one mother shook her head over the fact that her daughter never does any studying at home and is out every evening but gets A's in all her work."[5] Hollingshead reported a roughly similar pattern. High school students in Elmtown did very little homework: "The high schools' work load is so light that very few students have to study more than an hour or two a week outside of school hours . . . the typical youngster has hours of free time on his hands."[6]

If these accounts suggest that academic work was a low priority in high schools during the first half of this century, it doesn't mean that the schools were trivial. Both the Lynds and Hollingshead, as well as nearly every other contemporary source, make clear that the schools were important. In Middletown and Elmtown, for instance, many students spent an enormous amount of time and energy in socializing, in extracurricular activities, and in sports — even though some students worked at part-time jobs, or in family enterprises, or both. The Lynds listed a veritable cornucopia of nonacademic pursuits that Middletown youth pursued: clubs, dances, band, sports teams, social cliques, orchestra, school papers and yearbooks, drama clubs, class meetings, contests, fundraising for one activity or another, cheerleading, and so on. Adults supported these nonacademic pursuits, especially by boosting sports teams. Sports, and learning to get along, was what Americans really liked about high school, not the academic work. The Lynds found many Middletown adults who freely confessed that they could not imagine their children remembering, let alone using, most of what they learned in school.[7]

If this account of why most students went to school is correct, it is also ironic. We usually think of high schools as institutions that are in charge of students' lives: several historians have told the story of high school expansion as though the schools reached out to enroll and then control millions of adolescents.[8] But what the Lynds and Hollingshead were reporting was a system of secondary education that had in one sense been built from the outside. Schools were deluged with students who had nowhere else to go. Students wanted an undemanding academic program that would not interfere with their personal priorities for work and play. Their parents generally agreed. The schools complied.

There is no suggestion here of a golden age of high schools, a time when masses of students were taught well and studied hard. Nor is there much basis, so far, for concluding that high schools have in fact gone downhill since the good old days. If the 1920s and 1930s were the good old days, they look remarkably like the days we live in. Certainly the complaints of school critics today sound similar to the observations of the Lynds and Hollingshead a half century ago: too many electives, too much nonacademic work, too little homework.

There are elements of success in the story, though: the schools' growth was a great victory for democracy, for high schools rapidly became a mass institution, enrolling by 1940 roughly two thirds of everyone who was old enough to attend. But the story sketched here suggests that the victory was compromised precisely because the schools were democratically enrolled. Mass enrollment and unselective admissions meant that the schools had to cater to what students and their families wanted. These were not selective private schools that could admit the students they wished, to fit the institution's taste for academic work or for students' manners; rather, they were public schools that had to take what they got, and work with it — or so educators thought. Most students seem not to have wanted a heavy academic diet, and in general they got what they wanted. The high schools were doing what comes naturally in a popular democracy: paying attention to their constituents. Neither the Lynds nor Hollingshead found much evidence of community dissatisfaction with the high schools, nor did we find such evidence in the communities that we studied.

But even if Counts, Hollingshead and the Lynds correctly explained why most students went to school (and nearly all contemporary educators agreed with them), does it follow that the schools simply capitulated to students and parents? After all, high school students are not utterly inflexible. In the 1980s there are classes in which quite ordinary students work hard, engage the material, and learn. Is it not possible that there were once many such classes? In fact, American educators argued passionately about what they should expect from ordinary students eight or nine decades ago, as the schools began to grow toward mass attendance. We can tune in on those early debates and learn a little about how high schools responded to new enrollments.

The Early Debates

The arguments began at the end of the nineteenth century, but as a practical matter the public schools' position had begun to take shape before the debates reached full volume. For in the 1880s and 1890s entrepreneurial public educators began trying to attract out-of-school youth into high schools, or to lure established students away from private schools, by offering a variety of "modern" courses. Public high schools began to teach everything from book-keeping and mechanical drawing to French and physics, trying to increase their enrollments by offering the courses that educators thought students wanted. As enrollments grew, more and more schools permitted students to mix modern subjects with the inherited classical diet of Latin, Greek, natural philosophy, and ancient history. Some even permitted students to study only modern subjects.

By the 1890s the high school curriculum had begun to resemble a species of academic jungle creeper, spreading thickly and quickly in many directions at once.[9] This provoked great consternation. Some educators objected because the curriculum seemed untidy. Others objected because the spreading courses made it more difficult for colleges to figure out what their applicants had studied and how well prepared they were. Still others objected because they thought the new courses diluted the quality of secondary education, or because the critics' professional interests were directly threatened. Teachers of Latin and Greek, for instance, were persistent critics of flexibility in the secondary curriculum; they would have limited high school attendance to those who could manage the established program of classical studies.

These worries contributed to a great debate over secondary education, one that ranged over many issues between the 1890s and World War I. One early salvo was fired by a National Education Association panel — called the Committee of Ten — that was headed by Harvard's president, Charles W. Eliot. The Committee staked out the high ground in an 1893 report that argued for both greater quality and greater flexibility in secondary studies. The Ten supported certain recent additions to high school offerings — French, physics, and chemistry, for example — but opposed others, such as bookkeeping and clerical studies. The Committee wanted to simplify high school work and cut back the sprawl of course offerings; it did not want to do so, however, at the expense of those modern subjects that it considered desirable. The Committee wanted to encourage flexibility in high school studies — it argued that students

240

should have some choice about the subject areas in which they would specialize, rather than following an entirely prescribed set of courses — but it rejected the idea that anyone should be free to choose bookkeeping or stenography. The Committee proposed what amounted to a national high school curriculum, setting out the areas of study that would be acceptable, the sorts of courses and subject matter content that seemed appropriate, and even the scheduling of course sequences.[10]

These were bold steps by any standard, and inventive ones, but as a result there was something in the report for nearly everyone to hate. The argument for expanding modern subjects and pruning classical studies drove classicists and their fans into a fury, and these partisans were not impressed with Eliot's advocacy of serious study in science or math. Many were absolutely enraged by his view that students would gain as much intellectually from physics as from Latin. Nor were the advocates of classical studies much mollified by Eliot's eloquent opposition to vocational content in the secondary curriculum. Eliot had argued that all high school students should be educated with equal seriousness in the great areas of human knowledge, and that occupational decisions should be put off until after graduation, lest students from poorer homes lose out. But opposition to vocationalism was nothing new to the classicists, and it held little hope for them when it was coupled with support for other alternatives to their courses. And if Eliot's insistence on equality in secondary education won few friends among traditionalists, it made some solid enemies in the many high schools that were trying to build enrollments and reputations around diversified curricula that included vocational courses. The Committee's report was ingenious, but it managed to offend people on all sides of the high school issue.

As it turned out, not all the enemies were equally important. The classicists' opposition certainly did some damage, but within a few years their ideas and Eliot's were being overwhelmed by a much more radical approach, one that built on the schools' earlier efforts to respond to new students by diversifying offerings. One prominent advocate of this view was G. Stanley Hall, president of Clark University and a graduate of Eliot's Harvard. Hall argued that most of the students then entering high school had little interest in academic work for its own sake, no more for modern algebra or French than for old-time Greek or Latin. He had made the argument dozens of times, but on October 9, 1901, he made it again before President Eliot himself and an audience of New England educators. It was a dramatic occasion, one of those rare debates that lay bare some of the great issues of a time.[11]

Hall said that the high schools should adapt their curriculum to "the great majority who begin the high school [and] do not finish, instead of focusing our energies on the few who get to college." He worried that the curriculum Eliot had advocated would force students to become "disenchanted by difficulty or aridity" or would encourage them to "grow restless because they find other things in their new horizon more interesting." The way to avoid these problems, Hall argued, was to base the curriculum on the "nature and needs" of students, rather than on academic conceptions of subject matter. Hall placed himself among those who "hold that everything in the school — buildings, topics, and methods were made for youth, and not *vice versa.*" And he looked forward to a day when high school studies would be organized around the needs and interests of the many students who would leave high school directly for jobs. He closed with his vision of the future: "When the public high school really becomes, as it surely will, the people's college, permeated with the ideal of fitting for life, which is a very different thing indeed than fitting for college, then secondary education will have become truly democratic."[12]

Hall's argument for a curriculum adapted to what students needed or wanted to learn was presented with forcefulness, but his views were hardly singular. His was only one voice in a rising chorus that demanded either radical revision or elimination of academic courses of study, old and new.[13] He noted that most high school entrants did not graduate, staying two years or less, and that they, like many of those who finished, would go on to jobs that required practical skills and knowledge. What most of these students needed was short courses — one or two years — that would prepare them for the workaday lives they would actually lead, rather than studies that bored them with preparation for a college education they would never get.

Hall and other reformers were mistaken in saying that the inherited secondary curriculum prepared students for college or university study. By even the most generous estimate, only a modest fraction of high school enrollees went on to college at the turn of the century — perhaps 15 percent.[14] But this was not the point to which Eliot chose to respond. He bore in instead on Hall's notion that the high school should distinguish between college-bound and other students, and offer the latter an easier and more practical program of studies. Eliot argued instead that "public high school programs should make as little difference as possible between the studies of a boy or girl who was going to college and the studies of a boy or girl who was not." Eliot defended his view partly with an argument about the relations between school and life: "Human character in the college-trained person ought not to be a thing distinct in the least degree from human character in the laboring classes . . . [for] the intellectual powers which give success to a college student are just the same as those which give success to the manufacturer or the merchant. They are a firm will, good sense, alertness, industry, and high aims."[15] Those attributes, Eliot maintained, would be much better cultivated by an intellectually serious program, equally demanding for all, than by a program that made life in school easier for the children of workers and merchants on the grounds that their minds couldn't manage intellectual work or that their careers would not require it.

But Eliot's position did not rest only on his estimate of how the mind could best be cultivated, or on his ideas about school and life. He opposed Hall's arguments chiefly because they offended his vision of human dignity. All students should be encouraged to take serious studies because, he said, "the longer I live the more I am persuaded that the great sources of happiness are open to every creature." The distinctions among students which Hall proposed were invidious: "We do college life a great wrong when we try to separate it from other human life at the same age. We undervalue that other human life . . . when we think of it as something necessarily inferior."[16]

Between them, Eliot and Hall had politely laid out the greatest issue that divided American educators at the time: could all students be expected to pursue an intellectually demanding program of academic study, or should most be given an easier and more practical curriculum? This question was full of implications for schools and for political democracy, but it was quickly settled — in Hall's favor. Public high school enrollments skyrocketed, roughly doubling every decade beginning in 1890. Educators worried that the new enrollees were less able because they came increasingly from lower-class homes. They saw that many cities, and their elementary schools, were already crowded with immigrants from eastern and southern Europe. Like other Americans, many educators took for granted that the immigrants were intellectually inferior, that they came from racially — which was to say genetically — poorer stock than resident white Americans.[17] This notion even gained support from the work of early educational psychologists, preeminent among them Edward L. Thorndike of Teachers College. Thorndike and other early practitioners of "mental measurement" advertised the virtues of newly devised tests of intelligence for assessing students' capacity for learning. Dozens of studies done early in the century found that, on average, the children of immigrants scored less well on the tests than did "native" white American children.[18] Since the psychologists also held that the tests were good predictors — in other words, that children who did less well on the tests would do less well in school — these results convinced most psychologists and many educators that children's ability to succeed in school differed radically, and that it differed racially as well.

There was some opposition to these notions. Walter Lippmann and John Dewey argued that the tests were crude measures at best, that whatever they measured was very uncertain, and that the doctrine of racial traits was no less problematic for scientific reasons than for political ones. They might have added that the "prediction" of achievement from ability also was questionable, on several grounds. But their voices seem to have been lost in a rush of anxiety about changes in America's people and in her schools. Educators in the first decades of the century could see that spiraling elementary enrollments were already spilling over into high schools, and they correctly expected much more in the near future. Given their assumptions about the mental capacities of immigrants and poor people, it seemed reasonable to conclude that the high schools would have to revise their offerings radically if they were to cope successfully with the newcomers.

Few educators tried to check on the validity of these ideas about high school students' capacities. Those who did check found evidence to the contrary,[19] but no one paid attention. By 1910 educators everywhere were arguing that high school studies should be differentiated, with easier, more practical work being offered to students not bound for college. By 1920 the changes in curriculum, school organization, and coursework were well under way. And by the early 1930s the reforms were firmly in place. A new system of secondary studies had been installed, in which a small minority of college-bound students were expected to pursue intellectually serious work while everyone else was taking courses explicitly designed for these less able, less willing, or less interested. American educators quickly built a system around the assumption that most students didn't have what it took to be serious about the great issues of human life, and that even if they had the wit, they had neither the will nor the futures that would support heavy-duty study.

These ideas seem deeply pessimistic, both about the American people and about the possibility of political democracy, but school reformers in the early decades of this century embraced them in a brightly hopeful spirit. Reformers were convinced that if schools would adopt modern methods and scientific principles, they could do wonders with the new students. The reforms that laid the foundations of American secondary education were an odd, and oddly American, mixture of skepticism about the masses' capacity for serious work, and optimism about how easily schools could turn this poor material to socially useful ends. It pays to look a little more closely at the reforms, for they built the system in which students and teachers still labor.

The New System

One essential change was the invention of a few broad academic avenues within the high schools — curriculum tracks — that were tied to preparation for work. Those students who seemed cut out for higher education and the leadership responsibilities of the professions would enroll in an academic track; they would concentrate on such areas as languages, literature, and science. Those whose futures seemed to hold office work or lower management would enroll in a commercial curriculum; their studies would focus on accounting, clerical methods, and similar matters. Those who seemed likely to move from school to labor in the trades and manufacturing would enroll in one or another vocational program; they would take such courses as drafting or machine work. And those who had no evident destiny, or seemed incapable of settling on one, would enroll in a general curriculum that offered a smattering of studies in a variety of fields.[20] One school administrator summarized the principles of the new order succinctly: "We can picture the educational system as having a very important function as a selection agency, a means of selecting the men of best intelligence from the deficient and mediocre."[21]

This new organization spread very quickly in the early decades of the century. Thanks to several ingenious contemporary studies of high school organization, we can watch things change.[22] In 1906–11 and in 1929–30, nearly all the schools studied had at least one college-preparatory curriculum. Some had two, one to prepare students in the classical subjects and another to prepare those with a taste for science and math. The real changes came in the other courses of study. Early in the century only about one school in six offered a general curriculum, but by 1930 more than five of every six schools had installed a course of study for the uncertain or unspecial student. In 1906–11 half of the schools offered a commercial course of study; by the beginning of the Great Depression all schools offered such work, and several had more than one. In the earlier period only one school in six offered an industrial arts diploma, but by 1930 nearly five in every six offered such a curriculum.[23]

By 1930, then, almost all the schools in this study were offering quite extensively differentiated curricula. The average number of curricula in the schools studied had more than doubled in twenty years. The practical arts curricula (home economics, industrial and commercial arts) had the largest growth — they increased threefold — and the general curricula multiplied by nearly as much. But the average number of college-preparatory curricula had increased only slightly. The author noted that college-preparatory work was not declining absolutely, but argued that "the important point . . . is that other functions of the high school, especially . . . training

246

in the practical arts, have taken on more and more importance."[24]

These changes had several sources. For one thing, they were administratively useful; they tidied up a cluttered and often confused curriculum inherited from the late nineteenth century, when some schools had offered literally dozens of courses of study. The new organization also became a vogue, and educators are no less susceptible to the allure of fashion than anyone else. In addition, ideas about high schools' purposes were changing. Many educators argued that schools had to tie their work to new developments in American society: rapid industrialization, a knowledge explosion, and the efficient style of great corporations. Ellwood Cubberley, one of the two or three most influential figures in school administration at the time, nicely summarized the new ideas. He wrote in 1909: "Along with these changes [in industry] there has come not only a tremendous increase in the quantity of our knowledge, but also a demand for a large increase in the amount of knowledge necessary to enable one to meet the changed conditions of our modern life . . . A man must have better, broader, and a different kind of knowledge than did his parents if he is to succeed under modern conditions."[25]

Cubberley and many like him campaigned to get schools to prepare students for this new world. Those who had the wit and the will for work in the upper reaches of American society would be educated in serious subjects. Others with more modest endowments, or with different ambitions — or, in the case of most girls, with futures that were limited regardless of endowments — would learn the skills required for clerical work or housework, without any education beyond high school. And the rest would learn whatever was needed to prepare for competent work in the manual trades. The gradations of merit in academic studies would correspond to the gradations of skill, power, and status in the occupational structure. High schools would fit the young for their niches in that structure.[26]

This may have an aroma of unfairness to late-twentieth-century readers, but the ideas seemed democratic and progressive to educators at the century's beginning. In 1908 the superintendent of Boston's schools decried the old arrangements, in which schools "have offered equal opportunity for all to receive *one kind* of education."

The problem with that approach, he argued, was that students' abilities and interests differed, and the educational needs of various occupations differed as well. The old schools were single-minded and aristocratic, imposing one classical curriculum on diverse students with diverse requirements. He went on to assert that "what will make them [the schools] democratic is to provide opportunity for all to receive such education as will fit them *equally well* for their particular life work."[27]

These ideas inspired many educationists, but their appeal was not simply ideological. The new doctrine also promised to help solve some of the nasty problems that American school administrators — mostly men — faced on a daily basis. While their heads had begun to dance with visions of an expanding industrial society in which specialized knowledge and technical skill would count, their work was plagued with humiliating evidence of marginality. They wished to become professionals, but salaries were poor. Budgets were slim. The teachers were an embarrassment — poorly educated, mostly female, and drawn heavily from the lower orders of society. And most city schools were just another department of local government, pushed this way and that in painfully unprofessional struggles over patronage, corruption, and machine politics which convulsed municipalities earlier in this century. If schools could be reorganized to train students for the right jobs, school leaders would be at the heart of the industrial enterprise, making key decisions about who would work where, and how well. A new organization for high schools would help to turn educators into captains of industry and respected leaders of society.

School administrators were buoyed by the belief that education paid off, that it increased individual workers' productivity by improving their skills. School would make workers more valuable to employers, and this would raise workers' earnings. In addition, such individual improvements would add up, increasing prosperity overall by improving productivity. The U.S. Commissioner of Education advertised these ideas in the preface to a volume of studies on the "money value of education," which his agency published in 1917: "Comparatively few are aware of the close relationship between education and the production of wealth, and probably fewer still understand fully the extent to which wealth and the wealth-producing power of any people depend on the quality and quantity of education."[28] School leaders all over the country began to use Chamber of Commerce boosterism to convince America — and perhaps themselves — that education mattered.

Their arguments were reinforced by the first blush of enthusiasm for scientific tests of ability. Large-scale tests of this sort had been only recently devised, and were initially used to screen recruits for America's armies in World War I. The results revealed enormous variations in men's ability scores; analysis showed that the average IQ for men in professional occupations was higher than the average for those in manual trades. This finding was naïvely but widely interpreted to mean that occupations had a natural hierarchy of mental ability requirements, and that workers sorted themselves out accordingly. Educators seized on the finding as evidence that brains rose to the top, using it to support the notion that the top track in school would prepare students for the fast track in life; other tracks would fit the less able for less demanding work. Since most psychologists and many educators assumed that individual intelligence was fixed, they slid easily from the idea that tests measured innate ability and predicted occupational capacities to the idea that, if administered to entering high school students, test results would identify those who could manage advanced work and leadership, and distinguish them from those who had the lesser abilities required for labor lower down.[29] Psychology seemed to promise that educators' decisions about students' destinies would be made with the sure authority of science. Economics seemed to show that schools could be socially useful even though most students were intellectually limited. These were encouraging ideas for men at work in a women's field, a comfort for would-be professionals who wished to beat down the evidence of marginality that confronted them at every turn.

A second change, essential to the new high school education, was radical revision of academic requirements. Sorting students into tracks that led to the right destinations was a good first step, but courses that were irrelevant or boring could stymie students and stall schools' efforts to adapt to the new masses. So reformers sought to rid the curriculum of courses they deemed inappropriate for modern youth — such as "dead" languages and foreign history

— and tried to replace them with more modern courses, like mathematics, science, and American history. The battles were fierce, but classical languages and the history of foreign countries were well on their way out of the public high schools' required curriculum by the 1920s. An early 1930s national survey of secondary schools concluded that the old practice of requiring all students to take academically serious courses "is being abandoned."[30] The study reported huge reductions in the proportion of high school students who were taking foreign language courses. This didn't always mean that fewer students were taking those courses, for enrollments were growing like Topsy. But as students poured in, the schools relaxed their language requirements, and a diminishing proportion enrolled. In addition, many schools simply dropped required courses that had recently been staples. During the first several decades of the century, for instance, one third of the schools in the national survey abandoned ancient history. Two thirds abandoned medieval history. And by 1930–31 most senior high school students had to take math courses only if they were preparing for college.[31]

In a sense, then, Mr. Eliot had been on the winning side, for the old classical course of study had lost its hammerlock on high school work. But Eliot surely would have disliked the terms of the victory, for the new courses he had championed — math, chemistry, and physics, for example — had not been big winners. The courses that scored the greatest gains were the very ones he had tried to keep out of high schools: practical and vocational courses, and personal development courses such as health and physical education. Another big winner that Eliot would not have liked was watered-down academic courses intended for students not in the college track. By 1930, for instance, it seems that most high school students took only a "general math" course in the ninth grade, and after that no more mathematics. General math was intended to be an overview of the principles of mathematics, but it was more often a review of grade school arithmetic. Similarly, an eighth- or ninth-grade "general science" course was invented and substituted for the basic sciences. General science offered a smattering of material from all the sciences and was to be taken by students with no academic ambitions beyond high school. It also included personal hygiene, reproduction, and conservation, subjects that its fans thought would captivate adolescents. The course was a favorite of educational reformers, and it spread like a brush fire on a dry prairie. The number of junior high schools that required students to take general science literally doubled in the two decades before 1930. By the beginning of the Great Depression, between 60 and 80 percent of the schools in one study were requiring general science of non-college-bound students.[32] Thirty years before that — even twenty years before — the course didn't exist.

Roughly the same story can be told for offerings in history. As enrollments climbed, the older academic courses — ancient, medieval, and modern European history — either were dropped entirely or were removed as requirements. They were replaced in part by American history, but the big growth item was a new field called "social studies" — an amalgam of sociology, economics, and political science, with some history thrown in. Reformers argued that this new subject would draw on contemporary material rather than on dry data from a dead past. Social studies would focus students' attention on such problems as how local government worked, what the economy did, and how families were organized. Many educators believed that these subjects were more likely to capture students' attention than the Civil War, Teddy Roosevelt's trust-busting, or World War I. In a sample of junior high schools only one or two had required social studies in the 1915–20 period; by 1930 nearly one third required the subject. In senior high schools, required foreign history courses declined precipitously between 1906 and 1930, while courses in economics doubled, and courses in sociology grew from literally nothing to offerings in half the schools studied.[33]

Thus the nature of common requirements shifted quite dramatically during the first three decades of this century. First, schools did away with the old system of requiring all students to take courses in specific academic subspecialties, like physics or history, that built on each other and led, at least in principle, to deeper command of a subject. Instead, most of the new students were given general survey courses. They might have had meat, but got Pablum: not algebra, but general math; not history, but social studies; not physics and chemistry, but general science. The new surveys were both introductory and terminal. They were not a first step toward deeper knowledge, but a passing glance on the way to other, more practical matters.

Second, course offerings were vastly expanded in number, widely diversified in purpose and content, and sorted into tracks that aimed students at different social destinations. The high schools' center of gravity changed radically and quickly. In the period 1906–11 nearly 60 percent of high school curricula were of the standard academic sort; two decades later the academic curricula had fallen to one third of all the curricula offered. Two thirds of the curricula were commercial, general, and trade. The academic sector of high school studies had been cut in half in only twenty years.[34]

Third, academic demands on students were eased. Nearly all the new courses were intended for those believed to be academically less able or less interested, and these courses were specifically designed to be passed. Educators desperately wanted their new students to get by. After all, how could schools succeed in their new universal mission if many students failed? By 1930 radically different standards of academic performance had been established within high schools. One observer who studied English instruction concluded, in 1933, that "in general the trend seems to be away from a required minimum for everybody . . . Some systems have definitely abandoned the effort to bring everybody up to a given level of performance. Others have retained the minimum but have reduced the proportion of mastery to be expected from groups of different abilities."[35] A devastating comment, but one echoed in almost perfunctory fashion by other commentators. By 1930, when high schools enrolled half of those old enough to attend, they had given up the effort to maintain decent performance for all those attending.

These changes amounted to a revolution in high school studies, but it was not a revolution in which existing academic courses were swept away. George Van Dyke showed that the number of academic courses (math, science, English, social studies, language) in the high schools he studied increased modestly, from a school average of twenty-four in 1906–11 to a school average of twenty-eight in 1929–30. But during that same period, nonacademic courses (chiefly household arts, industrial arts, and commerce) grew from eight to thirty-eight, on average.[36] The revolution, therefore, consisted not in an absolute decline of enrollment in the academic curriculum, but in the much more spectacular growth of a much less demanding curriculum for everyone else.

252

Varied Views on Reform

The changes had some arguably positive features. Students did differ greatly in their academic ability and in their interest in academic work, and the new curricula and courses were one way to respond to that diversity. Working schoolpeople and reformers alike stressed that the high schools could not hope to "hold" their clientele, or enlarge it, unless they responded to students' interests. And when students were asked, many expressed an aversion to standard academic courses and a preference for more useful and practical subjects. Some were quite frank about their distaste for all schoolwork.[37] As some reformers asked, was there any hope of keeping such students in school, and ultimately of teaching them something, if their studies did not interest them?

Nor did the changes necessarily imply a fall from grace. One might think, for example, that the curriculum revolution described here degraded the quality of teaching, or that it encouraged teachers to care less about their students. But all the evidence about teachers' classroom work in the late nineteenth century suggests that it was regularly bad and frequently horrible. Joseph Mayer Rice, a shrewd observer of hundreds of classrooms in the 1890s, wrote that in general "the professional weakness of the American teacher is the greatest sore spot of the American schools . . . As a rule our teachers are too weak to stand alone."[38] His contemporaries regularly noted that high school teaching consisted chiefly of students cramming facts from dry textbooks and teachers' lectures. The distinguished American historian Oscar Handlin has argued that in most classrooms of the time, "learning consisted of the tedious memorization of data without a meaning immediately clear to the pupil."[39] There is simply no evidence that high school teaching in the late nineteenth century was, on average, even decent, and thus no reason to conclude that the reforms corrupted desirable standards of classroom performance. In fact, some of the impetus for reform stemmed from educators' wish to improve teaching.

But the changes had a price. For one thing, they channeled efforts to improve teaching into a dangerous path. Instead of encouraging teachers to focus on improving pedagogy in serious subjects, the

253

revolution tied better teaching to relaxed academic requirements and to the development of the practical aspects of academic subjects. Some reformers, chiefly university faculty members, sought to improve the teaching of serious subjects. But the changed standards and organization of curriculum, and the new sense of schools' purposes, pressed high school teachers — and their teachers in college — in the opposite direction.

Another price of the changes was the creation of a climate that discouraged serious academic work. For the new structure clearly distinguished between those who were presumed to be academically able and those who were not.[40] The top tracks were the places in which better work was expected and where it seems to have most often occurred. But such classes were a small minority, far outnumbered by the new vocational, personal development, and academic survey courses designed for the less able or less willing students. Much less was expected there, and students and teachers knew it. In addition, as several studies showed, there were big social class differences between the students who wound up at the top and those who found themselves at the bottom of the high school hierarchy.[41] This stratification of curriculum tracks along social and economic class lines restricted students' opportunities to socialize and helped to define serious studies as the business of more advantaged students.[42]

This organization of an academic institution seems patently self-defeating, for if serious work was not expected from most students, why would they do it? But of course that was the point: most were not expected to do such work. As it happened, the system caused problems even for the few who had been singled out as academic hot-shots. For if schools were designed explicitly on the assumption that most students could not hack serious work, and if all those students and their teachers knew it, how could high academic standards have been maintained among the select few? Wouldn't the indifference to serious work have been contagious? The Lynds and Hollingshead, at least, found that high standards were not maintained in any track.[43]

These seem to be serious problems, yet few educators raised questions about the fairness of the reforms or about their possible effects on teachers' work, on students' performance, or on schools' quality.[44] One reason for the absence of much critical comment may have been the terrific pressure that schools were under to do something — anything — about the huge increases in enrollment. Another probably was that high school expansion seemed to stabilize somewhat education's uncertain position in American society. Salaries had been very low, budgets very tight; and schools' performance had been under attack. Teachers in several cities had been locked in ferocious school wars with politicians and corporate leaders, struggles that sometimes seemed to threaten even the existence of public schools. Against this history, high school expansion seemed positive evidence that America was behind education, somehow. It also meant more jobs for teachers, and in the 1920s it even meant slowly growing salaries. With education on the defensive — the 1920s were years of unprecedented business influence on American life and of business-like critiques of inefficient education — any success at all must have seemed particularly sweet.

A final reason for the lack of much criticism is that educators appear to have sold America — and themselves — on the notion that the reform of secondary education was a great democratic crusade, a sort of academic populism. One early advocate from New York complained about the disparity between the economic realities of life and high school students' academic programs: "If rental is taken as a criterion [of family income] we find a class of pupils, whose parents are struggling for the bare necessities of life, pursuing at school for the greater part the remnants of an aristocratic secondary education." One problem with such a course of study was that it led in a direction that few high school students could follow. "We are preparing for a college to which few will ever go, and for a life of ease and refinement which few will ever enjoy, the greater part of our thirty thousand pupils." Economic necessity would drive most to work before high school was ever finished. There was a great disparity between "the democratic nature of the student body" on the one hand, and the "aristocratic" curriculum on the other.

What would a "democratic" solution be? Some might have said, Break down the economic barriers that prevented so many from pursuing the education that they wanted. But this writer, like scores of his fellows, argued that the solution lay in adapting the curriculum to economic realities: "The necessities demand a short [high school] course, [not] one twice as long . . . The necessities call for a better appreciation of modern social conditions, [not] . . . German or Latin grammar . . . The necessities indicate the advantage of turning boys and girls into some position where they can command respectable wages, [not] . . . Algebra or 'The Ancient Mariner.' "⁴⁵

Thus, making the curriculum of secondary schools easier and more practical was seen as part of a grand effort to break the bad habits of an older day. Secondary education once had been reserved for the few, but reformers wanted to bring the high school to all of America. They wanted to build a curriculum that would appeal to all comers. If high school reform was a political movement to broaden the appeal of education and the power of educators, then the new curriculum was the movement's party platform. Reformers wanted to be sure there was something in it for everyone.

The platform was laid out in an NEA report — *Cardinal Principles of Secondary Education* — that proved to be immensely popular. Democracy in education, the 1918 report asserted, meant education that would help every individual to "find his place" in society, by teaching him the things modern citizens needed to know. What were those things? The report mentioned, first, "worthy home membership, vocation, and citizenship"; then, "good health." Only after these did the report turn to academic work: "There are various processes, such as reading, writing, arithmetical computations, and oral and written expression, that are needed as tools in the affairs of life. Consequently, command of these fundamental processes, while not an end in itself, is nevertheless an indispensable objective." In a democratic education, academic studies would be "tools," designed to advance the other, practical and more important aims of secondary education. As the report noted at another point, these tool subjects should not be pushed beyond the point that they "will show results in practice."⁴⁶

The *Cardinal Principles* quickly became the bible of school reformers. It continues to attract enthusiasts today. It helped to popularize and rationalize the new studies and standards because it identified them with a great democratic advance. Everyone was enrolling, and everyone would find work to their taste.

The association of high school reform with democratic ideals also helps to account for some other changes in secondary schools.

One was the rise of extracurricular activities. Boys' sports were the first wave: between 1890 and 1910, baseball, football, and track and field teams were organized in many schools. Debating, drama, and student journalism (newspapers and yearbooks) also were an early enthusiasm. Then, between 1910 and 1930, public high schools welcomed a veritable avalanche of nonacademic activities: student council, glee club and chorus, band and orchestra, and a clutch of clubs — clubs for academic subjects, clubs for hobbies, special interest clubs, recreational clubs, and social clubs.[47] Some schools even had sororities and fraternities.

These activities were promoted by a variety of groups — everything from local football boosters to religiously oriented professional youth workers.[48] Some fans argued that the General Organization (student government) would provide opportunities for students to be of service to school and community, and would thus promote "character formation." Another booster wrote: "We are not especially interested in the intellectual attainments of the man we meet on the street, in the office, in the theater or at the ball game. We do not care about his classical knowledge when we are closing a business deal with him. But we are tremendously interested in his behavior."[49] The author went on to claim that academic work would not affect such behavior, but that the extracurriculum could. It would offer the "emotional training" that was an essential part of education. A high school principal argued that extracurricular activity "pulsates with life and purpose," while the formal curriculum "owes its existence to a coercive regime, loosely connected and highly artificial."[50]

While religious and social motives doubtless moved many, secondary educators embraced the extracurriculum for several additional reasons. The new activities helped schools to cope with students who were believed to be in school for reasons unrelated to education. Sports, clubs, music, drama, and other activities would offer alternatives; they would provide things to do that were interesting and possibly even uplifting. In addition, they would offer boys a way to get rid of "red-blooded" energies. They also would gain community support. Nonacademic activities thus would offer schools a way to mobilize attachment — from youth who found academics either dull or repulsive, and from communities. The new activities were another way to broaden the schools' appeal, to hold everyone in a scholastic embrace, to broaden the platform even further. With football, debate, cheerleading, and the Latin Club, high schools were providing something for everyone.

The extracurriculum became so important that by 1930 many schools were giving academic credit for work in it. George Counts wrote, in a mid-1920s study of high schools in fifteen cities, that this change was due in large measure to students' influence: "Through their extra-curriculum activities, they have profoundly influenced the curriculum. Activities which were formerly classified as extra-curriculum and which were largely the product of the interest and efforts of the pupils have been incorporated into the regular curriculum."[51] Student pressure helped to expand the definition of academic work, from vocational training to recreation and personal development.

In fact, student choice was an essential development in the new system. Reformers argued that students ought to be able to select their courses, and, within limits set by test scores and counselors' opinions, to select the curriculum in which they would work. They reasoned that if students could take courses in subjects that interested them, they would be more likely to be interested in their schoolwork. It was not a new idea in the 1920s — President Eliot had introduced an elective system at Harvard much earlier, and some high schools in the late nineteenth century had permitted choice. Student choice also gained support from newer ideas about pedagogy. John Dewey had written that schools go wrong when they "take the accumulated learning of adults, material that is quite unrelated to the experiences of growth, and try to force it upon children, instead of finding out what these children need as they go along."[52] Dewey and others had urged educators to remake the curriculum so that it exploited students' natural curiosity, responded to their real-life interests, and encouraged them to make choices about what to study, and how. The appeal of Dewey's ideas and the authority of his name certainly added luster to this development in high school studies, and his prestige may even have added some impetus to the changes. Student choice of courses and curricula spread rapidly in the first three decades of the century.

But Dewey also worried about student choice, for course selection took on serious meaning when it was tied to life's destinations. The Columbia professor argued against the vocationalized and stratified offerings to which high school reformers married his ideas, and he made it tolerably clear that his arguments against stiff and dusty pedagogy did not imply acquiescence in watered-down work.[53] Dewey believed that high school work could be intellectually serious yet deeply engaging for everyone.

But that was not the direction of change in secondary education. Dewey's wish to marry quality and equality was lost on most reformers, and choice in the high school became a way to evade academic responsibility. For choice was not equally available to all students. Some observers noted that the students who had the greatest choice were those in the general, commercial, and vocational tracks. These youngsters could select from a broad range of courses, electing to take either general science or more traditional science courses, for example.[54] But students in the academic track had fewer options. If they took general science or business math they would be defeating the very purpose of their track placement. For the most part such choices were closed to them, either by school rules or by college entrance requirements, or both.

Ironically, then, the students who were supposed to have the greatest capacity for schoolwork were permitted the least freedom to choose, while those who were supposed to have the least academic capacity were permitted the most choices. And it wasn't difficult to predict how things would work out. George Counts asked more than eight hundred high school teachers what sort of courses students chose. A little more than 30 percent of the teachers said that it depended on the student. A little less than 20 percent said, ambiguously, that students chose the "more valuable" courses. But roughly half said, unequivocally, that students chose "the easier subjects." When we put this observation together with Counts's earlier analysis of student influence on the curriculum, we can see that student choice within a curriculum that offered varying levels of difficulty would push out harder courses with easier ones. Lacking enrollments, difficult electives would simply die. Counts observed, "In many and diverse ways the pupils help in determining the content and even the fortunes of individual courses."[55]

So far, our picture of the high schools' response to mass enrollment suggests a curious mixture of hope and despair. From one angle, the reforms described just above added up to a massive revision of educational substance and standards, all of it designed to cope with a deluge of students who were believed to be incapable of serious academic work. But the reforms were not an exercise in cynicism. There was ebullient enthusiasm for the good work that schools would do with the new students. High schools would serve democracy by offering usable studies to everyone, rather than dwelling on academic abstractions that would interest only a few. It was easy to ignore the great inequalities in what students would learn — for a booming economy needed clerks as much as it needed corporate executives. The reformers' vision combined deep pessimism about most students' academic capacities with high optimism about schools' capacity to do good.

It would be difficult to exaggerate the appeal of that vision. For it permitted educators to face a task that was by their own description daunting, and even depressing — that is, do a good job of instructing hordes of students who had little academic talent — with hope, with the promise of doing much good, and with a vision of great new days for education. But the problems were as formidable as the appeal. For one thing, huge patches of the new curriculum were specifically designated for less capable and less interested students. Everyone in school knew it. Reformers nonetheless seem to have believed that students placed in such courses would want to learn, and that their teachers would want to teach. Why? Did no one think that the result would be demeaning for teachers and defeating for students? If most students were as incapable as reformers believed, how can we explain the reformers' astonishing faith in the schools' power to redeem them?

The answer lies, first, in the simple fact that the reformers were pedagogues. By profession they could not believe otherwise. Could doctors practice medicine if they knew that their patients would not respond to any treatment? Second, these educators had been raised in the faith of Horace Mann. Most were small-town men, drawn from the Protestant heart of the country, where a belief in education's saving power had deep religious as well as political roots. If education is America's civic religion, these men were among its leading evangelists, struggling to build institutions that would bring the untutored masses into the one true church. Faith of their sort is rarely diminished by evidence about the heathen's incapacity; if anything, such evidence only heightens evangelical zeal.[56]

Most important, though, was that educators believed their reforms would capture students' attention; they believed the new courses and curricula would be bright, lively, and relevant. As a result, they saw nothing strange in asserting that students with little academic talent or interest could be actively committed to four years of academic work. That was a remarkable faith, and one that placed a huge burden on the curriculum and on teachers. High schools could work, but only if "interesting" courses could be produced everywhere. An "interesting" curriculum was where educators' pessimism about students intersected their optimism about schools.

What convinced American educators that schools could produce commitment among the academically disaffected? Part of the answer lay in new doctrines about childhood and pedagogy. Dewey and others saw children as active, curious creatures. If they did not take much interest in schoolwork, their schools had probably taken the wrong approach, trying to cram dry packages of subject matter into young minds as if the growing brain were a musty warehouse. If schools would only connect their work with children's curiosity and use youthful experience as an entry to adult knowledge, then all would learn, irrespective of their abilities or their parents' social station.[57]

These ideas — reformers often referred to them as the "new education" — made it seem that any student could take a lively interest in learning, if only schools would get out of the way. Their appeal was reinforced by other developments in psychology which seemed to suggest that children, not books and teachers, ought to be the schools' starting place. For instance, Dewey's notion that the child was an active learner rather than a passive receptacle for teachers' lectures was broadly similar to the views of such leading authorities on scientific psychology as William James and George Herbert Mead. By the 1920s their view that human beings learned by making something of their experience, rather than by passively receiving messages from the senses, was diffusing widely in American psychology. The enthusiasm for orienting instruction to children's interests and experiences also was reinforced by growing acceptance of the idea that the minds of young children worked differently from those of adults. Psychologists and educators stressed, for example, children's more concrete modes of thought and their greater difficulty with abstract concepts. They argued that pedagogy should be adapted to these different mental operations. Teaching and schoolwork should be appropriate for the particular development each child had achieved; children could not be taught things that they were not ready to learn. These doctrines offered much support for the notion that pedagogy should be adapted, not only to the generally distinctive features of childhood but also to the particular developmental situation of each individual.

But psychology's most important new doctrine, for our purposes, was what Joseph Kett has called the "invention" of adolescence.[58] Around the turn of the twentieth century the notion began to spread that high school youth had an utterly distinctive psychological formation. James E. Russell, at the time a University of Colorado education professor, wrote in 1896 that psychology showed a "decided change" in children around the thirteenth year: "The child lives in a world essentially realistic . . . He seeks to add to his store of knowledge and to his stock of possessions; he makes collections of birds' eggs, postage stamps." In contrast, "the world of youth is essentially idealistic . . . He begins to ask the meaning of what he has done."[59] G. Stanley Hall, undoubtedly the most avid entrepreneur of adolescence, had a vaguely similar but much less restrained notion. Adolescence, Hall explained, was when "the best things are springing up in the human soul." Hall was never at a loss for enthusiasm, and this was a theme on which he could embroider endlessly: "It is spring in the soul. If the race is ever to advance, it will not be by increasing longevity . . . but by prolonging this period of development."[60] This was a rosy, if not purple, picture of the newly discovered creatures, but Hall and Russell, like many others, worried about the educational implications. Referring to the "physiological transformations" of adolescence, Russell put the matter delicately: "The individual comes into his inheritance, an embarrassment of riches." He thought that the most "important pedagogical consideration is the enormous accession of physical and psychical energy. What shall be done with it?"[61]

Russell's answer was pointed: "The American secondary school must go on multiplying courses (most likely by offering more elective studies) until every boy, and especially every girl, may find a course of study adapted to his or her peculiar needs."[62] His point, apparently, was that adolescent energy was so intense that schools could effectively work with them only by orienting education to youthful demands. If students could choose their courses of study, their restless energy would find a suitable focus. Russell did not explain why he thought this was so, or whether there should be any limits to student choice.

Hall's answer was a good deal less succinct — his writings on adolescence filled two fat volumes[63] — but he did agree that adolescence was a period "in which the method of freedom in instruction and the appeal to interest and spontaneity should be increased." He did not explain, any more than Russell, how this would help. But he did have a more extensive picture of the new creature. For one thing, he insisted that adolescents were not just idealists — they also were practical. Young men needed to be active, to move around, to build and do rather than to sit and listen. If they were to learn physics, they should be given lots of laboratory work that required physical activity and concrete problems instead of endless classroom exercises that required them only to learn ideas. Hall conceded that physics texts were perfect models of exactness, logically organized and full of good scientific material, but wrote that "boys of this age want more dynamic physics . . . They are interested chiefly in the "go" of things . . . [They] need wide acquaintance first with tops, kites, and other physical toys, then with clocks, dynamos, engines, machinery . . . taking apart and putting together almost anything that will go." In Hall's view the youthful mind was a tinkerer's paradise, not a philosopher's. Yet he also wrote that adolescents were passionate for "general principles and especially forces." They had no strength in precise description, though, and despite his point about "general principles," he offered as evidence the observation that adolescents hated mathematics.[64]

Precise description was not one of Hall's great strengths, either. If we took him literally, we should also say that youth were plagued by a flitting consciousness, a brief attention span, for his catalog of youthful attributes was so full that one wonders how any person could manage them all. Still another persistent note in his writing was the new sociability of adolescence. Gregariousness, or at least greater interest in association, was another mark of the new age: changes in biology drove changes in sociability. If schools were to succeed, they needed to capitalize on the adolescent requirement for more social contact.[65]

But the details are less important than the broad outlines; for one thing, Hall was wildly inconsistent, and for another, other writers stressed somewhat different points. The most important common elements in the portrait seem to have been activity, practicality, and sociability, and the leading argument was that these were inevitable features of a developmental sequence. Most writers depicted adolescents' attributes as "needs," mental and emotional configurations that were programmed by "laws of development," to which schools must respond or fail. All agreed that schools could succeed. They had only to organize instruction around issues that adolescents care about; to make sure that there was lots of activity; to replace abstract, academic material with concrete, practical problems; and to provide plenty of opportunities for students to express their social interests.

These ideas seemed made to order for a profession that was worried about the deluge of uninterested students. They showed that high schools could work for everyone; they showed that everyone needed high school; and they showed that practical education was needed most. Enthusiasm ran high among educators, and the ideas spread rapidly. One nice example was William H. Kilpatrick, one of Dewey's colleagues at Columbia's Teachers College, a popular writer on curriculum and teaching and an influential figure in teacher education. In the late 1920s Kilpatrick wrote that "the school must become a place where life, real experiencing goes on." Real learning occurs only through "actual experiencing," and the whole purpose of education should be to provide knowledge that would be useful in life; therefore, "the more nearly school life can be like life outside of school the better." This prolific professor taught at Columbia University, but he was militantly anti-academic: "The mind is best used when it is put to work now conducting enterprises and meeting problems." Teaching must be centered on "activities," or an "activities curriculum," in which students took responsibility for solving problems that interested them. Students would learn whatever academic content they really needed, because they would stumble on things they needed to know in order to solve the problems.[66]

One implication of these ideas, Kilpatrick argued, was the reconstruction of the schools' curriculum around practical, appealing activities. Another was the parallel reconstruction of teacher education, so that teachers would be qualified to guide problem-solving rather than studies of academic subjects. Still another was to "rid the schools of dead stuff . . . For most pupils, Latin should follow Greek into the discard. Likewise with most of mathematics for most pupils. Much of present history study should give way to study of social problems . . . Modern foreign languages can hardly be defended." English and the sciences survived in Kilpatrick's down-to-earth world, but only under the proviso that they needed "remaking from within."[67]

Another telling example of the new ideas is an essay on instruction in English that was composed in the 1930s by a Wisconsin curriculum consultant and published on the eve of World War II. Most high school teachers, the essay claimed, were already concerned with "pupils as people." They made "the student the hub of the literature program." One practical implication was that every teacher should "screen from his course abstract adult content, unrelated to the needs of the typical secondary school student." Literature, the authors argued, should not be seen as the study of an academic subject, for "literature plays a vital role in the life of a student only when it helps him to solve the problems of everyday living." Teachers would begin "where the student is."[68]

These ideas were part of a great sea-change in American education. They implied that students were by far the most important figures in the process of schooling, much more so than books or teachers. Teachers' effectiveness was tied to their ability to adapt methods and knowledge to the "needs" of students, for without children's active engagement and interest, nothing worth the name of education could occur. The new doctrines also helped to situate scientific psychology — rather than teachers' knowledge of subjects, or pedagogy — at the center of educational wisdom. Psychologists were convinced that they could unravel the puzzles of children's intellectual development, decipher their emotional needs, and untangle the implications for school operations. The new ideas thus sug-

265

gested that teachers should take their cues from students, or from those who could interpret students — experts in psychology or in curriculum construction — or both.

Did teachers get the message? Or rather, since we know that the message reached them in many forms, what did they do with it? How did high school classrooms look, after a few decades of reform? One point on which observers seem to have agreed was the considerable change in the way most subjects were presented in books and course outlines. A study of high school science instruction found many examples of increased "practical content" in course design and materials. A study of mathematics teaching reported extensive adaptation of mathematics to "practical uses and cultural aims" in junior high school science courses, but found much less in the senior high offerings for college-bound students. The high school science study made a similar distinction. Math and science had been made easier, more practical, and more relevant, especially for the majority of students who were headed for work rather than college.[69]

But both studies were much less hopeful about the quality of teaching. The science study — which included observation of more than fifty classes in fourteen cities — complained that only "traditional teaching" was found. Most high school science teachers used the old, lecture demonstration method: students did little experimentation themselves and instead passively watched teachers do the work. In the few classes in which students at least reported on their work, the reports were "dull" and got little attention from other students. Most classroom activity was either seatwork or taking notes on a teacher's lecture.[70] A survey of social studies, which reported the extensive adoption of new courses with more practical and contemporary materials, also commented that the old approach to teaching nonetheless prevailed in the forty schools that were visited. In junior high school classrooms the teachers seemed preoccupied "with form and machinery rather than with the realities of government." In general, "the question-and-answer recitation . . . still holds a dominant place as a classroom procedure in the social studies. Lesson learning and lesson hearing rather than cumulative learning and creative teaching are still prevalent."[71]

The picture that these studies present is mixed: much progress

266

had been made in making courses more practical and keyed to youthful needs, but teaching was still dull and lacking in invention and failed to stir students' interest. This situation was nicely summed up in a study of English instruction. On the one hand it reported that "analysis of courses reveals a definite tendency to looking on English as a tool subject, its primary object being to prepare boys and girls for the expressional activities of everyday life. More and more the literary aspects of writing are being reserved for pupils in superior classes . . . Course designs show significant changes in the direction of conversation, informal discussion, and simple explanation." But on the other hand, "classroom visitation . . . reveals few opportunities for actual expression of ideas, and disproportionate emphasis on grammar drills and exercises in punctuation."[72] The author of these lines juxtaposed them on the same page, but seemed to have little sense of their ironic contrast.

It seems, then, that the reforms discussed here produced the worst of both worlds: new courses, content, and academic standards that were less intellectual and more practical, and a style of teaching that was as dull as reformers had once complained of in Latin and medieval history courses. There was one difference, though: it was much easier for students to get through. Schools could thus be more successful, at least in the sense of increasing both enrollment and graduation rates. Students seemed to be no more committed to or interested in classwork, but the reforms made it much easier for them to finish. If high school reform had failed to liven up the classroom, it had at least greased the skids so that most students could easily slide through.

Just how hard schools struggled to get everyone through was revealed by a 1933 survey of high school marking and promotion. The study reported that most high schools made "strenuous efforts" to avoid failing their students. These efforts took many forms, chief among them performance standards that were much easier outside the academic track and in lower ability groups. Teachers could pass students who had learned little. But even when students failed, more than half the schools said that they were promoted anyway. The study noted, without any apparent ironic intent, that these marking and promotion systems were of recent origin.[73]

The practice of passing students through the grades on the basis

267

of age and attendance, rather than academic achievement, soon came to be known as social promotion. That was the final, crucial stone in the foundation of mass secondary education, for it meant that progress in school was detached from progress in learning. By the early 1930s high school students could succeed in school without succeeding in their courses. The schools could thus succeed in enrolling, "holding," and graduating students, without success in educating them. The schools had failed to solve the problem of mass education in the ways that reformers had hoped — by using better teaching and relevant courses to mobilize students' commitment to school. But by revising standards for grading and promotion so that students' success in school was only weakly related to their success in academic studies, the schools had succeeded anyway.

Why did so few teachers produce the lively, interesting courses for which reformers yearned? One reason was the great difficulty of such work, a difficulty that most reformers had underestimated. It is easy to water down the content of courses, or slacken the standards for passing, or lead discussions of baseball and the legal drinking age. But it is not at all easy to connect these topics of interest to students with systematic knowledge that is useful either vocationally or in the life of the mind. Interest and experience are only a beginning. Students' interest in studying politics might be aroused by discussing a current controversy or by voting on classroom decisions, and such procedures might even produce some political insight. But students would still be a long way from understanding American politics. To learn, students must make an intellectual leap from their own experiences to the experience of others and to abstract ideas about government. And they must be taught. Even teaching students such practical things as how to choose among candidates would require careful exploration of the choices that voters have, of differences among candidates, of the possible reasons for voting, and of the political alternatives implicit in various choices. All of it is practical knowledge for citizens in a democracy, but little of it is easy for teachers to figure out and present in an interesting way to students who find school tiresome.

Another reason for dull classes was that reformers' scribbling rarely helped teachers to take the next step. It was easy for Dewey to write about the importance of experience in education: experience for him was a broad category of discourse that included all possible experiences. It was easy for Kilpatrick and others to stress activities, practicality, and students' interests, for these also were broad terms that included a multitude of possibilities. But any given teacher had much less to work with. It requires considerable wit, imagination, and a broad grasp of subject matter to see the important points — practical or not — through the small and often confusing particulars of students' experiences. Building serious classroom work around the interest and experience of students and teachers was difficult and demanding. Few of the reformers explained how to do it. John Dewey confessed, after a try at running a school, that he knew much less about it than he had thought.[74] Teachers found it much easier to fall back on the familiar techniques — lectures, drill, question-and-answer recitations — or to organize classes around activities that had little content.

Most teachers' own educations did not prepare them well for the work of creating lively classes. Teacher education in colleges and universities grew enormously in the early twentieth century, but the growth was not oriented to exciting teaching. The big growth items were psychology, "foundations" courses in philosophy, history, and sociology, and "methods" courses. The first two sorts of courses dealt not at all with how to teach, while the latter offered only rudimentary introductions to professional practice. What is more, methods courses were generally limited to lesson making, not to lesson execution and then revision in light of teaching experiences. The methods courses were carried on in university classrooms; there were few chances to explore the connections between the lessons built and real students' interests or responses. Confrontation with real students came later, in a brief episode of practice teaching, without much help from professors who knew something about lesson building. In fact, as the century wore on, practice teaching requirements diminished.[75] Student teachers had less and less time to think about anything besides getting through the next hour.

The expansion of teachers' professional education thus offered little help in building the pedagogical skills that might have advanced the ideals of high school reform. And the growth of the "professional" programs for teachers limited the number of academic courses they had time to take, which made it even more difficult for them to teach lively classes. It is, after all, hard to be inventive with a subject one knows only a little. Intending high school teachers still took more academic than education courses in the early 1930s,[76] but subject matter knowledge was also limited by changes in those who taught teachers. For as the teacher education enterprise grew, more and more intending educators attended normal schools and state teachers' colleges, where they learned academic subjects from faculty members who had majored in education rather than in academic subjects. In addition, even when teachers attended universities and were required to take their academic courses in the relevant arts or sciences departments, their course requirements often were easier than those for regular departmental majors.[77]

Another reason for the easing of the emphasis on subject matter knowledge was that colleges and universities were changing — academic goals were becoming less important than vocational and personal development. A national study of college and university purposes in the late nineteenth and early twentieth centuries reported a "very sharp decline" in attention to such goals as "mental discipline," and a slightly less sharp decline in the goals of liberal arts education. There was a steep increase in such educational goals as "recreation," "training for life needs," education related to "health, home, and parental responsibilities," and the like. By 1930, a survey of teacher education institutions showed that only 35 percent of faculty and administrators thought that their institutions tried to train students "directly and specifically" in the liberal arts, but nearly all agreed that they tried "directly and specifically" to teach "the professional skills and knowledge of teaching" — an endeavor that was by then evidently regarded as quite distinct from liberal arts education.[78] The growing emphasis in higher education on practical, personal, and vocational purposes could not have stiffened intending teachers' resolve to master academic subjects.

Perhaps a more important reason that most high school teachers did not teach exciting classes was that they had not been taught that way themselves. Teaching is one of those activities — like being a parent — about which one learns a great deal long before one begins the work. Much of what teachers know about their trade is imbibed as students in school, watching how real-life teachers work. Unlike airline pilots, teachers therefore arrive in profes-

270

sional training with quite well developed ideas about how the job is done, what can be expected from most teachers and students, and how to survive in class. Because such ideas are the product of long experience, they are not easy to change. Six or eight education courses — the college diet of an average intending high school teacher in the 1930s — were unlikely to repack baggage of that sort, let alone replace it with an entirely new set. If public school teaching was routinely mediocre and often bad in the late nineteenth and early twentieth centuries, as nearly all contemporary observers reported, then we can more easily understand why teachers who sat through such classes as children grew up to teach the same sort of classes in the 1920s and 1930s.

This is not to say that teachers' minds petrify upon receipt of their high school diplomas. Many have learned to teach in a manner quite different from the way they were taught, and in some cases the change is due to their professional education. But such change seems to go best when teacher educators provide plenty of time for students to try and then revise classroom practices, when there is ample support and thoughtful supervision of such practice work, and when the intending teachers know their subjects, are able, and want to change. None of these conditions was typical of high school teachers' professional education earlier in this century. Those teachers were batch-processed. They were taught in large classes in increasingly large colleges and universities, in courses that were often quite superficial. One contemporary survey of teacher education concluded that teachers' college and university education often was so weak that "it is probable that many students at entrance to college have already acquired much of the knowledge and skill required in a college major." Moreover, they were educated under standards for certification that were judged to be so low as to "permit almost anyone with mediocre professional preparation to teach."[79] Such arrangements helped to build an entire system of public secondary education very quickly, at relatively low cost, but they also ensured that the education thus provided would be rather thin. And that meant that whatever was learned in four years of college or university preparation for teaching would not be much of a match for the things students had learned for six hours a day, five days a week, during the preceding twelve years. If we can believe teachers' own reports about their professional education, there was little in it that helped them to become teachers, let alone much that taught them how to excite their students.

A last reason why high school teaching was rarely lively was that the job was not designed with that end in view. For one thing, the administrators who hired high school teachers were apparently little interested in the candidates' ability to teach exciting classes, or their mastery of academic subjects. A study of education school placement officers reported instead that candidates' "general personality and ability to assist in extra-curricular activities are two qualifications stressed more than any others" by the superintendents who hired teachers.[80] The workloads of most high school teachers were another serious impediment to good work. By the early 1930s, for instance, two out of every three high school teachers were in class five or more hours a day, five days a week.[81] These teachers were facing five or more different classes of students every day, and given average class size at the time, that implies an average of more than 150 students a day. In addition, roughly two thirds of high school teachers regularly had to teach two or more different subjects.[82] This means that besides various preparations within the same subject — for example, preparing a class in business math at 8:30 and one in plane geometry at 9:30 — a teacher would typically have had to teach mechanical drawing or English at 10:30 and then at least two or three additional classes.

These were extraordinary teaching loads, many times the size of those in elementary schools or universities. Even if one considers such simple elements of the job as learning students' names and getting classes settled down for work, the large numbers presented some serious problems. The problems grew when teachers turned to more refined aspects of their work, such as giving some attention to each student's problems, interests, or talents. And when they turned to such academic tasks as homework, or exams, the implications of the daily load were staggering. If correcting each exam or homework paper takes only five minutes, then grading 150 would take more than twelve hours. Even if teachers assigned homework in only half their classes daily, it would imply six hours' worth of grading each day. Such workloads make it easy to see why teachers would quickly reduce homework demands and forsake essays or

272

complex problems in favor of multiple-choice assignments. Even if all teachers had been superbly qualified to excite their students, their efforts would have been crippled by a staggering workload. Like teachers' own college and university training, their high school teaching was organized to process students in great gulps. Most teachers fell back on the methods that made sense in a batch-processing enterprise: lectures, seatwork, recitation, and knowing most students superficially.

The Depression Years

There was thus no shortage of impediments to the sorts of exciting teaching that reformers wanted, but the advocates of change seem not to have noticed. Throughout the century's early decades they wrote as if blind to the enormous barriers to improved teaching, as if they believed that new books and new courses would do the trick. This curious contrast, between the great scale of the obstacles and the modest scale of the solutions, became even more stark as America sank into the Great Depression; then there were more students and fewer opportunities to improve instruction. Some students would have come anyway, but others came only, as one contemporary study delicately put it, because of "the lack of opportunities for employment of the population of high school age."[83] American educators embraced the new students, rejoicing that their domain grew. But the common perception that more and more students were in high schools only because they couldn't get jobs also fed the old anxieties about how to teach those who really didn't want to learn.

The obvious, well-worn answer was more interesting, practical courses, but practicality cut two ways. For one thing, the schools were being squeezed by Depression-induced tax shortfalls and by the consequent demands for reduced public-sector budgets. As a result, while there were more students, there were not more teachers. Teachers were being fired, or their salaries were being reduced, or both; school services were being cut or eliminated in many districts. Doing something practical thus meant doing something with the existing, already stretched resources.[84] It meant using extant materials or else inventing on a shoestring. Most of all, it meant doing

273

something with the teachers already in place. Familiarly, while there were real pressures to innovate there also were terrific pressures to contain or reduce costs. If high schools were to revise their curricula further to respond to Depression enrollments, they would have to do so within severe constraints.

Another problem with practicality was adult employment. The old practicality had meant training students for jobs — how to type or repair cars — but the reform program of the teens and twenties had an embarrassingly hollow ring in an age of mass joblessness. How could education be made useful under these new circumstances?

Here was the most basic question that the Depression raised for educators who worked in the tradition of the *Cardinal Principles.* It took a few years to sort things out, but an answer soon was presented, under a new banner: "Education for Life Adjustment." Ironically enough, the banner was first hoisted high at Harvard University, when Charles Prosser delivered the distinguished Inglis Lecture at the decade's end. One wonders what his Cambridge audience thought when Prosser began by asserting, "Little [high school] reform will be accomplished unless and until the subject matter of the high school becomes the subject matter for life." What high schools needed was a truly practical program of studies — an idea that hardly seemed new by 1939. But like many passionate ideologues, Prosser was convinced that too little had been done in the cause of reform: "Like Mark Twain's weather, there has been a great deal of talk about the curriculum of the secondary school, but nothing much has been done about it."[85]

In one sense Prosser was correct, for pedagogy had changed little from the bad old days of the 1890s. But in another sense his assertion was breathtaking, in view of the panoramic reforms of secondary studies that he had just lived through — indeed, that he had spent most of his career promoting. What further changes did he envision?

Focus education on useful knowledge, he said (a familiar answer). But he broadened the definition of usefulness so as to give the small details of daily life as much place as vocational training. Listen, as he addressed members of America's oldest, most prestigious, and most selective university: "Every subject taught in our secondary schools should be selected on its merits for use value . . . Business arithmetic is superior to plane or solid geometry: learning ways of keeping physically fit, to the study of French . . . simple science of everyday life to geology."[86]

It was a stroke of genius. Given that economic collapse had virtually confiscated the old reform program, Prosser redefined reform by redefining usefulness — to include all of life. His program gave plain living equal educational status with work. The old ideas about practicality were thus given new life, and the scope of practical education was expanded to include such things as daily conduct and physical fitness. Prosser pressed even further: instead of arguing, as reformers had in the preceding three decades, that a solid academic education should be reserved for those going to college, he insisted that academic studies were as useless for college students as for the boys who wanted to fix cars or the girls who wanted to keep house. The practical curriculum for everyday living that he wanted "would give both better mental and better social training to prospective college students than they are now getting."[87] There really was a perverse populist slant to this educational Babbittry, a democracy of anti-intellectualism.

Prosser's idea was a simple one, but it had startling implications for the secondary curriculum. English courses would not only teach students how to write letters but would also offer instruction in conducting polite conversation with one's friends. Social studies would instruct students not only about family sociology but also about how to behave on dates. Schools would replace much dry reading about government and economics with more practical and interesting matters. Future housewives would be taught how to sew, prepare meals, and keep house, bringing science and mathematics usefully down to earth for girls. These ideas solved all of the hard pedagogical problems that Dewey had posed — or, rather, pushed them aside — by purging the idea of experience of anything that was not utterly mundane.[88]

Prosser's ideas also implied that teachers would not need deep knowledge of their subjects, for the curriculum would only embroider the commonplaces of everyday life. Inventing materials for such work would be much easier, because there would be no need to build careful bridges between students' limited experiences and the great heritage of human knowledge and experience. The bridge-building would be much more modest — between students' school experiences and the demands of daily life for down-to-earth Americans. Teachers would have to learn more about some things — for instance, adolescent psychology and teenagers' social lives — in order to understand their charges better. To respond properly to young people's needs, teachers also would have to cultivate sympathy. And teachers would have to be sensitive to relationships with students, for if they remained merely academic figures they could never make the connections that a more human, practical curriculum required. But learning such things would be easier than physics, or American history — it would even be fun.

Prosser's lecture came at a remarkable moment in the history of American education. For one thing, by the time he spoke in Cambridge the high school system had been built. By 1940 these schools were fast approaching universal coverage, enrolling two thirds of those who were old enough to attend, roughly six and one-half million students. Only half a century before, high schools had been an elite institution, enrolling about 10 percent of those old enough to attend, a few hundred thousand students. Thousands of high schools had been erected, many more thousands of teachers had been educated and employed, and millions of students had been schooled and graduated — all in four or five decades. Simply in terms of scale — the ambitions for education, the energy turned loose, the hopes for democratic inclusiveness, and the size of the enterprise — the accomplishments were impressive.

Americans were impressed. The decades that Prosser's lecture closed seemed golden ones for secondary education. After all, education is one of our oldest enthusiasms, and vast enterprise is another. The combination was bound to please. Another reason that so many Americans found high schools to their liking was that the institution tied up many contrary threads in the country's character: great faith in the good work that schools could do, but little confidence in most students' academic interest or ability; great faith in the transforming power of curriculum, but modest budgets, and thus teacher workloads that would defeat most efforts to make classrooms exciting or challenging; great faith in the democratic extension of schooling to all, but an anti-intellectualism that severely limited educational content for most; great faith in the schools' potential for equality, but a school organization that created terrific inequalities.

These stunning polarities were the fundamental terms of reference for high schools — the treaties, if one likes, that Americans made in order to extend secondary school to all comers. Educators had managed to build a system of secondary schools in which the popular passion for education and the popular contempt for intellectual work were woven tightly together. That too was a remarkable achievement, one that Prosser's lecture threw into particularly plain relief.

Looking back from our later vantage point, that time seems less golden, and more puzzling. How much of the change was an improvement, and how much a loss? Some would answer that there was no change — because the organization of teaching and learning was no different. The curriculum was still sliced into discrete subjects, and schoolwork divided into the little bits called classes. Neither would stimulate real learning. Others would say that academic standards had slipped from an earlier day, and that therefore the expansion of secondary schools must be counted a loss. We can find no evidence of such slippage, though. Classes in the 1930s seem to have relied on textbooks no more than classes in the 1890s. High school teaching seems to have been generally poor in the 1890s, but there is no evidence that it got either much better or much worse.

Thus the image of loss and decline is misleading. There were big changes, but these lay more in the invention of questionable new purposes than in the degradation of fine old ones. In 1890 high school teachers worked in institutions that sought to provide a mostly academic education to a small fraction of those who might have attended. There was great controversy about the nature of academic studies, and vocational offerings were growing, but the curriculum was still overwhelmingly oriented to the study of academic subjects. By 1940, high school teachers worked in institutions with vastly inflated purposes: they sought to meet students' psychic needs, their needs for practical education including but ranging far beyond the vocational, and their social needs. Academic learning had expanded greatly, but it had become a much less important feature of high schools.

All of this was new, but even if we judge it to have been perniciously new, it would be difficult to portray it as a decline. For one thing, most of the students to whom such redefined education was offered also were new — they would not have had any secondary education a generation before. If education is good at all, whatever they got was an improvement. For another thing, academic studies expanded on the wave of enrollment increase. Many students who would have received no secondary education a generation before entered the academic track and received an education that was probably no worse and often better than that which had been offered five decades before. There were many distressing changes, but the vast enrollment expansion meant that the best in high school studies was growing, along with everything else.

My view of the changes in secondary education, then, is not one of decline, but of opportunities forgone. For the bargains that America made in order to extend secondary education to all simply assumed that most students neither wanted nor needed much education. Little effort was made to offer quality education to everyone. Reformers instead tried to invent education that would be useful, but in so doing created a doctrine of practicality that extended schoolwork into trivial details of daily living. As they made education relevant, reformers often made it ridiculous.

But these reforms were not entirely foolish. Many reformers were properly distressed at the poor teaching in high schools. They wanted schools to treat students compassionately, rather than like so many items to be processed impersonally. But when high school reformers spoke of taking students seriously as human beings, they did not include taking them seriously as intellects. This was a new problem, one that owed a great deal to the reformers' pop psychology, and to their doctrine of practical studies for everyday life. Together these produced a language of discourse about education in which humanity was divorced from intellectual seriousness. By denigrating serious intellectual work, and distinguishing it from a humane concern with students' lives, the early-twentieth-century movements to reform high schools created a new, crippling disability for American educators. It helped to keep them from developing an intellectual vocabulary — one that Dewey had tried to create — in which taking students seriously would include both serious thought and deep feeling, both practical and intellectual concerns.

This new problem was one of the great legacies of the old golden age of secondary education. Early-twentieth-century high school reform did not degrade existing standards and requirements, debasing a formerly fine educational system in return for including the masses. Indeed, few high school reformers ever tried to deliver on President Eliot's proposals. They never tried to turn the mostly mediocre collection of secondary schools which they inherited from the nineteenth century into a system of secondary education that would do its best to take all students seriously as thinkers, and to put them in touch with the great inheritance of human achievement. What is more, they neglected this opportunity in a conscious, deliberate, and thoughtful way, out of an odd combination of despair over the intellectual capacities of most young Americans, and hope for the saving social potential of schools. Their era of reform was full of promises about the democratic content of popular education, but also full of implied pessimism about the people's capacity for thought, and for thoughtful democratic participation.

One last remarkable feature of Prosser's lecture was its timing. For as that old high school warrior looked forward to a new epoch of reform, Europe was going up in flames, again. America was on the verge of being drawn in, and like the rest of the world that emerged from that inferno, this country would be irretrievably changed by it. Even the agenda of high school reform would be shaped and reshaped by the unfolding consequences of war.

The Postwar Years

If the prewar years were marked by general agreement about what a mass system of high schools should do, subsequent decades saw unremitting criticism of the system that had been built, and unprecedented divisions over schools' missions and priorities. Within a few years of Dwight Eisenhower's election, a broad national debate about the character of secondary education was under way. Self-congratulatory optimism was replaced by acrimonious criticism. College and university educators questioned the quality of the high school curriculum, and public officials worried about losing a competitive educational edge on the Soviets. By mid-decade high schools began to seem a major social problem — a cause of difficulties in America's social situation, her scientific establishment, and her international position — rather than a solution to social problems. The old, easy boosterism had vanished before Eisenhower had gotten far into his second term.

It has not been heard since, in public debate over schools. The firestorm of fifties criticism had barely died down when it was lost in a new wave of early sixties attacks. They focused first on racial discrimination and then more generally on the schools' inadequate response to the children of poverty. One hallmark of the decade was unprecedented pressure to eradicate school segregation and the effects of poverty in education. Another was a wave of studies that raised fundamental questions about the schools' effectiveness, chief among them James Coleman's historic report, *Equality of Educational Opportunity.* [89] Still another was expansion of the civil rights agenda to include other minorities. But even as these developments matured, they were overtaken by others. Students' political action increased in the wake of civil rights protest and an expanding war in Vietnam, and their protest soon turned from national politics to the schools. Academic experts decried denials of students' rights, and lawsuits challenged educators' infringements of students' civil liberties, their efforts to control students' dress and behavior, and their demands for political orthodoxy. Several panels of education experts urged high schools to treat students in a more grown-up fashion, and to stop acting *in loco parentis.*

This tide of reform was only a few years old when it was swamped by contrary waves of criticism. Several commissions — including the President's Science Advisory Committee — argued that schools damaged youth by separating them from work and other realities of adult life. Schools helped to create an isolated "youth culture" that encouraged drug use, irresponsibility, and political rebellion; they removed students from the real world of work and adulthood. Then, in the middle and late 1970s, concern about the social problems that schools caused gave way to worries about their academic problems — especially declining high school test scores. This renewed concern with academic quality was capped, in the early 1980s, by an avalanche of reports that criticized high schools for a decline in academic performance and fretted about the impact on industrial productivity. High school criticism plainly has become a national

280

pastime since World War II. What changes did critics press on public high schools? How did the schools respond? What effects did the criticism and reforms have?

The Reforms of the 1950s

The first episode in postwar efforts to improve secondary education was a 1950s coalition of university presidents, professors, foundation officials, and public educators who sought to improve academic work. This chapter in high school reform was replete with denunciations of academic weakness in the curriculum and with demands for stricter standards and stiffer courses. It began with a broad denunciation of the secondary curriculum by the University of Illinois's Arthur Bestor and an attack on the quality of science education by MIT's Jerrold Zacharias. The biggest high school book of the decade, and perhaps of our half-century, was written by President James Conant of Harvard. It identified many weaknesses in high schools' academic programs and set out a plan for repairing them.[90]

But if the fifties crusade was united by worries about academic quality, it had diverse roots and competing aims. Some critics sought to broaden the attack on Life Adjustment Education that a few academics had begun in the late 1930s, and to improve work for all students in all subjects.[91] Others were more concerned with science and mathematics education for talented students. Still others worried about military and scientific competition with the Soviet Union. These Cold War anxieties blossomed in the wake of the 1957 Soviet Sputnik: educational improvement was quickly tied to national defense, and the reforms that most easily made the connection — better work in science, mathematics, and languages — got a big boost. The Office of Education and the National Science Foundation sponsored professors' plans to build new curricula for secondary schools. Congress passed the National Defense Education Act, and NSF and OE used those monies and others to recruit students to science, math, and language studies with scholarships. The same two agencies also tried to improve teachers' knowledge of these subjects by various programs of subsidized study.[92]

Reform attempts extended well beyond federal efforts to improve math and science. Some leading colleges and universities, most of them institutions that either had ignored teacher education in the past or had supported it with distaste, sponsored master of arts in teaching and similar programs designed to draw bright students into teaching. In fact, all of the fifties reforms helped to recruit talented young men and women to schoolteaching, buoyed by the renewed evidence of national educational mission and the sense that teaching could be both intellectually respectable and socially important.

What were the reforms' other effects? The new curriculum materials probably were the most visible element in that decade's work, and from one perspective they were a great success: they made more thoughtful, more up-to-date treatments of academic subjects broadly available to high school students and teachers. Given the texts and other materials generally in use at the time, that was a considerable accomplishment. But when one considers the actual use of these new materials, the picture seems much less rosy. Most studies of the subject suggest that the new curricula have had a disappointingly mixed and limited effect on what teachers and students do and know.[93]

Much effort and talent was mobilized; why did they produce such apparently modest results? One reason seems to be connected with educators' attention span: adoptions of the new science texts increased for ten or twelve years after they were first released, but then declined. With a few exceptions, the initial enthusiasm for the new materials seemed to wear thin after a relatively short time; most of the new materials never achieved the wide use that regular commercial texts enjoyed. (More on that shortly.) In addition, most commercial texts do not appear to have been heavily influenced by the NSF-sponsored competition. For instance, one study of math texts reported that although the physical appearance of the top ten commercial math texts improved dramatically after the mid-1950s, their content was less encouraging. The texts, it reported, "are clearly traditional . . . all quite similar to each other in terms of instructional design." They were oriented to "covering the material" rather than to the values of mathematical thought and comprehension that reformers had pressed.[94] Another study reported that most of the math texts emphasized "low level cognitive processes . . . and an emphasis on computational skill."[95]

The new materials also had a modest impact because most teachers continued to work in traditional ways. One study of high school math teaching found that "teachers followed the textbook very closely . . . The major objective of observed lessons tended to be completion of the exercises presented at the end of the section." For most teachers in this study, mathematics was what the text presented, and learning math meant learning the text: "the subject was resolved into a sterile sequence of homework/discussion/new homework."[96] The teaching methods on which high school teachers had been brought up simply swamped the innovative approaches of the new books.

Another explanation for the limited effect of the curriculum reforms is tied to the reformers' approach to improving teaching. Most were university professors in arts-and-sciences departments. They cared greatly about recruiting good students to their disciplines, but cared little for the teacher education faculties in their universities. Many were openly contemptuous of education generally and of educators of teachers in particular. Few made much effort to find out what life in high school classrooms was like, to comprehend the constraints under which teachers worked, or to understand why their own universities paid so little attention to quality in teacher education. Fewer still tried to frame a strategy for reform that took the conditions of teachers' work into account, or that would improve the quality of most high school teachers' college education.

The reformers did support university efforts to attract bright new graduates of arts-and-sciences colleges to teaching, and these programs did help: many of the new recruits stayed to make important contributions. But they were a small band, and their training prepared them to work in the better schools and classes. Most seem to have done just that. Nothing in the MAT programs moved education for the great mass of teachers any closer to the mainstream of university life, nor did it improve the intellectual quality of most teachers' education. Reformers also helped to provide short-term university workshops and institutes for the cream of the high school teaching crop, and participants gave these generally good reviews. But for the rest of the teaching force, the curriculum designers had a different approach. They tried to devise texts that would be invulnerable to teachers' ignorance or incompetence. They did not involve teachers in the development of the new materials. Nor did reformers work out implementation strategies that would help teachers to improve their understanding while using the materials.

In general, the reformers did not seem to take account of the ways in which teachers and teacher education could impede the progress of their pet programs. This increased the chances that the new curricula would meet an uninformed or hostile reception within the education professions. One evidence of that reception can be found in university education faculties' response to the new curricula. In social studies, for instance, educationists were hostile: the new texts struck them as much too "scholarly, cognitive," and too oriented to the structure of the disciplines. They thought that curricula instead should be oriented to students' "affective" learning, to issues of "community," and to values.[97] A study of social studies education remarked that "one certainly cannot get the impression that the 'new social studies' was an important element in the lives of social studies educators during the sixties and seventies. One can barely detect from the work of these education school faculty that there even *was* such a movement."[98] Social studies specialists in education schools were of course the very professors who taught the undergraduates who would go on to teach social studies in high school.

Thus, the isolation and mutual distrust between university faculties — often arrogant arts-and-sciences professors on one side, often incapable or defensive educationists on the other — made it easy for education schools and departments to continue older and less demanding approaches to teacher education. A major national campaign to upgrade high school teaching and learning did not affect education faculties' isolation within universities. They went on preparing new social studies teachers in the same old ways, a point that seems to hold only a bit less well for other subjects.[99] So the movement for reform was accompanied by a continuing supply of new high school teachers who had learned the old ideas.

This may seem a terrible oversight on the curriculum reformers' part, but it was more than that. For one thing, it was easier for them to bemoan the quality of work in education schools than it was to do anything about it. That would have required time and engagement, distraction from their own disciplinary work, and quite likely a reallocation of resources within universities to the underfinanced education schools — possibly even the reformers' own departmental resources. For another, most of the curriculum reformers were interested chiefly in students with real academic talent, students who would at least go to college and do well, and especially those who might go on to academic or professional careers. The nation's problem, after all, had been advertised as a deficiency of scientific manpower, a lack of excellence among those who would go on to careers in science or related fields. In mathematics, for instance, reform efforts "focused on college-aspiring youth and the development of curricula appropriate for them. The motivation for the development of UICSM, SMSG, the Ball State Project and other curriculum development efforts were [*sic*] in terms of serving those students destined for college work in mathematics and science who were likely to become part of the scientific talent pool."[100] Reformers generally deplored Education for Life Adjustment, but their work was particularly focused on the most talented high school students and their teachers.

Another reason that the new curricula had only modest effects on what most high school teachers and students knew, then, is that their authors and sponsors were not much interested in most high school students. They cared chiefly about the best and the brightest. One even might say that there was an unknowing collaboration between reformers and professional educators: reformers decried the educationists but focused chiefly on the talented top of high schools, while educationists defensively ceded this remnant to the fans of rigor without disturbing either their own influence in schools and teacher education or their commitment to practical and "interesting" studies for most students. Neither party ever tired of extolling the virtues of the comprehensive high school, and one reason is probably that its divided organization made it easy for professionals and reformers to pursue their separate passions, just as it allowed students to go their separate ways.

This divided approach to reform thus made it possible for a new generation of reformers to argue against the old reform ideas while at the same time permitting those old ideas to march ahead in most of the secondary curriculum and in teacher education. The consequences were plainly visible in the curriculum. If one considers the small sector on which the fifties reformers concentrated, one sees genuine change. The most visible innovation was the Advanced Placement program. Created in the mid-fifties, this program permitted "exceptionally talented" high school students to take special, accelerated courses. The AP courses gave the talented few an extra edge on other students, both by more high-powered work and by preparation for the Advanced Placement tests. If students did well enough on the tests they would get college credit for their AP high school work, and thus advanced college standing.

The fifties reforms also stimulated other advanced and specialized courses. A national survey of changes in the high school curriculum between 1948 and 1961 reported the introduction of college-preparatory math courses organized specifically around the new materials. It also reported similar developments in physics and chemistry: "In 1961 a total of 973 schools in 49 states offered advanced chemistry, and 566 schools in 46 states offered advanced physics. In 1949 these subjects were offered in schools in 18 and 6 states respectively, with combined enrollments of 2,900 pupils, as compared with 53,800 pupils in the current survey."[101] While high school enrollments grew by about 50 percent between 1949 and 1961 — from about five and one-half million to about eight million junior and senior high students — the number of students enrolled in advanced math, physics, and chemistry courses grew by nearly 2,000 percent.

These were important changes. They contributed to noteworthy improvements in the quality of classroom work at the top, and that made a difference to thousands of talented students and to those fortunate enough to be their teachers. In effect, the pressures for reform helped to create a new track within high schools, a subdepartment of college prep designed for those select students who had the will — or the parents — to push for high-quality education. The survey of high school course offerings and enrollments aptly characterized these developments as an "extension downwards of the college program . . . for intellectually able students."[102]

But it would be a mistake to conclude that these important changes were fundamental; everywhere else in high schools, life went on much as it had. The late 1940s and 1950s saw a new surge of secondary enrollments. While increases were noted among all population groups, black high school enrollments soared, and so did high school graduation rates for blacks: the percentage of black adults who had completed high school tripled between 1940 and 1960.[103] Secondary educators embraced this move toward universal enrollment, and in that spirit they opened an attack on a new enemy: the high school dropout. Concern about this newly minted creature grew in education and the media, as did a plethora of programs aimed at keeping him in school for four years.

How did high schools cope with continuing enrollment growth and the increase in minority students? The 1949–61 survey of changes in courses and enrollments commented that "considerable attention was necessarily directed to the lower ability groups, since a larger proportion of the high school enrollment was coming from that segment of the population." The report noted that the growth in subjects designed to meet the needs of these students — what it termed "functional education" — had begun before World War II, but it suggested that this trend had continued and perhaps intensified since then: "High schools expanded their academic, vocational, and general programs in an attempt to challenge the minds and interests of these new enrollees. They introduced courses on an experimental basis . . . Courses of a practical nature in everyday living continued to proliferate . . . The English field provided courses in practical English, language orientation . . . In mathematics, such courses as consumer mathematics, economic mathematics, mathematics for modern living, refresher mathematics and terminal mathematics [!] were reported. Science offered household biology, science for modern living, everyday physics, and consumer science, among others."[104]

So while new courses were devised for a small fraction of top students, the old habit of inventing and adapting "practical" courses for the great mass of other students continued, apparently quite unaffected by the national crusade for excellence. One can roughly estimate the relative effort that high schools devoted to these two approaches to reform by comparing enrollment increases during the 1949–61 period. In those twelve years, course enrollments in "honors English" went from an unknown quantity (data on such courses were not collected in 1949) to 2,381. "College-level English" went from roughly 1,450 students in 1949 to a little more than

9,000 students in 1961. But remedial English alone enrolled about 36,000 students in 1961, and remedial reading enrolled roughly 240,000 high school students — a combined enrollment in remedial English courses of roughly 276,000.[105] In 1949, the total enrollment in courses with that label had been only 36,000.[106] The enrollment increase in courses for the uninterested or incapable student was thus astronomical, compared to the increases for exceptionally able students. The same point holds for other subjects. Enrollments in advanced chemistry increased at a dramatic rate during this period — from about 1,800 to about 33,000 — but the numbers were tiny by comparison to those in general science, which grew from about 2.1 million to about 4.2 million during the same period.[107]

These figures show that the high schools' response to new pressure for excellence was really quite modest when compared to their continuing production of courses for less able or less interested students. The differentiated curriculum made it possible for secondary schools to accommodate demands for improvements at the top while still continuing the older, massive commitment to a weaker curriculum for everyone else. The old ideology was in eclipse in public debates about education, but it was obviously alive and well in professional decision-making about course offerings and student advising.

One might argue that this story reveals a nice compromise. The differentiated curriculum made it possible for schools to accommodate new pressures for reform without reducing the momentum of an older reform movement, whose ideas were by then part of routine decision-making everywhere in secondary education. The new reformers got what they most wanted — better quality for a select few — and secondary educators could continue, more or less undisturbed, their older tradition of massive curriculum relaxation. One even might argue that the compromise represents a sensible prototype for anyone interested in improving secondary schools: Pursue a policy of selective excellence. Focus on the most able students and teachers, where progress is both fairly easy to make and visibly important. Leave the rest alone.

Is this a plausible view? To answer we must ask if selective excellence worked. And to find that out we must consider the fate of the 1950s reforms during the 1960s and 1970s. One important development that transformed schools in those decades was an astonishing expansion of higher education. In 1939 just less than 1.5 million students were enrolled in colleges and universities, but by 1960 that number had more than doubled, to 3.2 million students. A decade later higher education enrollments had more than doubled again, to 7.1 million students.[108] These huge increases were mostly absorbed in the less selective public colleges and universities. In 1930 just half of the higher education enrollments were in public institutions, but forty years later the fraction had risen to two thirds.[109]

The fastest growing sector of higher education was thus the one that was least discriminating about students' high school records. Perhaps the best token of this point was junior and community college enrollments. In 1939–40 these institutions enrolled roughly 230,000 students — about 15 percent of American post-secondary students.[110] By 1970, however, two-year institutions accounted for 31 percent of higher education enrollments, and by 1979 the figure had risen to 37 percent.[111] These community college places were open to all students who had high school diplomas — grades were irrelevant. And many more places opened up in the only slightly more selective state universities and state university branch campuses. By 1960 hundreds of thousands of American students were attending something called a college or university without having done good work in high school. By 1970 millions were doing it.

While the 1950s reformers were pressing for higher standards in high schools, then, the growth sectors of higher education were pressing the other way. The effects on high schools were enormous. One effect was informal: incentives for academic work in high schools were sharply eased. Students and teachers could see that college admission did not depend heavily on the quality of students' academic work in high school, and that made it harder — and less necessary — to press students for good work. A second was formal: many colleges and universities that sought more students adopted easy requirements for college admission; many high schools that sought to improve their records in graduating students and sending them to college eased graduation requirements.[112]

These changes also altered the role of high schools in relation to higher education. Only about 12 percent of the students who made it to the fifth grade in the mid-1920s went on to enter college.

289

Most fifth-graders — more than 60 percent — never made it through high school in those years.[113] Colleges and universities were very selective: even if they didn't reject lots of applicants, only a small and generally advantaged fraction of the people who were old enough to attend college ever got there. High schools were chiefly concerned with students who would never get beyond the twelfth grade. The education that they provided was, as one eminent sociologist put it, "terminal."[114] But as more students stayed in high school and went on to college, things changed. By the late 1940s and early 1950s, more than half of the students who had made it to the fifth grade graduated from high school, and roughly three in ten went on to college. Twenty years later nearly three quarters were graduating from high school, and nearly half of all high school graduates were going on to college.[115] High schools were becoming a preparatory agency for higher education, and on a mass scale.

These changes meant that college preparation became much less special. To accommodate the change, many high schools developed two or three college tracks. There were the AP and honors courses for the tiny fraction of students who wanted demanding work and who would apply to selective colleges and universities. There was the old general track, growing rapidly, from which more and more students were going on to unselective colleges. And then there was the college track, which many teachers described as the new general track — one could find a great range of talent in it but no special press to work hard or do well; students from it went on to quite a variety of schools.

What college preparation had come to mean was thus quite different from what it had meant in the 1930s, or even the early 1950s. Most students who would go to college didn't need to take four years of science and four years of math, for instance — they needed only another year of science beyond general science, and introductory biology sufficed. By the early 1970s enrollments in that course were nearly twice those of the early 1960s.[116] Chemistry and physics, which required some knowledge of mathematics, had tiny enrollments by comparison.[117] Only a small fraction of college-bound students went beyond algebra I.[118] As the meaning of college education changed in an age of unselective mass attendance, the meaning of college-preparatory work in high school followed suit.

The expansion of higher education thus had a dramatic effect on high schools, but it was not the effect that reformers sought. In principle, the terrain for the fifties reforms might have been vastly expanded by the growth of colleges and universities, simply because there were so many more high school students preparing for college. But in practice the incentives for good work were weakened in the largest sector of college preparation because so much of the higher education expansion was in the least selective institutions. Most of the fifties reformers were college and university men, and it is ironic that the great expansion of their sector of education should have had such an unexpected and generally unhappy effect on their efforts to improve high school quality. But it was an irony that few seemed to notice at the time, perhaps because the same tidal wave of enrollment that carried many hundreds of thousands of poorly prepared high school students into unselective colleges and universities also carried along many talented and ambitious students. They swelled the crack courses at the top of the college track, while their less talented or pushy fellows created a huge bulge just below. Things were getting better and worse in the college track at the same time.[119]

A related irony concerns America's lone effort to address seriously the problems of teachers' college educations. James Conant published *The Education of American Teachers* in 1963, and it set out an agenda for change still worth consideration: higher standards for admitting undergraduates to study for the profession; a more thoughtful and demanding university education for those admitted; stiffer standards of professional responsibility, to which teachers and their universities could be held accountable.[120] But Conant launched these ideas on the sea of educated opinion just as the universities and colleges that educated teachers were digesting the huge enrollment bulge. The great engines of teacher education — the state university education departments and the state-operated teachers' colleges — were racing along at top speed, turning out the teachers that schools needed. It was not unusual for one of these institutions to graduate thousands of new teachers each year. Under the best of circumstances it would have taken an enormous effort for American higher education to close the destructive divisions within itself and sharply improve its work with intending teachers. But as it turned out, the best of times were the worst of times. Everyone was busy, classes were overflowing, and there were lots of jobs for teachers and for their teachers. There were few incentives within the enterprise for a reconsideration of teacher education — save those arising simply from a concern with educational quality, broadly defined. They were pathetically insufficient.

Civil Rights

These developments alone probably would have been sufficient enough to swamp Conant's scheme for reforming teacher education, along with many of the other 1950s reforms. But one irony piled on another: the movement to reform civil rights in America quickly overtook the fifties reforms. In fact, the 1950s had not even ended before the nation's educational priorities began to shift. The Supreme Court had decided the *Brown* cases in mid-decade, and that decision quickly percolated through the body politic. Rosa Parks sparked the Montgomery bus boycott just a few years later — shortly after the NSF and NDEA programs began. Less than two years after that, John F. Kennedy was elected president. And at the same time the direct action movement for Negro civil rights picked up inspiration and momentum from black student sit-ins at Southern lunch counters. In the three years before Kennedy's assassination, racial discrimination became the country's biggest continuing saga, and inequality became the largest educational issue. Within a year after Kennedy's death, Lyndon Johnson and the Congress capitalized dramatically on the developing change. Legislation aimed at ending racial discrimination in public life and eradicating its accumulated effects through massive federal education and training programs had set new national priorities.

The fifties movement for excellence thus had been replaced at the top of the national education agenda, only a decade after it began, by an even more intense movement for equality. Interest in the reforms that had so recently been adopted soon faded. Congressional appropriations for the fifties programs briefly held steady, but then began to fall in the mid-sixties. Educators turned their attention away from improving quality to extending equality. And public pressure for improved quality faded as politically active

Americans turned to the problems of blacks and poor people.[121] The country was swept by waves of criticism of the public schools' work with poor and minority students, and courts and other government agencies pressed for more rapid desegregation.

These developments had enormous effects on education. They eroded the sense that public schools were a fair, progressive, and open enterprise — a sense that was everywhere evident in the expanding school system between the wars, and that partly accounted for the lack of much criticism then. They also helped to produce remarkably rapid racial change. By the late 1960s a broad campaign against segregation was proceeding in Southern schools, and in the next few years discriminatory practices of a slightly less blatant sort — in hiring, and in student sports and other extracurricular activities — came under attack in schools in both North and South. By the *Brown* decision's twentieth anniversary, race relations in public education were undergoing a revolution, even though many problems remained. Not only were historic patterns of discrimination in school assignment and access to education being swept away, but federal and state legislation was directing substantial additional monies for remedial education to schools with many children from poor families.

These changes were accompanied by others, stimulated in part by the movement for black civil rights. The late 1960s and early 1970s saw mounting pressures to deal with the school problems of Hispanics and other minorities. Several states and the federal government extended antidiscrimination efforts to cover some of these groups, and some launched programs to cope with their educational problems. Perhaps the most significant program was bilingual education. The same period also saw rapidly increasing political and judicial pressure to halt discrimination against disabled students and to improve their education. Again, state and federal legislation pressured schools to change past practice, and offered money and guidelines for new program development. Finally, in the wake of civil rights and antiwar protest, student political activism and a civil rights type of litigation turned directly on high schools. Many schools relaxed restraints on students' dress, speech, and political behavior.

Although we distinguish these movements for reform, in the late

1960s and early 1970s they were all jumbled together in the nation's political washing. What effect did they have on schools? Did they improve the quality of education, for blacks and everyone else? More particularly, what was their impact on the fifties reforms?

In a general sense, the quality of education for black and other minority students did improve. The sixties reforms attacked the consequences of centuries of racism and neglect. Education for minority students improved in part because many students gained access to courses and materials that previously had been denied, a development that was most striking in the South but noticeable in Northern cities as well. The new school improvement programs also improved education for blacks.

But these developments must be balanced against others that were less encouraging. Most of the nation's school improvement efforts were focused on the primary and preprimary years: the big programs were Title I of the 1965 ESEA, and Head Start. High schools had nothing comparable. And many of the possibly positive effects of the 1960s reforms were diluted by the high schools' routine response to postwar increases in minority enrollments. Most of the new students wound up in vocational, commercial, and general classes, in which academic demands were modest at best.[122] Some of this was due to active discrimination by teachers and counselors, but much of it was due to the difficulty that many poor and minority students already had with school. It would have taken fairly serious work to convince them that high school was a good place to invest their energies, and few schools made the effort. High schools already had a mechanism for dealing with this issue: they presented the array of some difficult courses and many easy ones, and let students choose.

The established school organization also provided a handy way to deal with other pressures for reform. Many new courses for non-English-speaking students were created, as a way both to accommodate demands for change and to absorb new monies from federal and state bilingual programs. Some schools developed virtually an entire curriculum for non-English speakers. Schools also improved and broadened their offerings for handicapped students, responding again to demands for change and opportunities to capitalize on new monies. Many used the new courses and teachers as a way of dealing with minority students who had problems in the other curricula. High schools also responded to student protest by further diversifying the curriculum: existing course offerings were modified to highlight their relevance; new courses in social problems and ethnic studies were invented. And student participation in curriculum decisions was solicited.[123]

How did these developments affect the high school curriculum? First, courses skyrocketed: the number offered in 1972–73 was nearly double that of 1960–61, increasing from 1,100 to 2,100. Just a little more than a decade after the 1950s efforts to stem the fragmentation of high school studies and reassert standards of quality had peaked, the secondary curricuum was much more fragmented. Second, educators continued their long-standing effort to deemphasize academic work. The U.S. Department of Education reported that by 1972, "although traditional academic courses still receive considerable emphasis, their prominence in the curriculum has been noticeably eroded." Between 1961 and 1972, the report went on, "the emphasis on making a high school education available for every youth . . . has continued, with added attention given to the lower ability groups. This has resulted in considerable experimentation with course offerings, and the introduction of many new courses . . . Courses of a practical nature in everyday living proliferated . . . and core courses, minicourses and interdisciplinary approaches to learning were introduced." Remedial courses continued to grow: for instance, remedial English grew at more than six times the rate of overall enrollments.[124] These courses were not preliminaries to required English courses, but replacements for them.

We noted earlier that advanced courses held their own or even expanded. Advanced chemistry and physics made some gains of this sort, as did advanced math.[125] But enrollment increases in all advanced science courses, taken together, did not equal the increase in remedial English alone. The effects of the 1950s reforms continued to be felt in the advanced sectors of the high school curriculum, but they were modest when compared with the steady expansion of courses for students judged capable of only a little academic work.

A third sign of continued slippage in high school studies was a general relaxation of course standards and requirements. Federal analysts noted a tendency to offer more courses on an "ungraded" basis — that is, for only pass-fail ratings. They also noted that more and more courses were being opened to students in two or three grades, suggesting a drift away from sequencing and increasing difficulty within the curriculum. They pointed out that the share of high school enrollments in traditional academic courses — such as twelfth-grade English and U.S. history — had dropped, sometimes quite sharply. And they noted that "graduation requirements were eased in many schools, and that elective courses became more prominent. As a result, in most of the subject areas a drift away from the basic courses was noted."[126]

One conclusion about the fate of the 1950s reforms, then, is that they were quite vulnerable to forces beyond the control of either schools or reformers. While honors and Advanced Placement classes survived the 1960s and early 1970s, they became a smaller and smaller segment of high schools' college-preparatory work. There even is evidence that some of the top classes were weakened, or canceled, during those tumultuous years.[127] One could not exactly say that the selective excellence strategy had failed, because the reforms had not been abandoned — enrollments in advanced courses even grew. But one could not exactly say, either, that the strategy had succeeded, because the fifties reforms did not even affect most college-bound students.

We have pointed to three broad explanations for this result. One was that a rapidly changing national political agenda simply diverted attention from high school quality to other important matters. A second was that educators responded to all reform efforts in the same fashion: diversify offerings to accommodate the pressures from new constituencies, and continue to ease standards and invent interesting courses for the still-expanding mass of students judged incapable of serious thought. Whether or not educators welcomed the 1950s and 1960s reforms, they did not need to hold out endlessly against them. The reform demands were simply added to the already long list of high school treaties.

A third explanation was that the fifties reformers encouraged this tendency in secondary education by not challenging it. Most of the university fans of high school quality were simply unwilling to do much more than denounce the intellectual weaknesses of education from afar. Here was one of the biggest bargains in the brief history of mass secondary education: intellectual quality would be acceptable to educationists and appealing to reformers as long as it was just another small item in that large cluster of accommodations called the comprehensive high school. In the first two decades of postwar high school reform, roughly from the mid-1950s to the mid-1970s, the schools were subjected to increasingly bitter criticism and pressures for improvement. From one angle schools responded with amazing alacrity and flexibility: as each wave of reform broke, each was rewarded either with a new subdivision of the curriculum or with an expansion of the existing large, undemanding division. From another angle we can see that the fifties reforms did establish an important beachhead for quality. But because that beachhead only added to a still-growing list of others, its net effect was to fragment the curriculum further and thus further weaken the schools' capacity to take all students seriously.

This flexibility is in one sense deplorable, because so many students have been shortchanged. But in another it is admirable, because the schools have faced so many demands from so many quarters, and have tried to respond helpfully and in a certain sense humanely — even though they have not had the resources to do the many jobs that they have embraced or have been assigned. This remarkably adaptive feature of American secondary schools is best illustrated by their response to the first wave of recent conservative attacks. In the late 1960s and early 1970s a new sense of the high school problem began to take shape as reports of student protest, school violence, and drug use mounted. Critics argued that these were only symptoms of the pathological conditions that schools created among youth by isolating them from the realities of life and work, keeping them apart from contact with adults, allowing them to develop a separate "youth culture" that was opposed to adult values, and thus preventing them from learning proper grown-up habits and ideas. A program of reform was proposed: Get students out of school. Expose them to adults. Provide them with opportunities to work, or to learn about work.[128]

These ideas fell in with a broader movement to "deinstitutionalize" social services. Reformers from various professions argued that herding people together in mental hospitals, prisons, and schools restricted normal contacts at work and in community life. Social agencies thereby created or compounded problems rather than ameliorating them. Reformers wanted to eliminate these institutions, breaking them up into small, community-based agencies or trading them in for voucherized services. These ideas appealed to some educators, but they posed a unique problem: if schools caused social pathology rather than curing it, should schools then be closed?

This seemed rather an extreme step. Instead, schools embraced parts of the reform movement. Federal agencies provided new support for internships in community agencies, apprenticeships, work-release programs, and career education programs. Proposals were made to reduce the length of high school studies, either by cutting the school day for many students or by reducing the scope of compulsory attendance. While the latter idea failed to be accepted, the former succeeded hugely. Cutting the school day was in fact only an informal way to reduce compulsory attendance. Some schools used these programs to get troublesome kids out of the building. Many more used the programs as a way to accommodate a large postwar boom in students' working. Between 1960 and 1978, the proportion of students who worked part-time increased by roughly one third. By the end of the 1970s, roughly half of all high school students reported that they worked part-time.[129] Many reported that their paid labor left only a little time for schoolwork.[130]

The schools' inventions varied a bit. Some created career education programs in which students took paid jobs outside of school, got academic credit for occasional reporting on their work, and carried a much reduced course load. Others adopted or expanded work experience programs that allowed students early release from school each day if they had a job. Still other schools devised internship programs that got students unpaid work in community agencies, and often gave them academic credit for their reports on it. Students reported that they liked the programs for the same reasons they liked their jobs — work helped them to ease the boredom of high school. A few programs were academically serious; most, however, were simply an ingenious way for schools to cope with students who wanted to be somewhere else.[131]

The episode is worth noting because it suggests the resilience of the schools and the strength of the ideas on which mass secondary education was built. Even a reform that was aimed at reducing

298

high schools' dominion over youth was turned to institutional advantage. The notion that experience should replace schooling became the rationale for adding yet another division to the schools' curriculum. Experience became an academic activity, a way to cope with difficult students within the framework of courses, credits, grades, and graduation. On the one hand this seems to carry the diversification of the secondary curriculum to its logical *reductio*. But on the other it seems only the natural conclusion of earlier arguments that the high schools' true mission is helping students to learn about the practical realities of everyday life, rather than teaching academic subjects. In either case, the reform was usable: in many of the schools we visited, experience-based programs were alive and well.

We conclude, then, that selective excellence has been flawed because the fifties reformers wanted to have their cake and eat it too. They embraced the comprehensive high school in the name of equality and efficiency, but focused chiefly on the top track in the name of excellence. These reformers did not want to challenge the popular commitment to common secondary schools, democratically attended by all sorts of students. They preferred instead to advocate excellence for a few students while acquiescing in mediocrity for the rest. Neither Conant nor other reformers ever seem to have considered a specialized approach to secondary education, in which schools would focus on arts, or sciences, or commerce, or something else, and in which each would try to do high-quality work in one thing.[132] Nor did more than a handful of critics argue for high-quality work across the board in comprehensive schools; most seem to have accepted both the comprehensive organization of high schools and the accompanying assumption that most students could not be taken seriously as thinkers.

If schools could be organized on the model of nuclear submarines, with watertight bulkheads sealing off some sections from others, the 1950s approach might have been less problematic. But the organization of a school is much more porous than that of a submarine — there are no bulkheads. How can seriousness and quality be sustained or improved in one small part of the organization when most other parts are specifically organized for work of inferior quality and seriousness? Few of the fifties critics seriously grappled with this problem. Only Arthur Bestor seems to have seen that American public schools probably could not be academically demanding unless

299

they were demanding for all, and he saw the reason as well: high schools are popular institutions.[133] They depend for funds on local voters and state legislatures, they are governed by locally elected officials, and they work on people — not on letters, or water, or streets. In all these ways schools depend on popular support, and they are therefore quite vulnerable to what the people want. Of course, if all people, or some very powerful segment of them, say they want high academic quality in one section of the schools and mediocre work in the rest, and if they say it firmly and consistently, then selective excellence might work. It began to work a little better in the 1950s than it had earlier. But what if most people withdraw support for quality, or become interested in something else about schools, or something else quite apart from schools?

The answer became apparent when political change came to American education, as it did with amazing speed and variety beginning in the 1950s. The constituency for quality was then revealed to be quite modest, hardly suited to expand its domain in the face of other pressures. The differentiated curriculum, which was a cheap way to manage diversity among secondary students, was a poor way to protect or expand quality in secondary education, for it gave great weight to the forces in schools that were not oriented to serious work. Selective excellence meant that the demanding small section of schools would be perennially threatened by the larger, explicitly undemanding, essentially anti-intellectual whole.

It is no novelty to see this flaw in selective excellence. Horace Mann, among others, pointed it out at the very inception of public education: if one wishes to create high standards of quality in public schools in a popular democracy, one has a hope of success only if the standards are broadly established and if the populace as a whole may therefore become committed to them. If most people are taught that intellectual seriousness is not for them, then they will probably grow up to behave accordingly, denigrating rather than supporting those small segments of school devoted to quality.

The Eighties Reforms

The last wave of criticism to break over American education was in some ways the largest. The early 1980s saw intense concern about the quality of high schools. Literally hundreds of reports and studies were published, many more recommendations issued, and many actions taken. A modest cottage industry of reporting on and studying the reports and studies sprang up, and a parallel effort to study and report on the implementation of reform is growing.[134] This level of agitation was remarkable even in a quarter-century of vigorous school reform.

Our analysis has a few implications for this last outbreak of reforming zeal. Perhaps the main point is that high schools have been remarkably durable and, in their own way, successful. Durable because they have lived through three decades of intense criticism and reform, and successful because they have managed to accommodate many of the demands made on them. Much as teachers have struck bargains with students, high schools have accommodated pressures for change. Most reformers got a piece of the action, but the schools managed to arrange these bargains within the organization and ideology that were adopted seven or eight decades earlier. One cannot read this history without remarking educators' persistence and ingenuity in pursuing their chosen course, and their great capacity to accommodate a growing list of often competing demands without wavering from their favored commitments. We have compared the modern secondary school to a shopping mall, but that metaphor rather understates the many complex and carefully balanced bargains that keep these overworked organizations running — and running in a way that seems to please most of their clients and constituents. If we knew nothing else about the schools, we would suppose it unlikely that the last wave of criticism and reform would change this pattern of accommodation.

We do know more, though, including more about the latest reforms being urged on high schools. There has been a blizzard of ideas and proposals, but the thrust of most recommendations and actions is more academic requirements: more time spent in school, to ensure more study; more credits required for graduation, to ensure that students take more "solid" courses; and more required courses, especially in science and mathematics, to ensure that students learn more in those subjects deemed to be of great domestic and international economic significance.[135] Many of the reports stress that more and better teachers are needed to help shoulder this added load, and that more money will be required to attract them. But it is easier to legislate requirements than to appropriate monies, and so far the second activity has lagged far behind the first.

What can be expected from such reforms? One point, already visible in our school visits, was more serious teaching and learning. This was more a response to critiques and discussions than a result of requirements imposed. The reforming mechanism resembles political osmosis rather than formal compliance: teachers read newspapers and magazines and watch television, and are sensitive to what their publics want. A great many of the possibly constructive effects of this latest wave of reform were already under way before the requirements were laid on.

But as educators respond, they walk in well-worn paths. One example is the means by which teachers reemphasized academic seriousness. Rising public concern about declining SAT scores and related criticism prompted them to stress "basics." This generally meant teaching students more facts. Some science teachers, for instance, reported that they stopped trying to get students to understand scientific inquiry and concepts — efforts that were inspired by the 1950s reforms — in favor of memorizing scientific facts. Social studies teachers reported a similar shift to more time spent on drill, worksheets, and the like.[136]

Another example is that the new required courses are mostly taught by the same old overworked and frequently undereducated teachers. Additional math courses are taught by physical education teachers who have seniority over new candidates trained in mathematics. New courses in physics and chemistry are being staffed from the long-standing surplus of biology teachers, many of whom never took a college course in chemistry or physics.[137] In addition, even when qualified teachers do teach the added requirements, nothing else about their job changes. No compensatory adjustments in their workloads have been reported, nor have there been many reports of significant adjustments in salary. At best, then, the new courses will be no better than most of the old ones. Some will be very bad, because the teachers are unprepared.

A third example of stability in change is that the reforms require only that additional courses be offered, taken, and passed. Competence in teaching and learning are not required. Our earlier chapters amply reveal students' and teachers' capacity to cope with such requirements, and nothing about the last wave of reforms changes that. Slightly restricting the range of choice among courses does little to restrict the opportunities for bargaining within them. The existing organization of secondary schools is admirably suited to accommodate the new requirements, without producing much improvement in the content of courses, the quality of teaching, or the bargains that students and teachers strike.

Our analysis also suggests that in certain respects the current proposals are profoundly misdirected. The reforms aim to improve education by ratcheting up school requirements, yet a large fraction of the students now in high school seem quite immune to such requirements. These students are educationally purposeless. They attend for reasons quite unrelated to learning: because they need to be kept off the street, because they cannot be allowed to compete with older workers, because most of their friends attend, or because the schools are handy places to solve such other problems as driving ability, health, or nutrition. Opinion surveys show repeatedly that most students, like most adults, do not regard academic work as the primary purpose of schools: they give greater importance to social and vocational matters and to personal development.[138] And whatever their reasons for being in school, students are frequently hostage to circumstances that tend to defeat learning. Many students know, for instance, that when they leave school they probably will not be able to find a job or, if they can find one, that it will require only minimal skill or knowledge. They will work on an assembly line, check out groceries, serve hamburgers, sell shoes. It is easy to say that all citizens need to think critically, reason mathematically, and read and write well, but what sort of learning do such dismal economic prospects imply? Perhaps high schools teach students what they most need to know: how to endure boredom without protest. These students' prospects hardly suggest rewards for hard work or for intellectual curiosity. Students who plan for college in part to avoid such a fate know that they do not need to do much high school work to gain college admission. This, too, does little to build academic commitment.

One consequence of these limits on reform is that most students and teachers will cope with the eighties requirements as they have coped with others. Teachers and students will bargain to ease the effects of the requirements. A second consequence, typically ignored by school reformers, is that educational requirements piled onto high schools cannot substitute for real economic and social incentives for study. If many demanding and rewarding jobs awaited well-educated high school graduates, lots of students who now take it easy would work harder. If college and university entrance requirements were substantial, many students who now idle through the college track would step on the gas. But when real incentives that make hard work in high school rational for most students are absent, requirements alone have an Alice-in-Wonderland effect, crazily compounding the problems that schools already have. For the requirements fly in the face of what everyone knows, inviting disbelief and evasion, creating a widespread sense that the enterprise is dishonest — and this sense is fatal to good teaching and learning.

Still, there is a certain logic to the requirements. It is easier to criticize high schools than it is to criticize great corporations. It is easier to impose educational requirements on high schools than it is to press higher education to devise and enforce stronger entrance requirements — especially when many colleges and universities are hungry for bodies. And it is easier to press requirements on public institutions than it is to repair labor market problems that arise in that diffuse entity called the private sector.

One encouraging feature of the eighties debate about high schools is that it presented an opportunity to raise these questions. But one discouraging fact is that they were raised so infrequently. It seems plain enough that apathy, a sense of irrelevance, and compulsion are not the ingredients of good education. It seems plain that compounding this stew of sentiments with more requirements cannot improve education much; it may only further corrupt it. But if all of this is well known to educators, few voices were raised to question their corrupting effects. Nor did many commentators point out that even if problems in labor markets and higher education will not be addressed, there are other ways to cope with youth who see nothing for themselves in secondary studies. One is a national youth service, open to students of high school age. Another is lifetime educational entitlements for those who cannot make good use of secondary school on the established schedule. Still another is a lowered school-leaving age. These ideas have all been advanced before, and in one way or another America has had experience with each. Yet they found little place in the eighties debate. Whether or not schools are the appropriate target for reform, they are available, visible, and easy to hit. They are an easy mark for officials who feel they must respond to popular dismay about education, but who have not the time or inclination to probe a little into the sources of dismay.

It seems odd that educators have failed to make these arguments and have instead insisted again that high schools can meet all students' needs. They repeated the old litanies about programs that are practical, interesting, and relevant. They urged that dropouts be pressed back into school. And they pleaded only that more money was required. In part this is a reflex of tradition: educators have long been committed to the evangelical notion that schools have something for everyone. In part it is self-serving: most school systems get state aid based on the number of students attending. And in part it is political strategy: educators have rarely pointed out the misdirection of reform efforts because they want to capitalize on public interest — even critical interest. Promising to do more has long been a way to avoid disappointing constituents while squeezing out more money, hiring more teachers, gaining more esteem, or improving working conditions. The strategy makes sense from one angle — appropriations to education have increased over the decades. But it has also been foolish, because the added resources have remained modest in comparison to the promises that educators have made and the demands that they have embraced. What the high schools delivered for most students therefore has always been much thinner and less effective than what was advertised. By promising to do everything well for everyone, educators have contributed to the growing sense that they can do nothing well for anyone.

There is one last, unhappy reason that educators have not pointed to certain misdirections in the current crop of reforms: one cannot point to an incorrect direction without some sense of the correct one. But American schoolpeople have been singularly unable to think of an educational purpose that they should not embrace. As a result, they never have made much effort to figure out what high schools could do well, what high schools should do, and how they could best do it. Secondary educators have tried to solve the problem of competing purposes by accepting all of them, and by building an institution that would accommodate the result.

Unfortunately, the flip side of the belief that all directions are correct is the belief that no direction is incorrect — which is a sort of intellectual bankruptcy. Those who work in secondary education have little sense of an agenda for studies. There is only a long list of subjects that may be studied, a longer list of courses that may be taken, and a list of requirements for graduation. But there is no answer to the query, Why these and not others? Approaching things this way has made it easy to avoid arguments and decisions about purpose, both of which can be troublesome — especially in our divided and contentious society. But this approach has made it easy for schools to accept many assignments that they could not do well, and it has made nearly any sort of work from students and teachers acceptable, as long as it caused no trouble.

Another way to put the point is to say that most of the foundation work of decent secondary education still remains to be done, seven or eight decades after the system began to take shape. High schools seem unlikely to make marked improvement, especially for the many students and teachers now drifting around the malls, until there is a much clearer sense of what is most important to teach and learn, and why, and how it can best be done. This is an enormous job, one that is never finished but should long ago have been started. We watched hundreds of teachers at work, but in most cases no sense of intellectual purpose shone through. The most common purposes were getting through the period or covering the material, or some combination of the two. But why does one cover the material? If the only answer is that it has been mandated, or that it is in the book, then how can the material be taught well, or learned more than fleetingly?

Americans will never completely agree on educational purposes. But educators could, through study and debate, have made some decisions to guide them in public argument and professional work. They might have decided, for instance, that their chief purpose was to produce students who could read well and critically, who could write plainly and persuasively, and who could reason clearly. Reading, writing, and reasoning are not subjects — they are intellectual capacities. They can be taught by studying academic disciplines, but only if the teachers possess the capacities in good measure, if they are trying to teach those capacities rather than to cover the material, and if the materials for study are arranged so as to cultivate those capacities — as opposed, say, to the capacity to remember a few facts, or write down disjointed bits of information.

We do not imply that these capacities are content-free, as so many approaches to "basic skills" seem to suggest today. But neither are these capacities the same thing as subjects or disciplines. In fact, the capacities we mention probably could better be cultivated if teachers were able to range across disciplines. Critical reading ability is as crucial to learning English as to learning history, and clear reasoning is no more the special province of mathematics than it is of physics or philosophy. Cutting the curriculum up into subjects makes it easy for students and teachers to forget the capacities that ought to be cultivated, and easier to pursue the illusion that education is a matter of covering the material. All of the standard academic subjects are good material for cultivating these capacities, but that is rather a different way of looking at them than as content to be learned.

This brief formulation leaves out a good deal, but it does reveal how much work remains to be done if high schools are to improve substantially. If educators could agree on such purposes, they would be better armed for debating about education and for deciding that some things cannot be done because others are more important. In addition, they would be in a position to think seriously about pedagogy — that is, about how to achieve educational purposes. Amazingly, high school educators have yet to take up this work as a profession. They have inherited a few catch phrases from the progressives: making studies practical; meeting students' needs; building the curriculum around activities — but even these have not been much developed. Perhaps there is little to develop. At the moment we don't know, because a pedagogy for high schools remains to be created.

There have been some beginnings, but most have remained very limited, or have fallen into disuse, or both. From time to time, various reformers have tried to reformulate educational purposes and to sketch out suitable pedagogy, usually from the perspective of one discipline or another. Many of these efforts — most recently, the 1950s curriculum reforms — have been promising. But these never spread very far, or cut very deep. Only a small number of teachers ever used the new materials as the basis for working out a pedagogy for secondary studies, and all reports suggest that most of these efforts have since been abandoned. Of course, every teacher has an approach to her or his craft, but each approach is practiced in isolation and does not contribute to a body of shared professional knowledge about how to teach. These separately practiced versions of the teacher's trade do not contribute to developing the skills of those entering the profession, or to deciding about when teaching is good enough, or to improving teaching when it is not good enough. This is an unfortunate list, one that many teachers regret. For every teacher must solve the problem of how to teach. But because the schools have embraced so many purposes, they have impeded the development of a body of professional knowledge about how to teach well. The high schools' many successes have helped to produce this failure.

What we outline is a tall order. We do so partly in the hope that it may help a little in current efforts to improve the schools. But our brief discussion of purposes and pedagogy also reveals just how far high schools are from such improvement. The high schools' greatest strength has been their embracing capacity to avoid these issues, to cope with many contrary visions of education by promising to pursue all of them. That has produced institutions that are re- markably flexible, ambitious, and tolerant, capable of making room for many different sorts of students and teachers and many different wishes for education. They are institutions nicely suited to cope with Americans' fickle political and educational sensibilities. All are important strengths, but they have had crippling effects. They have stunted the high schools' capacity to take all students seriously. They have blocked teachers' capacity to cultivate those qualities long valued in educated men and women — the ability to read well and critically, to write plainly and persuasively, and to reason clearly. And they have nurtured a constrained and demeaning vision of education among Americans, a vision that persistently returns to haunt the profession that helped to create it.

Conclusion: Renegotiating the Treaties

DEEPLY IMBEDDED in American history and deeply reflective of American preferences, the shopping mall high school is likely to withstand efforts to dismantle it: too many teenagers are served in the way they want to be served, and too many school professionals willingly provide the services. Many students are served very well indeed, and most graduate. Those are historic achievements. Whatever school participants and the public in general may think about high schools in the abstract, they seem generally satisfied with or tolerant of the educational accommodations made in their own local schools. Much of what is proposed as educational reform is thus designed to make the mall more appealing to sellers and shoppers alike, rather than to alter the educational assumptions on which it is based.

In most communities and for most students, the mall works well because it is so exclusively governed by consumer choice. Learning is voluntary: it is one among many things for sale. The mall's central qualities — variety of offerings, choice among them, and neutrality about their value — have succeeded in holding most teenagers on terms they and their teachers can live with. The will to learn is perceived, in a deceptively sensible formulation, simply as the responsibility of students and their families. Students who want to learn generally can do so, especially if they seek out or are sought out by specialty shops where a focused commitment to learning prevails. Pushy parents and pushy lobbies demand more for some, and if they succeed they also become satisfied customers. Dissatisfied but savvy parents seek out options such as fancier shopping mall high schools or private schools; having taken their business elsewhere, they are no longer dissatisfied. In a consumer society, attendance at one's local school is not automatic.

Of course high school does not hold everyone. Not everybody is satisfied. Especially in some of the largest cities, a high dropout rate is becoming a major educational dilemma. But the proposed solutions are familiar: make all the schools more like shopping malls, not less. The mall is the solution, not the problem. It suggests educational prosperity just as a new shopping mall in an old neighborhood signals economic prosperity. If not enough exciting courses or programs hold every student, more must be created. If not enough social services lay the groundwork for attachment to school, more must be offered. If many students are unspecial because there are few specialty shops, more shops must be developed.

But even where the shopping mall high school is working well and its prosperity is the envy of outsiders, many students — and especially many average students — do not learn. They avoid learning. The accommodations made to hold students and keep the peace permit this option. It is easy to avoid learning and still graduate. It is even easy to do so and graduate believing that one has learned. Avoidance can be wrapped in brightly packaged illusions. Behind impressive course titles lie the realities of very different classroom treaties. Students can accumulate endless credits without taking classes committed to engaging them in the subjects they are supposed to be studying. Nor are they pressed to engage in the realm of character and conduct. Most seem satisfied with this arrangement.

High schools thus solve many problems for themselves and their clients by saying, "It's here if you want it but it's all up to you." Yet this advantageous institutional treaty allows schools to abdicate responsibility for pushing all students to learn and to care about learning. If schools with high dropout rates reduce them by emulating more privileged shopping mall high schools, they may do little more than keep students off the streets. The unspecial majority will remain so, even while more of them pass through and graduate.

And many who participate in certain specialty shops may find immediate satisfaction and success without really learning to use their minds. Specialness in high school is often a temporary illusion.

Teachers have few incentives to change the system. It works for them just as it works for students. Most good teachers prefer to be with students who want to learn. Working usually in isolation from one another, without much institutional support, teachers find it hard to push students who do not want to be pushed. Pushing teenagers is especially difficult when it is framed as an isolated transaction between one teacher and his or her students. It is easier and often perfectly understandable for teachers to define their jobs as offering opportunities to those who want them. It is easier for them to explain classroom treaties for avoidance by arguing that students won't work or can't learn. It is easier for them to settle for a relaxed classroom atmosphere as an end in itself. It is particularly easy for those who resemble many of their students to do this. Lacking education and commitment to their work, they too prefer undemanding classes. They are satisfied, as long as students attend and are not disruptive.

Despite periodic cries for quality or excellence, there is little agreement in the society or among high school educators that teaching students to use their minds fully is either needed by most youngsters or possible for them. Most educators act as if they believe that feeling successful at something or feeling good about oneself is enough. Most act as if they believe that the "smarts" needed for life are not really taught in high school. Most high school classes reflect these beliefs. They suggest exactly what most people already believe: that thinking is the preserve of smart kids, and that the satisfactions to be derived from academic subjects are remote and esoteric, associated only with social or intellectual privilege.

Anti-intellectualism is often regarded by despairing intellectuals as an entrenched American trait, and high schools unwittingly reinforce rather than challenge it. They do not regard themselves as a countervailing force, a last citadel competing on behalf of students against the popular culture. The schools have done a masterly job at selling the importance of high school attendance, but have failed in the attempt to sell to most students the value of working hard to learn to use one's mind.

Ironically, education lacks the very vocabulary — the persuasive slogans — that might make the case more convincingly. Images of the "life of the mind" or of the "intellect" too often suggest a dry and dull life of distance from the world. "Cognition" or "higher-order skills" are technical terms that excite researchers more than consumers. "Academics" seem remote and — academic. These traditional words and phrases are the conventional weapons in the arsenal of advocates of excellence, but they have been weak and unpersuasive weapons. The catch phrase "life skills" is a revealing euphemism for anything schools teach that is not connected with students' minds.

In such circumstances, what incentives might be harnessed to rearrange the most educationally unproductive features of the shopping mall high school? Could the fact of individual differences, a fact that the shopping mall high school recognizes, be married to a commitment to help different individuals all learn to use their minds well, a commitment from which it withdraws?

Impatient reformers who underestimate public satisfaction with local schools often advocate change from the top. If students are not achieving enough, require them to work harder — or, more specifically, require them to take certain courses, do more homework, spend more days in school. Apply the stick with a vengeance, since for many the carrots of variety and choice do not seem to be working and the stick of mastery requirements for entry to jobs or colleges has broken into harmless splinters. Apply the stick to teachers, too: tell them exactly what must be covered, and hold them to other requirements as well.

Such measures are attractive to legislators and other policymakers in part because they can be done quickly and sometimes cheaply. And they have a compelling logic: if incentives to learn are not provided by the marketplace itself — by employers or universities — then public authority itself should provide them. But this approach contains several problems. First, top-down reform usually skirts the question of what students have actually learned in favor of emphasizing superficial symbols of learning: what courses are taken, how many credits are accumulated, how much homework is given, how long a student spends in school. "Standards" can thus be raised without much attention to actual performance. It

is easier to build a political consensus around such recommendations
— they seem responsive to the clamor to do something, they sometimes create additional professional employment, and they sometimes are linked with proposals to raise teacher salaries — than
to build a consensus about what high school graduates should know
and be able to do upon graduation, for such a consensus flies in
the face of the belief that high school graduation should be available
to everyone.

Further, there is no consensus about what performance standards
at the secondary level should be. One person's notion of minimal
mastery is another person's notion of unfair exclusion. This is not
surprising in a society which requires that the idea of standards
be linked to the idea that everyone can meet them. It is not surprising
in a pluralistic democracy where many notions of excellence prevail.
Even good schools with clearly focused purposes often do not have
the same purposes. They will resist standards imposed from above
— calling them unwise "standardization" — not because they dislike
standards but because uniform, mandated standards get in the way
of teaching those things they believe most worthy.

A second problem is that reform from the top too often attacks
the problem of standards from the extremes, where the short-term
stakes seem highest, and ignores the average or middle student,
where the major long-term problems lie. A variety of tests already
provide incentives for teachers and students at the top end of high
schools. Minimum competency tests attempt to provide a minimum,
if often vapid, standard at the very bottom. If the stick approach
is to change anything, it must be applied in particular to the average
child where, at present, there is far less consensus about what standards are most appropriate.

Finally, most top-down schemes can easily be subverted in schools
and classrooms if they have little support from parents, students,
and teachers. Such reform schemes have been frustrated for decades.
Requirements can be undercut by redefining what subjects mean
or by negotiating treaties inside classrooms. Many things can be
labeled as mathematics, for example, that have little to do with
it, and many courses with the same names and catalog descriptions
can be encountered inside classrooms in wholly different ways. It
is hard to mandate a new work ethic about academic studies that

commands the support only of politicians and academic reformers. The incentives to comply must be closer to the interests and commitments of the people directly affected. Much top-down reform may be popular precisely because it does not really affect engagement with learning at the classroom level.

What other grassroots incentives might be mobilized to do so? Shopping mall high schools are sensitive to market conditions and consumer demand, so one potential source of change is dissatisfied customers. Although they may have freely chosen to be taken to the cleaners, and although many feel they have received a good deal instead of a raw deal, the potential still exists for a consumer rebellion. What must be mobilized is greater consumer awareness: the shock of recognition that institutions which serve the savvy and the powerful well, serve others poorly.

Educated consumers have often created organized lobbies of one sort or another to modify the mall to meet their demands. Sometimes the modifications add shops to the mall; variety then increases. But more significantly, the modifications tighten the communal bonds between students and adults, and between students and other students. Both choice and neutrality diminish. Adult push and coherent purpose increase. The danger of anonymity, artfully disguised as individualization, is reduced by greater personal attention. These are crucial ways that specialness is encouraged inside the mall; they are the same features sought by families who withdraw children entirely from it.

Informed consumers of high school should understand when variety, choice, and neutrality become counterproductive for particular individuals. They should realize that the very factors that make many average youngsters unspecial — they are neither skilled enough nor problematic enough to stand out — also make them trouble-free, invisible, and taken for granted by schools. Parents of such children should become forceful advocates themselves, and should organize if they individually lack the means to send their children to another school. They will have to do what other parents and groups have done before them.

Nearly everyone wants to be special in some way; the embryonic incentives for such advocacy exist. Advocacy for "regular" or "normal" youngsters must realize that ordinariness is in part perpetuated and even welcomed by the shopping mall high school. Advocacy must demand that they not be left alone. Whether this will occur is highly uncertain: perceived specialness at either end of the spectrum creates momentum for parents as well as schools to do things that perceived unspecialness does not. Unusual gifts or unusual handicaps make people with them more visible, more problematic, more demanding of unusual attention, than people without them. But despite such built-in burdens, a movement on behalf of the average student is not unthinkable, perhaps not impossible.

It becomes less unthinkable if parents are not their only advocates. Pressure on schools to convert as many teenagers as possible to special status, rather than just to serve existing sorts of specialness, needs the advocacy of good teachers too. The most logical potential allies of these students and their parents are skilled and committed teachers; their greatest enemies are teachers who settle for avoidance of learning. Where skilled teachers are a small minority, they usually gravitate to students and families who already appreciate them and are committed to working hard. They respond to the absence of like-minded colleagues (assuming they themselves remain in teaching) by forming a tight little enclave of their own, a support group that includes only the most special students. They will normally avoid the average student if they can; but they usually cannot, particularly if top-track specialty shops are not that large. Not surprisingly, the greatest demands made on the least proficient students come from the best teachers.

Thus the presence of more good teachers — and especially of a critical mass of good teachers large enough to be a majority voice in a school — is especially important for average students. They are the teachers least inclined to tolerate unspecialness, the most inclined to expect more from everyone. There is no shortage of reasonable approaches to making teaching a more attractive calling; they include better pay, a more differentiated career ladder within teaching, the creation of working conditions attractive to educated adults, and changes in how prospective teachers are recruited and educated. All of these ideas can be pursued to good effect.

But teaching also can be made more attractive by renegotiating some of the treaties in the shopping mall high school. Indeed, the very items that might be renegotiated to improve the education of average students could also make high schools more desirable places for good teachers to work. We see three major areas for renegotiation — purpose, push, and personalization. All have in common the building of deeper ties among school participants and the aim of establishing more committed learning communities. They all assume that greater adult responsibility is necessary to educate students to assume responsibility. New treaties toward this end would make high schools more effective educationally and more attractive for good teachers.

The most obvious way to create more focused educational purpose is to expand upon existing practice: to create more specialty shops. More efforts along the general lines of the Beta program discussed in Chapter 4 would make more average youngsters feel special. Students of all kinds usually thrive by participation in institutions with distinctive purposes and common expectations. Magnet schools, examination schools, and schools-within-schools are expressions of the desire for communities of focused educational and often moral purpose. Because they are special places to begin with, teachers and students feel more special in them. Both are more likely to be committed to a purpose and the expectations that flow from it if they choose — and are chosen by — schools or subschools than if they are simply assigned to them. The existence of a common purpose has an educational force of its own, quite independent of the skills of individual teachers. It also helps good teachers do a better job and may soften the impact of less able teachers. Of course shopping mall high schools try to encourage purpose, but it usually is only school loyalty and spirit. Such a purpose may mobilize local pride, or maintain harmonious internal relations. But a sense of community — a precious lever for any school — is wasted educationally if not closely associated with the importance of learning.

Even if schools are prepared to risk some premature specialization or social isolation in return for greater commitment to learning, expanding the number and variety of specialty shops involves other risks. One is their tendency to be refined versions of enclaves for the already special. The programs may be terrific, but they tend to draw students who are already committed to learning; they rarely try to make the unspecial special. (Beta was a spectacular exception.) A related limitation is their voluntary nature. They allow the reasonably committed student to become better served, which is all to the good, but they touch the less committed average youngster hardly at all. Not only must more programs like Beta be created — clever and aggressive marketing will also be essential for success. Students may not flock immediately to such programs; patience and recruitment will be necessary. But greater supply may well create greater demand.

An essential ingredient in focused purpose for the less proficient or committed is a clear expectation that teachers push students. A good school must be morally averse to low expectations. Inside classrooms, the absence of students' skill in using their minds should never be an excuse for not trying to develop that skill, whether the subject is vocational electronics or academic algebra. The less proficient the student, the more engagement should be pressed. An attitude of push does not imply a barracks-like environment where students are forced to do as they are told. The goal is not to train dutiful soldiers but to develop responsible young adults. For most youngsters, some adult push is crucial to learning responsibility. Further, the existence of push does not imply an attack on therapeutic ideals of "self-esteem" in the name of academic austerity. But it does imply that, within schools, the ideal of self-esteem must be tightly linked with serious engagement in learning. Not all students will achieve the same. Some teenagers are in fact more special than others; some are profoundly ordinary and will remain that way. But teachers must believe that their students can do more than students think they can or say they will, and push them accordingly. That faith should be an important component of professional credentials.

It is especially crucial to substitute personal attention for anonymous individualization. Even if some teenagers say they prefer anonymity because they feel rejected, dejected, or just shy, abandoning them to make their own way should not be tolerated. Even if high schools continue a studied neutrality about what knowledge is of most worth, or what ethical principles are essential beyond basic civility, they need not be neutral about anonymous individualization. Parents who disagree about other things, or are passive and uninformed about school, usually agree that they want their children known seriously as individuals by key adults in school.

Personalization has a human and a professional dimension. The human side involves knowing students from the point of view of a concerned adult friend, while the professional side adds the element of specialized knowledge about particular strengths and weaknesses in learning. No one can know students seriously in these ways when the only adults charged with the task — the counselors — confront three or four hundred students and must spend most of their time on those who command special attention: the handicapped, the troubled, the top-track enclave. All teachers and indeed all school-based professionals should advise students on a regular basis. Therapeutic skills are not what most students need from advisers. What they need are adults who know them as unique learners, complex and distinctive.

Adults need time to play this role and need the institutional expectation that they play it. They must be able to talk with students privately, not just in a crisis, to discuss students with colleagues, and to prepare assessments of student work that go beyond letter grades. They must pay particular attention to families. As family commitment to school or knowledge about it diminishes, as it often does when students and especially low-income students enter high school, the obligation of schools to reach out to families should increase. This has been a remarkably low priority for shopping mall high schools.

In a more specialized way, schools and teachers should accommodate differences in how students learn rather than preferences about whether they should learn. It may be that the greatest impact of the special-needs movement will be to provide broad models for recognizing that every teenager is in some sense special and therefore requires some individual planning, based on assessments of the student's work, consultations among teachers, and discussions between schoolpeople and the student's parents. Testing may help here, if it aims to uncover specific problems and strengths rather than to rank students as life's winners and losers. But the very notion of individual diagnosis and planning is absurd in the face of the typical loads of 120–130 students that most teachers carry.

Renegotiating treaties to emphasize purpose, push, and personalization thus requires some reorganization of the shopping mall high school, a reorganization that goes beyond creating more specialty shops. Restructuring might begin with a rearrangement of how students and teachers spend time in school. Too much time is presently spent in classes. Both discussions and lectures are frequently unproductive and boring to students and teachers alike. Many seem to exist primarily for custodial reasons. Discussions are characterized by many kinds of avoidance, not only because discussions are difficult to conduct when students lack skills and commitment, but also because few teachers have the energy to fill class after class, day after day, with productive discussions. The hardest kind of class to teach well, a discussion can also be an easy way to avoid learning. In addition, most lectures we observed lacked drama or even excitement; they repeated material easily available elsewhere or were discursive and ill-informed.

Reducing the frequency of discussions and lectures would cause no major loss in any of the schools we observed. If they were less routine, they could be better planned, more special, and more effective. It may be more valuable for a student infrequently to encounter one intense discussion or lecture than to endure daily doses of a diet where it is well understood that everyone is going through the motions. Less may be more.

Reducing the number of conventional classes would allow school time to be used for more productive ends. For many average students, the kind of independent work often associated with homework — but work that rarely gets done at home or anywhere else — may productively be done in school. Teachers could then answer questions, check and correct work as it is done, demonstrate a correct procedure at the moment when a student needs to know it, and help students to learn on their own. Teachers could provide the kind of personal attention to students *at work* which parents or peers routinely provide for those students who take homework home and take it seriously. If courses met less frequently as conventional classes, teachers would also have more time for individual or small group tutorials, coaching sessions, or chances to connect directly with families. Everyone's day-to-day activities could be more varied and less routinized. Teacher schedules could resemble more closely the schedules of counselors and special-needs instructors.

Teachers also might have more time to discuss students with other teachers. Few things contribute to student anonymity more than the isolation of their teachers from one another. Teachers in such circumstances might even have the time and the obligation to talk to each other about education itself, and perhaps to watch each other teach. A sense of colleagueship, built around instruction, is indispensable for the creation of common educational purpose. Teachers need time for it, especially when fragmenting forces, such as departmental specialization, discourage it.

If teachers talked more with each other about both education and students, the chances for productive exchange about the effects of their efforts on students would increase. They could begin to discuss curriculum in its proper and broad context: what students should know and be able to do at the end of high school, not everyone to the same extent but everyone in the same direction. Many of the most serious "life skills" that high schools can teach — speaking cogently, writing clearly, reading with understanding, listening with empathy, having facility with numbers, solving problems — are not the exclusive domain of one subject. They need constant reinforcement in many subjects throughout high school. Facility with numbers, for example, is forever doomed to be the exclusive possession of the mathematically talented unless it is practiced in courses ranging from science to the arts. But it will not be so used until math teachers and other teachers know what each other is teaching, when, to whom, and why — and until they can seriously discuss these connections with each other.

It is more important to organize school time so that such conversations can occur, and are expected to occur, than to impose an ideal curriculum on schools from the outside. Effective treaties, for one thing, must be developed by those with a stake in compliance. Further, rearranging school time in this manner empowers teachers by placing them in the center of educational decision-making rather than on the periphery. It empowers good teachers by removing the protective isolation that allows the mediocre to survive and the competent to remain impotent. And it underscores that an effective school for students and a desirable one for teachers is a genuine community of learning for both. It thus helps make the job of teaching more attractive to the most able. Much depends on that.

The reallocation of school time is only an example of how the promotion of purpose, push, and personalization requires organizational change, in addition to commitment to the ideals themselves. It is an example of how change might take place through a tradeoff — we will do this instead of that — rather than through a massive infusion of new money or new requirements. And it is an example of the leadership that school professionals, teachers and principals alike, might exert.

But it is not necessarily an idea whose time has come. More parents, students, and teachers must be willing to press for new high school treaties, in these and other ways. Activists on all sides must engage one another, if new terms that can be honorably observed are to be found. The gains for education and democracy from such efforts could be large. But they could be hard to win. Present arrangements meet many preferences, and new agreements will emerge slowly.

Procedures

OUR EARLIEST RESEARCH DECISION was to examine a few schools in depth. This notion grew out of a year-long series of weekly seminars held with Mr. Sizer in 1980 to plan A Study of High Schools. Following readings, discussions, and several school visits, we adopted a two-pronged approach. First, we chose to look at schools primarily from the viewpoint of those who knew them best — the staff, students, and parents. We would study high schools from the inside out. Ms. Farrar had considerable experience observing school practice and talking to school participants. Mr. Cohen had done some similar work. He and Mr. Powell also were historians. Our backgrounds and interests inclined us to look closely and listen carefully, to treat the record of interviews and classroom observations as crucial documents in a rich archive.

We decided to concentrate on recurrent patterns in the voices of people inside schools. What were the central images or metaphors through which they understood the experience of school, and the central ways they dealt with each other and school subjects? This would not be a quantitative analysis. But as we surveyed the various efforts already under way — notably John Goodlad's large-scale Study of Schooling and the various projects of the High School and Beyond study — we were certain that survey and other statistical methods would not be neglected in the emerging rediscovery of high school as a subject for inquiry.

325

Procedures

Our second approach was to focus on themes that cut across schools, rather than on the particulars of life in each school. The latter method was admittedly tempting. Individual schools provide a compelling organizing principle even before any data about them are collected. Each school differs from others in revealing ways. Certain themes, such as how social class, family income and educational background, or school location affects the "culture" of schools, can usefully be explored through case studies. Important work along these lines, by Sara Lawrence Lightfoot, Philip Cusick, and others, was already under way. As the work progressed, we decided on a different but complementary strategy: to examine how issues, structures, and assumptions cut across schools, instead of how schools differed from each other. We chose a thematic rather than a case-by-case approach, in large part because the themes that emerged seemed so compelling.

The first practical task was to choose the schools. Within constraints of time and resources we sought a rough representation of the kinds of schools most American teenagers attend, along with a deliberate overrepresentation of schools that a minority attend — private schools. Private schools had rarely been studied before, were increasingly in the news as an alternative to some public schools, seemed particularly prone to stereotyping, and were the primary constituency of one of our sponsoring organizations. The inclusion of three private schools that charged substantial tuitions — our fourth private school contained a larger fraction of poor students than all but three of the public schools — guaranteed that economic affluence would not be underrepresented. (Real estate values in one community indicated that the most economically selective of all the fifteen schools was a public high school.) Analytically these selections were advantageous: in schooling, as in much of American life, present reality for the more privileged is also future wish for the less privileged. A good way to learn what the educational experience for the many may be tomorrow is to examine what it is for the few today. On all of these grounds, inclusion of several unambiguously privileged schools in a total of fifteen seemed both novel and sensible.

Representativeness beyond this factor required attending to several criteria. We sought a national distribution; an urban, suburban,

326

and rural distribution; a distribution by family income; a distribution by school size; and a distribution according to the racial and ethnic mix of student bodies. We emphasized comprehensive public high schools more than special-purpose ones (we excluded separate vocational/technical schools, magnet schools, and examination schools), and emphasized mainstream rather than special-purpose private schools (we excluded boarding and single-sex schools, and we underrepresented religiously affiliated private schools to facilitate comparisons with secular public schools).

Large numbers of schools met these criteria. We limited somewhat the potential pool by one further criterion, to group schools in geographical clusters where possible. This was a practical way to minimize the wear and tear on a field staff who would be spending much time away from home, and also a way to exploit the economic efficiencies in working with groups of schools close together. Equally important, we hoped to study the interaction among certain schools in the same community — especially public and private schools. In particular, we sought out students and parents who had direct experience with more than one school in the inquiry. Eleven of the fifteen schools finally chosen were clustered.

The actual choices were made largely for logistical reasons. Based in Boston, we chose a cluster of nearby schools. Cambridge Rindge and Latin School was a large institution enrolling 2700 students, the only public high school in a small but remarkably diverse city. (For this and the other schools, enrollments are rounded estimates for the 1981–82 school year. Since then several three-year high schools have gained additional students by adding a ninth grade.) Newton North High School was also sizable. Its 2300 students in grades 10–12 resided in a large suburban community traditionally known as an educational lighthouse, but the school served a more heterogeneous population than its reputation might have indicated. With 1300 students, Watertown High School described itself as a predominantly blue-collar, working-class, white ethnic community. Buckingham, Browne & Nichols, a Cambridge independent school, drew many of its 400 secondary students from Cambridge, Newton, and Watertown.

Denver was attractive because we had personal contacts with several of its schools, because it had problems of population transition in common with many cities, and because of its location. East High School (1500 students) possessed a long tradition of academic excellence in Colorado, but had undergone traumas of transition in the 1960s and 1970s. Manual High School (1000 students) had recently been integrated by court order from a primarily black school to one quite diverse in class and race. Colorado Academy, a small independent school in suburban Denver, drew some of its high school enrollment of 200 from the East and Manual districts and also sent some students to those schools.

The San Diego area, in which one of us had conducted research before, satisfied our wish to include a cluster of schools from the growing Sun Belt region. San Diego High School, one of the oldest in California, attracted a predominantly Hispanic population of some 1300 students, and had many of the problems characteristic of inner cities. La Jolla High, also part of the San Diego school district, was by contrast an affluent institution enrolling 1300. Nearby, The Bishop's Schools represented a church-affiliated independent school of 500 students. Considerable student movement in both directions existed between La Jolla and Bishop's. A few miles to the northeast, Vista High School was a large (2300 students) and growing school in a growing town.

With these clusters established, we sought additional schools to fill gaps of representativeness. In northwest Ohio we chose Findlay High School, an institution of 1700 students in a relatively stable large town. And in Cleveland, we selected Cleveland Central Catholic High School, whose primarily white ethnic student body of 900 also included a significant fraction of black students. In the south, Andalusia High School enrolled some 700 students in a rural Alabama town, while the predominantly black Williamson High School served 1000 students in urban Mobile. These selections by no means captured the full diversity of American high schools, but we were satisfied that, given the constraints, our basic criteria had been reasonably met.

Finding the field research staff was of equal importance. All of the field staff were former teachers or school administrators, although teaching experience in a few cases was primarily at the elementary level and in one case at the college level. Several also had well-established reputations in educational research. Some were advanced doctoral students in education who planned to return to schools to assume positions of increased responsibility. Just as we sought diversity between research and practitioner backgrounds, we also sought diversity in other qualities that mirrored the characteristics of the schools we would observe — for example, sex, race, ethnicity, and type of school in which major professional experience had been obtained. Two field staff members took responsibility for each of the fifteen schools, and we attempted to include in each team one individual with research experience and another with school experience as a teacher or administrator. To ensure overall continuity Ms. Farrar and Mr. Powell conducted field research in all the schools, and Mr. Cohen in some of them.

Most of the field work was carried out in three rounds during the fall, winter, and spring of 1981–82. Teams typically spent three to five consecutive days in each school during each round, visiting all schools in a cluster or region on each trip. The research consisted of individual and group interviews, along with classroom observations, during each period of the school day. School administrators arranged the schedules according to our requests, which became more specific (for example, requests to observe particular teachers teaching particular types of classes) as the investigation progressed. In addition to school staff and students, interviews were conducted with parents and district-level administrators.

Interviews were tape-recorded, and the field staff often took notes simultaneously. Notes on classroom observations were made by hand. Afterward, staff members listened to the tapes, reread notes, and then wrote a "field note" for each interview or observation, relying on the tapes for direct interview quotes. A typed field note ranged in length from one page to more than twenty. After all the field notes for each visit had been transcribed, distributed, and read, the team members plus one or more of the three authors met together to discuss the visits and the field notes. These "debriefings" allowed teams to elaborate and explain, and to report events or interpretations not in the notes. Sometimes additional internal papers were prepared as a result of debriefings.

An orientation program for the field staff, devised and primarily conducted by Ms. Farrar, paid special attention to the problem of observer bias and to the first round of visits. The main goal of round one was to learn what people in schools thought was most important about their schools and how they did their daily business. This open-ended charge was implemented through a set of interview guides for teachers, administrators, and students, and a guide for observing classrooms. The first-round guides were relatively unstructured, since we wanted to have issues and themes emerge from the schools rather than to impose too many preconceived ideas upon them. These visits emphasized issues to explore more than specific questions to ask. Field staff members were encouraged to use judgment and deviate from the guides if additional important concerns surfaced. The metaphor of the high school as a shopping mall, among other themes, emerged from this round.

After round one it became clear that the staff had been struck particularly by classroom interactions between teachers and students that varied greatly within schools but less so between schools. We focused the second round on classroom interaction, and especially on instruction at different levels or tracks. The interview and observation guides were less open-ended than in round one. We asked administrators to arrange, where possible, observations of the same teacher — in English, social studies, and a science — teaching a high-, a middle-, and a low-level class. We arranged interviews with these teachers, often more than one interview, and also interviews with students in each of the classes. We attempted to follow groups of students who together attended more than one of the classes. And we asked staff and parents about differences and similarities among the classes in instructional technique, grading, homework, and similar matters. Many of the field notes that suggested the notion of treaties were written during round two.

The third round primarily addressed nonacademic dimensions of school life, dimensions that had been neglected in round two but were considered very important by many school participants. These included extracurricular activities, special programs and services, and social interaction among different student groups. Round three helped to sharpen the emerging idea of specialty shops within high schools and also produced, from schoolpeople, the concept of the unspecial student.

The result of this effort was more than 1400 field notes about interviews and classroom observations, plus a collection of published and unpublished materials from each school. After the visits were over we continued our efforts to find order and meaning in this abundance of material. The authors divided the schools among themselves, and each wrote several papers about particular schools. These papers formed the basis of various discussions about how themes in them cut across schools, and how they did not. The final product of these discussions was a long outline of how the themes fit together, initially drafted by Mr. Powell, and an outline of how they could usefully be understood in the context of modern American history, initially drafted by Mr. Cohen. Subsequent discussions led to revisions, amendments, and finally general agreement.

Each author then chose the chapters he or she would write: Mr. Powell Chapters 1, 2, and 4, Ms. Farrar Chapter 3, and Mr. Cohen Chapter 5. The author who had special familiarity with the notes on a particular school, gained from the preparation of the internal papers, assumed responsibility for sharing with the other authors the most pertinent data relevant to the master outline. In certain cases they were assisted in this effort by Martha Landesberg and Robert Hampel. But each chapter was written by only one of us; if the argument is a joint product, the text itself is much more individual.

All descriptions of classes or people, along with all direct quotations in Chapters 1–4, come directly from the field notes and attempt to be faithful to the context of complete interviews or observations. There are no composite portraits of any sort. Every character in the book represents a real person and every class an actual class. But to preserve confidentiality all names have been changed and, in a few cases, sex as well. Any resemblance between a name used in the text and the name of anyone observed or interviewed, or the name of anyone else, is completely coincidental. The system of name selection was not entirely random, as those connected with a certain boys' soccer team may notice, but no association of any kind was intended between particular text names and particular individuals. The intention throughout has been to preserve complete confidentiality.

Our method is thus eclectic, and is best understood as closer to traditional historical research than to much of contemporary social science (indeed, one chapter is explicitly historical). By this we mean that we read carefully, again and again, many documents to seek patterns and meaning in different voices. The argument was constructed incrementally over a two-year period, through constant interaction with the documents and each other. It is only one of several complementary arguments that might have been constructed with the same data. But it is the one that best seemed to capture what we had seen, heard, and read.

Several research reports that appeared or were in preparation during the course of writing this book cast additional light on themes we attempt to develop. Philip A. Cusick's *The Egalitarian Ideal and the American High School: Studies of Three Schools* (Longman: New York and London, 1983) insightfully explores the processes of accommodating in one institution those who do not want to be there as well as those who do. John I. Goodlad's *A Place Called School: Prospects for the Future* (McGraw-Hill: New York, 1983) is not about high schools exclusively, but provides a wealth of wisely interpreted material on secondary school classroom life. Part of what we call treaties is thoroughly explored in the studies of Linda M. McNeil, most recently summarized in *Contradictions of Control* (Routledge and Kegan Paul: Boston and London, 1985). A comprehensive review of the research literature, plus a full bibliography bearing on many of our themes, is in Michael Sedlak, Christopher Wheeler, Diana Pullin, and Philip Cusick, *Classroom Perspectives on High School Reform: Bargains, Student Disengagement, and Academic Learning* (Teachers College Press: New York, 1985).

Acknowledgments

TWO GROUPS of remarkable people are mainly responsible for this book's existence and substance: the members of fifteen high school communities who opened their minds, hearts, and classrooms to our inquiries; and the ten research associates who did most of the field work, wrote most of the field notes, and helped us begin to understand what we had all seen. None of these people — the first group numbers in the hundreds — bears any responsibility for our final argument, but their imprint on the work is fundamental.

Time is precious to people involved with high schools — everyone is always busy at something, or almost late for something — and therefore it is a source of genuine satisfaction that so many teachers, students, administrators, counselors, and parents gave us so much time. We are grateful to everyone who talked with us and welcomed us to their classes, often on several occasions, and regret that we cannot list them all by name. Many of our key themes and specific metaphors — the shopping mall, the unspecial — were first suggested by people in the cooperating schools. We have tried to preserve their voices in the text. Readers should know we have also built upon their ideas.

Our commitment to confidentiality is a double-edged sword. It permits necessary candor, but it also denies recognition to those whose remarks were unusually perceptive or whose classrooms were unusually excellent. To the latter group — to Mike, Rita, Glenn, Carlos, Kara, Eric, Brad, and Andy, as well as to Ms. Fish, Dr. McBride, Mrs. Zukowski, Mr. Snyder, Mr. Rodriguez, Mr. Glynn, and many others like them — we owe a special if private debt.

Field work in schools cannot be organized unless school officials make the complicated scheduling arrangements that permit outside researchers to conduct their business in the limited time at their disposal. We owe special thanks to the principals and other administrators who took on the logistical tasks and did their best to meet our many and sometimes confusing requests. In particular, we thank Clayton Bryant (Andalusia High School); Peter Gunness and Richard Emmet (Buckingham, Browne & Nichols School); Edward Sarason, Diane Tabor, and William Mangan (Cambridge Rindge and Latin School); Rev. Neil O'Connor (Cleveland Central Catholic High School); Sister Rosemary Hocevar (Diocese of Cleveland); Frank Wallace and Terry Macaluso (Colorado Academy); John Astuno and David Strodtman (East High School); Robert Shamp (Findlay High School); Charles Clapper (La Jolla High School); Mary Gentilé and Galen Vanderlinden (Manual High School); Richard Mechem and Norman Gaudet (Newton North High School); Robert Amparán and Johanna Plaehn (San Diego High School); Dorothy Anne Williams and Mark Campaigne (The Bishop's Schools); Alan Johnson and Sandy Williamson (Vista High School); Manson Hall and Joseph Bannon (Watertown High School); and Fred Green, Jr. (Williamson High School).

We were privileged to have as colleagues ten experienced research associates with very diverse but complementary backgrounds. Their task was crucial, for doing good field work requires skills that are poorly captured in the term "data collection." And writing good field notes is an additional creative act of analysis and synthesis. The research associates gave us many of the lenses through which we could see, and we acknowledge here their first-rate work and our immense debt to all: Richard Berger, Ruben Carriedo, Helen Featherstone, Diane Franklin, Ellen Glanz, Peter Holland, Barbara Neufeld, Patricia Wertheimer, Lauren Young, and Mary Jane Yurchak. Insightful background papers on issues in particular schools, written by Helen Featherstone, Diane Franklin, Peter Holland, and Barbara Neufeld, further deepened our understanding.

Other individuals played crucial roles at the beginning or end of the project, and sometimes throughout. When the idea for this book was first conceived, Harry Judge of the University of Oxford arranged for Mr. Powell to visit six British high schools to develop fresh perspective on broad educational issues and on how to observe high schools. We are grateful for his many courtesies and to the principals for their thoughtful cooperation: John Sayer (Banbury School); John Phillips (Bicester School); Derek Seymour (Bloxham School); Derek Glover (Burford School); Brian Derbyshire (Peers School, Oxford); and John Thorne (Winchester College).

We appreciate the consistent encouragement and steady support of our sponsoring organizations, the National Association of Secondary School Principals and the Commission on Educational Issues of the National Association of Independent Schools. Scott D. Thomson, the director of NASSP, offered useful suggestions on big questions and practical logistics. John C. Esty, Jr., the president of NAIS, backed the project in numerous ways beyond the call, not the least of which was a detailed and insightful reading of portions of the manuscript. We are indebted to both of these Commission members, as well as to other Commissioners for helpful feedback at several meetings where we presented work in progress: Carl Dolce (North Carolina State University); Joseph Featherstone; Chester E. Finn, Jr. (Vanderbilt University); Gerald Grant (Syracuse University); Earl Harrison, Jr. (Sidwell Friends School, Washington, D.C.); Robin Lester (Trinity School, New York City); Thomas Minter (Herbert H. Lehman College); Cynthia Parsons (*The Christian Science Monitor*); and Blair Stambaugh (Baldwin School, Bryn Mawr, Pennsylvania). We further appreciate the opportunities given Ms. Farrar, by Christopher Berrisford and Frank Wallace, to present at an early stage the book's argument at meetings of school heads in New Jersey and Colorado, and Robert Colwell's Denver suggestions.

Without the financial assistance of five foundations, the project could not have been attempted. The early confidence of Helen Johnson and Philip Drake (Charles E. Culpeper Foundation) permitted the initial exploration of British schools. The Culpeper Foundation and the Commonwealth Fund (Carleton Chapman) supported our planning efforts. The assistance of Charles Froelicher and Peter Grant (Gates Foundation) allowed us to include schools from the Denver area. The interest of John Klingenstein and Robert N. Kreidler (Esther A. and Joseph Klingenstein Fund) permitted the inclusion of private schools. The commitment of Alden Dunham (Carnegie Corporation of New York) at a critical moment allowed the project to begin on schedule. And the Edward John Noble Foundation (John F. Joline III) provided important general support.

During the year of data collection the Study's administrative assistant, Pat West-Barker, handled effectively a myriad of logistical details ranging from school visits and travel arrangements to the transcription of field notes. Subsequently Cal Kolbe carried out similar responsibilities with competence and enthusiasm. Rick Belding solved many financial problems with a relaxed good humor rare in his trade.

We are much indebted to those who read portions of the manuscript. In addition to John Esty and Scott Thomson, they include Philip Cusick, Paula Evans, Helen and Joseph Featherstone, Patricia A. Graham, Gerald Grant, Cal Kolbe, Marvin Lazerson, John Ratté, Michael Sedlak, and Theodore R. Sizer. From Houghton Mifflin, we acknowledge Austin Olney's support of the entire Study from its inception, Larry Kessenich's juggling of disparate drafts from three authors, and Katarina Rice's thorough professionalism in editing.

A small band of comrades was intimately involved with virtually every aspect of the project from beginning to end. Robert Hampel and Martha Landesberg reanalyzed field notes and read all drafts with care. Besides ideas, they contributed exemplary sustenance and loyalty. Ted Sizer's formidable analytic and interpersonal skills were tested fully. He passed both tests with flying colors, and we gratefully recognize both his unwavering support for the book and his unswerving determination that the complex collegial association it embodied be nurtured.

Spouses, children, and other friends contributed more than they knew. Lisa Cohen assisted with the research for Chapter 5. Susanna Knott and Elizabeth Coxe argued with persistence and good humor for a book from which noneducators with children in schools could learn. They helped keep sections of the manuscript consistent with that principle. Barbara Schieffelin Powell read everything with insight, debated everything with verve, and gracefully endured her husband's midlife affair with a computer. With support from so many quarters, we can blame errors and deficiencies in the result only on ourselves.

Notes

THE NOTATION SYSTEM of this book is designed to protect the confidentiality of our sources and to record the evidence we used. Evidence for Chapters 1–4 came entirely from field notes and from a few published and unpublished school documents. Each field note was coded by letter and number to facilitate data analysis and citation. The final manuscript provides full citation of all field notes used in the text at the places where the notes are used; both direct quotes and supporting material are annotated. These coded citations refer to confidential material, cannot by themselves be understood, and are very extensive; hence they are not included in the published text. Fully annotated copies of the book are on file in the project's archive. We intend that they, and the field notes themselves, will become available to qualified scholars at an appropriate time under conditions acceptable to the project and the participating schools. The endnotes printed below include substantive notes from all chapters and references to sources (primarily in Chapter 5) that can be consulted independently.

1. The Shopping Mall High School

1. The movie *Fast Times at Ridgemont High* also makes the comparison of high schools to shopping malls. Its opening titles come up over scenes of a mall, not a school, and the mall continues throughout as the main setting where students live out their adolescence. See Pauline Kael's review in *The New Yorker*, November 1, 1982, p. 146.
2. These four elements subsume the ways that high schools attempt to educate teenagers, but not all the ways that teenagers use high schools. Those in active rather than passive rebellion against even the broadest notions of legiti-

mate educational variety often participate in an illicit curriculum. This curriculum is not "hidden" in the sense that no one except researchers is aware of it. Rather, it is hidden only because participants usually disguise illicit or illegal activities. For a few participants the agenda of the illicit curriculum may include vandalism, theft, smoking, drinking, or consuming drugs. For a somewhat larger number it includes active efforts to avoid the legitimate curriculum entirely without officially dropping out. Sometimes there are particular places — bathrooms, sections of the corridor, exits, lunchroom corners, locations on or near school grounds — where the illicit curriculum is consumed. Since high school is a setting for consumption, it is no surprise that a few students not only refuse any of the "official" goods offered but go beyond refusal to consume things against school rules or the law. We will not describe the illicit curriculum directly but only its consequences for the providers of the services curriculum.

3. In rare instances a semester's work in a foreign language may be offered over two semesters for those who learn languages slowly. The level of mastery aimed for in the spread-out version is the same as that in the one-semester course. A longer time is provided to reach the same end. But levels rarely have this intention.

4. In some schools, however, there was far less sensitivity to gender differences. We found numerous examples of male teachers using sexual innuendo with female students. In one physical education class it was common knowledge that the way to get a good grade was not to wear a bra. Despite mandated equality, the treatment of females is surprisingly and routinely chauvinistic.

5. In this school the attendance officer reported that one in six students was absent for one period a day. On a randomly chosen early morning, one in seven students was absent, late, or received excuses to be absent for the day. This excluded those who cut classes during the day.

5. Origins

1. National Center for Educational Statistics, *Digest of Educational Statistics, 1982* (Washington, D.C.: U.S. Government Printing Office, 1982), table 35, p. 44. In 1900 public high schools enrolled only about 8.4 percent of those old enough to attend (aged fourteen to seventeen); by 1940 they enrolled 67 percent of that age group. These figures reported here do not include private school enrollments. Their inclusion increases the enrollment percentages a bit but does not dramatically change the picture.

2. J. K. Van Denberg, *Causes of the Elimination of Students in Public Secondary Schools of New York,* Contributions to Education No. 47 (New York: Teachers College, Columbia University, 1911), p. 82.

3. George Counts, *The Selective Character of American Secondary Education* (Chicago: University of Chicago Press, 1922), p. 155.

4. August Hollingshead, *Elmtown's Youth, and Elmtown Revisited* (New York: Wiley, 1975), p. 108.

5. Robert Lynd and Helen Lynd, *Middletown: A Study in American Culture* (New York: Harcourt Brace and World, 1929), p. 195, note 9.

6. Hollingshead, *Elmtown's Youth,* p. 199.

7. Lynd and Lynd, *Middletown,* pp. 211–22.

8. David Nasaw, *Schooled to Order* (New York: Oxford University Press, 1979), especially pp. 114–39; Colin Greer, *The Great School Legend* (New York: Viking, 1977), pp. 116–29; Joel Spring, *Education and the Rise of the Corporate State* (Boston: Beacon Press, 1971).

9. R. B. Stout, *The Development of High-School Curriculum in the North Central States from 1860 to 1918* (New York: Arno Press, 1969; originally published by the Department of Education, University of Chicago, 1921), table XIV, pp. 90–91, 100–108, 249–59. On the situation in high schools in this period, see Theodore R. Sizer, *Secondary Schools at the Turn of the Century* (New Haven: Yale University Press, 1964).

10. See Sizer, *Secondary Schools,* for a discussion of the report and its origins and content, pp. 73–147. The report itself was printed by the U.S. Government Printing Office in 1893 and reprinted in New York in 1969 by the Arno Press and Columbia University's Teachers College.

11. The exchange was published in *School Review,* 9, no. 9 (Nov. 1901): 649–81, as "How Far Is the Present High School and Early College Training Adapted to the Nature and Needs of Adolescents?" by G. Stanley Hall, and an untitled response by Charles W. Eliot.

12. Hall, "How Far," pp. 657, 658, 650, 664.

13. Joseph F. Kett, *Rites of Passage* (New York: Basic Books, 1977), offers a lively and succinct discussion of Hall and others' role in this development, during the first few decades of this century (pp. 215–44).

14. Some evidence on this point can be found in *Report of the Commissioner of Education, 1910* (Washington, D.C.: U.S. Government Printing Office, 1911), tables A, B, C, pp. 1139–41. These tables show that in the academic year 1899–1900 only 10.8 percent of all students enrolled in public high school were preparing for college. It might be objected that many students failed to complete high school and that a fairer way to look at the matter would be to compute the proportion of high school graduates who actually went on to college. Figured this way, in 1899–1900, 30.2 percent went on to college. This still means that roughly seven of every ten high school students did not go to college, and that hardly makes the high schools chiefly college-preparatory institutions. It might be objected further that a large fraction of secondary students were then enrolled in private schools, and that more of them might be expected to attend college. And in fact, 31.8 percent of private high school students were preparing for college in 1899–1900, and 46.5 percent of graduates went to college in that year. But when public and private enrollments are combined, 14.5 percent of all secondary students were preparing for college, and 32.9 percent of graduates attended college. Thus, even on the most generous interpretation, high schools were not chiefly enrolled by a college-going population.

15. Eliot, untitled response, pp. 670, 671.

16. Ibid., p. 672.
17. David Tyack, *The One Best System* (Cambridge: Harvard University Press, 1974), pp. 109–214.
18. David Cohen, "Immigrants and the Schools," *Review of Educational Research,* 40, no. 1 (Feb. 1970): 13–27, especially pp. 18–24.
19. One of the most curious yet least examined issues in the history of secondary education concerns the common perception that as enrollments rose, high schools were flooded with students of low ability. There is not abundant evidence on this point, but everything seems to point in the other direction. For instance, E. L. Thorndike published a study, "Changes in the Quality of Pupils Entering High Schools," *School Review,* 30 (May 1922): 355–59, which examined the extent to which public secondary schools were intellectually selective. In 1890 he found that about 10 percent of those eligible by age attended secondary school, and 95 percent of those attending had above-average intelligence. Two decades later, in 1910, roughly one third of those eligible by age attended high school, and 83 percent of those attending had above-average intelligence. This result showed that while secondary enrollments expanded dramatically in twenty years, the proportion of students with above-average IQ declined only modestly. Yet this study was cited to support the assertion that there had been a dramatic change in the high school population, from one that was "fairly homogeneous in ability, interests, aims and needs . . . [to] a present student body highly heterogeneous in every respect . . . The new conditions may lead to a disaster if the secondary school is not modified to make the period of secondary education worthwhile for the pupils." *National Study of Secondary Education* [henceforth *NSSE*]: *Provision for Individual Differences,* U.S. Office of Education Bulletin No. 17 (Washington, D.C.: U.S. Government Printing Office, 1933), p. 3. These seem inappropriately strong words to describe a student body that the statistics showed to be only a bit less selected than had been the case in 1890. But the contrast between the evidence and the interpretation nicely conveys the strength of contemporary ideas about shattering changes in the intelligence of the high school population.

   Other studies also seem to show that high schools were still quite selective intellectually, through the early 1920s. The evidence that George Counts presented, in *The Selective Character of Secondary Education,* certainly supports that view. In addition, the NSSE staff did some other research on selectivity, comparing high school average IQ scores between 1919 and the early 1930s. Such comparisons are of course crude, but they showed "there is no evidence of a tendency toward decreasing selection." Yet the authors of those words concluded that a "high degree of intellectual democratization is being achieved" (*NSSE: The Secondary School Population,* pp. 22–24).

   It seems that contemporaries vastly overstated the degree of intellectual democratization in high school enrollments prior to 1930. One likely reason for this was the increasing participation by working-class and lower-middle-class students, whom educators probably mistook for less capable students. The available evidence suggests, as would experience, that these early representatives of the lower classes were in high school precisely because they had solid academic talent.

20. This program was announced most plainly in the *Cardinal Principles of Secondary Education,* pp. 21–27, perhaps the single most important document in the early twentieth-century high school reform movement. The report was printed, among other ways, as Bulletin 1918, No. 35, by the U.S. Bureau of Education, Department of the Interior (Washington, D.C.: U.S. Government Printing Office, 1918). For a discussion of the report's conception and execution, see Edward A. Krug, *The Shaping of the American High School,* vol. 1 (New York: Harper & Row, 1964). Lawrence Cremin, *The Transformation of the School: Progressivism in American Education, 1876–1957* (New York: Knopf, 1961), is still the best general treatment of this period.

21. W. B. Pillsbury, "Selection: An Unnoticed Function of Education," *Scientific Monthly,* 12 (Jan. 1921): 71.

22. We refer here to a study by George Van Dyke, "Trends in the Development of the High School Offering," *School Review,* 39 (Nov. 1931): 657–64 [Part I], and 39 (Dec. 1931): 737–47 [Part II]. Van Dyke replicated elements of Stout's earlier, classic study of curriculum structure (see note 9 above), in thirty-five districts. Both Van Dyke and Stout were associated with the Department of Education at the University of Chicago, and this may have had some bearing on Van Dyke's use of replication to capitalize on earlier studies.

23. All the comparisons reported in this paragraph are based on table II, p. 662, in Van Dyke, "Trends" [Part I]. His study included schools in the North Central region, which reached from Missouri in the south to Michigan in the north, from Kansas in the west to Ohio in the east. Thus, while it was not a national sample, the study seems likely to have captured developments in the United States at least in a rough way — with two exceptions. While the study included schools of many different sorts and sizes, in everything from small towns to big cities, both Van Dyke and Stout underrepresented very small rural high schools — because their curriculum record-keeping was so poor — and Negro schools in the South. *NSSE* (Washington, D.C.: U.S. Government Printing Office, 1933) showed that there were many schools of this sort; in one of the USOE surveys, roughly 75 percent of all the high schools enrolled fewer than 250 students (*NSSE: The Horizontal Organization of Secondary Schools,* p. 16). But small rural schools enrolled only a modest fraction of all high school students. *NSSE* estimated that in 1930–31 nearly three quarters of all secondary enrollments were in urban areas, with the remainder rural, despite the fact that the size of age-eligible population was roughly the same in rural and urban areas (*NSSE: The Secondary School Population,* pp. 6–7). Since the rural schools were small, they had fewer courses and curricula. So we can say that the argument in the text here is based on a census of North Central high schools that were in places with more than 2,500 population, and that existed in both 1906 and 1929. We also can say that the argument probably holds roughly for most

other schools in the country, save those that were in rural areas, or black schools in the South.

24. Van Dyke, "Trends" [Part I], p. 664.
25. Ellwood P. Cubberley, *Changing Conceptions of Education* (Boston: Houghton Mifflin, 1909), pp. 18–19.
26. *Cardinal Principles,* pp. 21–27. See also David Tyack and Elisabeth Hansot, *Managers of Virtue* (New York: Basic Books, 1982), pp. 110–13; David K. Cohen and Marvin Lazerson, "Education and the Corporate Order," *Socialist Revolution,* 2 (March–April 1972): 47–72; and Joel Perlmann, "Curriculum and Tracking for the Transformation of the American High School: Providence, R.I., 1880–1930," *Journal of Social History* (Fall 1985).
27. Boston School Committee, *Documents of the School Committee,* no. 7 (1908), pp. 48–53.
28. P. P. Claxton, "The Money Value of Education," in C. Ellis, ed., *Bulletin No. 22,* U.S. Bureau of Education (Washington, D.C.: U.S. Government Printing Office, 1917), p. 3.
29. Tyack and Hansot, *Managers;* Cohen and Lazerson, "Education," pp. 50–58; Raymond Callahan, *Education and the Cult of Efficiency* (Chicago: University of Chicago Press, 1962).
30. *NSSE: The Program of Studies,* pp. 166–67. It also commented that "only English, American History, and Physical Education are required by half the schools."
31. Ibid., table 97, pp. 247–48; table 60, pp. 164–65; p. 166. College-bound students took algebra in ninth grade and then other math courses. For more detail on this point see *NSSE: Instruction in Mathematics,* Bulletin 1932, No. 17 (Washington, D.C.: U.S. Government Printing Office, 1933), pp. 67–69.
32. Information on the general math and general science courses is in *NSSE: Instruction in Mathematics.*
33. *NSSE: The Program of Studies,* table 11, p. 39; *NSSE: Instruction in the Social Studies,* table 3, p. 13, and table 4, p. 18.
34. Van Dyke, "Trends" [Part I], table III, p. 663.
35. *NSSE: Instruction in English,* pp. 41–42.
36. Van Dyke, "Trends" [Part II], figure II, p. 739.
37. Lynd and Lynd, *Middletown,* pp. 188–205.
38. Joseph M. Rice, *The Public School System of the United States* (New York: Arno Press, 1969 [reprint]), p. 14.
39. Oscar Handlin, *John Dewey's Challenge to Education* (New York: Harper, 1950), p. 42. Sizer, *Secondary Schools,* chap. 3, offers a thoughtful and detailed discussion of these points.
40. The *NSSE* volume *Provision for Individual Differences, Marking, and Promotion* reported that just under half of all secondary schools used differentiated curricula; p. 9, table 4. If we bear in mind that most schools were very small rural schools, and that they were therefore much less differentiated, this estimate probably implies that most high schools outside rural areas

used differentiated curricula. The results reported by Van Dyke support this view, as do those in other studies of the same subject. See, for instance, George Counts, *The Senior High School Curriculum* (Chicago: University of Chicago Press, 1929), chap. 2. Less than universal reporting of curriculum differentiation also is partly explained by terminological problems, for many of the schools that didn't report differentiated curricula did report "ability grouping," or "special classes for failures," "opportunity plan for slow students," and the like; *NSSE: Provision,* p. 9, table IV. In addition, some of the reporting problems arose from variations in practice. For instance, high schools that definitely employed curriculum and ability group distinctions in grades nine and ten used them less or not at all in grade twelve, because during these years there was terrific attrition in high school enrollments, from grades nine to twelve. Since the dropouts were usually less able students, the need to make distinctions based on ability or destination became less acute in the higher grades; *NSSE: Provision,* table 11, p. 63. For such schools, which included nearly all high schools, deciding whether or not they used ability grouping or tracking would have been a real puzzle.

41. Counts, *The Selective Character.* See also Hollingshead, *Elmtown's Youth,* pp. 122–29, and *NSSE: The Secondary School Population,* pp. 8–11.
42. Hollingshead, *Elmtown's Youth,* pp. 155–75.
43. Lynd and Lynd, *Middletown,* pp. 193–95, 211–22; Hollingshead, *Elmtown's Youth,* pp. 199–200.
44. There was a terrific blow-up in Chicago, in the teens and twenties, over these issues; see George Counts, *School and Society in Chicago* (Chicago: University of Chicago Press, 1925). But there appear to have been no other local battles over high school curriculum tracking. A few academics did raise questions about the practice, at least implicitly, by studying the results: Hollingshead, the Lynds, and Counts chief among them. But apart from Chicago, there seems to have been little political opposition to tracking, and little criticism of it.
45. Van Denbergh, *Causes of Elimination,* pp. 82–83.
46. The version of the report cited here was published as a circular by the U.S. Bureau of Education, Bulletin 1918, No. 35 (Washington, D.C.: U.S. Government Printing Office, 1918), pp. 9, 10, 12. The report also identified "ethical character" and "worthy use of leisure" as objectives of schooling.
47. G. Jones, *Extra-Curricular Activities in Relation to the Curriculum,* Teachers College Contributions to Education No. 607 (New York: Teachers College, Columbia University, 1935), table V, p. 17.
48. Kett, *Rites,* pp. 214–44.
49. P. S. Lamar, "Extra Curricular Activities," *NEA Proceedings,* 153 (1925): 609–11.
50. V. K. Froula, "Extra Curricular Activities: Their Relation to the Curricular Work of the School," *NEA Proceedings,* 43 (1915): 737–39.
51. Counts, *The Selective Character,* p. 128.
52. John Dewey and Evelyn Dewey, *Schools of Tomorrow* (New York: E. P. Dutton, 1915), p. 3.

53. Dewey published several pieces on the subject of class and education. One was a broadside aimed at a plan devised by E. G. Cooley, a Chicago school superintendent, which would have established a separate system of vocational schools for that city: "An Undemocratic Proposal," *Vocational Education,* 2 (1913): 374–77.
54. See, for example, *NSSE: The Program of Studies,* pp. 148, 150, table 56.
55. Counts, *The Selective Character,* p. 134, table 41; p. 128.
56. Tyack and Hansot, *Managers,* pp. 105–40.
57. In Dewey and Dewey, *Schools of Tomorrow,* pp. 5–14, a succinct overview of Dewey's ideas about pedagogy and child development is also offered.
58. Kett, *Rites,* p. 242.
59. James B. Russell, "What Constitutes a Secondary School" (letter), *School Review,* 4, no. 7 (Sept. 1896): 529–31; p. 529.
60. Hall, "How Far," p. 649.
61. Russell, "What Constitutes," pp. 529–30.
62. Ibid., p. 530.
63. G. Stanley Hall, *Adolescence: Its Psychology and Its Relations to Physiology, Anthropology, Sociology, Sex, Crime, Religion and Education* (New York: Appleton, 1905).
64. Hall, "How Far," pp. 649, 652–53, 661.
65. Hall, *Adolescence,* chaps. 10, 11, 15.
66. William H. Kilpatrick, *Education for a Changing Civilization* (New York: Macmillan, 1927), pp. 85, 112, 103, 122.
67. Kilpatrick, *Education,* pp. 111–12.
68. Bernice Leary and William Gray, "Reading Problems in Content Fields," in *Readings in General Education* (Washington, D.C.: American Council on Education, 1940). The quotes below are taken from a version of the essay that was republished by the National Society for the Study of Education, chap. 8 in *Reading in the High School and College,* ed. Nelson Henry (Chicago: University of Chicago Press, 1948), pp. 137–39.
69. *NSSE: Instruction in Science,* pp. 9, 39; *NSSE: Instruction in Mathematics,* pp. 67–69.
70. *NSSE: Mathematics,* pp. 50–54, 48–53, 62.
71. *NSSE: Instruction in the Social Studies,* pp. 40, 101–2.
72. *NSSE: Instruction in English,* p. 85. All historical studies that we have found on the character of instruction support both the observations about classroom work reported here and the idea that, on average, classroom teaching has changed little, and slowly. The most recent and comprehensive study is Larry Cuban, *How Teachers Taught* (New York: Longman, 1984).
73. *NSSE: Provision for Individual Differences, Marking, and Promotion,* pp. 466–67, 426.
74. Katherine Mayhew and Anna Edwards, *The Dewey School: The Laboratory School of the University of Chicago, 1896–1903* (New York: Atherton Press, 1966), chap. 1.
75. U.S. Office of Education, *National Survey of the Education of Teachers*

[hereafter *NSET*], 6 vols. (Washington, D.C.: U.S. Government Printing Office, 1933), vol. 3, pp. 80–88.

76. *NSET*, vol. 3, reports extensively on teachers' academic and professional preparation. It reveals that in the early 1930s, teachers' college education consisted, on average, of 30–40 percent of courses in major and minor academic subjects, and 20–25 percent of courses in education subjects; pp. 84, 88. It also reports that these fractions were roughly similar whether students attended normal schools, teachers' colleges, colleges, or universities. But *NSET* also notes that in 1930–31 roughly 80 percent of all students enrolled in normal schools and teachers' colleges were in short courses (less than AB or BS programs). Thus, even teachers who attended for the full four years in teachers' colleges and normal schools did so in institutions that were organized chiefly to serve students who would be less well prepared; vol. 3, p. 46.

77. *NSET*, vol. 3, reports one survey of college teaching which showed that university and college teachers consistently gave greater stress to instruction in academic subjects than did teachers in teachers' colleges; pp. 38, 40, 46. The volume also reports on visits to teachers' colleges. These included classroom visits, and the observations revealed that in nearly half of all academic subject courses that were offered in teachers' colleges and normal schools, the instructors oriented the presentation to "professional" issues (i.e., how to teach the subject in school, how to make up tests, and the like), rather than only to subject matter; p. 134. This implies a considerable difference between the coverage of so-called academic courses in normal schools and teachers' colleges, as compared with those offered in colleges and universities. In addition, in teachers' colleges and normal schools these methods courses were counted as academic, not professional subjects, which further deflates the academic content of teachers' education in such places.

78. *NSET*, vol. 3, pp. 32–33; p. 34, table 1. By 1930–31, *NSET* reports, more than one third of the presidents and faculties of teachers' colleges and normal schools responded (to an NSET survey) that one chief aim of their work with future teachers was "training for life needs."

79. *NSET*, vol. 2, pp. 84, 21.

80. Ibid., p. 108.

81. *NSET* reports that between 50 and 60 percent of secondary school teachers (50 for junior high and 66 for senior high) had five or more clock hours of teaching every day; vol. 2, p. 66. This implies no fewer than five classes. By contrast, only about 8 percent of college and university faculty had similarly heavy loads in the same years; p. 182, table 28.

82. *NSET* reports that by 1930–31, between 34 and 37 percent of secondary teachers taught only one subject, and that another 51–52 percent taught two subjects. The rest taught more than two subjects; vol. 2, p. 66.

83. *NSSE: The Secondary School Population,* p. 5.

84. David Tyack, Robert Lowe, and Elisabeth Hansot, *Public Schools in Hard Times: The Great Depression and Recent Years* (Cambridge: Harvard University Press, 1984), pp. 42–91.

85. Charles Prosser, *Secondary Education and Life* (Cambridge: Harvard University Press, 1939), pp. 1–2.

86. Ibid., pp. 3, 15–16.

87. Ibid., p. 3.

88. Barry Franklin, "The Social Efficiency Movement Reconsidered: Curriculum Change in Minneapolis, 1917–1950," *Curriculum Inquiry,* 12, no. 1: 9–33.

89. James S. Coleman et al., *Equality of Educational Opportunity* (Washington, D.C.: U.S. Government Printing Office, 1966).

90. Zacharias went on to head a group of scientists who produced PSSC Physics. Arthur Bestor's book was *Educational Wastelands: The Retreat from Learning in Our Schools* (Urbana: University of Illinois Press, 1953); Conant's contribution, *The American High School Today* (New York: McGraw-Hill), was published at the end of the decade, in 1959.

91. The two best examples of this tendency were Arthur Bestor's book and J. F. Latimer's *What's Happened to Our High Schools* (Washington, D.C.: Public Affairs Press, 1958), especially pp. 114–35. Diane Ravitch, in *The Troubled Crusade* (New York: Basic Books, 1983), gives a brief account of the early 1950s reaction against progressivism, pp. 70–80. Patricia A. Graham, *Progressive Education: From Arcady to Academe* (New York: Teachers College Press, Columbia University, 1967), provides an illuminating account of the ideological struggles and puzzles of progressivism.

92. Ravitch, *The Troubled Crusade,* has a few useful pages on the 1950s reforms (pp. 228–32) and a helpful bibliography.

93. The most detailed single study of science teaching in the wake of the 1950s reforms is Robert Stake and Jack Easley, *Case Studies in Science Education,* 2 vols. (Washington, D.C.: U.S. Government Printing Office, 1978). It reports that there were plenty of text adoptions and NSF-sponsored workshops following on the fifties reforms (vol. II, pp. B:28–B:29) but that by the mid-1970s few evidences of the sort of instruction intended by the reforms could be found (vol. II, pp. II:4–5 ff).

94. EPIE, "Research Findings: More About NSAIM," *EPIEgram,* 5, no. 2 (Oct. 15, 1976).

95. M. Suydam and A. Osborne, *The Status of Pre-College Science, Mathematics, and Social Science Education, 1955–1975: Mathematics Education* [hereafter *Status-Math*] (Washington, D.C.: U.S. Government Printing Office, 1977), p. 100.

96. J. K. Brown, cited in *Status-Math,* p. 101.

97. J. Tucker, "Teacher Educators and the 'New' Social Studies," *Social Education,* 36, no. 5 (May 1972): 548–54.

98. K. Wiley and J. Race, *The Status of Pre-College Science, Mathematics, and Social Science Education, 1955–1975: Social Science Education* (Washington, D.C.: U.S. Government Printing Office, 1977), p. 208.

99. For example, a review of teacher education in the sciences noted that the 1960s had seen some increase in college science course requirements for secondary teachers, but that "changes in science education courses and materials for the elementary and secondary levels appear to have made little, if any,

impact on college course requirements for certification." S. Hegelson, P. Blosser, and R. Howe, *The Status of Pre-College Science, Mathematics, and Social Science Education, 1955–1975: Science Education* [hereafter *Status-Science*] (Washington, D.C.: U.S. Government Printing Office, 1977), p. 50.

Established professional ideas continued to influence teacher education in many other ways as well. One instance is the texts for education courses in the principles or foundations of secondary education, which were required of intending secondary teachers. The old ideas were carried on in new texts, as well as in 1950s and 1960s revisions of old texts. Some examples are: R. Faunce and C. Munshaw, *Teaching and Learning in Secondary Schools* (Belmont, Calif.: Wadsworth, 1964), where in pp. 1–19 the fifties criticisms are attacked and the Life Adjustment goals reasserted; S. Collins and A. Unruh, *Introduction to Secondary Education* (Chicago: Rand McNally [no date, but from footnote citations we estimate mid-sixties]), also reviewed the fifties critiques and, with a few concessions, reasserted the old ideas in pp. 1–25; N. Bossing, *Principles of Secondary Education* (Englewood Cliffs, N.J.: Prentice-Hall, 1959), revised a 1949 original text, and in the first chapter (pp. 3–14) dismissed the criticism of academic weakness; R. Bent, H. Kronenberg, and C. Boardman, *Principles of Secondary Education* (New York: 1941, 1970), follow suit, in pp. 1–22, and later (p. 43) identify the *Cardinal Principles* statement of high school purposes as the "most comprehensive, functional and influential"; L. Crow, H. Ritchie, and A. Crow, *Education in the Secondary School* (New York: American Book Co., 1961), also follow suit, pp. 39–41.

100. *Status-Math,* p. 68.
101. Grace Wright, *Subject Offerings and Enrollments in Public Secondary Schools* (Washington, D.C.: U.S. Government Printing Office, 1965), pp. 8–9.
102. Wright, *Subject Offerings,* p. 21.
103. V. Grant and L. Eiden (National Center for Education Statistics), *Digest of Education Statistics: 1981* (Washington, D.C.: U.S. Government Printing Office, 1981), table 11, p. 17.
104. Wright, *Subject Offerings,* pp. 19–20.
105. Wright, *Subject Offerings,* table 8, p. 100; table 4A, p. 38; table 4A, p. 35.
106. U.S. Department of HEW, *Offerings and Enrollments in High School Subjects* (in *Biennial Survey of Education in the U.S., 1948–50*) (Washington, D.C.: U.S. Government Printing Office, 1956), table 2, p. 31.
107. Compare U.S. Department of HEW, *Offerings and Enrollments,* table 2, p. 33, with Wright, *Subject Offerings,* table 4A, pp. 49–50.
108. Grant and Eiden, *Digest,* table 95, p. 104.
109. Seymour Harris, *A Statistical Portrait of Higher Education* (New York: McGraw-Hill, 1972), figure 2.2–2, p. 312.
110. Compare Edmund Gleazer, "Trends in Junior College Education," in Edmund Gleazer, ed., *American Junior Colleges,* 7th ed. (Washington, D.C.: American Council on Education, 1967), p. 5, with Grant and Eiden, *Digest,* p. 95.
111. Compare Grant and Eiden, *Digest,* table 96, p. 105, with table 95, p. 104.

112. For a good brief discussion of academic standards in community colleges, see H. London, "Academic Standards in the American Community College: Trends and Controversies," *ERIC* (July 1982).

113. Grant and Eiden, *Digest,* table 10, p. 16.

114. M. Trow, "The Second Transformation of US Secondary Education," *International Journal of Comparative Sociology,* 2 (1961): 144–66.

115. Grant and Eiden, *Digest,* table 10, p. 15.

116. L. Osterndorf and P. Horn, *Course Offerings Enrollments, and Curriculum Practices in Public Secondary Schools, 1972–73* (Washington, D.C.: U.S. Government Printing Office, 1976), p. 15.

117. Osterndorf and Horn, *Course Offerings,* table A; compare enrollments for these courses in column 6, p. 37.

118. Compare these math enrollments in Osterndorf and Horn, *Course Offerings,* p. 36, with the figures for college attendance cited in Grant and Eiden, *Digest.*

119. This story remains to be told. Few historians or sociologists have explored the recent connections between university expansion and high school quality. A brief but spotty overview is offered by Frederick Rudolph, "Educational Excellence: The Secondary School-College Connection and Other Matters," *ERIC* (1982).

120. The book was published in New York, by McGraw-Hill.

121. *Status-Math,* pp. 71, 142.

122. For some crude evidence on this point in a 1965 national sample of northern urban schools, see the case bases in table VII of D. K. Cohen, T. Pettigrew, and R. Riley, "Race and the Outcomes of Schooling," in Daniel P. Moynihan and Fredrick Mosteller, eds., *On Equality of Educational Opportunity* (New York: Random House, 1972), p. 353. For rough data on one city, see Robert Havighurst, *The Public Schools of Chicago* (Chicago: Board of Education, 1964), pp. 206–9. See also Christopher Jencks et al., *Inequality* (New York: Basic Books, 1972), pp. 32–35, and the studies cited there.

123. Osterndorf and Horn, *Course Offerings,* pp. 6–7.

124. The quotations are from Osterndorf and Horn, *Course Offerings,* pp. 4–6, 22. For the figures on remedial English, compare Osterndorf and Horn, *Course Offerings,* table A, p. 34, with Wright, *Subject Offerings,* table 4-A, pp. 51–52.

125. Compare Osterndorf and Horn, *Course Offerings,* table A, pp. 36–37, with Wright, *Subject Offerings,* table 4-A, pp. 51–52.

126. Osterndorf and Horn, *Course Offerings,* pp. 5, 22.

127. J. Hertling, "Test Score Decline Caused by Drop in Academic Rigor," *Education Week,* Dec. 12, 1984, p. 10.

128. The centerpiece of this line of thought was James Coleman's report for the President's Science Advisory Committee, *Youth: Transition to Adulthood* (Chicago: University of Chicago Press, 1974). A few of the other reports with similar orientations were: John Henry Martin et al., *National Panel on High Schools and Adolescent Education* (Washington, D.C.: U.S. Government Printing Office, 1974); Ruth Weinstock, *The Greening of the High School: A Report on a Conference* (New York: Educational Facilities Laboratory,

1973). For a critique, see Michael Timpane et al., *Youth Policy in Transition* (Santa Monica: RAND, 1976).

129. N. Lewin-Epstein, *Youth Employment During High School: An Analysis of High School and Beyond* (Chicago: NORC, 1981).

130. Linda McNeil, *Lowering Expectations: The Impact of Student Employment on Classroom Knowledge* (Madison: Center for Education Research, 1983).

131. For a report on some of these programs, see Eleanor Farrar and D. K. Cohen, "Career Education: Reforming School Through Work," *Public Interest,* no. 44 (Spring 1976).

132. Burton Clark argues for such an approach in an illuminating unpublished paper, "The School and the University: What Went Wrong in America" (UCLA, 1984).

133. *Educational Wastelands,* cited earlier (note 90), especially pp. 25–39.

134. By the summer of 1984 there already had been dozens of reports, and the Education Commission of the States reported that there were about 275 state task forces at work on education reform. Some of these developments are summarized and critiqued by Joseph Featherstone, "Change Thy Ways: Reflections on the Reform Movement in Education," *Boston Phoenix,* Aug. 14, 1984, section IV, p. 6.

135. Featherstone, "Change Thy Ways"; Edward Fiske, "States Gain Wider Influence on School Policy," *New York Times,* Dec. 2, 1984, p. 1.

136. Stake and Easley, *Case Studies,* vol. II, pp. 12:3–12:11.

137. Thomas Toch, "Teacher-Shortage Realities Seen Thwarting Reform," *Education Week,* Dec. 5, 1984, p. 1.

138. Evidence on popular priorities for schools has been presented by the Gallup polls on education for more than a decade. A more focused account can be found in Kenneth Sirotnik, "What You See Is What You Get: Consistency, Persistency, and Mediocrity in Classrooms," *Harvard Educational Review,* 53, no. 1 (Feb. 1983): 26–28.

Index

Index

Class ditching, 77, 142, 178–179, 190, 191, 222–223
Class participation: for intense discussion, 100; in private schools, 214, 231; students' reluctance toward, 19, 93–94; in top-track vs. regular classes, 122
Classroom treaties. *See* Treaties
Coaching, 30, 136, 166
Cold War, 279, 281
Coleman report, 280
College entrance: as incentive, 107–108, 122, 304; 1960s/1970s expansion in, 288–289; and role of high school, 119–120, 255, 289–291; and student choice, 42–43, 160; and top-track admission, 154; as unspecial, 119, 174–175
Commitment: as curricular-reform problem, 261; and curriculum revolution of early 20th century, 267, 268; from extracurricular activities, 134; irrelevance of, 106; in private schools, 201; in specialty shops, 309–310; by specialty-shop teachers, 144, 149, 163, 164, 165; of top-track students, 122, 123, 124, 155–156; variety of levels of, 106, 111, 117; voluntary nature of, 5, 199
Committee of Ten, 240–241
Community, sense of: among learners, 117, 316, 320; in private school, 205, 206, 230; and purpose, 316; tolerance as basis of, 3, 58, 199; among top-track students, 169
Community support: and academic quality, 299–300; as extracurriculum rationale, 257–258; for specialty shops, 150, 166, 176–177; and sports/band, 135, 137, 150–151, 238
Competency tests, minimal, 61, 183, 313
Comprehensive high school. *See* Shopping mall high school; Variety
Conant, James, 281, 291, 299
Conflict prevention: as first duty, 116; and treaties, 67–68, 108–109, 110; and troublemaker specialty shop, 139–140
Consensus, lack of: on goals and values, 3, 4, 56, 57; on performance standards, 313; in private schools, 225–228; in society's view of high school function, 65; and treaties, 4
Consumer choice, and shopping mall high school, 3, 39, 309–310. *See also* Shopping mall high school
Consumerism: in junior English classes, 29; and unspecial students, 195, 196; and vertical curriculum, 23
Consumer rebellion, and reform, 314

Consumer resistance, in courses, 67
Consumer satisfaction: as high school goal, 1; and private schools, 203, 222, 225
Consumption, 12, 38–39
Counseling (advising): as consumer good, 48; high school course in, 13; personalization through, 318; in private schools, 219–220; psychological orientation of, 49–50; in service curriculum, 34, 35–37; for special-needs students, 164; and student choice, 45–50; students' needs missed by, 47–49, 179; for top-track students, 163–164; for troublemakers, 141, 162; and unspecial students, 183. *See also* Guidance counselors
Counselors and administrators, descriptions of: Ms. Devlin (social worker), 34–35; Miss Lowell (administrator), 172–173, 174, 216; Dr. Nelson (guidance counselor), 39–40, 181
Counts, George, 235, 236, 239, 258, 259, 344n44
Courses: created by 1980s reforms, 301, 302–303; intentions of participants in, 67. *See also* Curriculum
Courses, descriptions of: Advanced Physics, 17–19, 74–75; American history, 100–103, 114, 114–116; AP science, 23; Asian Studies, 84–85, 100; in Beta program, 193–194; Child and Family, 14–15, 16, 21; communications and media, 130–131; Constitutional Law, 72–74, 96; in Delta Program, 120; English and literature, 23–29, 68–69, 71–72, 74, 75, 85, 89–90, 97–100, 103, 104, 184–185
"Coverage," as avoidance of thinking, 102
Critical thinking. *See* Thinking; Questioning
Cubberley, Ellwood, 247
Curriculum: in Committee of Ten report, 240–241; as consumption-based, 38–39; from early debates, 245; Hall's plan for, 242; intellectual capacities vs. subjects in, 306–307, 320; as lacking for unspecial, 187; levels of commitment to, 117; in 1950s reforms, 282–286; 1960s/1970s effect on, 295; for non-English speakers, 294; of pre-1900 high school, 240; in private schools, 210; of specialty shops, 159; variety in, 1, 2, 38; work experience in, 298–299
Curriculum, types of, 12–13; extracurriculum, 2, 13, 29–33 (*see also* Extracurriculum); horizontal, 2, 12–13, 13–21, 31, 43; illicit, 338–339n2; services, 2, 13, 33–39,

352

220, 339n2 (of ch. 1); vertical, 2, 13, 21–29, 31, 43 (*see also* Standards, grading)

Curriculum revolution of early 20th century, 245–252; and academic requirements, 249–252, 253–254; and Depression years, 273–276; and extracurriculum, 257–258; faith in, 260–261; intellect denigrated by, 278–279; Life Adjustment in, 274–276; and 1950s reforms, 285, 288; and pedagogy, 253–254, 261, 262, 265, 269; and performance standards, 252, 254, 259; postwar criticism of, 279–281; rationales for, 247–249, 253, 254–256, 260; results of, 266–268, 277–279; and student choice, 258–259, 263; and student needs or interests, 247–248, 253, 260, 261–266, 268, 274–275; and teaching quality, 266–267, 268–269

Curriculum tracks. *See* Tracking

Customer satisfaction, as high school goal, 1. *See also* Consumer satisfaction

Deaf students, 13, 15, 37, 127, 147–148. *See also* Handicapped students; Special-needs programs

Deinstitutionalization, and school reform, 297–298

Delinquents. *See* Dropouts; Troublemakers; Truants

Delta Program, 120–123

Democracy: and early debates on high school role, 244; and early 20th-century reforms, 245, 247–248, 255–256, 260; in Hall's view, 242; and individuality, 39–40; and uses of high schools, 239. *See also* American society; Pluralism

Depression years, 273–276

Dewey, John, 244, 258–259, 261, 268–269, 275, 278

Discipline problems: and Child and Family class, 16; disagreement over, 53; and junior English class, 26; and teachers' avoidance, 108–109. *See also* Conflict prevention; Troublemakers

Discussion classes: in advanced vs. unspecial English, 184–185; avoidance in, 319; in Beta program, 194; in Constitutional Law, 73; intensity of, 100; mechanical, 100–101; in private schools, 214, 221; self-contained responses in, 101–102, 103; in top track, 122; unwillingness toward, 93–94, 194. *See also* Class participation; Questioning

Ditching. *See* Class ditching

Diversification of curriculum. *See* Variety

Diversity of students, 2, 3: and attitude–change class, 96; and neutrality, 53–54; and private schools, 203, 225–226; and treaties, 110; among unspecial students, 187; and variety, 38–39

Diversity of teachers, 39, 57

Do-your-own-thing attitude. *See* Neutrality

Dropouts: and anti-truancy efforts, 142; concern with, 287, 305, 310; and troublemakers' enclave, 158; unspecial students feared as, 180–181

Drugs: as problem, 50, 51, 297; school response to, 139

Education of American Teachers, The (Conant), 291

"Education for Life Adjustment," 274–276, 281, 285

Egalitarianism: in civil rights reforms, 292; in Eliot's report, 241, 243; and function of high schools, 276–277; and specialty shops, 159. *See also* Democracy

Eliot, Charles W., 240, 242, 243–244, 250, 258, 279

Employment of students, 9–10, 77, 298

Engagement: academic vs. intellectual, 215, 231; and conflict prevention, 109; and top-down reform, 313–314; in private schools, 215. *See also* Avoidance and engagement; Intensity

Equality of Educational Opportunity (Coleman), 280

Ethnicity, 58

Excellence: for all levels of ability, 183; in music shop, 136–137; 1950s pressure for, 281, 285, 288–289, 299, 300; pluralistic notions of, 313; and sports, 134; vocabulary of, 312. *See also* Mastery; Standards, performance

Exceptional students. *See* Special needs programs; Top-track students

Expectations. *See* Standards, performance

Extracurriculum, 2, 13, 29–33; and college admission, 122; course credit in, 30, 32; early 20th-century rise of, 257–258; and intensity, 96; in Lynds/Hollingshead studies, 238; in private schools, 211; as specialty shop, 133–138, 157; and teamwork, 95

Facts, vs. thinking, 102

Faculty. *See* Teachers

Failure: need to avoid, 52, 61–62, 110; and special-needs students, 128. *See also* Success

Index

Family: course on, 14–15, 16, 21; outreach to, 318. *See also* Parents

Family background: counseling problems from, 50; and Mrs. Jefferson's students, 15; of Kara/Eric vs. Robert, 20; and school discipline, 53; and school performance, 79–80; and special vs. unspecial, 178; and student choice, 44–45. *See also* Low-income students; Social class

Federal programs: in 1950s reforms, 281; and 1960s/1970s reforms, 294; for special-needs students, 33, 158, 167; vocational, 133

Females, chauvinistic treatment of, 339n4

Football: community support for, 135, 150–151; as specialty shop, 135–137. *See also* Sports

Freedom of choice. *See* Choice

"Functional education," 287

Funding, outside: and program for unspecial students, 175; for special-needs programs, 33

General math courses, advent of, 250

General science courses: advent of, 250–251; 1950s growth of, 288

Goals. *See* Purpose

Grades: and college entrance, 43; as goal, 122; and parental pressure, 147; and self-esteem, 224. *See also* Standards, grading

Grassroots reform, 314–315

Great Depression, age of, and curriculum revolution, 273–276

Groupwork, avoidance in, 94–95

Guidance counselors, 35–36, 45–50, 146. *See also* Counseling

Hall, G. Stanley, 241–244, 262, 263–264

Handicapped children: class discussion on, 14; lobbying for, 151–152; 1960s/1970s reforms for, 294; in special-needs shop, 126; tolerance toward, 57–58. *See also* Deaf students; Special-needs programs

Handlin, Oscar, on 19th-century teaching, 253

High school: as adolescent social center, 236–237; alternatives for, 304–305; commitments to, 1; community satisfaction with, 239, 309; durability of, 301; early debates on, 239–245; in "good old days," 238–239, 248, 255, 277–278; as haven from "street," 63, 152; and industrial society, 188, 235–236, 247–249; 1960s/1970s criticism of, 293, 297; 1980s criticism of, 300–301; postwar criticism of, 279–281; as teenag-er's right, 64, 106. *See also* Shopping mall high school; Teaching quality

High school expansion (1900–1940): causes of, 234–236; curriculum revolution in, 245–252, 254–255 (*see also* Curriculum revolution of early 20th century); extent of, 234, 239, 276; lack of criticism of, 293; immigrant enrollees during, 244; and intellectual democratization, 244–245, 341–342n19; and uses of high schools, 236–239

Hollingshead, August, 236–237, 237–238, 238, 239, 254, 342n44

Home life. *See* Family; Parents

Homework: and conflict prevention, 109; and feeling of failure, 110; in-class performance of, 80; in-school performance of, 319; in Lynds and Hollingshead studies, 237–238; McBride's policy on, 19, 74–75; in private school, 207, 212; and proficiency gaps, 81–82; and students' home life, 79–80; and teacher workload, 104, 272; treaties on, 78–82; for unspecial students, 191

Honors courses. *See* Top-track specialty shop

Horizontal curriculum, 2, 12–13, 13–21; and Andy, 31; and college entrance requirements, 43; and social gap, 20–21. *See also* Requirements, academic

Incentives to learn: college entrance as, 107–108, 122, 304; consumer orientation in, 64–65; in desire to be special, 314–315; neither carrot nor stick as, 107, 312; and top-down reform, 312–314. *See also* Commitment; Pushing of students; Students' needs or interests

Inclusiveness: accommodation to, 2–3, 11, 38; extent of, 38; high school expansion as, 276; as private-school trend, 225. *See also* Diversity; Variety

Individual differences. *See* Diversity; Personalization

Individualization: and ambitious parents, 5; as anonymity, 314, 317; as choice vs. personalization, 216–217 (*see also* Personalization); as commitment to intellect, 312; in Delta Program, 120; in learning style vs. preference for learning or not-learning, 318; in private schools, 197; and unspecial student, 181; and variety, 38

Individualized education program, 126–127, 147; and average students, 176, 318

Industrial society: and curriculum revolution of early 20th century, 247–249; and high

Index

Racial integration: school improvement
from, 145; and top-track enclave, 156
Reasoning. *See* Thinking
Reform: and accommodation, 6, 309; diversification as response to, 288, 294–295, 296,
297; grassroots, 314–315; required parenting class seen as, 16; students' immunity
to, 303–304; top-down, 312–314; as
tradeoff vs. infusion, 321
Reform movements: pre-1900 debates, 240–
243, 245; curriculum revolution of early
20th century, 245–252 (*see also* Curriculum revolution of early 20th century); of
1950s, 281–292, 295, 296–297, 299, 302,
308; of 1960s/1970s, 292–299; of 1980s,
300–306
Relationships: avoidance of, 92–93; change
in, 87; in private schools, 216, 220; and
teachers' backgrounds, 112; in top track,
121–122, 162–163; treaties on, 85–96, 116;
unspecial students on, 191
Religion, and private schools, 225, 226, 229
Remedial education, as employment opportunity, 108
Requirements, academic: vs. choice, 40, 41–
42, 52; and curriculum revolution of early
20th century, 249–252, 253–254; vs. incentives, 304; and 1960s/1970s trends, 289,
290, 295–296; students' immunity to, 303.
See also Standards, grading
Responsibility: and choice, 2–3, 50–51; toward classmates, 95, 96, 221; schools' abdication of, 65, 183, 310; schools' assumption on, 180; in treaty renegotiation, 316
Rice, Joseph Mayer, 253
Roll call, 142
Russell, James E., 262–263

Sales promotion, classtime homework as, 81
Satisfaction of public, 239, 309. *See also*
Community support
Satisfaction of students, 309; from extracurricular activities, 134; with mediocrity,
233; as social-class-dependent, 311
Schools. *See* High school; Shopping mall
high school
Selection, as school function, 230, 231, 246
Selective excellence, as 1950s policy, 288,
296, 299, 300
Self-esteem or self-respect: as course objective, 62, 110; and minority students, 156;
and push, 224, 317; from special-needs
programs, 126; from sports, 30; for unspecial students, 189, 224, 317. *See also* Success, feeling of; Therapeutic mentality

Services curriculum, 2, 13, 33–39; and illicit
curriculum, 339n2 (of ch.1); private-
school rejection of, 220
Shopping mall high school, 3, 6–7, 8–11,
309–310; avoidance and engagement in,
70, 76, 310 (*see also* Avoidance and engagement); choice in, 2–3, 11, 39, 41, 159,
211 (*see also* Choice); community of tolerance in, 3, 58, 199; consumer orientation
of, 1, 3, 38–39, 65, 309–310 (*see also* Consumerism); curricula in, 2, 12–13 (*see also*
Curriculum, types of); and dilemma over
indifferent students, 64–65 (*see also* Incentives to learn; Passivity of students; Students' needs or interests); individualization in, 216 (*see also* Individualization);
and intellectual quality, 59, 61, 297, 300,
311–312 (*see also* Requirements, academic; Standards, performance); neutrality of, 3, 11, 53, 58 (*see also* Neutrality);
private schools as tending toward, 228–
229, 232; reform of, 312–321 (*see also* Reform); restructuring schemes for, 319–321;
and society's views, 1, 65, 239 (*see also*
American society); as something for everyone, 2, 65, 305–306; specialty shops in,
4–5, 118–119, 143–145, 169 (*see also* Specialty shops); standardization vs. privilege
in, 164–165; strengths and weaknesses of,
308; treaties in, 4, 66–70, 111, 301, 303
(*see also* Treaties); truants and troublemakers in, 143 (*see also* Troublemakers);
unspecial students in, 173, 195, 197, 222
(*see also* Unspecial students); variety in,
2, 11–12, 38, 41, 53 (*see also* Variety);
vertical curriculum in, 21; as way of looking, 6–7. *See also* High schools
Shops. *See* Specialty shops
Social class: and academic satisfactions, 311;
and attitude-change course, 96; and curriculum tracks, 254; and estimates of intellectual democratization, 244, 341–342n19; in
intelligence testing, 244; and parental involvement, 44; and specialty shop admission, 170–171; and special vs. unspecial,
178; and top-track enclave, 156, 165–166.
See also Family background; Parents;
Low-income students
Social promotion, 267–268
Social services. *See* Services curriculum
Social studies: advent of, 251; under life-
adjustment plan, 275; and 1950s reforms,
284; for special-needs students, 128; survey on method in, 266

Index

Special education. *See* Special-needs programs

Specialization: as disguising ignorance, 104; and specialty shops, 316

Special-needs movement, individual specialness shown by, 318

Special-needs programs, 4–5, 33, 125–129; admission to, 157, 157–158; extra attention for, 164; lobbying for, 151–152; new curriculum for, 128, 149; and school social worker, 35; and unspecial students, 175–176. *See also* Deaf students; Handicapped students

Specialness: encouraging of, 314, 315, 316; of every teenager, 318; as illusion, 311; of specialty shops, 144

Specialty shops, 4–5, 118–119, 143–145; admission to, 143, 153–159, 170–171; advocacy for, 143, 145–153, 165, 170, 176–177; attention to, 144, 162–164; belongingness of, 169–170; commitment in, 309–310; extracurricular, 133–138, 157; private schools as, 196–197; resentments toward, 169, 190; special needs, 4–5, 33, 125–129 (*see also* Special-needs programs); and student choice, 144, 159–162; teachers in, 144, 148–149, 163, 164–169; top-track, 4, 119–129 (*see also* Top-track specialty shop); for troublemakers and truants, 138–143, 157, 161; and unspecial students, 176, 195, 316–317; and use of mind, 311; vocational/technical, 129–133, 157, 159

Spectatorship, of unspecial students, 176

Sports: and college admission, 122; community support from, 150–151, 238; early 20th-century rise of, 257–258; in extracurriculum, 30, 37, 134–137, 138, 157, 161–162; and intensity, 96; in private schools, 211; and unspecial students, 176. *See also* Football

Standards, grading: and curriculum revolution of early 20th century, 267; failure-feeling avoided through, 61–62; performance minimized in, 58–61; for special-needs students, 128, 149; and spelling, 104; treaties on, 60, 68. *See also* Grades

Standards, performance: vs. actual performance, 312; and college expansion, 289, 291; consensus lacking on, 313; and curriculum revolution of early 20th century, 252, 254, 259; in debate on high school role, 243–244; Dewey on, 259; differentiation as eroding, 300; and 1950s reforms, 299; and 1960s/1970s trends, 295–296; for

unspecial students, 317. *See also* Excellence; Mastery; Requirements, academic

Standards, teacher certification, 271

Structure, and unspecial students, 187

Student choice. *See* Choice

Student council, 30–31, 32

Students: alternatives to high school for, 304–305; curriculum decided by, 9; diversity of, 1–2, 38, 53–54, 110–111 (*see also* Diversity; Inclusiveness); as ignorant of options, 44, 45, 182; part-time employment of, 9–10, 77, 298; reasons for treaties by, 106–108 (*see also* Treaties); responsibility by, 51, 95, 96, 180, 221 (*see also* Responsibility)

Students, descriptions of: Andy, 30–31, 39, 68; Beth, 32–33; Bill, 139–140; Brad, 31–32, 33, 39, 83; Brent, 128, 129; Bruce, 222–224, 225, 228; Carlos, 198–199, 207–208, 211, 213–214, 215, 218, 222, 231; Chris, 125–126; David, 139, 140; Derek, 47; Eileen, 133–134; Eric, 17, 18, 20, 75, 92, 194, 231; George, 46–47; Glenn, 198, 199, 202, 206, 207, 208, 213–214, 214, 215, 222; Kara, 17, 17–18, 20, 21, 75, 92, 194, 231; Matt, 133–134; Mike, 192–193, 193–195; Pete, 133–134; Peter, 72, 73, 74, 75; Randy, 121–122; Rita, 192–193, 193–195; Robert, 14, 15, 20, 21; Thomas, 224–225, 228

Students' motivation: through peer pressure, 203; pushing required for, 213 (*see also* Pushing of students); in troublemaker case, 55; and unspecialness, 173, 179, 186–187, 188. *See also* Commitment; Engagement; Incentive to learn; Passivity of students

Students' needs or interests: vs. academic requirements, 303; accommodation to, 2, 10–11, 61 (*see also* Accommodation); and avoidance, 107; and choice, 51–52, 61; and curriculum revolution of early 20th century, 247–248, 253, 260, 261–266, 268, 274–275; difficulty in teaching to, 268; in extracurriculum rise, 257–258; in Hall's proposals, 242; in Hollingshead's study, 236–237, 238; in Lynds' study, 238; and teacher education, 269; and view of unspecial students, 186. *See also* Boredom

Student-teacher relationships. *See* Relationships

Student turnover, and personalization, 217

Success, feeling of: need to impart, 38, 58–59, 62, 189, 228, 311; private-school atti-

Index